29

THE JAPANESE CONSPIRACY

THE
JAPANESE
CONSPIRACY

The Oahu Sugar Strike of 1920

MASAYO UMEZAWA DUUS

Translated by Beth Cary
and adapted by Peter Duus

University of California Press
Berkeley   Los Angeles   London

Translated and adapted from *Nihon no inbō:
Hawai Oahu Shima daisutoraiki no hikari to kage*,
originally published by Bungei Shunjū, Tokyo,
Japan, 1991.

The publisher gratefully acknowledges the support
of the Suntory Foundation for the translation and
publication of this book.

University of California Press
Berkeley and Los Angeles, California

University of California Press, Ltd.
London, England

Library of Congress Cataloging-in-Publication Data

Duus, Masayo, 1938–.
    [Nihon no inbō. English]
    The Japanese conspiracy : the Oahu sugar strike of 1920 /
Masayo Umezawa Duus; translated by Beth Cary and
adapted by Peter Duus.
        p.   cm.
    Includes bibliographical references and index.
    ISBN 0-520-20484-0 (alk. paper).—
ISBN 0-520-20485-9 (pbk. : alk paper)
    1. Strikes and lockouts—Hawaii—Oahu—History.
2. Aliens—Legal status, laws, etc.—Hawaii—Oahu—
History.   3. Japanese—Legal status, laws, etc.—Hawaii—
Oahu—History.   4. Emigration and immigration law—
United States—History.   5. Oahu (Hawaii)—Social
conditions.   I. Title.
HD5326.O23D8813   1999
331.892'83361'099693—dc21   99-17701
                                                   CIP

Manufactured in the United States of America

08 07 06 05 04 03 02 01 00 99
10 9 8 7 6 5 4 3 2 1

The paper used in this publication meets the
minimum requirements of ANSI/NISO Z39.48-1992
(R 1997) (Permanence of Paper).

To Dr. Clifford I. Uyeda
whose fairness has impressed and
inspired me over the years

CONTENTS

Preface / ix

Prologue: A Dynamite Bomb Explodes / 1

1   The Japanese Village in the Pacific / 13

2   A Person to Be Watched / 26

3   The Oahu Strike Begins / 42

4   The Japanese Conspiracy / 67

5   The Conspiracy Trial / 138

6   Reopening Chinese Immigration / 230

7   The Japanese Exclusion Act / 300

Notes / 341

Bibliography / 351

Index / 357

PREFACE

My interest in how the history of Japanese Americans has intertwined with that of U.S.-Japan relations began with my first book, *Tokyo Rose: Orphan of the Pacific,* about the trial of Iva Toguri, a Japanese American woman accused of treason for making wartime propaganda broadcasts for the Japanese government. Since then I have published other books on this theme: a history of the 100th Battalion and the 442d Regimental Combat Unit, the Japanese American army units in World War II; and a biography of Tazuko Iwasaki, the first Japanese woman to work as a labor contractor on a Hawaiian sugar plantation. And with this book I return to that theme again.

During the years following World War I, relations between the United States and Japan, though cordial on the surface, were troubled by unresolved tensions. Many Americans distrusted Japan because of its aggressive policies in China, and many Japanese resented discrimination against Japanese immigrants in the United States. The immigration issue was a highly emotional one for the Japanese, whose attempt to include a "racial equality clause" in the League of Nations charter had been rebuffed by President Woodrow Wilson. The anti-Japanese movement in California and other parts of the West Coast has attracted the attention of many historians, but the immigration issue in Hawaii, then not yet a state, has not. A critical event that revealed anti-Japanese sentiment in Hawaii was the 1920 Japanese plantation workers' strike on Oahu, the subject of this book.

I first heard about the 1920 Oahu strike while interviewing Japanese American veterans whose families had been forced off the plantations at the time of the strike. But it was during my research on Tazuko Iwa-saki that I first sensed that a thread might link the strike with the anti-Japanese immigration law passed by the American Congress four years later. That thread was the alarm of the Hawaiian plantation owners, who were upset by the defiance of the Japanese cane field workers. While the planters succeeded in waiting out the strikers, who eventually aban-doned their demands for higher wages, they were determined to reas-sert control of the labor force. Not only did the plantation owners work with the Hawaiian territorial government to indict the strike leaders on trumped-up conspiracy charges, they went to Washington, D.C., to lobby for lifting restrictions on the immigration of Chinese laborers. As I argue in this book, their testimony that a large Japanese immigrant community in Hawaii threatened the national interest contributed to the passage of the so-called Japanese Exclusion Act of 1924.

What confirmed my commitment to this research project was my dis-covery of the transcripts from the trial of the 1920 strike leaders, charged by the territorial government with conspiring to dynamite the house of Jūzaburō Sakamaki, the Japanese interpreter on the Olaa Plantation. I had despaired of finding the transcripts after I learned that the First Cir-cuit Court of the State of Hawaii had thrown out many old records be-cause it no longer had space to store them. By chance I discovered that Professor Harry Ball of the Sociology Department at the University of Hawaii collected documents discarded by government agencies. Thanks to his help I was able to find the transcripts in the basement of the Ham-ilton Library at the University of Hawaii, where he had stored them, and began to pursue the project in earnest.

In conducting research for this book, I found materials in several other archives. After several years of effort, under the Freedom of Infor-mation Act I obtained Federal Bureau of Investigation (FBI) and Depart-ment of Justice documents on Noboru Tsutsumi and other strike lead-ers; the record of the House and Senate hearings on the renewal of the importation of Chinese labor was in the National Archives; other official documents came from the Department of the Interior and the Territorial Government of Hawaii; and the diplomatic archives of the Foreign Min-istry in Japan provided important source materials on the Japanese side. To the staff persons who helped me in these archives I would like to of-fer my thanks.

I interviewed many individuals in Japan and Hawaii, including the widows of three of the strike leaders, to learn as much as I could about the strikers. I would like to express my deep gratitude to the following persons who cooperated with me in my research. In Hawaii: Yasuki Arakaki, Hiroshi Baba, Violet Fujinaka, Tom Fujise, Mitsu Fukuda, Ryūzō Hirai, Tokutarō Hirota, Magotarō Hiruya, Edward Ishida, Kōji Iwasaki, Ten'ichi Kimoto, Takashi Kitaoka, Victor Kobayashi, Masao Koga, Kumaichi Kumasaki, Lefty Kuniyoshi, Masaji Marumoto, Spark Matsunaga, Gyoei Matsuura, Yoshie Mizuno, Michiko Nishimoto, Warren Nishimoto, Harold Oda, Franklin Odo, Asae Okamura, Nobuko Okinaga, Shōichi Okinaga, Kiyoshi Ōkubo, Moon Saitō, Ben Sakamaki, Kenji Santoki, Kameyo Satō, Minoru Shinoda, Shigeru Sumino, Sakae Takahashi, Tomiji Togashi, Ryōkin Toyohira, Hatsuko Tsuruta, Seiei Wakikawa, Reizō Watanabe, Tsuneichi Yamamoto, Shigeru Yano, and Paul Enpuku.

In Japan: Maino Baba, Mutsui Baba, Kaoru Furukawa, Akiko Fujitani, Kaichi Fujitani, Masao Gotō, Takeshi Haga, Yoshie Hashimoto, Chiso Ishida, Michiko Itō, Genshichi Kogochi, Kiyoshi Kondō, Ō Koyama, Susumu Koyama, Kimiko Kurokawa, Setsu Makino, Tōru Makino, Masami Takizawa, Masao Tsutsumi, Mihoko Tsutsumi Allilaire, Norio Tsutsumi, Tamotsu Tsutsumi, Tsuruyo Tsutsumi, Yasuo Tsutsumi, Sachiko Ueda, and Toyo Yokoo.

As many of those I interviewed were of advanced age, some have since passed away. I respectfully express my wish that their souls rest in peace.

I would like to thank Beth Cary for her preliminary translation of the original Japanese volume and my husband, Peter Duus, for revising and adapting her translation. My thanks go as well to Laura Driussi, Sheila Levine, and Rose Anne White of the University of California Press for shepherding the manuscript through production and to Sheila Berg for meticulously copyediting it.

Finally, I would like to thank the Suntory Foundation for its generosity in supporting the translation of the Japanese edition of this book.

Masayo Umezawa Duus
Stanford, California
June 1998

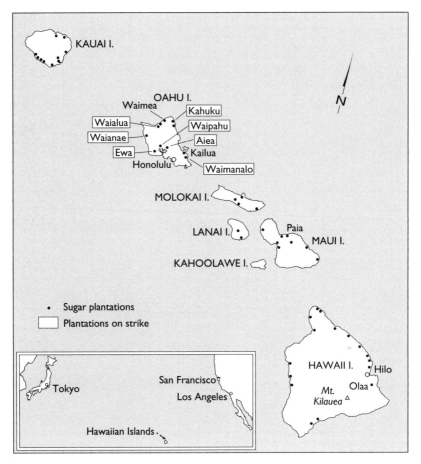

Map 1.   Hawaiian Islands

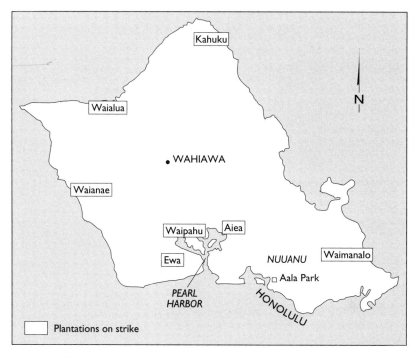

Map 2.   Oahu

A DYNAMITE BOMB EXPLODES

Olaa Plantation, Hawaii: June 3, 1920

AN EXPLOSION IN THE NIGHT

On April 15, 1920, on a street in South Braintree, Massachusetts, the paymaster of a shoe factory and his security guard were assaulted at midday while delivering the employees' payroll. The guard died instantly, the paymaster the next day. Three weeks later, on May 5, the shoemaker Nicola Sacco and the fishmonger Bartolomeo Vanzetti were arrested on suspicion of robbery and murder. Both men were Italian immigrants known to be anarchists. Thus began the "Sacco and Vanzetti Case," notorious in American labor history.

Less well known is an incident that began six weeks later, on June 3, 1920, at Olaa Plantation on the island of Hawaii, five thousand miles and five time zones from South Braintree. The journey by train across the continent and then by ship from the West Coast took half a month. To mainland Americans, Hawaii seemed closer to East Asia than to America, and the islands were still a territory, not yet recognized as a state.

A small item in the June 4 *Honolulu Star Bulletin* noted, "The home of a Japanese eight miles from Olaa was blown up with giant powder last night." The newspaper did not give the name of the victim, but it reported that the man was in a back bedroom at the time and was not killed, even though the front of the house was destroyed.

It is not surprising that no name was mentioned. Laborers who worked in the sugarcane fields, the main industry in Hawaii, were anonymous to the companies that employed them. Because their names sounded unfamiliar to their haole bosses, they were forced to wear aluminum neck tags engraved with numbers. It was by these "bango" numbers that they were recognized when they received their semimonthly pay, charged items at the company store, or were punished for violating regulations.

The man unnamed in this incident, however, was not a mere laborer. He was Jūzaburō Sakamaki, the interpreter for the Olaa Sugar Company, who was paid a salary under his own name just as the haole employees were. At the time the forty-nine-year-old Sakamaki was known to the haoles as Frank Sakamaki.

During the trial over the incident, Sakamaki recalled the explosion. "It was about eleven o'clock P.M. that night of the third of June; maybe a little before or maybe ten or fifteen minutes," he said. "I didn't take a look at the clock that time; the clock was fallen down. I was awokened by sound and, of course, didn't realize that it was an explosion; first thought it was water-tank fell or something; anyway, I was awokened by the sound, and my wife was in another room and she called me, 'What was that sound? What was that noise?' Then a little later my boy said he smelled powder; then I realized it was an explosion." [1]

The *Star Bulletin* was wrong when it reported that Sakamaki was in a back bedroom. All of the bedrooms in the Sakamaki house were on the second floor; none were at the rear of the house. According to Sakamaki's testimony, after he heard the blast, he jumped out of bed and rushed downstairs with a flashlight. When he reached the first floor, it was so full of smoke he could not see clearly. Somehow he made his way outside and ran to the house of the inspector (the security guard hired directly by the plantation). Even running through the field of sugarcane taller than a man so fast that he got out of breath, it took him five or six minutes to get there. The inspector's wife, wearing a muumuu as a nightgown, came to the door. The inspector himself had just dashed out of his house, thinking that something had occurred at the mill.

Instead of following the inspector to the mill, Sakamaki ran to the Olaa Sugar Company office, grabbed the wall telephone, and called Charles F. Eckart, the manager of Olaa Plantation, at his home. After Sakamaki apologized for waking him in the middle of the night, Eckart calmly responded that he would contact the local police and then go to the Sakamaki house right away. Approximately twenty minutes later, Henry Martin, deputy sheriff of the Olaa district police station, arrived there by car.

In the meantime Sakamaki had run home and found that the smoke had cleared considerably, revealing what had happened inside. In the parlor, the table was overturned, and legless chairs were strewn all over the room. It looked as if a toy chest had been dumped onto the floor. In the living room next to the parlor, shards from vases and other objects were scattered everywhere. Then Sakamaki noticed for the first time that the side of the house had been blown off.

In the seventy years since the explosion, Hawaiian society has undergone great changes, but today the only way to reach the Olaa Sugar Company from the city of Hilo is by following the old road. About eight miles from Hilo, Volcano Road, the route taken by tourist buses going to Mount Kilauea, crosses a road so narrow that one could easily miss it. The road curves gently for a mile or so toward the ocean. Since it was a private company road, it is not named on the map, but the local people still call it Plantation Road. Unlike the paved Volcano Road, it remains a gravel road just as it was in 1920. According to the confession of the perpetrator, it was the road he used to flee after setting the explosives.

When I visited Olaa in 1987, the road was overgrown on either side with sugarcane gone wild. After turning onto it, I saw in the distance beyond the golden cane the tall smokestack of the mill. As the mill was to be closed two months later after eighty-five years of operation, no smoke rose from it. The mill consisted of several dilapidated tin-sided structures. The suffocatingly sweet smell so peculiar to sugar refineries, produced by the filtering of the boiled juice pressed from the cane, was long gone. Next to a huge concrete water tank was a tall water tower. It was not the same one there at the time of the incident, but the location and height were similar. When Sakamaki and the inspector heard the blast of the explosion, both had mistakenly thought that the water tower had fallen down.

The Olaa Sugar Company building, referred to by the local people simply as the "Office," is four times larger than it was at the time of the incident. It is a very long single-story wooden structure with peeling white paint and a deep eave along the front to offer protection from the heavy rainfall throughout the year. The distance between the Office and the mill is about one hundred fifty meters across the sugarcane fields. Looking diagonally right behind the Office, the roof and smokestack of the mill are visible and the water tower tank seems to be floating on a sea of sugarcane.

The Sakamaki house was in the middle of the cane field, on the border of north district fields 390 and 370, near Olaa Eight Mile Station on the rail line from Hilo. Hiroshi Baba, a trucking company owner in Hilo who formerly worked on the administrative staff at Olaa Sugar Company, lived in the former Sakamaki house until he retired. "It was a large house," he recalled, "just like one for the haoles." It stood by itself at a distance behind the company buildings. There were only three other houses nearby—company houses for haole technicians and a Portuguese engineer—but they were still at some distance across the cane fields. The camps where plantation laborers lived, grouped by their countries of origin, were even farther away. The closest, Eight Mile Camp, was half a mile away. The inspector's house at Eight Mile Camp, where about forty skilled mill workers lived, was about four hundred meters from the Sakamaki house.

The plantation workday started before sunup. The plantation laborers awakened at 4:30 A.M. and were in the fields by 6:00. The administration staff were at the Office by 7:00. Because they started so early in the morning, workers went to bed soon after sundown, and the lamps in their houses were turned off early in the evening. Sunset in Hawaii on the day of the incident was 6:38 P.M. When Sakamaki had run along the paths through the sugarcane fields on the night of the explosion, the moon was two-thirds full.

Houses on Hawaii, where the climate is always warm and humid, are set above the ground. The floor of the Sakamaki house was raised about 70 centimeters above ground level on the Hilo side but as high as 160 centimeters on the volcano, or *mauka,* side. The dynamite had been set under the floor between the parlor and the dining room on the mauka side. The impact of the explosion can be seen vividly in the photographs taken for the police by a Japanese photographer from Olaa on the morning after the incident. The outside of the house was faced with vertical boards. In the section with the worst damage, sixteen of these boards had been blown off, leaving a large hole that looked as if a cannon shell had hit. In other sections, the boards were cracked up to the roofline or were nearly falling off. The window glass had splintered, and the second floor window frame was twisted and dangling. Strewn on the ground were jagged fragments of wood, their ends seemingly sharpened, and scattered about were pieces of what looked like steel pipe. A kerosene tank under the floor had once piped in the oil for the lamps inside the house, but at the time of the explosion it was not being used. If this tank had been full of kerosene, the dynamite blast would have been considerably more destructive.

Plantation workers' living quarters in the camps were mostly row houses, and families even lived in one room, sleeping on mats on the wooden floor. By contrast the Sakamaki family lived in luxury. The house had running water. On the ground floor were a parlor, living room, and dining room across the hall from a kitchen, bath, and storage room. On the second floor were Mrs. Sakamaki's sewing room and four bedrooms. At the time of the blast, Sakamaki had six children. His eldest son, Paul (Tokuo), a seventeen-year-old junior in high school who had smelled the gunpowder right away, was the only one with his own bedroom. On the other side of the sewing room Sakamaki's wife, Haru (36), slept with their sixth son, Noboru (3), their oldest daughter, Masa (8), and their fifth son, Charles (Yūroku, 5). (Their fourth son had died in infancy.) Across the hallway was the room where their second son, George (Jōji, 15), and third son, Shunzo (Shunzō, 13), slept, and next to it was Sakamaki's bedroom. At the trial, Sakamaki recalled seeing cracks in his oldest boy's bedroom. "It was a narrow escape for us," he said. "We all think ourselves very fortunate we escape this."

The only Sakamaki children still living are Masa and Ben, a seventh son born ten months after the incident. Masa is the only witness who can describe the dynamiting incident as she saw it, but even now she does not wish to speak of her memories. Ben told me that at the time the Sakamaki garden was full of hibiscus and other colorful plants. "On the banana tree, which was the tallest tree by far," he said, "one of the fragments of wood was stuck like a knife into the trunk."

WHO WAS JŪZABURŌ SAKAMAKI?

After Sen Katayama, an early socialist and influential labor leader, visited Hawaii, he wrote an article in his journal, *Tobei,* devoted to promoting emigration to America.

> In my tour of various locations on Hawaii Island, I have been struck beyond my imagination by the many Japanese who are involved in independent businesses and progressing to greater levels of prosperity. In particular, the Japanese like those at Olaa Plantation are actively growing sugarcane in trial cultivation, and so naturally are proud of their accomplishments and full of confidence and high morale. . . . Two men most likely to become well known at Olaa are Mr. Jirō Iwasaki of Eleven Miles and Mr. Jūzaburō Sakamaki at Nine Miles [author's note: mistake for Eight Miles]. They are the star actors in local business circles.[2]

Japanese Americans who remember Olaa in its early days still mention the names of these two close *furen* (friends), Jirokichi (also known as Jirō) Iwasaki, the contract labor boss with two thousand immigrant laborers under him, and Jūzaburō Sakamaki, the plantation interpreter. Many photographs donated to the Bishop Museum in Honolulu by the descendants of Jirokichi Iwasaki show just the two of them, with the tall Iwasaki seated on a cane chair and the shorter Sakamaki standing next to him. Sakamaki, who always wore a suit, stood upright with hands on hips. Other photographs show the two men with important visitors, such as the consul general of Japan on his way to view Mount Kilauea, a succession of haole managers, or Emō Imamura, the head priest of the Hawaii mission of Honpa Honganji and a powerful presence in the Japanese immigrant community. As these photographs make clear, Iwasaki and Sakamaki were men of status in the local Japanese community.

Sakamaki's distinctive feature was his eyes. In every photograph, Sakamaki stares intently straight at the camera lens, his gaze, beneath bushy eyebrows, penetrating and almost hostile. His eyes seem to reveal a suspicious nature. Even in family photographs in Ben's album, Sakamaki clenches his fists and furrows his brow as if he was in some pain. Ben remembers that his father, who was fifty when he was born, "was extremely short-tempered."

According to Tomiji Togashi, who was born in 1911 and reared on Olaa Plantation where his father had come from Niigata, Sakamaki was feared as a man of strong likes and dislikes. "He boasted that he was from a samurai family," said Togashi. When Sakamaki's house was blown apart in the explosion, his collection of samurai swords, spears, and helmets was flung onto the floor. But after leaving Japan as a youth, Sakamaki had never returned, and according to Ben, all the "samurai things" had been collected in Hawaii.

Records of the retainers in the Tsugaru domain of the Hirosaki City Library in Aomori prefecture show that generations of the Sakamaki family served in Edo as clerks. The sixth-generation Hisao Sakamaki, a samurai with an upper-middle-rank stipend, had six children. Jūzaburō, the youngest child of his third son, was born in Tokyo in 1869, the year after the Meiji Restoration. Jūzaburō's father died when he was four years old, and the family's life became difficult when the old domains were abolished in 1871. His mother had to run a private boardinghouse to make ends meet. As the youngest son raised by his widowed mother, Jūzaburō was uncommonly headstrong. When he was fifteen, without telling his mother, he stowed away on a ship bound overseas from Yoko-hama, hiding in the hold for a few days until the ship set sail.

In a way Sakamaki was following in the footsteps of Sen Katayama, who had landed a year earlier in San Francisco at the age of twenty-six, inspired by a letter from a friend who had gone to the United States ear-lier. America, his friend had written, was a place where you could study even if you were poor. Taking jobs as school boy, dishwasher, janitor, and servant, Katayama persevered until he finally obtained a degree in theology from Yale University's Divinity School. Life as a "school boy," working as a live-in servant helping with housework in the morning and evening while going to school during the day, offered the best opportu-nity for study, he later observed, but it was all too easy to become bored. "It is regrettable," he noted, "that the students who graduate are ex-tremely rare."

After arriving in the United States, Sakamaki went East to Pennsyl-vania, where he spent nine years studying and working. But unlike Kata-yama, Sakamaki did not graduate from college. Although he was ad-mitted to one, he did not stay to graduate. Receiving word that his mother was ill, he decided to return home. But by the time he reached Hawaii he learned that she was already dead, so he canceled his plans to go on to Japan. Just at the time, the Olaa Sugar Company was estab-lished, and he was hired as the company's only regular interpreter.

As interpreter, Sakamaki was the only pipeline between the company and the Japanese immigrants who made up the majority of the labor force at Olaa Plantation. Even a labor contractor like Iwasaki had to go through Sakamaki for all his contacts with the plantation manager. The outcome of discussions with plantation management very much de-pended on what the company interpreter said, so it is not surprising that Iwasaki kept on close terms with Sakamaki, calling him "Jū-chan" and "furen."

Workers who cultivated a few acres of cane fields as tenants of the company as well as field laborers had to go through Sakamaki in all their dealings, from advances on fertilizer to bargaining for wages. Quite a few people called themselves interpreters, but Sakamaki had more clout than the others. As assistant postmaster of the Olaa post office, Saka-maki was involved in all the daily activities of the Japanese in Olaa. The post office was in a corner of the company office. The plantation man-ager was nominally the postmaster, but in actuality all the work was done by Sakamaki. As the agent of the Consulate General of Japan in Honolulu he was also in charge of administering the immigrants' family register items. In this capacity, he not only dealt with registrations of births, deaths, marriages, adoptions and other family matters, he handled remittances that workers sent home. (A 1918 study conducted by the Consulate General showed that two-thirds of the monies sent back to Japan was handled through the plantation post office. Banks were inconvenient for plantation laborers as their branch offices were located in town.) Clearly the rebellious young stowaway, as Katayama reported, had made himself into a man of considerable local importance.

TWO SUSPECTS ARE ARRESTED

Deputy Sheriff Martin rushed to the Sakamaki residence immediately after the explosion, but it was still dark, so there was nothing he could be do. He left quickly. Sakamaki's eldest son, Paul, and his second son, George, both high school students, took turns standing guard, pistol at the ready, until the sun rose. Early in the morning of June 4, Martin returned with a photographer to conduct his investigation. The senior captain of the police of the island of Hawaii, H. T. Lake, who had been posted previously at the Olaa police station and knew Sakamaki, also arrived from Hilo.

Arrests came quickly. The *Honolulu Star Bulletin,* whose June 4 article treated the explosion as a local event, gave it a mere ten lines, reporting that the case had been resolved. "Two Japanese have been arrested on suspicion," the paper reported. "The dynamiting, it is said, was the result of a row over cane contracts." The Japanese-language newspapers reported the case briefly too, but they gave the suspects' names. The *Hawaii hōchi* reported, "The police authorities suspect that those who set the dynamite were laborers with a grudge against the interpreter Sakamaki and intended to kill interpreter Sakamaki. They have arrested two men as suspects, G. Fujioka and S. Iwasa, and have taken them to the police station for questioning." The *Hōchi* article was dated "June 4, 11:34 A.M.: (Honolulu) head office." Since the news was telephoned from Hilo, that means that the suspects had already been arrested at the latest by 11:00 A.M. on the morning following the explosion.

No records of the Sakamaki incident remain in either the local police station or materials related to the history of Hilo. A directory of Japanese residents from the 1920s lists only one Fujioka with the initial G., a tenant field worker from Hiroshima prefecture. The other suspect was Sueji Iwasa, a labor contractor who had risen very rapidly, in competition with Jirokichi Iwasaki. A native of Fukuoka, he controlled several hundred laborers from Kyūshū. Natives of Kyūshū had a reputation for being hot-tempered, and Iwasa was particularly well known for his high-handed methods. He was thirty-one years old at the time, some twenty years younger than Sakamaki. Sakamaki may have seen Iwasa as an up-start who, unlike his friend Iwasaki, did not understand the line between what was permissible and what was not.

Jirokichi Iwasaki had died the previous year. At the time of the explo-sion his widow, Tazuko, a total novice, had become the chief contract-ing agent for Olaa with the help of her husband's subordinates. Her hus-band's furen, Sakamaki, was also helpful to her in bidding on contracts. According to Tazuko Iwasaki's recollection, she worried that grudges arising over the bidding might result in sabotage, such as fires set in the cane fields during the harvest. She had her men take turns standing watch over the fields night and day. Other disturbances occurred as well. She mentioned that Sueji Iwasa was responsible for this kind of harass-ment. Naturally, Sakamaki did not make decisions to award labor con-tracts by himself. However, it was he who stood between the Japanese contractors and the company manager and other company officials. At the very least, Sakamaki was clearly in a position that made him the tar-get of dissatisfactions and misunderstandings.

NOBODY SAID MUCH

A few days after the dynamiting incident, Charles Eckart, the Olaa Plan-tation manager, gathered the local Japanese contractors and representa-tives of the tenant farmers at his home. It was located about two miles south of the company office on a rise with a distant view of the ocean. The mansion still stands, its landmark a huge banyan tree that is said to date from the era when native chieftains held power. Along the private road leading to the mansion dozens of tall coconut trees pierce the sky. The three-story white structure sits on the crest of a rise surrounded by an extensive lawn. On its grounds were a stable for a few riding horses and a shed for a dozen or so dairy cows kept for milk and butter. Al-though the mansion is weathered and worn now, it is still imposing enough to hint at the status and power of the plantation manager, who the Japanese laborers likened to a daimyo, or feudal lord, and who they regarded as the "owner" of the plantation. At the front was a wide porch with a carved bannister from which the ocean could be seen. Hiroshi Baba, who grew up in a cottage behind the mansion, where his father worked as a cook, recalls that his father told him that it was on that porch that the Japanese representatives assembled.

Charles F. Eckart (age forty-five at the time) had come to Hawaii from California, a state where anti-Japanese feelings ran high. Of the successive managers of the plantation he enjoyed a particularly high reputation among the Japanese immigrant workers, who regarded him as a man of good character. After studying agricultural chemistry in college, he was invited to work at the Hawaii experiment station of the Hawaiian Sugar Planters' Association, where he eventually became the director. Even after he was hired away in 1913 to become the manager at Olaa, he continued to be active in research on prevention of damage by insects. In 1919 he set up a plant to produce paper from the cane fiber remaining after straining. The paper was used to cover cane sprouts to prevent the growth of weeds. This innovation brought savings in labor costs. Later widely used in pineapple fields (where vinyl sheets now substitute for paper), this method earned Eckart a place in the history of Hawaiian sugar production. The 1918 Hawaii Meikan, a Japanese-language directory, noted, "[Eckart] obtains good results by working hard and diligently [as plantation manager] without making distinctions among regular workers, contract workers, or independent tenant farmers [and] promotes mutual benefit to the satisfaction of both sides without clashes of opinion at contract renewal times." (These words are testimony to the capabilities of Jūzaburō Sakamaki, who, as interpreter, acted as mediator between the company and the Japanese.)

From the start Eckart faced the explosion incident squarely as a sign of discord among the Olaa Plantation workers. Through a young nisei (second-generation) interpreter, Eckart asked the assembled contractors and tenant representatives, "I'd like to have you tell me without hesitation if you have any pilikia [trouble] or complaints about Frank Sakamaki." But no one said much to the "plantation owner." Sakamaki was neither dismissed nor demoted as a result of the incident. He remained the authority who stood between the Japanese and the company.

After June 4 no further reports on the explosion appeared in either the English or the Japanese newspapers. According to the June 4 Hawaii hōchi, Iwasa and Fujioka, the two men arrested for "attempting to kill Sakamaki by setting dynamite," were eventually released for lack of evidence. There were others who may have wanted to harm Sakamaki, but they may have felt that their grudges were satisfied by the dynamiting incident. Even though many deplored the use of dynamite, no one sympathized with Sakamaki. As the days gradually passed, the Olaa laborers, weary from their grueling work, spoke less and less about the incident, and then not at all.

THE TRUE NATURE OF THE SAKAMAKI INCIDENT

Dynamite, an extremely explosive nitroglycerin compound, can blow apart solid rock in an instant. Today it is still indispensable in mining and in dam, tunnel, and road construction. It also was one of the essential tools of the Hawaiian sugar industry. It was used in the volcanic terrain of Olaa to break up rocks in the cane fields and to construct roads through them. But dynamite can also be used as a weapon, and it is very much part of the history of labor strife in the United States. Indeed, numerous well-known labor struggles involved the use, or rather the alleged use, of dynamite. The Pennsylvania coal mine strike (1875), Chicago's Haymarket Square riot (1886), the Pullman Train Coach Company strike (1894), the assassination of the governor of Idaho (1905), the *Los Angeles Times* bombing incident (1910), the Lawrence textile workers' strike (1912), the Ludlow coal mine strike (1913), the Tom Mooney case (1915), and more—in many of these cases labor leaders were arrested and convicted on suspicion of killing or attempted killing by dynamite blasts, often on charges trumped up by the authorities, even though the true perpetrators remained unknown.

The dynamiting of the Sakamaki house should be considered part of this history of violent labor strife. Five months before the incident a strike had begun on a scale that Hawaii had not previously seen. Known as the second Oahu Island strike, it spread to all the Hawaiian islands. The strike was organized by the Japanese immigrant laborers who formed the majority of the sugarcane field labor force. At the time of the dynamiting incident no one on the plantation suggested that the explosion at the Sakamaki house might be related to this strike, nor was there any indication that the local authorities viewed the event in that light. But the significance of the Sakamaki dynamiting incident can only be understood against the background of labor struggles in the United States.

Neither the dynamiting incident nor the 1920 Oahu strike has received much, if any, attention in the history of American labor. The likely reason is that these events occurred in Hawaii, a territory distant from the mainland, and involved Japanese immigrant workers who remained outside the mainstream of American society. Nor have historians of the Japanese immigrant community in Hawaii delved into either event despite the importance of the strike in the lives of so many Japanese American families.

This book attempts to situate the events surrounding the 1920 Oahu strike in the framework of both labor history and immigrant history. But to treat them solely within these frameworks may blind us to their true significance. The Oahu strike captured public attention on the mainland in August 1921, when it became an issue before both houses of Congress in Washington, D.C. The struggle between the immigrant Japanese workers and the powerful Hawaiian sugar plantation owners became part of a process that led to the passage of the so-called Exclusion Act of 1924, an event that was to cast a long shadow on future relations between Japan and the United States.

By the early 1920s many Americans had begun to look at Japan and the Japanese with deep suspicion. In late 1921 a long feature article on U.S.-Japan relations captured some of those feelings.

> The most important country in the world to Americans today is Japan. . . . Japan is the only nation whose commercial and territorial ambitions, whose naval and emigration policies are in direct conflict with our own. . . . With the temporary eclipse of Germany as a world-power, Japan is the only potential enemy on our horizon, she is the only nation that we have reason to fear. The problem that demands the most serious consideration of the American people and the highest quality of American statesmanship is the Japanese Question. On its correct and early resolution hangs the peace of the world. . . . What is needed at the present juncture is an earnest endeavor on the part of each people to gain a better understanding of the temperament, traditions, ambitions, problems, and limitations of the other, and to make corresponding allowances for them—in short, to cultivate a charitable attitude of mind. . . . [T]he interests at stake are so vast and far-reaching, the consequences of an armed conflict would be so catastrophic and overwhelming, that it is unthinkable that the two people should be permitted to drift into war through a lack of knowledge and appreciation of each other.[3]

But far from nurturing a "charitable attitude of mind" among the American public, the Oahu strike deepened distrust of Japan. And in doing so it marked a step toward the "unthinkable" conflict that many on both sides of the Pacific already saw on the distant horizon.

ONE

THE JAPANESE VILLAGE IN THE PACIFIC

JAPANESE IMMIGRATION TO HAWAII

The first Japanese immigrants to Hawaii, known as the *gannen mono* (first-year arrivals), arrived in 1868. The Hawaiian Kingdom's Board of Immigration had asked Eugene Van Reed, an American merchant who had served as the Hawaiian consul in Japan, to recruit contract laborers to work in the cane fields. Van Reed recommended the Japanese as excellent laborers and spoke in the highest terms of their industry and docility, their cleanliness and honesty, and their adaptability.

It proved difficult to gather the anticipated number of 350 immigrants, and in the end only 148 (of these 6 were women) were actually recruited. Their pay was to be $4 per month with room and board provided for a three-year period, and Hawaii covered their round-trip ship passage. Many of the gannen mono were gamblers and idlers recruited from the streets of Yokohama who knew nothing about farming and were ill-suited for hard work in the sugarcane fields. When misunderstandings arose about their pay, this first effort at bringing in Japanese labor ended in failure. No additional contract workers came from Japan for another decade and a half.

By that time sugar had become king in Hawaii. In the late eighteenth century James Cook, the first Caucasian to set foot on Hawaiian soil, had noted in his ship journal that he had seen sugarcane. Half a century later, in the 1820s, missionaries arrived by sailing ship from New England, not only to convert the natives to Christianity, but also to teach them how to write and farm. It was the Hawaiian-born descendants of these missionaries, called *kamaaina*, who saw the potential for sugar-cane production in Hawaii. In 1848 foreigners, who had previously leased cane fields from the Hawaiian kings and chieftains, were allowed to buy land. Haole ownership of land increased rapidly. Not only did the scale of the sugar industry change suddenly, the social structure of Hawaii was transformed as well. The power of the Hawaiian royal dynasty, established by King Kamehameha I ten years before the missionaries' arrival, began to decline.

From the beginning the greatest problem for the Hawaiian sugar industry was the lack of a labor force. Native Hawaiians worked only when they felt like it—a custom they called *kanaka*—and were not inclined toward heavy labor in the fields all day long. Their numbers were also rapidly reduced by epidemic disease brought by foreign whaling ships. In 1850 a labor contract law was enacted to increase the labor supply. Workers from China were the first outsiders to be sought out as cheap labor. Docile and hardworking, they gradually constituted the majority of cane field laborers. But after working diligently and saving money, these Chinese workers would leave the fields when their contracts were up (five years initially, three years from 1870 on) to open up businesses. Some also went to the American mainland.

From early on Chinese laborers had gone to California to work on building the continental railroad. The Taiping rebellion and other disturbances that wreaked havoc in China produced a continuous stream of immigrants seeking work in America. But the Chinese newcomers were soon perceived as a threat by Caucasian laborers. Not only did they put up with exploitation and work hard for low pay, they held fast to their own ways of life. They still wore their pigtails, they lived in their own separate Chinatowns, and they continued to gamble and smoke opium. Seeing the Chinese as immigrants who could not be assimilated, the Caucasians began to demand that the Chinese must go. When a recession in the 1870s led to severe unemployment, Caucasian labor unions took the lead in the movement opposing Chinese immigration to the United States. Gradually the quota for Chinese immigrants was decreased, and in 1882 Congress passed the Chinese Exclusion Act.

By this time only a quarter of Chinese laborers who had migrated to Hawaii were left in the cane fields, and the sugar planters of Hawaii had already begun to seek other cheap labor to take their place. The Japanese government signed a formal immigration agreement with the kingdom of Hawaii in 1885. During the next nine years, nearly thirty thousand Japanese crossed the ocean to work under three-year contracts for wages of $12.50 per month. Most were poor tenant farmers from the bottom economic strata in Japan. Unlike the gannen mono, these Japanese contract workers were accustomed to working in the fields. Seeing that the Japanese worked as strenuously as the Chinese, the plantation owners soon competed to hire them. (Plantation managers ordered the procurement of "Japs" in the same memoranda in which they ordered macaroni, rice, horses, and mules.)

The Japanese government backed the contract labor system as a way of earning foreign exchange. It declared, "If we send 3 million workers out into the world and each one of them sends back to Japan $6 per year, the country will benefit." In fact, money remitted by the immigrants to Japan during the Meiji period amounted to more than 2 million yen annually. For a Japan struggling under foreign debts incurred to procure military equipment and other foreign goods, the foreign currency sent home by the immigrants, who hoped to return home "clad in brocade" after enduring hard labor under the broiling Hawaiian sun, was not an insignificant sum.

The United States was in a period of rapid industrial growth after the end of the Civil War. A great wave of European immigrants were pouring into the East Coast as unskilled factory workers, just as the Japanese were pouring into Hawaii, still an independent kingdom. There was a significant difference, however, between the Japanese and the European immigrants. The Europeans had forsaken their homelands and had placed their hopes in the New World, where they intended to stay permanently. By contrast, the Japanese immigrants to Hawaii expected to return home. In fact, they were indentured as contract immigrants, a practice forbidden by law in the United States. Japanese Foreign Ministry documents referred to the immigrants as "officially contracted overseas laborers" (kanyaku dekaseginin), and they were admitted into Hawaii solely to work in the sugarcane fields.

After 1893, when the Japanese government entrusted the immigration business to private immigration companies, the number of privately contracted overseas laborers increased. The following year the Hawaiian monarchy was overthrown with the help of American marines supporting the haole sugar planters. Hawaii became a "republic." Four years later, in 1898, the republic was annexed by the United States. For the sugar planters, who engineered the whole process, joining the United States was a long-cherished goal. Annexation meant an end to tariffs, enabling Hawaiian sugar to compete better with Cuban sugar or beet sugar from the U.S. mainland.

Nearly all the sugar plantations in Hawaii were under the control of five major sugar factoring companies organized by the powerful and unified kamaaina elite. Dominating all aspects of sugar marketing and management, as well as procurement of the labor force and seeds, these companies gradually absorbed small-scale growers with meager capital. Known as the Big Five, they became the new royalty of Hawaii and exercised enormous influence over the Hawaiian territorial government.

The annexation of Hawaii coincided with the extension of American sovereignty over the territories of the Philippines, Guam, and Puerto Rico, acquired as a result of the Spanish-American War, and with the enunciation of the Open Door policy in China. These developments marked a full-fledged American advance into the Asia-Pacific region, just at a time when Japan was expanding its power on the Asian continent after its military victory over China in 1895. In a clear display of its national strength, almost annually Japan had already been sending its imperial fleet, with rising sun flag unfurled, to Hawaii, a strategic spot in the Pacific Ocean.

Olaa Plantation, where Jūzaburō Sakamaki was hired as an interpreter, was established as a corporation capitalized at $5 million in May 1899, a year after annexation. Anticipating capital infusion from the U.S. mainland, much new plantation land was opened up after annexation. The development of Olaa was unprecedented in scale. An enormous land reclamation project opened some 20,000 acres (8,093 hectares) of cane fields extending from a point eight miles from Hilo to the Kilauea volcano. Originally owned by the Hawaiian royal family, the Olaa area was a jungle thick with ohia trees, ferns, and shrubs. The land had been sold to private individuals, and coffee cultivation had been attempted some ten years before but had ended in failure because of too much rainfall. The climate, however, was very suitable for sugarcane cultivation.

The first person to be hired for the Olaa reclamation project was the labor contractor Jirokichi Iwasaki. Gathering about fifty Japanese laborers and with the help of three horses, Iwasaki cleared 40 acres (about 16 hectares). He was the first contractor to undertake not only clearing the land but also the entire process of sugarcane cultivation, from *kanakou* (planting of cane), *hanawae* (irrigation of planted cane), *holehole* (cutting of dried grass), and *kachiken* (harvesting the cane) to *furubi* (transporting the cane by waterways) and *hapai ko* (loading). And it was Jūzaburō Sakamaki's job not merely to act as interpreter but to enable the Japanese laborers and the company to understand each other.

Within six months of the opening of the plantation, the number of laborers at Olaa swelled to 1,829. The vast majority were Japanese (1,268 were Japanese, 132 were Chinese, and 429 were Hawaiian). Still there were not enough. Workers were needed not only to grow sugar cane but also to lay a railroad line to carry the cane to the port at Hilo.

Annexation advanced the interests of the sugar industry, but it was not all to the producers' advantage. When Hawaii came under American law, contract labor immigration ended immediately. Finding themselves unexpectedly free, many Japanese workers left Hawaii in search of "gold-bearing trees" on the American mainland, where working conditions were vastly better. The Hawaiian sugar producers, who had expected that American law would not apply in Hawaii for three years, grew alarmed. To deal with the exodus of Japanese laborers, the Hawaiian legislature enacted a high business tax on the go-betweens who supplied laborers to the mainland, but even this did not halt the flow of workers out of Hawaii.

In the meantime anti-Japanese movements gained momentum on the West Coast. The California Japanese Exclusion League circulated pamphlets alleging that Japanese immigrants "don't mind low pay and long hours of work"; that they "have a strong sense of patriotism, and send money to their homeland without contributing to the American economy"; that they "do not make efforts to learn English"; that they "do not throw off their own culture, and refuse to assimilate"; and that they "engage in public urination, gamble with *hanafuda* cards, and, even on Sunday, get drunk and buy women." When there was an economic downturn, Caucasian workers targeted Japanese immigrants just as earlier they had worked to exclude Chinese low-wage workers.

Against this background, in 1907 President Theodore Roosevelt issued an executive order on termination of labor migration from Hawaii. Since Japan showed its ambition to dominate East Asia with its victory in the Russo-Japanese War two years earlier, American wariness toward Japan was rapidly on the rise. In 1906 the San Francisco School Board had resolved to segregate Japanese pupils in the public schools. When the Japanese government objected, the federal government in Washington, D.C., forced the city of San Francisco to rescind its resolution. But at the same time Roosevelt issued his executive order preventing Japanese immigrants from going to the mainland from Hawaii.

In 1908 the so-called Gentlemen's Agreement was reached to appease anti-Japanese feelings. The Japanese government agreed to voluntarily restrict emigration to the United States to reentering immigrants and their parents, wives, or children. Until the Gentlemen's Agreement the majority of Japanese immigrants had been single men, and with so few women, relations between the sexes in the Japanese immigrant community provided one source of anti-Japanese feelings among the Caucasians. To put an end to this situation "picture bride" marriages—marriages of convenience contracted by prospective partners who exchanged photographs—were encouraged.

ON THE EVE OF THE FIRST OAHU STRIKE

The Hawaiian consul in Japan, Van Reed, who had sent the first group of Japanese immigrants to Hawaii, assured the Hawaiian authorities that the Japanese were "docile." From the time the first shipload of government contract immigrants arrived, however, they constantly called for improvements in their harsh working conditions. The *lunas,* the overseers in the cane fields, were mostly Scottish, Portuguese, and Hawaiian. The Scottish, many of them former ship hands, in particular, were known for their mercilessness. They patrolled the fields on horseback, occasionally wielding their long snakeskin whips. A Department of Labor official sent to investigate labor conditions in the cane fields in 1910, reported that callous exploitation and abuse by the lunas were common on many plantations. He concluded that psychological oppression of cane field workers in Hawaii was no different from that suffered by black slaves in the South.

The Japanese laborers reacted to brutal treatment by the company by escaping, setting fire to cane fields, and other hostile acts. When contract labor was outlawed after annexation, the number of strikes, formal protests marked by organized negotiation, suddenly increased. For example, all the Japanese workers at Olaa Plantation struck on June 25, 1905. The origin of this strike was the death of a laborer who had taken medicine given him by the plantation hospital doctor. In those days plantation hospitals were often hospitals in name only, staffed by doctors with questionable qualifications, who sent workers home with laxatives for stomach- or headaches and Mercurochrome for cuts. The main work of the plantation hospital doctor, it was said, was to judge whether a worker was feigning illness.

The details of the 1905 Olaa strike are sketchy, but remaining documents indicate that the laborers demanded the dismissal not only of the plantation doctor and the clinic janitor but the plantation company interpreter, Jūzaburō Sakamaki, as well. The disturbance subsided the next day, however, and Sakamaki was not dismissed. Calling this protest a "strike" was clearly overreaction on the part of the company, but strikes on other plantations occurred around the same time. In 1901 cane cutters on Ewa Plantation struck for higher pay, and similar strikes took place at Waialua and Lahaina plantations in 1905 and Waipahu Plantation in 1906. But plantation workers also protested other kinds of exploitation and abuses as well.[1]

The first Oahu strike occurred in 1909, the year after the Gentlemen's Agreement. Approximately seven thousand Japanese laborers in all plantations on Oahu abandoned the cane fields for three months just before harvest, and the resulting collective bargaining was on an unprecedented scale. For the first time strikers called for the abolition of racial discrimination in treatment of workers and demanded wage increases to improve living conditions.

From the outset the sugar planters' policy toward laborers was based on racial discrimination. When the plantation owners imported Chinese low-wage labor, one of their motives was to raise the competitive spirit of the Hawaiians, who they thought took things too easily. On the plantations workers of each nationality set up their own living areas, forming Japanese camps or Chinese camps. Immigrant workers preferred to live together with their fellow countrymen. The plantation owners turned this to their own advantage by cleverly manipulating the competitiveness among the different nationalities to increase productivity. In the order of their arrival, the nationalities were Chinese, Japanese, Polynesians, Portuguese, Germans, Norwegians, Spanish, Australians, Italians, Puerto Ricans, African Americans, Koreans, Filipinos, and Russians.

As the Asian worker population grew, the plantation owners attempted to balance the labor force by hiring at least 10 percent white workers. They offered Europeans much better conditions than the Asians. The white workers were technicians and skilled workers in the mills, not manual laborers in the plantation fields. Records for 1896 show that while Japanese were given transportation costs plus wages, Germans were paid three times the wages of Japanese and given board as well. Rather than the shabby row houses allotted to Japanese, single-family houses were the norm for whites.

Although European workers were treated preferentially, most of them left for the American mainland when their three-year contracts expired.

Few stayed on in Hawaii. The Portuguese were the exception. The majority had come to Hawaii with their families intending to settle. The Portuguese came from a country close to the African continent and were swarthy, so the Hawaiian sugar planters did not recognize them as 100 percent white, but they did consider them best suited to oversee Asians in the fields.

Three months before the start of the first Oahu strike on January 29, 1909, a committee investigating agriculture in Hawaii sent a report to the secretary of agriculture in Washington, D.C.:

> There are some things about the Japanese situation in Hawaii that I believe the President should know. We are having industrial troubles with this race and there have been threats on the part of the Japanese of murder, assassination and destruction of plantation properties by fire, although thus far nothing more serious than to be a concerted effort to get all the Japanese laborers in Hawaii to go on a strike, has come of it.

The report, conveying the sugar planters' alarm about the Japanese laborers, was forwarded by the secretary of state to the secretary of the interior and on to the president. It forecast that strikes were coming in Hawaii. From the planters' perspective the attitude of the Japanese laborers was threatening.

When the 1909 strike began, for example, it was not unusual to see editorials such as the following in the Japanese-language newspapers.

> Now is the time to act in the spirit of national unity to assert our comrades' prestige and our comrades' rights. Even if, as you might say, we must endure coarse food, as subjects of the greater Japanese empire we will not flinch in standing up for a righteous cause. The Japanese are a people with the world's most fearsome perseverance. As long as they have rice and salt they can keep alive. In the Sino-Japanese and Russo-Japanese Wars, our heroic officers and soldiers sustained themselves for many months eating almost nothing but rice and pickled *ume* plums. That demonstrated our national glory in the world.[2]

During the 1909 strike opponents called those demanding wage increases "agitators," "irresponsible men," "opportunists," and "outlaws"; similarly, those who were against the strike were called "planters' dogs," "planters' pigs," "insurgents," "traitors," and "Czarist spies."

The number of Japanese immigrants increased sharply after the Russo-Japanese War. In 1906, 30,393 Japanese immigrants arrived in Hawaii, slightly more than the 29,669 who had come during the nine-year government-sponsored contract labor system. The majority were younger sons of farming families, who had returned safely from the war front but were unable to find work or inherit land. The government in Tokyo as well as prefectural governments fanned an "American fever" among these returning veterans. But the arrival of these immigrants, who had survived the battlefield, not only incited anti-Japanese feelings on the American mainland, it brought a sudden increase in the number of Japanese groups with patriotic names in Hawaii as well.

The book most often packed in the trunks of these former soldiers was Sen Katayama's *Tobei annai* (Guide to Going to America), a slim volume of seventy-nine pages first published in 1901. The initial printing of two thousand copies sold out in one week, and the book went through many subsequent printings, becoming a best-seller of the day. Its message was forthrightly patriotic. "For our country Japan to build up a strong power in the Orient and to attempt to achieve an independent destiny, Japan must promote thriving industries," the author noted. "That is to say, our country Japan should not remain an isolated island in the Orient but should pursue its advantage by expanding into the rest of the world. . . . *It is my deepest belief that our fellow Japanese who depart their country and brave the vast wild ocean to enter another land, engage in business abroad, and make themselves economically viable are the most loyal to the Emperor and patriotic among our countrymen."*

Katayama, who had returned to Japan after spending more than a decade living and studying in America, was a Christian Socialist. He founded Kingsley Hall, the first modern settlement house in Japan, participated in forming Japan's first labor union, became the editor of the first trade union paper, and joined with Shūsui Kōtoku and Isoo Abe to organize the Society for the Study of Socialism (Shakaishugi Kenkyū-kai). As he traveled throughout Japan publicizing the labor movement, Katayama urged Japanese youth to emigrate to America, and he established the American Emigration Association (Tobei Kyōkai), which held monthly meetings at Kingsley Hall. Readers who subscribed to his trade union paper, *Rōdō sekai* (Labor World), automatically became members of the society.[3] Not only did Katayama want to stabilize the paper's finances by gathering readers interested in going to America, he also hoped to inform these youths about labor issues and socialism. The back cover of *Tobei annai* carried an advertisement for *Rōdō sekai*. "Those who have been tyrannized by authority, come and enjoy *Labor World*," it said. "Those who are oppressed by the wealthy, come and make your appeal to *Labor World*." While Sen Katayama was a socialist, he was also a thorough realist. His argument for emigration was well within the bounds of a nationalist argument, which expected the emigrants to return to Japan.

SUSPICIOUS JAPANESE IN AMERICA

Not all the Japanese immigrants who crossed the Pacific were field laborers or ambitious students. The United States, particularly the West Coast, was also a haven for those whose political views were too radical to be tolerated by the authorities at home. At first many were refugees from the "popular rights movement," which had fought to force the Japanese government to adopt a constitution establishing a popularly elected national assembly. By the early 1900s Japanese with more extreme views began to arrive on the West Coast. The San Francisco region, including the city of Oakland across the bay, became a hotbed of antigovernment political malcontents. It is likely that the activities of these Japanese on the West Coast heightened the anxieties of the Hawaiian sugar planters and territorial officials.

In 1907, two years before the first Oahu strike, an open letter addressed to "Mutsuhito, Emperor of Japan from Anarchists-Terrorists" was posted at the Consulate General of Japan in San Francisco. It began, "We demand the implementation of the principle of assassination." After claiming that the emperor was not a god but, like other humans, an animal who had evolved from apes, it went on, "[The first emperor] Jimmu, the most brutal and inhumane man of his time, ruled as sovereign; under the name of being ruler he relished in every kind of crime and sin; his son followed his example and his grandson after him followed the example of his father; and so on and on down until 122 generations later." The "open letter" concluded, "Hey you, miserable Mutsuhito. Bombs are all around you, about to explode. Farewell to you."

This head-on attack against the authority of the emperor system shocked both Prime Minister Kimmochi Saionji and elder statesman Aritomo Yamagata, who immediately called in the head of the supreme court and the chief prosecutor to demand a review of the control of socialists. The incident sharply changed the attitude of the Japanese government toward leftist movements. The following year secret documents identifying "dangerous persons requiring close scrutiny" were prepared by the Police Bureau of the Home Ministry for distribution within the government. Socialists, anarchists, and communists were to be put under secret surveillance, but all those who criticized the existing national political system were targeted as well.

It is of particular interest that in this secret document are to be found many reports about "those residing in the U.S." According to an August 31, 1909, report by the consul general in San Francisco, "The anarchist movement had its origin in young men who gathered in San Francisco to hear Denjirō [Shūsui] Kōtoku advocate socialism on his visit to the U.S."[4] Shūsui Kōtoku spent eight months in San Francisco after arriving in November 1905. He had been imprisoned for five months for violating press ordinances in articles written for the *Heimin shinbun* (Commoner's Paper), and after his release from jail he left for America to recover his health. In San Francisco he relied on the help of Shigeki Oka, a former colleague at the newspaper *Yorozu chōhō*, who headed the San Francisco branch of the Heiminsha, a radical organization, and eked out a living in the freight business. With Oka's help, Kōtoku made contact with American socialists and anarchists. What most influenced him during his stay were San Francisco's Great Earthquake, which occurred six months after his arrival, and his contacts with the Industrial Workers of the World (IWW), an organization that found its way into the Police Bureau's top secret report.[5]

The mainstream of the American labor movement was represented by the American Federation of Labor (AFL), the largest labor union since its founding in 1886. The AFL took as members only skilled laborers and tended to exclude people of color. The IWW was formed in opposition to the AFL and welcomed members regardless of nationality, race, religion, or gender. An epoch-making federation, it included those abandoned by the AFL, those at the bottom of society, unskilled laborers, blacks, and new Asian immigrants unable to speak English. Unlike the moderate AFL, which put cooperation between labor and management first, the IWW adopted a strong ideology stressing that there were no common interests between employer and employee and that the mission of the working class was to "abolish the capitalist system." The IWW proclaimed that the sole road toward working-class liberation was through direct action such as strikes and boycotts. From its inception, the American authorities put the IWW under close scrutiny as a radical group.

Kōtoku contrasted his impressions of the IWW and AFL as "idealistic versus realistic, revolutionary versus reformist, radical versus moderate, those that put weight on the propagation of ideology versus those that place emphasis on winning elections." He confessed, "If I were to choose between these two, I prefer the idealistic, revolutionary, and radical."[6] On his return to Japan, Kōtoku squarely denounced the parliamentarianism of the moderate socialists and declared that the only strategy for the workers was to mount a general strike. He had become an advocate of the revolutionary methods of syndicalism. By urging a strategy of direct action imported from America, Kōtoku hoped to reinvigorate the socialist movement, which was being stifled under intense repression from the authorities.

In San Francisco, Kōtoku had again met Katayama with whom he had organized the Society for the Study of Socialism. Although the two men were opponents within the socialist movement, and although their personalities and ways of life were quite different, they were cordial toward one another in a foreign land. Katayama had been in the United States and Europe since December 1903. He had just returned to America after attending the Sixth International Socialist and Trade Union Congress in Amsterdam, where he served as vice-chairman along with the Russian representative. The congress had unanimously passed a resolution opposing war. During his stay in the United States, Katayama had planned to lead a group of immigrants to open up rice cultivation in Texas, but this plan ended in failure. However, he had succeeded in forming socialist groups among Japanese immigrants in Seattle and other areas on the West Coast.

Just before his return to Japan in 1906 Kōtoku had organized a socialist revolutionary party whose party membership register included the names of fifty-two persons from San Francisco, Oakland, Berkeley, Sacramento, Chicago, Boston, and New York. Among them was Sakutarō Iwasa, who later became a central figure along with Sakae Ōsugi in the anarchist movement. The incendiary open letter posted on the consulate door in San Francisco was instigated by a member of this group. Having promoted his ideas freely in the United States where he could evade the Japanese authorities, in what seems to be an irresponsible decision, Kōtoku summarily returned to Japan. The explosion of free thought he stimulated drew the attention not only of Japanese officials but also of American authorities.

Even before the open letter incident, the socialist revolutionary party had created a furor by publishing an article suggesting the assassination of the American president in its organ, *Kakumei* (Revolution). The *San Francisco Chronicle* ran the headline "Secret Servicemen on the trail of

Japanese publishers—Japs favor killing of President Roosevelt."[7] And across the bay, the *Berkeley Daily Gazette* warned, "Hotbed of Japanese Anarchists located here—the Yellow Peril."[8] The author of the radical statement, Tetsugorō Takeuchi, a member of the revolutionary party, was forced to move to Fresno, where he organized the Japanese Fresno Federation of Labor and published its magazine, *Rōdō* (Labor). In 1908 he led five thousand Japanese seasonal migrant grape pickers in a strike demanding better working conditions and wage increases. It was supported by Italian and Mexican members of the IWW. Four months before, Japanese immigrants had participated in a strike started by Mexicans in the sugar beet fields of southern California. Although the strike was quickly suppressed, the new involvement of Japanese laborers with the IWW attracted the notice of American authorities.

It was against this background of radicalism and labor unrest among Japanese workers on the mainland that the 1909 Oahu strike began. Sakutarō Iwasa and other Japanese sympathizers in San Francisco, calling themselves the Japanese Federation Strike Investigation Committee, sent a reporter from the newspaper *Nichibei* to Hawaii. An editorial in the paper strongly supported the strike: "This strike is the only way to struggle against capitalists."[9] Although the Japanese supporters on the mainland showed extraordinary interest in the Oahu strike, the largest ever mounted by Japanese immigrant workers, neither Japanese leftist activists nor the IWW became involved. Neither did the Police Bureau's secret report list any activists related to Hawaii.

The first Oahu strike ended in failure when all of its leaders were arrested. Soon after the strike, however, working conditions improved when treatment of workers on the basis of racial discrimination lessened and wages were increased. But the strike also spread anti-Japanese sentiments among the Hawaiian governing elite. The "Japanese problem" in Hawaii eventually came to the surface in the late 1910s in the controversy surrounding the oversight of the Japanese-language schools. As a participant in World War I, America had gone through a campaign of "one nation, one flag, one language." It was vital that an awareness of being an American was instilled in a nation made up of immigrants from so many countries. At a time when this "100% American movement" was at its height, the Japanese-language schools in Hawaii became the object of attack.

TWO

A PERSON TO BE WATCHED

Honolulu: 1918–1919

According to the records of the Japanese Consulate General in Honolulu, on February 28, 1918, twenty-eight-year-old Noboru Tsutsumi
arrived in Hawaii to take up a post as principal of a local Japanese-
language school. Two and a half years later his name also turned up in
the records of the General Intelligence Division of the Bureau of Investigation (renamed the Federal Bureau of Investigation in 1935) in Washington, D.C. The division had been established by Attorney General
A. M. Palmer in June 1919 after a series of bombings at the homes of
high-level government officials. Charged with gathering information
about revolutionary and ultra-radical groups, the General Intelligence
Division was placed under the direction of J. Edgar Hoover, who had
entered the bureau a scant two years before. Fulfilling Palmer's expec-
tations in short order, Hoover set up a master file of all radical activities, making it possible "to determine or ascertain in a few minutes the
numerous ramifications or individuals connected with the ultra-radical
movement."

Bluntly put, the activities of the Bureau of Investigation were the by-
product of the "red scare" that followed the Russian revolution. Fearing political subversion, the bureau specifically targeted labor movement leaders who were foreigners. Those suspected of being "Red" or
"foreign spies" were interrogated mercilessly. Two days before Sacco
and Vanzetti were arrested, for example, a suspected anarchist fell to his
death from the fourteenth floor of the bureau's New York branch office
where he had been detained. It was rumored that unable to endure the
severity of his interrogation he had committed suicide, or that he was

pushed by G-men. Among the comrades active in the movement demanding his release had been Sacco and Vanzetti.

The Bureau of Investigation compiled a Weekly Summary of Radical Activities from reports sent in by branch offices in major cities throughout the United States. These reports contained information about anarchist and socialist groups, the Communist party, labor union activities, and strikes, but they also covered the American Legion and other patriotic and right-wing groups. Reports about labor strikes were nearly always stamped "Attention of Mr. J. E. Hoover." The bureau also collected detailed reports about matters related to public security overseas. Naturally developments in the Soviet Union constituted the bulk of the information, but reports on "Japanese Affairs," including domestic strikes in Japan, gradually increased. Reports on activities of Japanese in the United States were limited, however, and information about Japanese in Hawaii was essentially nonexistent for this period. But the bureau did maintain files on Japanese "non-immigrants," or *hiimin* (the category used by the Japanese government under the Gentlemen's Agreement). Apparently suspecting all such people of espionage activities, the names of all Japanese on passenger lists of ships putting in to port were reported. No attention was paid to Japanese like T. Tsutsumi who disembarked in Hawaii. But his name did turn up in reports from the Los Angeles branch office of the Bureau of Investigation in reports of labor unrest on the West Coast of the mainland:[1]

> T. Tsutsumi; a strike leader and one of the leaders of the Japanese Federation of Labor. (January ?(unknown), 1921)
>
> Tsutsumi, Takashi; subject attended the conference of the Hawaii Laborers' Association. (December 1, 1919)
>
> Tsutsumi, T.; subject was Secretary of Hawaiian Laborers' Association at the time of strike in 1920, and was principal figure in directing strike activities. (September 10, 1921)

As there was no bureau branch office in the district of Honolulu and the Hawaiian Islands, the investigative reports were issued by the Los Angeles or San Francisco office.

The Los Angeles branch office investigative file on "T. Tsutsumi" dated January 13, 1921, reads as follows:

> Tsutsumi one of the leaders of the Japanese Federation of Labor is considered by Informants as a very dangerous agitator and a Radical *Socialist*. He is highly educated in Japanese, being a graduate of the Imperial University at

Tokio [mistake for Kyoto Imperial University]. . . . He is a very fluent speaker, very radical in his views. The laborers at present worship him like a god and believe whatever he tells them. . . . Tsutsumi, in a speech, told the Japanese that if they did not win he would commit Hari Kiri, that it would be *unpardonable* sin if the Japanese did not win and that in that event he would suicide. He said that the Sumitomo bank had agreed to advance $200,000 to the strikers in *case* of an *emergency* and that the Yokohama Specie Bank stated that this is false as the bank will not advance money without good *security*.[2]

In short, Tsutsumi was put on the bureau's blacklist as one of the most radical Japanese residing in America and requiring special observation.

A JAPANESE NAMED "T. TSUTSUMI"

The Bureau of Investigation files all refer to Takashi Tsutsumi or T. Tsutsumi, but English-language newspapers in Hawaii sometimes referred to him as N. Tsutsumi and treated him as an entirely different person. When Tsutsumi took the stand at the Sakamaki dynamiting trial, he was first asked by the prosecutor which initial was correct. The character for his given name was pronounced "Noboru," but it is more commonly read as "Takashi." The mistake followed him around even in Japan.

Noboru Tsutsumi was born on April 8, 1890, in Kōzuhata, Eigenji town, Kanzaki-gun, Shiga prefecture. Kōzuhata is a village nestled in a mountain valley of lotus fields bordering on Mie prefecture. Most of the inhabitants made their living from woodcutting and charcoal making. The number of families living in the village today is 168, three times that in the 1890s, and the village is now famous as a place to view maple foliage in the autumn. One of the two temples in the village, Jōgenji of the Higashi Honganji sect, was administered by the family into which Noboru Tsutsumi was born. He was the third son, with two older brothers and two younger sisters. As he grew up the villagers called Noboru "temple boy."

Since his father, Reizui Kurokawa, the fifteenth-generation chief priest, had a weak constitution, he was not a very dominant force in the family. His mother, Masano, who had come from the neighboring village's temple, took charge of everything. Masano was Reizui's cousin. According to her nephew Hajime Furukawa (b. 1897), second son of her oldest brother who inherited the temple where Masano was born, Masano was the one who actually ran the Jōgenji temple and cultivated some fields as well. Since Furukawa's mother had died when he was an infant, Masano took on that role. She never raised her voice to scold him or her own children.

According to Furukawa, his cousin Noboru was the child most like Masano, not only in appearance but also in personality. Furukawa was attached to his cousin, whom he called "Nō-san," and often followed him around. It was Nō-san who took him into the nearby mountains and taught him which leaves and berries were edible. Nō-san was extremely adept at catching loaches in the rice paddies. Noboru was also known as a "bright boy" from his days at Kōzuhata primary school, which still stands at the crest of the hill above Jōgenji temple.

The temple raised silkworms as a side business. Shelves for spring and summer breeds of silkworms lined all the rooms but the main worship hall. Noboru and the other children diligently gathered mulberry leaves for the silkworms in large baskets on their backs. Silkworms were the only source of the temple's cash income. In a poor village like Kōzuhata, offerings to the temple consisted of rice and vegetables harvested in the fields. The priest's family did not want for food, but there was never much cash on hand. The eldest son, Eseki, who knew he was to succeed his father, did not study hard. But the second son, Ekan, and Noboru, four years younger, were gifted students, and their school tuition came entirely from the income earned by the silkworms. After graduating from upper primary school both went off to normal school.

On finishing fourth grade many of the boys from this area were sent to Kyoto and Osaka to become apprentices, dreaming of the day when they would set up their own shops and become full-fledged merchants in the Ōmi region.[3] Unlike the other village families, the priest had his dignity to consider and could not send his children off to be apprenticed to shopkeepers. Neither did the family have the means to provide their sons with advanced education. Normal school was the only place they could receive more schooling without paying tuition. Normal school students boarded for one year of preparatory subjects and four years of regular work, and all fees, from books to uniforms, were covered at public expense. When there were other necessary expenditures, public-spirited temple parishioners helped out.

Following in his brother's footsteps, Noboru enrolled in the Shiga normal school in Ōtsu. Though he did not spend all his time at his desk, Noboru's grades placed him consistently at the top of his class for the five years he studied there. Not only was he popular among his fellow students, he was also uniformly liked by the teachers and the house masters. He was also known for antics like putting a frog into the bed of the instructor who had overnight duty in the dormitory and for being suspended from school when he was discovered smoking. His cousin, Hajime Furukawa, who also attended the normal school because of similar family circumstances, was surprised and proud to find out that the legendary student known as "Dragon Tsutsumi,"[4] about whom stories were handed down even after his graduation, was his cousin Nō-san.

After completing Shiga normal school, Noboru entered Hiroshima higher normal school, where he majored in biology and agriculture. His mentor was Shigenao Konishi, a scholar of education who taught there after study abroad in Germany and later became a professor at Kyoto Imperial University. On graduating, Noboru entered the liberal arts department at Kyoto University in 1913. The campus was in the midst of strife, thrown into disorder when professors opposed President Seitarō Sawayanagi on a personnel matter and the entire faculty of the department of law submitted its resignation. Ultimately, the education minister intervened to settle the matter, and the president was relieved of his duties at his own request. The Sawayanagi incident, as it later became know, was the first step toward establishing the autonomy of university faculty self-government in Japan. The incident may have influenced Tsutsumi's later thinking.

Noboru entered the university as an education major, but according to a résumé he wrote later on, he graduated as a philosophy major. The star of the philosophy department at the time was Professor Kitarō Nishida, whose philosophy contrasted traditional Eastern thought such as Zen Buddhism with Western philosophy and whose volume *A Study of Good* (Zen no Kenkyū; 1911) was widely read. After World War II, Nishida would be criticized as an ideologue of imperial absolutism, but in those days many students gathered to hear his lectures. Such an ideological climate may well have affected Noboru's intellectual development.

During his days at the university it is unlikely that Noboru's interest lay in social causes. His cousin Furukawa recalls Noboru mentioning that he had caught a glimpse of Fumimaro Konoe, a future prime minister, and Kōichi Kido, a future cabinet minister and imperial court official, at Nishida's lectures. Yet there is no talk that Noboru, like Konoe and others, was ever interested in the classes of Hajime Kawakami, who became a leading Marxist economist and thinker in the 1920s. Neither did Noboru show any particular interest in leftist incidents and activities, such as the High Treason incident (1910) that stirred the country while he was at Hiroshima higher normal school, the formation of the Yūaikai (Friendly Society) by Suzuki Bunji in 1912, or the labor movements led by Sen Katayama and others.

While at Kyoto Imperial University, Noboru was a member of the riding club. He counted horseback riding among his great pleasures. It is said that he cut a dashing figure and turned heads as he rode. Conspicuously tall for a man of that period, Noboru was slender, with a high forehead, straight nose, and deeply etched features set in an elongated face. His eyes had a straightforward gaze, extremely intelligent yet gentle.

To all appearances Noboru led a carefree and easygoing student life, but he was already a married man with a wife and daughter. When he entered Kyoto Imperial University he changed his name from Noboru Kurokawa to Noboru Tsutsumi. He was adopted into his wife's family on the condition that they would take care of all his tuition and living expenses. His older brother, Ekan, after graduating from Shiga normal school and Tōhoku University, also was adopted into his wife's family and was studying at the faculty of medicine at Kyoto Imperial University. Only the firstborn son, Eseki, inherited the family profession of temple priest. Adoption into another family was one way for superfluous second and younger sons to survive. It was quite common for a promising student to be adopted into his bride's family and to have his tuition paid for.

The Tsutsumi family lived in Nagahama on the shores of Lake Biwa in Shiga prefecture. It was an old family that traced its history back seven generations. The head of the family, Taizō Tsutsumi, a prominent local figure, was a physician, and his wife, Koto, was Noboru's father's older sister. Noboru's bride, their youngest daughter, Chiyo, was his cousin. Noboru had been critical of his own parents' marriage between cousins, but he found himself pushed into a similar one.

The Tsutsumi family was in no particular need of a successor. Chiyo had two older brothers. The elder was already a practicing physician in a branch clinic of his father's in Nagahama, and the younger was in medical school. Chiyo's two older sisters had married into wealthy families. Raised as the youngest child, basking in her parents' love, Chiyo was so gentle that her mother had not wanted her to face the difficulties of marrying into another family. Koto had long since set her eyes on her personable and bright nephew Noboru as a prospective husband for her younger daughter, who was one year older than Noboru.

Even after the wedding Chiyo continued to live with her parents in the Tsutsumi clinic. Noboru boarded in Kyoto, returning to the Tsutsumi house during term breaks. Chiyo often asked her mother when Noboru-san was coming home, but she showed no eagerness to look after him in Kyoto. At her parents' home the housework was done by several maids, so she continued to live as the young lady of the house. The only person Noboru could complain to was his brother Ekan, who also disliked being an adopted son. "I try to rise up [noborō], rise up, but my other half says fall down [ochiyo], fall down," he said. Ochiyo's nature was gentle, but to Noboru she was "the daughter of the house" and a wife who always asked her mother's advice first. Noboru once told his niece, Kimiko Kurokawa, "They say if you have three cups of rice bran don't get adopted by marriage into another family." To be sure, Noboru had no financial worries. Not only was he given enough money for living expenses, he could go occasionally to the geisha houses with his brother, even though both were still only students. Noboru should have had no reason to be discontent. Even his father-in-law, Taizō, was not someone to make him feel ill at ease. Yet the better Noboru was treated, the more he seemed to have reproached himself at being beholden to his wife's family.[5]

After his father's death Noboru's oldest brother inherited the family temple, but troubles ensued when this brother brought a woman from the pleasure quarters into his household. In 1914, in the midst of these difficulties, his mother, Masano, died, and the next year Chiyo bore Noboru's eldest daughter, Michiko. A year and a half later, graduation from Kyoto Imperial University put an end to Noboru's long years of student life.

The world outside Japan was caught in the vortex of war and revolution; the United States entered the fight against Germany; in Russia the Romanoff dynasty was destroyed by the February Revolution; and in October the Bolshevik Revolution led to the establishment of the Soviet Union. Noboru, however, was making plans to go to Hawaii. His eldest daughter, Michiko, recalls hearing that for about six months after graduation her father helped out at the local bureau of the newspaper Osaka mainichi shinbun, but his plans for going to Hawaii were already under way, so the job must have been temporary. His brother Ekan, who graduated from medical school at the same time, left the adoptive family that he so disliked and took back the name Kurokawa despite having a daughter. His mind was set on pursuing his studies in Germany. It is said that Noboru proposed his own plan to go abroad while drinking with his brother. "If you're going by way of the Indian Ocean to Germany, I'll go across the Pacific Ocean to America." he said. "Let's have a reunion in New York. That will mean we two brothers will have circled the world."

In any case, in February 1918 Noboru boarded the *Shunyō-maru,* a Tōyō Steamship vessel leaving the port of Yokohama. Among those seeing him off was his wife, holding the hand of his charming three-year-old daughter, Michiko. "I'll send for you in a year's time," Noboru promised Chiyo. Six months later Chiyo bore their oldest son, Toshio. Though he did not leave his adoptive family as Ekan had, Noboru went abroad to escape his status as adopted son-in-law. On reaching Hawaii, however, he noted on his immigration entry forms that Taizō Tsutsumi, his father-in-law, was his household head. His trip abroad was possible only with funds provided by the Tsutsumi family.

It is said that Noboru Tsutsumi consulted his professor Shigenao Konishi about going abroad. Perhaps thanks to Konishi's introduction, the entry card preserved at the Honolulu Consulate General states that the purpose of his voyage was his employment as the principal of the Japanese high school in Hilo. To be more accurate, since there was no independent high school in Hilo, he was employed in the upper division of Hilo middle school. He listed as his initial contact person Kikuzō Tanaka, principal of the Japanese primary school in Hilo. Tanaka, who was also a graduate of Hiroshima higher normal school, had been Konishi's student and must have been acquainted with Tsutsumi during their school days. For Noboru Tsutsumi, Hawaii was merely a convenient stepping-stone to the American mainland.

THE JAPANESE COMMUNITY IN HAWAII

The *Shunyō-maru* docked in Honolulu on Thursday, February 28, 1918. The disembarking passengers were hurried into an immigration office surrounded by a wire fence. Along with the immigrant laborers, Noboru Tsutsumi had to submit to a literacy screening, a stool test for hookworm, inspection for trachoma, and checks for other diseases. But the Hawaiian Islands had become a comfortable place for newcomers from Japan. As *Saikin Hawaii annai,* a guidebook published in Hawaii for newly arrived Japanese noted, "Of the 240,000 population of Hawaii, Japanese residents form a majority; as a crossroads of the Pacific, the arrival and departure of Japanese is daily increasing in frequency."

According to the guidebook, Hawaii, "the paradise of the Pacific," had an average annual temperature of 75°F. In the torrid summer months of August and September the temperature rose into the nineties, but in February, when Tsutsumi arrived, temperatures could dip lower than 60°. "Men can wear Western clothes with melton lining the year around," the guidebook noted, "and women can go through the entire year with a cotton *yukata* and *haori* half coat." Hawaii was also a place where Japanese travelers could take care of their daily affairs without using English. Once safely through the immigration office, newly arrived Japanese found that not only the coachmen in the carriages taking passengers from the Honolulu piers to the inns but also the drivers of the streetcars crisscrossing the city were mostly Japanese. Lining the streets of Honolulu were inns and shops displaying signs written in Japanese characters. According to a Consulate General survey, the number of Japanese in Hawaii in the year Tsutsumi arrived was 102,479. As *Saikin Hawaii annai* noted, Hawaii was truly "a Japanese village in the middle of the Pacific."

At Honolulu Noboru Tsutsumi boarded a small ship of the Inter-Island Navigation Company headed for the largest of the islands, Hawaii, nicknamed "the Big Island." It left Honolulu in the evening and arrived at Hilo the following morning, usually after a rough crossing. The port of Hilo was frequented not only by ships plying the waters between the islands but also by merchant ships from the American mainland, Yokohama, and South America. With a population of more than ten thousand, more than half of them Japanese, Hilo was the second-largest town in the Hawaiian Islands.

In Honolulu the business district was dominated by Caucasians, whose imposing brick or stone buildings symbolized their economic and social power, but most of the three hundred or so shops in Hilo were single-story wooden structures, nearly all of them displaying Japanese signs. On Front Street, the town's main street, which the Japanese called Motomachi, more than a few shops were owned by Japanese. Among them were rice, noodle, and soy sauce makers, but most were fish stores. The wholesale fish market was run by Japanese.

Disembarking at Hilo, travelers headed for one of the Japanese inns, such as the Okino, Matano, Yamato, or Koizumi. Among the restaurants in downtown Hilo were Okino, Baigetsu, Anegawa, Nomuratei, Daikokutei, and Seaside Club. There were even half a dozen women who made a living as geisha—professional entertainers. Most likely the welcoming party for Noboru Tsutsumi, the new principal of the high school, was held at one of these restaurants. Among the theaters in Hilo were the Yūrakukan (considered larger than any in Honolulu), the Yamatōza, the Kaisui-za, the Teikoku Gekijō (Imperial Theater), the Moheau-za, and the Kilauea-za. Religious establishments included the Yamato Shrine, the Honganji mission, the Jōdo sect's Meishōin, the Shingon sect's mission, and a Christian church.

Newspapers and magazines from all over Japan arrived in Honolulu. The local Japanese-language newspapers carried articles from Tokyo, and international telegrams were received twice a day. Even in Hilo there were three daily Japanese-language newspapers, the *Hilo mainichi,* the *Hilo asahi,* and the *Hilo shinpō,* and a weekly, *Kazan* (Volcano). From these papers Tsutsumi would have learned the peculiar words the Japanese used daily in Hawaii: "plantation camp" (*kōchi kyanpu*), "(Buddhist) missionary" (*kaikyōshi*), "Japanese clothes" (*Nihongi*), "arrival in Hawaii" (*rai-Fu*), "return to Hawaii" (*ki-Fu*). And although Hawaii was an American territory, the local Japanese immigrants called the Americans "foreigners" (*gaijin*), the Hawaiians "natives" (*dojin*), and the Hawaiian-born Japanese "second generation" (*nisei*).

In addition to the local English-language public school, there were seven Japanese-language schools in and around Hilo: the Honganji-affiliated middle school, girls' school, and elementary school; the Jōdo sect-affiliated girls' school; and three independent elementary schools unaffiliated with any religious institutions. Only a few pupils, however, went on to high school.

The first appearance of Noboru Tsutsumi, the Hilo Japanese school principal, in materials related to Japanese in Hawaii is on July 22, 1918, when as the representative of the Hawaii Island Education Research Group he attended the Third Hawaii Educational Representatives' Meeting held by Japanese-language educators. It was a mere five months after his arrival in Hawaii.

In a keynote speech to the meeting, Consul General Rokurō Moroi cautioned his audience,

The many problems brought about by the state of current affairs are now weighing on the shoulders of educators. Especially since entry of the United States into the Great War in Europe, a variety of new issues have been raised, which put the close relations between Japan and the U.S. in an entirely different light from before the war. Now is a time when you should do more than devote yourselves to furthering Japanese-language education. You must realize that you have the power to deal with other grave and momentous matters as well.

A month before the meeting Secretary of the Interior Franklin N. Lane had arrived in Hawaii on an observation visit. On the surface his visit was to look into Hawaiian land problems, but when he stopped off in Los Angeles on his return trip he announced, "It is extremely important to Americanize the foreigners who were born in Hawaii and the resident aliens too."[6] His strong tone focused attention on the foreign-language schools.

The "foreign-language schools problem" had already emerged as a major social issue in Hawaii. At its core was concern over how to educate second-generation Japanese. In effect, what was at stake was the way Japanese immigrants should live in the American territory of Hawaii. Tsutsumi, who decided so lightly to cross the Pacific in the hope of being reunited with his brother in New York, unexpectedly found himself in the eye of the storm over these issues.

CONTROL OVER THE JAPANESE-LANGUAGE SCHOOLS

It was said that the first things that Japanese immigrants on the plantations wanted to build were a temple and a school. At the Iwasaki camp at Olaa Plantation, where Jirokichi Iwasaki was boss, the Olaa Eleven Mile Jōdoin temple was built within the first year, and a Japanese-language school affiliated with the temple went up the next year. It was the third such school established in all the Hawaiian Islands, the first on a sugar plantation. Initially the sugar companies cooperated in establishing Japanese-language schools, providing land and even monetary assistance. Though this may have been a conciliatory policy to pacify the workers, we should not overlook the philanthropic spirit of the sugar planters, instilled in them as the descendants of missionaries.

The first Japanese-language school in Hawaii was founded in 1896. The government contract workers who arrived in Hawaii in the 1880s did not have much time or energy to worry about their children's education. Their only aim was to make enough money to return to Japan. With mothers going to work from early in the morning the children were virtually left to themselves all day long. Takie Okumura, posted in Hawaii as a minister after his graduation from Dōshisha University, was astonished as he made his pastoral rounds at how little communication the immigrant children had with their parents. When a young man with a teaching certificate arrived from Hiroshima, Okumura seized the opportunity to make an appeal for contributions to establish the Honolulu Japanese school (later Hawaii Chūō Gakuin, or Hawaii Central School).

The Honganji sect, which had already established temples in each plantation, followed by setting up temple-affiliated schools, and so did other competing Buddhist sects. In a few years' time, the Japanese-language schools far outnumbered the public schools in Hawaii. Second-generation Japanese children attended Japanese-language school for an hour early each morning before going to public school, and for an hour or two afterward as well. They heard recitations of the Imperial Rescript on Education and sang the "Kimigayo," the Japanese national anthem, just as schoolchildren did in Japan.

It was not an easy matter for the parents to pay school tuition fees, but they could rest easy that when they returned to Japan their children would be accepted as Japanese. The Japanese-language schools became the locus of community activities, promoting ethnic solidarity among those who endured laboring under white employers. Parents developed extraordinary enthusiasm for the schools. Attaching great importance to school ceremonies or Japanese holidays such as the emperor's birthday, they had their children take the day off from public school. Their support for the schools grew stronger in the wake of Japan's victories in the Sino-Japanese and Russo-Japanese wars, as if in proportion to the national strength of their homeland. The Consulate General encouraged the schools in an ambivalent way. On the one hand, it touted assimilation as a way to enhance harmonious relations between the United States and Japan; on the other, it contributed funds to the establishment of the schools and directed them to display the imperial chrysanthemum crest at the front entrance.

The first trouble over the Japanese-language schools was rooted in disputes between Buddhist and Christian groups within the Japanese community. The two religious sects feuded with each other on every plantation, and they became embroiled in local power struggles within the immigrant community. It was not unusual for violence to break out as one side tried to snatch teachers or students from the other.

But the school problem attracted the attention of the haole elite as the number of pupils rose. After the Gentlemen's Agreement was signed, the number of picture brides arriving in the Japanese immigrant communities increased annually. In the view of some, these brides "bore children like rabbits." In 1918 when Noboru Tsutsumi arrived in Hawaii, 9,404 infants were born in the Hawaiian Islands. Approximately half (4,534) were Japanese, far greater than the number of Portuguese infants (1,032), the next largest group. By contrast, a mere 365 white infants were born. Though these Hawaiian-born second-generation Japanese infants all acquired American citizenship at birth, they were also entered into family registers in Japan, making them dual citizens.

Within the Hawaiian elite many were worried that the parents of the Japanese children, whose teachers came from Japan and who used textbooks edited by the Japanese Ministry of Education, thought only of sending their children back to Japan to receive a Japanese-style education without becoming assimilated. "Are we to hand over Hawaii in the future to the Japanese?" they asked.[7] Voices were raised that the Japanese-language schools were preventing the Americanization of the nisei.

When the United States declared war on Germany in 1917, German-language schools on the American mainland were closed one after another. In Hawaii, in response to a campaign by the English-language newspapers, the legislature passed a resolution ending the use of German in newspapers and magazines. It was these same English-language newspapers that fanned opposition to the Japanese-language schools, against a background of rising diplomatic tension between Japan and the United States.

In 1914 Japan quickly entered the First World War on the side of Great Britain and its allies. Japanese troops occupied the German concession on the Shantung Peninsula and took over German Pacific Island possessions. But when the Japanese government presented its Twenty-one Demands to China, requesting expansion of Japanese rights and interests, it met with strong American disapproval. In November 1917 the Lansing-Ishii Agreement recognized Japan's "special interests" in China but also reaffirmed the American Open Door policy, based on the principles of Chinese territorial integrity and equal opportunity in commerce and industry for all countries in China. While the United States took "special interests" to mean economic interests, Japan interpreted them to include political interests. This difference in views cast a continuing shadow over relations between the two nations. Japan remained an ally of America, but it was already viewed as a country requiring careful watching.

When the United States entered the First World War, the Japanese community in Hawaii actively supported the war effort. Many bought Liberty Bonds, and volunteers enlisted in the American army, forming a "Japanese" company. As many immigrants were veterans of the Russo-Japanese War, this kind of cooperation was easy for them to understand. But when it came to the Japanese-language schools their attitude was different. As before, they continued to place greater importance on the

Japanese schools than the public schools, and disputes related to sectarian differences continued unabated.

In 1918 there were 15 Japanese-language schools in Honolulu and a total of 146 in the Hawaiian Islands. Of those, 141 were elementary schools and 5 were middle schools. (On Olaa Plantation there were 4 schools: the Honganji mission-affiliated school, the Jōdo sect-affiliated school, Nine Mile Japanese elementary school, and Mountain View Japanese elementary school.) By sect, the breakdown was 33 Honganji affiliated, 16 Jōdo sect, 3 Sōtō sect, 8 Christian, and 86 independent. The independent schools included those run by a combination of several Buddhist sects as well as those with few students at small plantations. The total number of students enrolled in the Japanese-language schools was 18,166. The number of teachers was 401, 32 of them middle or girls' school teachers. But there were only a few high school teachers like Tsutsumi.

Six months before Tsutsumi's arrival, the Honolulu immigration office had refused entry to six teachers of Japanese-language elementary schools affiliated with Honganji. Declaring them to be contract immigrants prohibited by the immigration law, the immigration bureau took a tough new stand. Although the teachers eventually were allowed entry, the problem of the Japanese schools moved beyond the level of public criticism to demands in the Hawaiian legislature that the schools be abolished.

Since the issue directly affected their livelihood, the Japanese-language school teachers were the first to attempt a response to the foreign-language schools issue. They organized educational study groups on each island and established the Japanese Educational Association of Hawaii. The first objective of the association was the compilation of a textbook more relevant to pupils born in Hawaii than the Japanese textbooks that stressed loyalty to the emperor and patriotism. The new textbook, written by a Tokyo University professor, was put into use in the year Tsutsumi took up his position. Indeed, the newcomer was put in charge of the new textbook study committee.

When Tsutumi attended the meeting of the Japanese Educational Association for the first time, on July 22, 1918, he spoke about his observations on Japanese-language education during the five months since his arrival. "In the postwar [World War I] development of the American people," he said, "a confrontation with the Japanese people is unavoidable." But both nations should take heed of their differences about Japanese-language education and work to avoid misunderstandings. In the spirit of the Meiji emperor's Charter Oath and of George Washington's Farewell Address, the Japanese and the Americans should aim at conciliation between their two cultures for the sake of world peace. Responsibility to do so lay on the shoulders of the Hawaii-born second-generation Japanese who learned both languages and knew the customs of both countries. For this reason alone, he said, America should be grateful for Japanese-language education. "Twenty years from now there will no doubt come a time when [American] public schools will see the need for Japanese language instruction." He ended with a proposal to establish a training organization for second-generation instructors who would take over from the native-born Japanese instructors. His eloquence made a striking impression on those attending the conference, but his speech reflected an overly idealistic Japan-based viewpoint. It did not take into account the position in which Japanese in Hawaii had been placed.

In his opening address Consul General Moroi warned, "Sending Hawaii-born boys and girls to Japan to receive a Japanese-style education and having them return again to Hawaii as citizens who do not know English will incur the deep ill feelings of Americans." He pointed out that "real power over education [in Hawaii] is in the hands of parents who do not understand education. They always control education from behind the scenes, and are apt to undermine the tireless efforts and faultless educational methods of the educators." He urged teachers to see themselves like the traditional village headmen in Japan, making it their first priority to lead these "obstinate parents."

As far as the Hawaii territorial government was concerned, the Japanese schools were permitted to operate only after public school hours. The Japanese immigrant community, which made up close to half of Hawaii's population, was apt to forget this fact, and continued to mishandle the Japanese-language school problem. In the meantime, in January 1919 the *Honolulu Advertiser* published the proposal by Albert F. Judd to extend government control over foreign-language schools. The Judd proposal would place the Japanese-language schools, then operated by the Japanese parents, under the administrative control of the Territorial Board of Education. It would require that certification examinations for English, American history, and other subjects be given to the Japanese teachers. It was clear, of course, that if the proposal was implemented, most of the Japanese teachers would fail such examinations.

In March 1919 the Judd proposal, with some additions, was submitted as a bill to the Hawaiian House of Representatives by Lorrin Andrews, the Oahu representative. This threw the Japanese community into an uproar. At meetings of Japanese residents all over the islands resolutions were passed opposing the territory's plan to control the schools. The Japanese Educational Association appealed to newspapers, religious groups, and other organizations, and it issued a resolution to "cooperate . . . with the Americanization of the boys and girls" that was published in the English-language press. On April 7 leaders of the association met with Governor Charles McCarthy to make a direct appeal. The association meeting in July debated new regulations for the Japanese-language schools that would encourage the Americanization of their pupils. "Americanization" was raised frequently at the meeting, but the situation had already moved too far to do much about it. The foreign-language school bill eventually passed the House of Representatives of the Hawaiian territorial legislature, but it was narrowly defeated in the Senate.

When Noboru Tsutsumi attended the July meeting of the Japanese Educational Association, he was no longer the principal of the Japanese-language school. He was an observer, attending as the editor-in-chief of the *Hawaii mainichi shinbun*. In the days before radio, the Japanese-language press was the only way for Japanese immigrants to find out what was going on in the community. Not a few Japanese newspaper reporters were semi-hooligans with odd personal quirks, but for better or worse, the Japanese newspapers led opinion in the Japanese community. Tsuneichi Yamamoto, who dropped out of middle school in Hiroshima to go to Hawaii and was hired as a reporter at the *Hawaii mainichi* at the age of seventeen, recalled that Tsutsumi was respected by other reporters as an intellectual who had graduated from an imperial university. Indeed, Tsutsumi took the young Yamamoto under his wing and taught him everything about writing newspaper articles.

By this time Tsutsumi had become deeply interested in the labor conditions of the immigrants, visiting the plantations whenever he had time. As he delved into the Japanese-language school problem he must have started to wonder about the position of Japanese immigrants in Hawaii. It was only natural that he soon shifted his attention from education to the conditions of plantation labor. Around the time that the territorial legislature took up the foreign-language school bill, the Japanese press began to call for wage increases for plantation workers. Noboru Tsutsumi was the first to take up his pen for this cause.

THREE

THE OAHU STRIKE BEGINS

Honolulu: 1919–1920

When the United States entered the European war the country was in a skittish mood. In 1916 Woodrow Wilson had been reelected with the slogan "He kept us out of war." Unable to resist pro-war agitation after a German submarine sank a British passenger liner with many Americans abroad, in April 1917 the president declared the United States would go to war against Germany. A patriotic fever to "make the world safe for democracy" suddenly swept the country, and young men lined up to volunteer for military service, but the American labor movement was badly split in its reaction to the war. Without hesitation the American Federation of Labor had issued a declaration supporting entry into the war, and its president, Samuel Gompers, joined the advisory board of the Council of National Defense to align organized labor with national policy. As military demand heated up the economy, jobs were suddenly plentiful and unemployment dropped.

The radical wing of the labor movement, however, was adamantly opposed to the war. The Industrial Workers of the World, led by "Big Bill" Haywood, had already mounted an antiwar campaign, and the IWW joined with socialist, anarchist, and pacifist groups to condemn the country's entry into the European conflict. The IWW, whose organizers had been condemned as "outside agitators" when they rushed to join labor struggles wherever they could, was now branded as a nest of "foreign spies." Neither of the two anarchists, Sacco and Vanzetti, were official members of the IWW, but they had fled to Mexico to avoid the draft.

Suspicion of the radical wing of the labor movement, especially the IWW, with its reputation for confrontational strike tactics and sabotage activities, was deepened by the February 1917 revolution in Russia, then by the October revolution led by the Bolsheviks under Lenin. The IWW leadership was as quick to declare its support for the new Bolshevik government as it had been to condemn the American declaration of war against Germany. The federal authorities, made nervous by a rising number of large-scale strikes and labor demonstrations, marked the IWW as a target for investigation. In June 1917 Congress had passed the Espionage Act to crack down on spying and other acts abetting the enemy, and a year later amendments were added to limit free speech.

In the summer of 1917 the FBI raided the Chicago headquarters of the IWW as well as its local branches, seizing documents and any IWW leader they could lay their hands on. Several IWW members were lynched by company-hired detectives, the Ku Klux Klan, and right-wing patriots, and foreign-born labor leaders were deported. The IWW was hit hard. Haywood, an American and a Westerner to the core, so despaired of his prospects that he defected to the new Soviet Union while on bail and eventually died in Moscow.

Sen Katayama, who had returned to America in 1914 after his release from prison, where he was sent for his involvement in the 1906 Tokyo streetcar workers strike, sent a secret report on the situation in the United States to his socialist comrade, Toshihiko Sakai: "Several hundred IWW members have been seized. . . . However, though there is oppression, this is indeed a free country. We can work to collect donations for legal fees by advertising in magazines and newspapers, forming groups and holding speeches. This has become part of our movement." [1] Katayama was already persona non grata with the Japanese authorities in the United States. In 1915, despite a warning from the Japanese consulate, Katayama had denounced the credentials of Bunji Suzuki, the moderate labor leader of the Yūaikai, who arrived from Japan to attend the AFL convention in San Francisco. Suzuki had been sent by Eiichi Shibusawa and other Japanese industrialists to promote friendly relations between Japanese and American workers in the face of growing anti-Japanese sentiment on the West Coast. In a speech to a meeting of the Japanese day laborers' union in San Francisco, Katayama described working conditions in Japan and said that Suzuki, bankrolled by Japanese capitalists, did not represent Japanese labor. Under pressure from the consulate, Katayama was forced to move to New York.

The Ministry of Home Affairs took note of Katayama's activities in its report on "dangerous persons": "Led by Sen Katayama and others, the Japanese socialists in the U.S. are using New York as their base of operations to further their plans to engage in coordinated actions with radicals." Already in his late fifties, Katayama continued to work as a dishwasher or cook while gathering around him youths who would later become active in Japan's socialist movements, including Tsunao Inomata, Mosaburō Suzuki, and Eitarō Ishigaki. He also published the magazine *Heimin* (Common Man). Gradually he drifted toward communism.

Before 1919, however, the Home Ministry reports on the "movements of Japanese radicals resident abroad" hardly mentioned the Japanese in Hawaii. This was because Katayama and other activists went directly to the mainland without staying in Hawaii.

There were also very few American files on "foreign agitators" in Hawaii. Given the power of the sugar plantation interests, there was little chance for the IWW to grow in Hawaii. Three years after the 1909 Oahu strike, white telephone operators from the mainland gathered Japanese workers of Waialua Plantation to urge them to join the IWW, but their talk of capitalists, exploitation, individual rights, and labor struggles rang unfamiliar to the ears of the Japanese, who themselves were wary of "suspicious outsiders." Another IWW organizer who arrived in Hawaii at about the same time took a job on the Kahuku plantation as a sugarcane worker, but he disappeared suddenly. It was rumored at the time that he was killed by plantation company agents, but the truth of the matter remains unknown to the present day.

Another reason that American government agencies paid little attention to the foreign laborers in Hawaii was that there were no significant labor movements after the 1909 Oahu strike. Since it ended with the defeat of the strikers, the solidarity among the Japanese laborers quickly dissolved.

THE RICE RIOTS OF 1918

In the latter half of 1917, in response to rising prices, demands for wage increases were heard once again in the Hawaiian sugar plantations. In 1918 a declaration demanding wage increases was issued by the joint youth organization on five plantations in the Hamakua area of the island of Hawaii. The consciousness of the young cane field workers was fired by the activities of mainland laborers roused by the Russian revolution. Yet what made the greatest impact on these youths was the rice riots in their homeland.

During the wartime boom, prices in Japan rose and rice prices soared. The Terauchi cabinet proclaimed a policy of restraint on cornering the market, export prohibition, and control over rice imports, but the situation was out of control. Stockpiling of rice for the military in anticipation of the Siberian intervention caused the price of rice to rise even further. The rice riots began on August 3, the day after the Siberian intervention was announced. Fishermen's wives in the village of Uozu, Toyama prefecture, protested the shipment of rice out of the prefecture to Osaka. Protest demonstrations quickly spread throughout the country. The Honolulu Consulate General issued a notice that "due to the rice famine in Japan, imported Japanese rice should only be sold to Japanese." When he spoke to immigrant workers, Bunji Suzuki of the Yūaikai was surprised to find that they were eating high-quality Japanese rice from Yamaguchi and Kumamoto prefectures. No matter how strained their budgets, they wanted Japanese rice on their tables. It was not surprising that they reacted with panic when they heard that the supply would be depleted two months after the consulate's warning.

In Hawaii the price of rice jumped to twice what it had been the previous year. When it was revealed that the four large trading companies with headquarters in Japan had been hoarding rice in Hawaii, rumors flew that the four shops were going to be "wrecked." Not only rice prices, but the prices of other indispensable imported Japanese foods—soy sauce, miso, dried fish, pickled ume plums, pickled *daikon* radishes—had risen sharply in the half year after Noboru Tsutsumi had arrived in Hawaii. One Japanese-language newspaper called for "the overthrow of the pickled daikon millionaires."

News of the rice riots had as much impact on the Japanese in Hawaii as the Russian revolution had on Japanese leftists like Sen Katayama in New York. A few, believing that revolution was afoot in Japan, immediately prepared to return home. The riots affected Japanese of all social classes. What finally brought together the Japanese laborers working in the cane fields was the impact of the protest by fishermen's wives and tenant farmers in Japan, who like themselves were at the bottom of society.

The time was ripe for action, but it was Noboru Tsutsumi who put the anxious feelings of the Japanese immigrant laborers into words and who encouraged them to organize. The cane field workers lived in camps on the plantations, bought items necessary for their daily lives from the stores operated by the plantation companies, and deducted those charges from their wages. It was a life in which food, clothing, and shelter were all controlled by the company. Tsutsumi summarized the awakening consciousness of the workers: "When the company behaves in such an autocratic manner controlling production, livelihood, and society, the workers' spiritual life is never calm. This is because human beings have in themselves a constant desire for freedom. Even in the face of uncertainty, they do not like interference and restriction by others." The immigrants, he said, were about to "become self-aware of their position in society" under the stimulus of the "trends in the labor world." Tsutsumi put words in the mouths of the workers:

To live in society as a human being. These times compel me to realize that I am a laborer. The sunlight of democracy shines and labor groups are blossoming. I'm the same as other human beings, so I would like to pluck the beautiful flowers of real society. . . . There were at least a few who realized this and many more who were about to come to this realization.

If the company cannot survive because the price of sugar is low, we could understand the need to help each other and would put up with eating rice gruel. But at a time when the price of sugar is going from $60 a ton to $80, then to $100, to $150, and to more than $200, our bosses are full of idle talk that they are flush, have money left over, are getting large dividends; and they're lording it over us by living in grand houses and riding around in big cars.

It's not as if we had drawn our fortune from the gods that we would *hō hana* [do hoeing work] all our lives from the time we come bawling into this world. We must do something to be able to bear it. If we stay quiet, no matter how many years go by we will stay sunk like a hammer in the river and we will not be able to raise our heads in pride. Brothers, let's think about this. Laborers threatened by economic distress are forced to consider their present circumstances and the future of their descendants.

The single word *pau* [finished; fired] ruins the foothold gained over several decades, forcing a household to keep from uttering it. The bosses are trying to oppress us by treating us as they treated government contract immigrants or ignorant laborers in the past. This is unacceptable to progressive thinking youths and laborers who are in touch with current trends. And yet, in the struggle between employer and employee, we are weak as individuals.

Using the plain words spoken by cane field workers, Tsutsumi captured their attention, and he eventually won their admiration and absolute trust as well.

Through his eloquence, Tsutsumi played the role of standard-bearer for the cane field workers. Liberated from the constraining social structure of Japan and his status as adopted son-in-law, he was feeling more freedom than when he rode horses across the Kyoto Imperial University campus. The struggles of the workers gave his life a goal.

The year 1919, after the rice riots had subsided in Japan, saw unprecedented labor struggles throughout the United States; 3,630 strikes were carried out by some 4.16 million workers. This was twice as many strikes as in 1916. The biggest reason for the strikes was the economic hardship that accompanied the increased cost of living. In February 1919 a shipyard strike in Seattle turned into a general strike, crippling the entire city's services. After that was settled, a San Francisco Stevedores' Association strike in May sparked other strikes in Los Angeles, San Diego, and other ports on the West Coast. Streetcar strikes occurred in Denver, Chicago, and Nashville; and in September telephone operators and police struck in Boston. At year's end there was a great steel strike by 370,000 steel workers in fifty cities in ten states, centered in Pittsburgh. Federal troops and state militia engaged in bloody clashes with the workers.

The news of these strikes was reported in detail in Hawaii's Japanese-language newspapers. Since Hawaii was dependent on the mainland for many necessary goods, strikes on the West Coast delayed shipments for months and had a great impact on daily life. In 1919 there were eight small-scale strikes in Hawaii.[2] Two were longshoremen's strikes; the others involved telephone operators, machinists, lumber workers, and golf caddies. Japanese carpenters and plasterers also protested wage cuts proposed by the Japanese Contractors' Association, but this dispute did not turn into a major one.

In April 1919 the Japanese-language newspapers, led by Tsutsumi, began to discuss the cane field workers' demand for wage increases. The Hawaiian territorial government, however, did not show much interest in the issue. The workers' discontent was overshadowed by a series of local celebrations: in July, the centennial of the death of King Kamehameha; and in August, the opening of the U.S. Navy dry dock at Pearl Harbor on Oahu. The cane field workers' movement for increased wages and improved working conditions was gradually taking shape against the background of these festivities.

FORMATION OF THE HAWAII FEDERATION OF JAPANESE LABOR

Of the 43,618 workers in all the sugar plantations in Hawaii, 19,474, or almost half, were Japanese. Filipinos constituted the next largest group, with 13,061 workers, and it was they who first rose to demand higher wages. On August 31, 1919, at a rally of the Filipino Labor Union of Hawaii (initially called the Filipino Labor Association) in Aala Park in Honolulu, the Filipino laborers elected Pablo Manlapit as their chairman. A graduate of a mainland college, Manlapit was hired in 1916 by the planters' association to take charge of relations with Filipinos. He was fired when he was found to be recruiting workers to go to the mainland. He soon became a well-known figure among the Filipino laborers. He organized a longshoremen's strike on Maui, eloquently arguing down strike breakers despite being injured, and helped out Filipinos as an interpreter for the Honolulu police department. With his dark complexion and taut physique, Manlapit was an imposing man. After becoming president of the Filipino Labor Union, he started making the rounds of Oahu's sugar plantations campaigning energetically for a wage increase. From newspaper photographs, it is clear that Manlapit emulated the style of the IWW's Wobblies by making his speeches on a soapbox.

As recent arrivals in Hawaii, the Filipinos did not yet have their own schools or theaters. Refused the use of plantation meeting halls, Manlapit spoke at train depots on the outskirts of town. When he made a speech in front of a Japanese store at Waimanalo Plantation, he was arrested and held overnight by the police for gathering people on a private road. Undaunted, he not only continued his speaking tour but also took and passed the bar examination.

On October 15 Juan Sarminento, editor-in-chief of the Filipino newspaper *Ang Filipinos,* called for the presentation of a wage increase demand in late November. If no reply was received within a week, he said, then the three thousand Filipino workers in Oahu should begin a strike on December 1. Sarminento was a leader of a faction within the Filipino community that did not entirely trust Manlapit because he had worked for the planters' association in the past.

The unification of the Philippines is said to have been delayed in part by the division of the islands among ethnic groups using different languages, such as Visayan, Tagalog, and Ilocano. Filipino workers who went to Hawaii took these divisions with them, and the Filipino Labor Union likewise suffered continual internal discord. Nevertheless, at the union delegates' meeting on October 20, Manlapit was chosen president and it was formally decided to submit wage increase demands by December 1. Manlapit immediately went on a speaking tour of the islands, pointing out that the success of the wage increase movement depended on the solidarity of workers throughout Hawaii.

On November 18 Manlapit arrived on the Big Island, which had been shaken by earthquakes for nearly two months because of an eruption of the Mauna Loa volcano. But the fiery lava flow had headed in the direction of Kona, on the opposite side from Hilo, and residents breathed a sigh of relief. The rally for the Filipino workers, which was held in the Gaiety Theater in Hilo, drew Spanish and Portuguese workers as well. As Manlapit toured the plantations after the meeting, Noboru Tsutsumi was always at his side, proclaiming the need for Japanese workers to support Manlapit's campaign. A month and a half earlier Tsutsumi had organized the Federation of Japanese Labor on Hawaii, the only island to organize.

The center of the Hawaiian Islands, however, was Honolulu on Oahu. One-third of Hawaii's population, many of them Japanese, lived in Honolulu. The city was a microcosm of "the Japanese village" in the middle of the Pacific. The downtown area near Alala Park was dotted with Japanese shop signs, and only Japanese was heard on the streetcars. On the streets Japanese women wore cotton *yukata* and wooden *geta* clogs. Those in Western-style dresses were a rarity.

Members of the Japanese Association in Honolulu, which was dominated by upscale shop owners, school principals, religious leaders, newspapermen, and other professionals, thought of themselves as the elite within the Japanese community. Taking the lead, the association joined with other groups to form the Plantation Labor Supporters' Association in Honolulu. It was made up of representatives from various occupational groups, including the craftsmen's union, the automobile association union, the barbers' association, the fisheries association, the pawnshop, cleaner, and tailor industries, the young men's association, and various prefectural associations. Of the twenty officers of the supporters' association, nine were newspapermen working for Japanese-language papers.

On the U.S. mainland miners' strikes were spreading across the midwestern states. Despite the intervention of AFL President Gompers, no settlement had been reached. On November 7 Attorney General Mitchell Palmer issued a strict warning to end the strike. Two days later, on November 9 at 7:00 P.M., a lecture meeting on current issues was held under the sponsorship of the Plantation Labor Supporters' Association at the Asahi Theater in Honolulu. (The resident Japanese had met here to discuss the Japanese-language schools problem the previous March.) The meeting was attended by a crowd of some one thousand Japanese, far greater than the number of seats in the theater. Many were forced to sit in the aisles.

The first to take the stage was Takeshi Haga, a nineteen-year-old youth from the Palama area youth association. Brought over to Hawaii from Yamanashi by his father two years earlier, he spoke about his experience working on Waipahu Plantation:

> This is no time to put up with being treated like livestock. Merchants in Honolulu who sell the sugar plantation laborers rice and miso they import from Japan are making a big profit. At a difficult time like this, when our blood compatriots on the islands are sweating away at hard labor day after day under the scorching sun, we must as a body censure those who ignore their plight. I respectfully urge you to contribute all forms of aid, material and spiritual, to encourage the sugar plantation laborers.[3]

Haga spoke passionately, even referring to the Russian revolution. (In preparing for his speech, Haga had wondered whether he should speak in the style of Seigō Nakano or Yukio Ozaki, two prominent orators of the day, and he had practiced repeatedly, like Demosthenes, projecting his voice over the crash of the waves on Ala Moana beach.

In 1919 many prominent Japanese stopped over in Honolulu on their way to the Paris Peace Conference. Although their ships were in port for less than a day, they were invited to speak at lecture meetings sponsored by the newspapers. It was a rare chance for the Japanese in Honolulu to listen directly to Japanese leaders from various circles, and often the speakers inflamed the audience's patriotism from the stage. For example, Seigō Nakano, editor-in-chief of *Tōhō jiron*, declaimed that "a clash between Japan and America" over the future of Japanese interests in China would be "difficult to avoid." Calling the white man a villain and waving the rising sun flag were dangerous in a society dominated by Caucasians, but the Japanese audience greeted Nakano's speech with applause and cheers. The Japanese newspapers, reporting these events in florid language, made them the topic of the day at barber shops and public baths or at lunchtime in fields of the sugar plantations.

But many visitors urged prudence. Baron Shinpei Gotō, one of the country's most prominent officials, who stopped on his return trip from the Paris Peace Conference a week before the meeting on current issues, told his audience to tread softly on the Japanese-language schools problem and labor problem: "The fortunate Japanese here in Hawaii must adopt the standards and ideals of the American nation. They must realize that they are part and parcel of the body politic of the United States and not of the body politic of Japan." The *Honolulu Advertiser* reported his speech on November 4, 1919, under the headline "'Become American' word of Goto to Japanese, Says 'English Education is best.'"

As the former head of civil administration in Taiwan, Gotō had promoted sugar production. Given this background, it is likely that he better understood the feelings of the Hawaiian Sugar Planters' Association (HSPA)—those with the ruling power—than the feelings of the Japanese immigrants. His remarks were made at a welcoming reception held at former Governor Walter F. Frear's residence and attended by fifty prominent citizens of Hawaii. A skilled diplomat, in supporting the assimilation of immigrants, Gotō was not speaking directly to the immigrants themselves but making a gesture to please his American hosts.

Several Japanese leaders had stopped in Hawaii on their way to the first International Labor Conference convened in Washington, D.C., in October and November 1919. As labor problems were troubling the whole world, President Wilson proposed a conference aimed at easing labor-management relations. Chaired by Samuel Gompers of the AFL, it was attended by representatives from forty-one countries who discussed the freedom to unionize, the minimum wage system, the eight-hour workday, and other issues making up the nine principles of the Labor Bill of Rights. The eight-hour workday, adopted five years before by the Ford Motor Company to shut out the IWW, had gradually taken hold in the United States, and nearly half the workers had secured this right. The government and industry representatives from Japan, opposing the eight-hour workday, pressed the other nations' representatives to give Japan "special treatment." Just before departing from Honolulu, Shinpei Gotō explained, "Since the Japanese have long torsos and short legs in comparison to Caucasians who have short torsos and long legs, the Japanese tire more easily and are inferior in their working power. Shortening working hours to eight hours is suitable for the Caucasians, but we must look at the Japanese in light of their physiology. This is why under the current labor system in Japan hours are somewhat longer but include many breaks."[4] In the sugarcane fields of Hawaii, the ten-hour workday was normal.

Although many Japanese attended the November 9 meeting in Honolulu, the movement for wage increases on Oahu's sugar plantations did not easily fall in step with the movement on the Big Island. The memory of the 1909 strike ten years before, when only the Japanese workers on Oahu had struck and then been miserably defeated, was a stumbling block. Finally, however, a branch of the Federation of Japanese Labor was organized on Waialua Plantation.

On December 1, 1919, under the sponsorship of the Honolulu Plantation Labor Supporters' Association, worker delegates met to organize the Japanese laborers on all the islands. The meeting, held in the Honolulu Club, whose entrance was decorated with Japanese and American flags, was attended by two delegates from each of the six major plantations on Oahu, eight delegates from Hawaii, three from Kauai, five from Maui, and thirty from the Honolulu Plantation Labor Supporters' Association.[5]

From the start there were disputes about voting rights. In fact, the night before the meeting began delegates from Hawaii, Maui, and Kauai had gathered at the Kyōrakukan restaurant on Nuuanu Avenue to hold a three-island council. Ostensibly it was a social gathering, but its real purpose was to discuss how to rein in the Honolulu Plantation Labor Supporters' Association, which tended to plunge ahead without consulting the laborers themselves. To be sure, without the supporters' association, the meeting in Honolulu would not have been funded or even held, but the laborers' delegates were extremely wary of the participation of all the Honolulu Japanese newspapers. At the November 9 meeting, for example, five of the nine speakers had been newspapermen. As the *Hawaii hōchi* asserted on December 1, the newspapermen believed that "making changes in society depends on the organs of public opinion." The newspapermen took the attitude that the workers could not do much without the "intelligentsia." And their attitude suggested that their involvement might reflect a struggle for leadership among the newspapers.

The English-language press saw the wage increase movement not as one arising from among the laborers but as an affair stirred up by the Japanese-language newspapers. The labor delegates feared that if the Japanese-language newspaper reporters led the attack at the meeting, it would only reinforce the views of the English papers and play into the hands of the planters' association. "This is our movement," they felt, "so we will carry it ourselves. We appreciate sympathy and understanding, but we reject any interference."

In the end, the question of voting rights was resolved by allocating votes on the basis of the number of laborers, with eight votes going to Hawaii and six votes to each of the other islands. As this was a workers' struggle, the supporters' association had the right to speak out but did not participate in the votes. One newspaperman, disgruntled at this resolution of the voting rights issue, immediately challenged the qualifications of Noboru Tsutsumi, the delegate from Hawaii.

The Honolulu newspapermen found it difficult to deal with Tsutsumi, a man whose education was superior to their own. Tsutsumi had never made the round of greetings to the Japanese-language newspapers, considered customary for anyone seeking to do anything in Honolulu. It was Tsutsumi, moreover, who had warned against the involvement of the Japanese newspapermen in the wage increase movement and insisted that it should be a labor movement with "true laborers" as its members. Irritated that "peasants" had arrived in Honolulu to dominate the movement while they were forced to the sidelines, the newspapermen made Tsutsumi the object of their attack.

Tsutsumi had already resigned from the *Hawaii mainichi,* but there was certainly a problem with his qualifications as a "true laborer." Among delegates from the other islands were newspaper reporters or schoolteachers, but all of them had had experience working in the cane fields. Nevertheless, the labor delegates from the islands, brushing aside interruptions by the supporters' association, resolved, "It is not essential that those entrusted by laborers to be their delegates be laborers."

On the third day of the meeting, the delegate from Ewa on Oahu directly criticized Haga (nicknamed "Fighter Haga"), editor-in-chief of *Hawaii hōchi,* who had strenuously criticized the 1909 strike in a newspaper bought out by the planters. He continued to publish vehement views on the labor movement, incurring the anger of the Japanese laborers. The consulate in Honolulu still has in its archives a threatening letter, with a photograph of Haga showing in red ink blood flowing down from the tip of a Japanese sword stuck in his throat.

Despite such disputes the delegates finally managed to debate the main issue: how much of a wage increase to demand. On December 5 they issued a declaration announcing the formation of the Federation of Japanese Labor in Hawaii (also called the Japanese Labor Federation by English newspapers). President Manlapit of the Filipino Labor Union, who attended that day, stressed the importance of cooperation between the Japanese organization and the Filipino workers. In response, the Japanese promised solidarity. But when the Japanese delegates met that evening to decide on the details of the wage increase agenda, the main topic was put aside as discussion shifted to warnings about the Filipinos until late into the night.

"GIVE US $1.25 A DAY"

At 10:00 A.M. on December 6, five Japanese labor representatives visited the office of the Hawaiian Sugar Planters' Association and handed over a written wage increase demand to its executive secretary, Royal D. Mead. It read:

> We are laborers working on the sugar plantations of Hawaii.
>
> People know Hawaii as the Paradise of the Pacific and as a sugar producing country, but do they know that there are thousands of laborers who are suffering under the heat of the equatorial sun, in field and in factory, and who are weeping with ten hours of hard labor and with a scanty pay of 77 cents a day?

The statement included demands for an eight-hour workday as well as for contract changes for contract workers and tenant workers. But the most urgent demand was revision of the basic wage. "The wages of common man laborers, which at present are 77 cents per day, shall be increased to $1.25. . . . And minimum wages for woman laborers shall be fixed at 95 cents per day."

According to surveys undertaken by the Japanese workers, the minimum living expenses were about $34 per month for unmarried men and $75 for a family composed of a husband, a wife, and two children. This was an increase of more than 40 percent over what was needed four years before, and education expenses for the children were not included. Projecting needs into the future, Tsutsumi and other Hawaii Island delegates pressed for wages of $3 a day, but all the delegates from the other islands insisted that the wage increase should be an amount acceptable to the planters. In the end, the delegates agreed on a demand for a minimum wage of $1.25 a day.

Compared to the demands for wage increases on the American mainland, this was not a great deal. Seattle longshoremen were demanding $5.25 per day for unskilled laborers; San Francisco stevedores, $8.80 per day. The 1915 Report on the Survey of Labor in Hawaii concluded that "the laborers in Hawaii earn low wages in comparison to laborers in California; and there is little opportunity for future advances."

Though they were provided with housing, the wages of the Hawaiian laborers were shockingly low.

The $1.25 a day demand took into consideration the bonus system. It was only with bonuses that plantation workers were able to eke out a living. Under a formula that said laborers should benefit from profits, the bonus rate was calculated according to the current market value of sugar. To receive a bonus, a laborer had to work twenty days or more per month. Plantation owners, who regarded the bonus as a way "to encourage diligent work and savings," used it as a worker incentive. The bonus system had the effect of discouraging workers from changing jobs or moving to another plantation. It also encouraged workers to continue on the job even when they were injured by the knives used as tools or by sharp cane leaves, or when they became ill from working under the scorching sun. To qualify for a bonus, sick or injured workers forced themselves to go out to the fields.

Tsutsumi and the Hawaii delegates thought that the bonus system should be abolished, the paternalism of the company side should abandoned, and the laborers should insist on $3 a day as a fair basic wage. What delegates from all the islands agreed on, however, was a demand for $1.25 a day and for a decrease in the number of workdays needed to qualify for bonus pay to fifteen days per month (or ten days for women).

At its 1919 annual meeting on December 8, the Hawaiian Sugar Planters' Association discussed the wage increase demand from the Federation of Japanese Labor. The HSPA was formed in 1883, fourteen years before the American annexation of Hawaii. Its membership included forty-four Hawaiian sugar companies, but the real power within the association was held by a handful of kamaaina, large plantation owners who controlled all phases of the industry—harbor facilities, railroads, buses, major banks, insurance companies, electricity, and fuel. Indeed, these sugar magnates held the actual power in the territory, and they were a formidable opponent for the cane field laborers to challenge.

It is clear from the minutes of the 1919 annual meeting that the planters knew living costs and prices had increased and that they tacitly recognized the need for a wage increase. Nevertheless, at noon on December 11, the final day of the annual meeting, John Waterhouse, president of the HSPA, firmly rejected the wage increase demand the Japanese and Filipino laborers had made. (The formal reply to the laborers' union was dated December 16.)

Arguing that housing, lighting, and fuel costs were borne by the companies and that the bonus system would be revised, the HSPA refused to budge from a basic wage of 77 cents per day. They proposed to revise the bonus system by changing the base from the annual price of sugar to its monthly average price. Since an increase in sugar prices was forecast, the HSPA said that this was the maximum concession it could make. The annual meeting also decided to establish a bureau for handling housing facilities, sanitation, and social welfare of workers. "Besides sound business reasons," they announced, "there is an ethical obligation, that we properly care for those whom we have brought here, and the further obligation that their standard of living and social conditions be such that their descendents will be qualified to become useful American citizens." [6] In other words, the HSPA absolutely refused to recognize collective bargaining with a labor union, no matter what was going on on the American mainland or in the world. As in the past, the planters attempted to deal with the workers in a paternalistic manner.

On December 14 the Filipino Labor Union, which had submitted similar wage demands, held a delegates' meeting that voted unanimously to strike. The union also sent a telegram to AFL president Gompers—"Deliberating strike. Hope for your utmost support"—and it also sought support from the headquarters of the Manila labor organization. [7]

On the plantations rumors spread that the strike might start in a week, but the Japanese federation, thinking that the first stage in the negotiations had just started, hesitated to support the Filipinos' decision to strike. From the start the Japanese labor delegates from all the islands agreed on the principle of cooperation between labor and management, and they held out hope for a lawful settlement based on "temperate discussion."

The Federation of Japanese Labor had just opened an office on the second floor of the Sumitomo Bank at the corner of Smith and King streets in the downtown area near Aala Park. Tsutsumi had returned to Hilo to straighten out his own affairs, but when he received a telegram about the Filipino decision to strike, he rushed back to Honolulu. So did the delegates from the other islands. Since the office was still bare of tables and chairs, the delegates had to discuss their plans while standing. The first order of business was to request a loan of $500 from the Japanese-owned Pacific Bank.

The man who had found the office was Ichiji Gotō, a native of Kumamoto prefecture. Gotō was the same age as Tsutsumi, but he had worked on a sugar plantation after his father brought him to Hawaii when he was fifteen years old. He attended an English-language night school in Honolulu while working as a house boy, and he became a fervent Christian as well as a member of the youth association of Nuuanu Church. After a stint as a reporter for the *Maui shinbun*, he became a reporter for the *Nippu jiji*, one of the leading Japanese newspapers in Honolulu. Gotō resigned from his job and became secretary of the federation headquarters when it opened its new office. Short in stature, with the round rugged face of a farm boy, Gotō made a favorable impression on everyone. He was usually a man of few words, but at the meeting on current issues held the previous month he had attracted attention with his denunciation of the "tyranny of the plantation owners who regard laborers as beasts of burden."

To fight against the unyielding HSPA, the federation's most urgent task was pulling together a strong organization. The worker delegates asked Seishi Masuda, principal of the Kakaako Japanese-language school and a man regarded as an upstanding figure in the Japanese community, to become secretary-general of the federation. According to the FBI files, "Masuda is deeply interested in labor questions and in the past wrote several articles concerning labor questions in the local Japanese newspaper. Masuda was quite willing to accept the position [of secretary-general of the federation]. However, his fellow teachers advised him to keep away from labor agitation as it will arouse misunderstanding."[8] Despite his colleague's misgivings, Masuda agreed to take the job. On December 21 sixteen directors selected from the islands attended the first directors meeting. Tsutsumi proposed a temporary headquarters organization consisting of an administrative committee (to coordinate communication with the labor organizations on each island), a negotiating committee (to negotiate with entities outside the federation), and a finance committee (to handle accounting matters). Together with secretary Gotō, Noboru Tsutsumi and Hiroshi Miyazawa, both from Hawaii, were appointed to the secretariat as superintending secretaries.

While the federation was engaged in this flurry of activity, the shopping district of Honolulu was being draped in red and green Christmas decorations. Christmas Eve in Honolulu was celebrated with a paper blizzard instead of snow. On the main street a lively parade of immigrants from various countries marched in their native costumes, and American troops posted from the mainland participated as well. On Christmas Day the English-language newspapers carried a full-page announcement on the front page, "Joy and Peace to All Hawaii upon this

Christmas Day," as well as prayers for peace in the coming year. After all, the Hawaiian Islands had been developed by missionaries.

On December 26 the Federation of Japanese Labor submitted its second wage increase demand to the HSPA. At the same time the federation leaders called for "unity, resolution, frugality" by the laborers. It also warned against acting like *okintamamen*, a word said to be derived from a term referring to sumo wrestlers who curried favor with higher-ranking wrestlers by washing their private parts. In this case, it meant those in collusion with the planters.

At year's end a theatrical troupe from Japan toured the islands, with a beautiful magician blowing kisses to the crowds. It was the talk of the Japanese community. The festive New Year's mood was dampened by news of a severe influenza epidemic, but on New Year's Eve the haole social elite, decked out in expensive evening gowns and tuxedos ordered from San Francisco and New York, danced out of the hotel ballrooms into the streets to the rhythms of the bands, showered at the stroke of midnight by blizzards of confetti.

On the second floor of the Sumitomo Bank, oblivious to the New Year's festivities, the Federation of Japanese Labor continued its heated debates. Noboru Tsutsumi, who was staying in the Kobayashi Inn across from Aala Park with the other delegates from Hawaii, was hard at work at federation headquarters from 7:00 A.M. until late into the night preparing for negotiations with the HSPA in the new year. He had resolved to forgo New Year's celebrations.

Meanwhile on the day before New Year's, the territorial governor, Charles McCarthy, together with several legislators, had departed Honolulu by ship to deliver a petition to Washington. Although this trip was to have significant repercussions later, the federation leaders paid no attention to their departure.

THE PALMER RAIDS

On January 3, 1920, the *Honolulu Advertiser* carried the following article:

Arrest 5,000 to thwart plot against U.S.—Washington, Jan. 3—(AP). Agents of the Department of Justice and police officials had arrested 3,896 radicals at midnight in raids on headquarters of the Communist Labor parties in 70 cities throughout the United States in an effort to upset a plot for the establishment of an American soviet government. At that hour it was believed that fully 5,000 disciples of radicalism would be behind bars by daylight.

These so-called Palmer Raids, reported on front pages all over the country, continued under the direction of U.S. Attorney General Palmer for several months. They led to the arrests of some ten thousand men and women in seventy cities throughout the United States. The purpose of the raids was to deport foreign radicals. The American Communist party, formed the previous September, was targeted along with socialists, anarchists, and labor unions such as the IWW. In actuality, the raids were a general roundup of "Reds." The American press, starting with the *New York Times,* approved of the prompt handling of the red scare and reported that the danger of a government overthrow had been narrowly averted. Most historians now consider the Palmer Raids a violation of the civil rights of innocent persons unprecedented in American history.

The origin of the Palmer Raids lay in the discovery of thirty-eight bomb packages mailed to prominent Americans, including financier J. P. Morgan and Supreme Court Justice Oliver Wendell Holmes, just before May Day in 1919. Claiming this was to be the start of an attempted revolution, the FBI spread fears of political subversion. Nothing happened on May Day, but after the commotion had died down, on June 2 a bomb exploded in front of Attorney General Palmer's house. That night there were explosions near the homes of several judges, one of which killed a night watchman. Dynamite blasts occurred in front of immigration offices and churches as well.

President Wilson, who was campaigning for the League of Nations, was facing strong domestic opposition from the Republican party. During a speaking tour to win public support for his plan, Wilson collapsed from a stroke. Hiding news of his paralysis from the nation, his aides and his wife, a political novice, took over the affairs of state. It was after this that the Palmer Raids began at the attorney general's initiative. Nineteen twenty was a presidential election year. Palmer's name had been raised as a possible Democratic candidate to succeed the incapacitated Wilson, and the raid raised his political profile. The raids were also an opportunity for Palmer's right-hand man, J. Edgar Hoover, to sniff out "radical red elements" and anarchist assassination plots and to increase his political influence by "ridding America of the red menace." Although the majority of those arrested in the Palmer Raids were associated with the Communist party, the real purpose of the raids was the arrest of anti-American activists whom Hoover and his subordinates judged to be politically dangerous. In the background were the long-lasting miners and steel workers strikes, which involved four hundred thousand workers and were led by former IWW organizers. Six days after the Palmer Raids began, the strike was called off.

At the time of the Palmer Raids Hawaii was not yet under Hoover's jurisdiction. Even so, the two major English-language newspapers in Honolulu, the *Honolulu Advertiser* and the *Honolulu Star Bulletin,* explained to their readers how to protect Hawaii from the dark shadow of Bolsheviks and IWW radicals. Both newspapers served as mouthpieces for the HSPA, but they had not yet connected their antiradical arguments to the Federation of Japanese Labor. It was obvious to the HSPA that the demand for wage increases by the federation did not involve either ideology or the IWW.

The Japanese in Hawaii had little understanding of the impact of the Palmer Raids. Teisuke Terasaki, a reporter for *Hawaii hōchi,* who had made a habit of writing daily entries in his diary noting memorable events in a concise, unemotional manner, is a valuable source on daily life in Hawaii at the time. But Terasaki's diary does not contain a single sentence about the Palmer Raids on the mainland. Instead the entry for January 2 reads, "Delegates to the labor convention enter port on the Siberia-maru. Talks at the young men's association by Sanji Mutō (industry representative) and Eikichi Kamada (government representative)."

These two men were part of a twenty-five-member Japanese labor delegation on their way home from the International Labor Conference held in Washington, D.C., two months earlier. The Japanese delegates had incurred criticism from the European and American delegates by petitioning that Japan be given special treatment on labor issues. After attending a luncheon meeting on January 2, they were on their way to Yokohama in the afternoon. A report on the International Labor Conference by the U.S. Department of the Interior called the meeting a failure, saying it had widened the gap between capitalists and laborers.

On Sunday, January 4, the Federation of Japanese Labor sponsored a mass meeting at the Asahi Theater in Honolulu to report on the conditions of plantation workers. The last speaker, Noboru Tsutsumi, described the basic stance of the federation headquarters. "The capitalists cannot treat laborers as machines, " he said. "As long as they think laborers are satisfied with getting just enough food to keep from starving and receiving a bonus as if they were machines being oiled, they have not recognized laborers as people. Desiring improvements in production, we are prudently stressing harmony between management and labor. However, if the capitalists are determined to destroy production and oppress laborers, it is inevitable that we strike." [9]

After the meeting, the federation planned to collect "righteous contributions" from the general public to support the strike. The very next day, however, the Oahu branch called for the provisional dissolution of the temporary federation headquarters and the halt of the money-raising campaign. The Oahu labor leaders were worried about the existence of an "advisory committee" for the federation headquarters, made up of newspapermen who were also the principal members of the strike supporters' association. From the start neither Tsutsumi nor the other leaders in the federation headquarters had been able to control the advisory committee, whose members vented their conflicting opinions as they pleased in the competitive spirit of newspapermen. Any action by the federation headquarters also needed to be approved by the advisory committee.

Since withdrawal of the Oahu workers would mean a halt to any concerted labor actions, the federation headquarters now had an excuse to disband the advisory committee. Ichiji Gotō, who was involved as a reporter selected by the supporters' association, played the central role in the negotiations, and on January 7 all the members of the committee resigned. The federation secretary, Seishi Masuda, who had lost trust by being too deferential to the advisory committee, also stepped down. It was after this turn of events that the *Hawaii hōchi* began to attack the ineffectiveness of the federation headquarters. The Honolulu branch offices of the Yokohama Specie Bank and the Pacific Bank, founded by the leading Japanese merchants with support from Eiichi Shibusawa and other Japanese industrialists, also refused to lend money to the federation. The capitalist plantation owners were not their only enemies.

On January 14, the day the United States demanded the withdrawal of Japanese troops from Siberia, the HSPA notified the Federation of Japanese Labor headquarters that it rejected any further negotiations. That night the federation directors gathered at the Kyōrakukan restaurant to discuss whether to strike. The Kyōrakukan was located at the corner of Nuuanu Avenue and School Street, about twenty minutes by streetcar from the federation headquarters. In the garden behind the main restaurant building was a detached cottage, ideally suited for clandestine meetings. It had a Japanese-style bath, and guests could spend the night there.

Heated discussion lasted late into the night, but by 3:00 A.M. the directors pledged to one another that when the time came, they would stake their lives on the strike. As Noboru Tsutsumi later noted, it was the first time that the directors from the various islands had made a unified decision. But the federation leaders thought that there was still room for negotiation. The Filipino Labor Union had announced that it would strike in two days, but with a serious influenza epidemic spreading through the community, the federation leaders wanted to proceed with caution. They feared being dragged along by the hasty actions of the Filipinos. Hiroshi Miyazawa, whose English was fluent, was in charge of close liaison with the Filipinos. He worked hard to rein them in. At the same time, the directors of the federation directors, making preparations just in case a strike took place, went on "observation trips" to the islands.

Terasaki's diary entry for January 16 noted in English, "Hōchi begin attack upon staff labor Union because they do nothing for labor but themselves." The Hawaii hōchi had reported that day, "The headquarters directors are busily seeking contributions, taking compensation of $6 per day from the amounts donated." This was a false report intended to damage the federation directors, but it forced a temporary halt to the fund-raising campaign on Oahu, and the federation was forced to print an open letter in the Hawaii hōchi to dispel suspicions.

On January 17 a document signed by Gotō requesting reconsideration by the HSPA was sent. Meanwhile Hiroshi Miyazawa was at the Filipinos' headquarters on the second floor of a Japanese wholesalers' shop about three blocks from the federation headquarters, trying to persuade Manlapit to postpone the strike. The thirty-two-year-old Miyazawa was the second son of a farming family in Nagano prefecture who had come to Hawaii when he heard that he could work his way through school. As a "school boy" working during the day, he studied English and Episcopalian theology at night school. On a tour of the plantations to do missionary work, Miyazawa was hired by a labor contractor as an interpreter, and he thus became thoroughly familiar with the living and working conditions of the plantation laborers. Since Miyazawa had worked with Tsutsumi in organizing the Federation of Japanese Labor, the FBI file dated August 2, 1921, noted, "Miyazawa has become more or less radical in his views through influence of Tsutsumi."

"WE'RE NOT WORKING": THE STRIKE BEGINS

Although the Filipinos had issued a strike statement, they had not made any strike preparations. They did not even have a fund to cover food expenses for striking laborers. Since no Filipinos in the islands were successful enough to give financial help to the strikers, they sought aid from the Japanese Chamber of Commerce of Honolulu, which rebuffed them. On the evening of January 17 Manlapit issued an order to postpone the strike planned for January 19, stating that he had failed to get assurances of cooperation from the Federation of Japanese Labor of Hawaii. But on January 19 Terasaki noted in his diary, "Filipinos at Ewa, Waipahu, Aiea, Kahuku start their strike. At Ewa Portuguese and Puerto Ricans join in. There may be a total of 3,000 people." Why did the strike start even though it was to have been postponed?

It began when a Hawaiian luna sneered at Filipino laborers at Kahuku Plantation, "No can strike, you, Filipino, *hila hila* [cowards]." At the close of work on January 18, the agitated workers gathered at the Filipino camp at Kahuku Plantation. Ignoring Manlapit's order, at 6:00 P.M. they made an independent announcement that they were on strike. This action spread immediately to other plantations on Oahu, and all the Filipino laborers left the cane fields the following morning.

Ironically, the Filipino workers had been brought in great numbers to Hawaii as strikebreakers during the first Oahu strike in 1909. They had arrived in Hawaii to control Japanese laborers who were "dangerous and didn't know their place." At the time, the HSPA noted, "The outcome of this strike movement, while calling for great expense to the Planters' Association and the territory, has the promise of proving a blessing in disguise. Too long have the vested interests of the territory permitted the dominating nationality to insidiously dispossess others in the varied lines of higher grade work." [10] Ten years later, however, the Filipinos, now the second-largest labor force after the Japanese, were ready to take on the HSPA with all its power.

Most Filipino laborers were single. About 40 percent had wives and families, whom they had left in the Philippines. Although many looked forward to being reunited with their families, statistics show that only 48 percent actually returned to their homeland. Under these circumstances cockfights and "three-minute dances" were their only fleeting pleasures. They eagerly looked forward to the arrival in camp of dance troupes from the Philippines. For the price of a ticket they could dance the tango, pressing their bodies against the dancers for three minutes. Some Filipino workers were also said to engage in homosexual activities, and for that reason Japanese immigrants held them in contempt. At festivals and celebrations Filipino workers sometimes danced with each other to the beat of the rumba whose intense rhythm blended the native music of Cuba with the music of the African slaves taken to work in Cuban sugarcane fields.

The example of the Filipino strike that began on January 19 stirred the Japanese laborers but they were slow to take action.

"Japanese cane workers threaten general strike" ran the lead headline in the January 20 *Honolulu Advertiser*. From the start of the strike the English-language press focused attention on the Japanese. Indeed, they treated the strike by the Filipinos as though it had been instigated by the Japanese. In fact, the Federation of Japanese Labor had announced that if the Filipinos went on strike, "Our position and intentions are wholly legal and orderly. If a strike of Japanese labor shall be called, [the laborers are] cautioned to quit their places in a quiet and peaceable manner." The Japanese plantation workers in Oahu were equally cautious. Flatly refusing to follow the Filipinos, whom they looked down on, they chose to work in the fields even though the Filipinos were on strike.

"Pau hana, *no go work*"

The Filipino laborers, who had never doubted that the Japanese would stand with them, were enraged. At Waipahu Plantation several dozen Filipinos attacked Japanese workers boarding a train to go to the cane fields on the morning of January 21. The anger of the Filipino workers was so intense that the Filipino Labor Union was hard-pressed to calm them down. The Japanese workers, fearing that the Filipinos were ready to pull out knives at any provocation, returned to their camp houses with their lunch boxes in hand. At Ewa Plantation, six kilometers west of Waipahu, Filipino workers wielding scythes and knives swarmed around a train traveling through the cane fields. The Japanese engineer and the Hawaiian plantation guard fled into the field of tall sugarcane and hid there until the sun went down. A similar incident occurred at Aiea Plantation near Pearl City between Honolulu and Waipahu. Special officers from the Honolulu police force were rushed to these plantations to arrest numerous Filipinos.

Hiroshi Miyazawa, the federation's man in charge of relations with the Filipinos, went to the large Waipahu Plantation for a workers' rally at noon the same day. Fearing that harm might come to their families, many Japanese workers concluded that things had come to such a pass that they had no choice but to back the Filipinos and to stop work. Noboru Tsutsumi, who had returned from a trip to Maui, and the other directors, who had returned from observation trips to the other islands, met immediately. After hearing reports from the four islands, they decided to issue a work lay-off order to all the plantations on Oahu—Ewa, Aieia, Waialua, Waipahu, Kahuku, Waianae, and Waimanalo.

Even at this stage, the federation's work lay-off order was considered to be quite different from a strike order. Continuing to negotiate with the planters, the federation sent Gotō and Miyazawa to the HSPA to give Mead, the HSPA's secretary, a third written demand for wage increases. The two men also requested that they be allowed to attend the regular meeting of the HSPA to explain the laborers' position. Mead turned them down. It was "no use," he said.

The federation's first delegates' meeting, composed of representatives from plantations from all the Hawaiian Islands, was held on January 25 at the Palama Japanese-language school. At about 4:00 P.M. it went into a secret session closed to outsiders under tight security, guarded by directors carrying pistols. At 10:00 A.M. on the morning of January 26 the Federation of Japanese Labor in Hawaii resolved unanimously to "carry out a walkout by the Federation as of February 1" if there was no change in the attitude of the HSPA.

Secretary Noboru Tsutsumi, as representative of the participants, read aloud the resolution. After waiting for the applause to die down, he explained the organization of federation headquarters. He said that the three secretaries, Tsutsumi, Miyazawa, and Gotō, would remain in their positions as agreed upon when the federation was established. The meeting also reconfirmed that the strike would be held only on the island of Oahu, with workers on the outer islands raising support funds. They also needed to be prepared to assist in covering the strike expenses of the Filipinos.

On the following day, January 27, the HSPA gave its final response. The planters' association said that it did not recognize the laborers' union or its right to collective bargaining and that it would not respond to "any demands." In response, the usually moderate *Nippu jiji* printed a large headline, "110,000 comrades, carry out collective duty; we have an obligation to support the laborers who stand on the front lines so that they may be free of anxieties." The *Hawaii hōchi* also showed its support of the federation's strike resolution in an editorial with the title "A Courageous Struggle."

On January 30, at a noontime rally at Waipahu, the three federation secretaries were in attendance. In response to Miyazawa's speech in English to the Filipinos, Manlapit appealed for unity between the Japanese and the Filipinos. Gotō then explained the procedures and cautions to be followed by federation members. Speaking last, Tsutsumi urged the workers on, "We'd like you to settle in and treat this as a five to six month vacation and hang on until your promised wages are paid." [11] To a man, the laborers in their denim overalls rose with a long and vigorous round of applause. Noboru Tsutsumi had become the indispensable man at rallies on every plantation.

At 2:00 P.M. on January 31 an official strike declaration for "realization of wage increase demands" was issued for the plantations on Oahu island. Beginning on the morning of February 1, Japanese and Filipino laborers, who together made up 77 percent of the plantation workforce on Oahu, boycotted the cane fields.

Figure 1. Jūzaburō Sakamaki (second from left); Jirokichi Iwasaki (fourth from left). (Courtesy of Bishop Museum)

Figure 2.   "Fred" Kinzaburō Makino.
(Courtesy of Hawaii hōchi sha)

Figure 3.   Noboru Tsutsumi.
(Courtesy of Tsutsumi family)

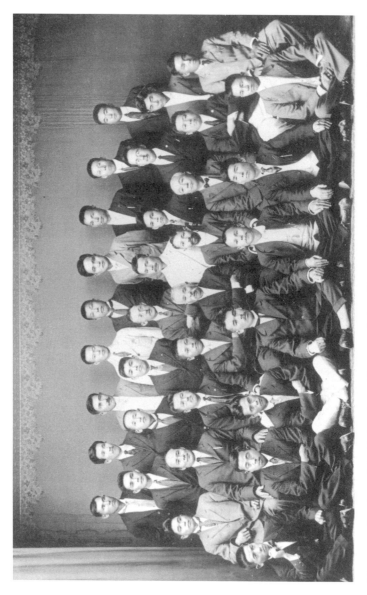

Figure 4.   Leaders of the Federation of Japanese Labor. First row: Ichiji Gotō (second from left), Tokuji Baba (third from left), Honji Fujitani (fourth from left), Chūhei Hoshino (sixth from left); third row: Yasuyuki Mizutari (first on left); fourth row: Shoshichirō Furushō (first on left), Noboru Tsutsumi (second from left), Hiroshi Miyazawa (fourth from left). (From Tsutsumi, *1920 Hawaii satō kōchi rōdō undōshi*)

Figure 5.   Posters distributed by the Hawaiian planters during the 1920 strike: (top) Filipino strike leader leaving Hawaii with a sack of money; (middle) striking Japanese worker receiving a pittance from "agitators" versus worker on the job receiving regular wages; (bottom) cigar-smoking Federation of Japanese Labor leaders riding in a rented touring car. (From Tsutsumi, *1920 Hawaii satō kōchi rōdō undōshi*)

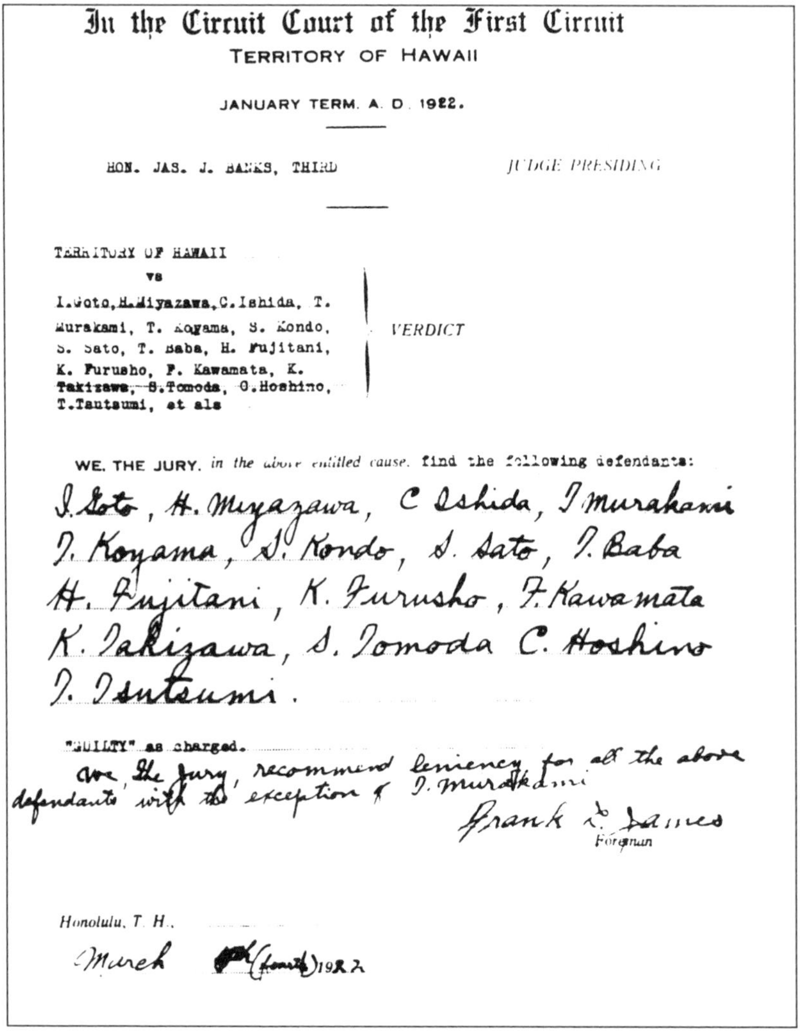

In the Circuit Court of the First Circuit

TERRITORY OF HAWAII

JANUARY TERM. A. D. 1922.

HON. JAS. J. BANKS, THIRD   JUDGE PRESIDING

TERRITORY OF HAWAII

vs

I. Goto, H. Miyazawa, C. Ishida, T.
Murakami, T. Koyama, S. Kondo,   VERDICT
S. Sato, T. Baba, H. Fujitani,
K. Furusho, F. Kawamata, K.
Takizawa, S. Tomoda, C. Hoshino,
T. Tsutsumi, et als

WE, THE JURY, in the above entitled cause, find the following defendants:

I. Goto, H. Miyazawa, C Ishida, T. Murakami
T. Koyama, S. Kondo, S. Sato, T. Baba
H. Fujitani, K. Furusho, F. Kawamata
K. Takizawa, S. Tomoda C. Hoshino
T. Tsutsumi.

"GUILTY" as charged.

*We, the jury, recommend leniency for all the above
defendants with the exception of T. Murakami*

Frank L. James
Foreman

Honolulu. T. H.

March ___ *(fourth)* 1922

Figure 6.   Guilty verdict in the Sakamaki dynamiting trial. (In author's
possession)

FOUR

THE JAPANESE CONSPIRACY

Honolulu: 1920

FEAR OF JAPANIZATION OF HAWAII

On the eve of the strike Terasaki noted in his diary, "The English-language newspapers are playing up their view that the Japanese government is instigating the strike." Indeed on January 31 the *Honolulu Advertiser* carried an editorial asking, "What is Hawaii going to do about it? What is the Government of the U.S. going to do? Is Hawaii ruled from Tokio?" The next day, it ran a front-page political cartoon depicting a man dressed in *yukata* (cotton kimono) and *geta* (wooden clogs) hurling a brick labeled "strike" at a ducking plantation owner who lets the brick hit the head of Uncle Sam. The same day the *Honolulu Star Bulletin* splashed a large headline accusing "priests of Asiatic paganism, foreign language school teachers and Japanese editors" of seeking to control Japanese laborers so they could become the "masters of Hawaii's destiny." A few days later, in an article carrying the headline "Control of Sugar Industry at Stake," the *Honolulu Advertiser* warned of a "Japanese conspiracy" jeopardizing the future of the territory. All the local newspapers had begun to speak of a "Japanese conspiracy" and to accuse the Japanese government of working behind the scenes to incite the laborers to strike.

It was actually a specific event, the "red flag incident," instigated by the Japanese-language newspapers in Hawaii, that prompted the English papers to raise the Japanese conspiracy theory. For historians of modern Japanese history, the "Red Flag Incident" refers to the 1908 case in which Sakae Ōsugi, Toshihiko Sakai, Kanson Arahata, and several other socialists received prison sentences for waving red flags to celebrate their comrades' release from prison. In the aftermath of this incident the Saionji cabinet was forced to resign; and the succeeding Katsura cabinet, dominated by conservative officials, adopted a policy of strengthening control over socialists and strictly regulating strikes. The incident is often considered a prologue to the High Treason Incident of 1910.

In Hawaii the red flag incident was sparked by an editorial in the *Hawaii shinpō* of January 21, just before the Federation of Japanese Labor issued its stop work order. The editorial read,

> We feel keenly the need to hold demonstrations with flag processions. Striking laborers should parade through towns, each hoisting a red flag with the slogan "77 cents for a day's wage" or "77 cents for ten hours of hard labor." This is a demand for a wage increase to the merciless plantation owners; and it is an excellent method to gain understanding and sympathy from the general public and the gradually increasing numbers of tourists.

The day before the newspaper had already urged the workers to go on strike in support of the Filipinos who had begun their strike expecting the support of the Japanese.

> History throughout the ages proves that the reason one tiny, small nation in the Far East has been able to overcome the tyranny of a mighty nation and achieve the greatness it has today is not its military force, much less its monetary power, but rather its spirit which combines a sense of justice with chivalrous virtue. You must accept with pride and honor the fact that you are people of such a country, the Land of the Rising Sun. Japan, where cherry blossoms bloom, is a country of spirit, a country where blossoms scatter quickly and bear fruit.

The American Legion, represented by its territorial executive committee, vigorously protested the *Hawaii shinpō* for encouraging "a red flag parade of Japanese strikers in American territory," and the English-language press criticized the *Hawaii shinpō* for being an organ of the Federation of Japanese Labor. The president and editor-in-chief of the paper, Takeshi Hattori, who had written the pieces, was summoned for questioning by the police.

Hattori, who had a good command of English, had once worked for the Hawaiian Sugar Planters' Association. In secret reports sent to the Ministry of Foreign Affairs by Consul General Rokurō Moroi, who had returned to Japan in 1919, Hattori is frequently identified as a "secret agent." It is not clear whether Hattori joined the HSPA as a secret agent of the Japanese consul general from the start, nor is it known whether he was fired from the HSPA or resigned. Whatever the case, he had acquired enough capital to purchase the *Hawaii shinpō* immediately after he left the HSPA. If the HSPA suspected that Hattori's red flag incident involved the Consulate General of Japan, that would clearly add weight to the English press's charge that the Japanese government was inciting the strikers.

The Federation of Japanese Labor responded with a statement in the Japanese press: "We have no connections with the Japanese government, Japanese language newspapers, or any other newspapers and magazines." Acting Consul General Eiichi Furuya declared in a statement dated January 31 to both English-language newspapers, "I wish to state that the Japanese has under no circumstances any connection or relation with the Labor Union in this Territory."

As local representative of the Japanese government, the consulate had always been involved in troubles related to immigrants. Consular officials usually adopted a prudent peace-at-any-price principle that was not always to the advantage of the immigrants. When the consul general tried to dissuade the workers from striking at the time of the 1909 strike, they responded with fists raised in anger and shouts that he was parroting the planters. After that the HSPA had stopped conferring with the consul general when labor issues arose.

The English-language newspapers brushed aside the consul's statement as "weak denials" and continued to argue that the strike was a Japanese conspiracy. The *Honolulu Advertiser* condemned the pending strike by the Federation of Japanese Labor and its "cat's-paw," the Filipino Labor Union, as against American interests. On February 1, 1920, it forecast a "practically complete paralysis of the Hawaiian sugar industry at a moment when the nation is facing a serious sugar shortage and when the highest prices in history are being secured for the product and the laboring men are sharing the profits on a scale unheard of elsewhere." A few days later the newspaper announced, "Uncle Sam cannot afford to have Hawaii under the domination of an alien race."

As evidence for the claim that Japanese field laborers were receiving sufficient wages, the *Honolulu Advertiser* pointed out that at Aiea Plantation alone nearly $900,000 in money orders had been sent to Japan during the previous year. The paper suggested that this proved the Japanese were refusing to assimilate and that they maintained primary loyalty to Japan. The English-language press also pointed out that the federation dealt with potential defectors by warning them that betrayal of the union would bring disgrace on the whole Japanese people. According to article 3, clause 6, of the constitution of the Federation of Japanese Labor, "Should a member be found guilty of the act of contravening the interest of this Federation, . . . he should be reported to several affiliated branches . . . and to the mayor of the offending member's permanent domicile in Japan." This regulation was decided by a vote on January 25, a week before the strike began. Manjirō Yamakawa, the director of the Oahu federation (and the former Aiea Plantation federation chairman) was immediately expelled from the federation because he was suspected of leaking the deliberations of its meetings to the planters.

The Japanese newspapers regarded this disciplinary action against Yamakawa as an object lesson. The *Hawaii hōchi* went so far as to expose his real name, stating that Yamakawa was an alias he was using in Hawaii. Measures adopted to maintain a rocklike organizational solidarity included not only expulsion, denial of membership, and repayment of debts but also "social discipline" and "notification in Japan." Not only would a turncoat and his family be ostracized from the Japanese community in Hawaii, his kinfolk in Japan would be stained by the dishonor of his betrayal too.

This method of ensuring unity, which stifled minority opinions and symbolized a culture of collectivism and shame, was very Japanese, but it appeared shockingly alien to the haole sugar plantation owners. The Hawaiian Sugar Planters' Association charged that "reporting to the Japanese government of a member's dismissal" was a manifestation of fanatic nationalism.

Once the strike began, the English-language press hammered away at the theme that the strike was "un-American" and that it had been instigated by the leaders of the Japanese community. The *Honolulu Advertiser* declaimed on February 20, 1920, "Hawaii is an American territory. Hawaii's sugar industry is an American industry, owned and controlled by Americans. And this condition is not going to be changed to satisfy a few Oriental newspaper editors and foreign language school principals. The Americans of Hawaii can't be terrified by a threat." The paper's February 3 editorial repeated this view:

> The constitution of the United States guarantees the right of free speech and a free press. But free speech and a free press do not mean license to attack Americanism. Certainly it does not give to a foreign press the right to work for the overturning of American institutions, nor does it contemplate the use of any portion of the press to stir up industrial trouble with the purpose of subjecting our industries to the domination of an alien race. . . .
> The Japanese press, the Japanese language schools and the Japanese priesthood have demonstrated that they are dangerous to American institutions and hostile to American principles. . . .

Let's fight this thing out to a finish. Let's have the issue decided once for all—the issue of whether Hawaii shall remain American or become Japanized. That is the real issue, the only issue that counts.

The Japanese conspiracy theory that claimed Japan aimed at upsetting the Hawaiian sugar industry and gaining control over it escalated day by day. A February 3 editorial in the *Honolulu Star Bulletin,* under the headline "Alien Agitation," went so far as to say that the situation was "as if the Mikado had the power to name our Governor and direct our political destiny." And on February 6, HSPA president John Waterhouse issued a short statement condemning the strike: "The action taken by the Japanese Federation of Labor is, as we see it, an anti-American movement designed to obtain control of the sugar business of the Hawaiian Islands. The Hawaiian Sugar Planters' Association feels that it is absolutely necessary to oppose this movement to a finish no matter how long it takes, how much it may cost or how much inconvenience it may cause."

During the labor struggles on the mainland the usual rhetorical trump card played by management or the authorities was to fan public fears by labeling strike leaders as "Bolsheviks" or "IWW leaders." But the HSPA used a slogan familiar from the First World War: "Fight for democracy." They transformed the strike, an economic conflict between labor and capital, into an international conspiracy by defining the issues as "whether Hawaii was to be controlled by Asians or Anglo-Saxons" and "how American territory was to be protected from pagans." The tone of racial conflict was unmistakable.

The Japanese conspiracy theory advanced by the HSPA cannot be dismissed simply as propaganda warfare to crush the strike. Anti-Japanese sentiments were strong in the United States. After the Russo-Japanese War, for example, an English-language newspaper in Hawaii had run a political cartoon showing a vicious-faced "Japan" with its wide-open mouth about to swallow up the "Sandwich Islands" (Hawaii). Since Japan had taken colonial control over Korea and Taiwan, the question of "Japan's ambition" was of real concern to those living in Hawaii, the American territory closest to Japan.

Wartime tensions between Japan and the United States over Japan's Twenty-one Demands in China and later over the Siberian intervention intensified the anti-Japanese movement on the U.S. mainland. Newspapers in Japan occasionally ran headlines such as "Anti-Japanese Agitation by Americans."[1] However, the anti-Japanese movements that concerned them in 1919 and 1920 did not refer to anti-Japanese movements on the West Coast or to the great strike of the Japanese workers in Hawaii. Indeed, the strike in Hawaii was reported only twice in Japan, and then only in articles of a few lines.[2] The "anti-Japanese policies" that the Japanese government was frantically dealing with were happening not in the United States but in Asia. In May 1919 Chinese students mounted demonstrations to protest the Japanese occupation of Shandong, and in Korea the March 1 "independence movement" triggered daily bloody incidents on the peninsula for several months. In the view of many Japanese, the British and Americans, especially the missionaries, were assisting these anti-Japanese movements. What is more, many American missionaries sent to Asia were affiliated with the same denominations that had sent missionaries to Hawaii. Hawaiian sugar plantation families often had brothers or sons who followed in the footsteps of their forefathers to become missionaries in Asia or sisters and daughters who married missionaries there. From these witnesses the planter elite in Hawaii heard bloodstained testimony about the meaning of Japanese domination in Asia.

But there was another reason the HSPA advanced the Japanese conspiracy theory. Of Hawaii's population 48 percent were ethnically Japanese, and more than half were nisei, American citizens who would have the right to vote some day. It was obvious from the birthrate statistics that political power in Hawaii would eventually shift to these dual citizens. But the parents of these "American citizens," the first generation, or issei, placed primary importance, and most of their enthusiasm, on educating their children as Japanese. Wouldn't an increase in the second-generation population lead to their control de facto over Hawaii's sugar industry; and wasn't this the ultimate aim of the "pagan priesthood"? In the eyes of the haole governing class, the Japanization of Hawaii had already begun.

ACTING GOVERNOR IAUKEA MAKES A DECLARATION

Royal Mead, the HSPA assistant secretary, dealt directly with the Federation of Japanese Labor. But the federation side, which seems to have taken the title "secretary" to mean a clerical office worker, slighted Mead. In fact, his actual position was executive director in charge of the HSPA's finances and administration. The forty-four-year-old Mead was from San Francisco, a city where anti-Japanese feelings ran strong. After qualifying as a lawyer, he had gone to Hawaii, where he was later hired by the HSPA.

Mead had negotiated with the Japanese side during the 1909 strike. No doubt it was partly because of Mead's experience that the HSPA claimed that the new Oahu strike was not a spontaneous movement by the workers but an affair instigated by the Japanese-language newspapers. In fact, the first strike was led by Yasutarō Sōga, president and editor-in-chief of the *Nippu jiji* (at that time named *Yamato shinbun*) and Kinzaburō Makino, later president of the *Hawaii hōchi,* among others.

In handling the 1920 strike Mead kept in close contact with Frank Thompson, the HSPA's lawyer. Terasaki noted in his diary that a Japanese clerk from Thompson's office often went to purchase several copies of the *Hawaii hōchi.* The HSPA propaganda campaign against the strike began as a fight against the Japanese-language newspapers, using the two English newspapers as a foil. The *Hawaii hōchi* countered this attack with headlines such as the following, which appeared on February 5: "Officers of the HSPA should calm down" and "Crazed commentary by the English-language newspapers." The battle between the Japanese and English newspapers ran on, leaving the federation sitting on the sidelines. As a result, a labor-management struggle that should have been no different from that on the U.S. mainland was transformed into a race issue and an anti-Japanese issue.

Worried that this situation might cast a long shadow on Hawaii's future, on February 3 Acting Governor Curtis Iaukea issued a statement denying the involvement of the Japanese government in the strike: "There is not a shred of evidence to connect the government of Japan with this industrial conflict." On February 19 he sent a document to the representatives of both houses of the territorial legislature, stating that he was "convinced that the racial issue [had] been deliberately emphasized to cloud the economic issue."

The territorial governor of Hawaii was appointed by the U.S. president, but it was the HSPA that recommended a suitable person to the White House. The governor was always someone who had associations with the HSPA. Governor McCarthy, who had departed for Washington on New Year's Eve, was no exception. But Acting Governor Iaukea, who took charge of the territory during the governor's absence, was different. Already seventy-five years old, he had worked for the royal household of King Kamehameha. He was managing trustee and treasurer until Queen Liliuokalani's death, and for a long time he was also responsible for foreign affairs. It was Iaukea who had gone to Japan to conduct the final negotiations for bringing Japanese contract immigrants to Hawaii in the 1880s.

The kamaaina oligarchy had granted certain privileges to the native Hawaiians after the overthrow of the Hawaiian monarchy. Iaukea as well as other members of the Hawaiian royal family and Hawaiian chieftains were elected to the territorial legislature, where they had some political clout. At the time of the strike, of the legislature's fifteen senators and twenty-nine representatives, one-third were Hawaiian or part-Hawaiian. After serving as a legislator for many years, in 1916 Iaukea had been appointed secretary of territorial Hawaii.

Known popularly as "Colonel," the elderly Iaukea was a thin man, unusual for a Hawaiian, who displayed dignity and composure. He was also a troublesome opponent of the HSPA. Not only was he familiar with how Japanese immigrants originally came to Hawaii at the urging of the sugar planters, he also knew very well who had overthrown the independent Hawaiian kingdom. The day after issuing his statement that there was no evidence of a Japanese government conspiracy, Iaukea turned down a request by the plantation owners to call out the local American army garrison and the territorial forces to suppress the striking laborers. But the HSPA dismissed Iaukea as a mere figurehead who was filling in for the absent Governor McCarthy. The English-language newspapers disparaged his actions. On February 5 the *Honolulu Advertiser* criticized "the weak-kneed attitude of the territorial government" and went on to write, "It is extremely unfortunate that in this crisis there is not at the head of the territorial government a man with backbone and sound judgment able to understand that the plantation strike is not a conflict between capital and labor merely but a fight to decide whether Hawaii shall remain American or become a Japanese province."

One of the purposes of Governor McCarthy's long-pending trip to Washington was to petition Congress for Hawaii's statehood. When the news arrived in Hawaii that the statehood bill had no chance of passage, the English-language newspapers immediately blamed not only the Japanese strikers, whose agitation had made a bad impression on the mainland, but also the "weak-willed" Acting Governor Iaukea.

Having dealt with the kamaaina many years, Iaukea was not surprised at being disparaged, nor was he upset in the least by pressure from the HSPA. Despite their repeated requests, he continued to refuse to call out military troops. The accomplishment of Iaukea, who appealed to the racial harmony and aloha spirit of Hawaii and who tried to prevent violence and needless provocation, should not be underestimated. For the

Federation of Japanese Labor, his presence as acting governor during the initial days of the strike proved an unexpected advantage.

By contrast, the brashness of the Japanese-language newspapers, starting with their reporting of the red flag incident, worked against the strikers, and so did the penchant of the Japanese community to veer toward narrow-minded nationalism. The advisory committee, made up mostly of Japanese-language newspaper reporters, had already detached itself from the federation headquarters, but it continued to function as the Honolulu strike supporters' association. The association consisted of the leaders of Honolulu's Japanese community, and its influence was great. According to the FBI files, the organization "forced donations to the Federation from all Japanese in Hawaiian territory, from maids to gardeners."[3]

Japanese religious leaders, both Buddhist and Shinto, quickly made public their support of the federation, but they irritated the HSPA by sending a "letter of caution" in the name of "charity and benevolence." When the strike supporters' association formed a group to collect donations for the striking workers, many religious leaders gave their names to the cause. Governor McCarthy later sent the authorities in Washington a list of contributions made at this time as evidence of the Japanese patriotism of Japanese residents in Hawaii.

While the cane field workers' strike was unfolding in Hawaii, on the mainland the usually conservative Railroad Brotherhoods were rumored to be planning a nationwide strike in support of a plan to nationalize the railroads as the Soviet Union had. Attorney General Palmer received coded secret telegrams from FBI branch offices around the country about this planned action. But the office of the U.S. Attorney in Hawaii reported, "It is not probable that there will be any difficulty with the few railroads in this district (Oahu Railway, Maui Railway, Hawaii Consolidated Railway)." The territorial attorney general, Harry Irwin, could be confident of this assertion. In mid-January the largely Caucasian railway workforce had received the wage increases they demanded in negotiations with management. It was the powerful sugar planters who operated the railways on the Hawaiian Islands, and the railroad operators were members of the HSPA. But although the HSPA approved wage increases for Caucasian workers, it refused to recognize the right of Japanese and Filipino sugarcane workers to bargain collectively regarding their demands.

THE MACHINATIONS OF HSPA LAWYER THOMPSON

On the morning of February 8 Acting Governor Iaukea summoned Pablo Manlapit, the Filipino workers' leader, to the territorial government office to meet with officials, including Harry Irwin, the territorial attorney general, and Dr. Frederick Trotter, president of the territorial Board of Health. They urged Manlapit to call off the strike temporarily for public health reasons. The number of influenza patients was increasing daily at an alarming rate. In Honolulu many churches had canceled their services because of the epidemic. On the plantations, however, the separation of workers into camps on the basis of nationality kept them isolated from one another and slowed the spread of the disease. The Board of Health wanted to limit the movement of people as much as possible. It thought that the HSPA would soon issue orders to evict the Filipino strikers from the plantations and feared that a movement of evicted workers off the plantations would accelerate the epidemic. The Board of Public Health had pleaded with the HSPA to postpone eviction, but Secretary Mead refused. On the afternoon of February 8, the day the eviction order was served, Manlapit convened a special meeting of the Filipino delegates and immediately called off the strike. Only 257 Filipino laborers on Oahu followed Manlapit's order. The rest of them, thrown off the plantations, boarded trains for Honolulu to seek protection from the Federation of Japanese Labor.

News of struggles within the Filipino union had already reached the federation headquarters. Just two days before the strike was called off, Manlapit had expelled the leader of an opposition group, the newspaper publisher Juan Sarminento, on suspicion of spying for the HSPA. The Filipino union leaders, moreover, never made clear how they spent support monies given them by the Japanese federation; and, though the HSPA eviction order had been anticipated, they had made no concrete plans to deal with the situation. Antipathy toward the Filipinos was on the rise among the Japanese workers. Although the Filipinos had rushed ahead in calling for a strike, their resolve had collapsed in just twenty days.

On February 11 and 12 the *Hawaii hōchi* published a series under the title "The Truth Behind the Back to Work Order" that was based on Manlapit's revelations to Kinzaburō Makino, the paper's editor. According to these articles, on the day before he was called in by Acting Governor Iaukea, Manlapit was invited to the residence of Frank Thompson, the HSPA lawyer. After offering Manlapit some whiskey,

Thompson asked, "What would you do if I put $25,000 on this table?" "If there were $50,000 I'd think it over," Manlapit answered, intending to draw Thompson out. But Thompson was more cunning than Manlapit. "Your words have been recorded by my secretary," he said. When Manlapit looked into the next room, he saw a Caucasian woman taking shorthand. The trap set by Thompson, combined with the intrigues of Sarminento, who had gone over to the HSPA after expulsion from the Filipino union, left Manlapit with little choice but to order an end to the strike.

But that was not all. Two days after the strike ended, a Chinese messenger who said he was sent by Thompson told Manlapit, "There is a booking in your name on the *Matsonia* which departs tonight. Go to the mainland on this ship." He handed over an envelope containing $500. Manlapit sent his eldest daughter to return the envelope, but two hours later Thompson himself arrived with an English-language newspaper reporter. He said to Manlapit, "I hear that more than a few Filipinos are so enraged at your order calling off the strike that they are aiming to kill you. For your own safety, it's best if you leave Hawaii."

Thompson also claimed that the envelope had contained $5,000, not $500. Manlapit decided that the only way he could escape from this trap and make public his innocence was to confess everything to Makino.

The day after the *Hawaii hōchi* ran its story, the *Honolulu Star Bulletin* printed Thompson's version of what had happened. According to Thompson, on January 26, the day before the Japanese went on strike, Manlapit called to request a meeting. Shortly after, Manlapit arrived with Esquerez, treasurer of the Filipino Labor Union.

"We don't have funds to continue the strike," Manlapit said. "The Japanese promised us $50,000 at the start and $100,000 later, but they haven't given us any money. If the HSPA can pay us $50,000, we can call off the strike as early as tomorrow." Thompson turned down the offer, saying he couldn't engage in that kind of deal. "Then I'll fight to the end whether I die or am put in prison," said Manlapit angrily. As Manlapit started to leave Thompson called out, "If you call off the strike, I'll personally cover your travel expenses."

About two weeks later, on February 10, according to Thompson, Manlapit arrived at Thompson's law office at 1:15 P.M. He said that his life was in danger and asked for $500 to go to the mainland. Thompson gave him the money, but Manlapit must have changed his mind, for that night he came at 8:00 P.M. to return the money. These being the facts, explained Thompson, charges of threats or bribes were way off the mark.

Putting the lie to Thompson's story, the *Hawaii hōchi* ran an article revealing that it was not Manlapit who had reserved cabin 36 on the *Matsonia* bound for San Francisco. On February 14 Manlapit issued a new strike order to the Filipino workers. The *Hawaii hōchi* promptly observed, "the measures to separate the Japanese and Filipinos have ended in failure."

Can the HSPA's efforts to disrupt the strike using cultural and racial differences be considered a failure?

On October 28, 1919, as Noboru Tsutsumi and other Japanese leaders were beginning to organize the Federation of Japanese Labor, William Sheldon, a haole lawyer deeply interested in labor issues, warned, "The Japanese are making a serious mistake, because if they want to make the movement a success they have got to eliminate the national line and cooperate with laborers of all nationalities."[4]

Sam Nishimura, a nisei who was fifteen years old at the time of the strike, later recalled the viewpoints of both Japanese and Filipinos. "You know, whatever Japanese do, they're persistent. They're hard working guys. And the other guys, *molowa* (lazy), so they don't work, so naturally, Japanese would advance. Up and up. So, they didn't like the idea. But nothing they can do, because Japanese is such nationality that they're industrious, and they try to make a go no matter how hard a time they have, so they didn't like the idea, I think."[5]

Many writers on Hawaiian history have concluded that the Oahu strike of 1920 was a revolutionary labor struggle that transcended the bounds of race. But this interpretation is simply wishful thinking based on a current perspective. In actuality, the gears of the Japanese and Filipino sides had not meshed from the start. In particular, Manlapit's decision to call off the strike deepened the Japanese laborers' contempt for the Filipinos and widened the rift between them. The Federation of Japanese Labor continued to provide the Filipinos with monetary assistance, but they no longer trusted or relied on them.

THE TRUMPED UP "TSUTSUMI STATEMENT"

What inspired the striking Japanese plantation workers in Hawaii was the labor movement back home. In 1920 demonstrations demanding universal manhood suffrage centering on labor organizations were held throughout Japan, and the military police had been called out to deal with a major strike of thirteen thousand factory workers at the state-run Yahata Iron and Steel Works. On February 12 the front pages of the Japanese newspapers reported the arrest and detention of the leaders of the Yahata strike. That morning Noboru Tsutsumi was called to the Consulate General in Honolulu.

Late in the previous afternoon Tsutsumi had received a summons to appear with one other director. He had just returned from Kauai, where he had gone to rein in the Kauai Federation of Labor, which had declared their intention to strike. Kiyofumi Nakabayashi, the director from Kauai, accompanied Tsutsumi to the Honolulu consulate, which was located in an expensive residential neighborhood lined with prominent palm trees, about twenty minutes by car from the federation headquarters. The consulate still stands there today, but in 1920 it was a two-story wooden building with the gold imperial chrysanthemum crest glittering on the front.

Acting Consul General Eiichi Furuya and a secretary by the name of Kumazawa met the two men. The previous consul general, Rokurō Moroi, had been called back to Japan the previous August, but his successor, a former consul general in New York, Chōnosuke Yada, was still at the Foreign Ministry in Japan, and for some reason his posting had been delayed. The forty-five-year-old Furuya was fifteen years older than Tsutsumi. After graduating from an English-language training school, he had worked for a time at the Customs Office in Yokohama. Although not a typical career diplomat, he had been posted to Seattle, Shanghai, and Liaoyang as vice consul and had arrived in Honolulu six months after Tsutsumi.

In his three-piece linen suit, the long-jawed Furuya gave the impression of being relaxed. His manner of speaking was courteous. Pulling the English-language newspapers on his desk toward him, he began to question Tsutsumi. The February 11, 1920, *Honolulu Advertiser* that he held in his hand carried a lengthy report on the "Tsutsumi statement." It alleged that Tsutsumi had made speeches on Kauai to the effect that the strike was instigated by the Japanese government and that "the strike . . . is in line with Japanese policy wherever they colonize. It is of a part with the Japanization of Korea, Manchuria, Eastern Inner Mongolia, Shantung and Formosa." Since the statement implicated the Japanese government, the consulate could not ignore it.

The following report of the questioning is based on what Tsutsumi noted down immediately after he talked to Furuya. Neither the director,

Nakabayashi, nor the secretary, Kumazawa, who were in attendance, contested the contents when the summary was made public.

FURUYA: "Did you say anything about being connected to the Japanese government?"

TSUTSUMI: "I am such an advocate and promoter of the principle that workers should organize themselves that others criticize me vigorously for excluding third parties. I am confident that labor struggles can be won by the laborers. I am always eager to accept the support of those who understand and sympathize with our struggle, regardless of nationality. But there is no need to promote Japanism nor do I feel the need to call in the Imperial government. I am not a narrow Japanese imperialist, but a nationalist socialist [*minzokuteki shakaishugisha*] in the broad sense.

"It would be a great mistake to shout about Japanese imperialism in Hawaii. But even though this is a free Hawaii under the American flag, only the workers are forced to put up with a half-baked Japanese-style paternalism. So I started this movement to demonstrate the American spirit and to build a Hawaii for Hawaii.

"Whoever dragged the Japanese government into this is like the bureaucratic politicians in Japan, who hide behind the mask of paternalism to protect feudalism. It must have been some famous political trickster, some obstinate and narrow-minded petty official. I feel no need to bring in the Imperial government to the strike. Therefore I have no reason to say such things in my speeches and have no recollection of doing so."

FURUYA: "What about the matter of taking over the power of the industry?"

TSUTSUMI: "If wages are increased from 77 cents to $1.25, will industrial power in Hawaii shift? The Federation headquarters has barely $3,000 in funds even if its pockets are turned inside out. If we could buy a $100 million sugar production company with this kind of money it would be cheap. This could only happen in an adventure novel or a fairy tale, and at this point we don't have the time to waste on such fantasies. But there are capitalists who are using this as an opportunity to buy up stock on Oahu. I am impressed by such clever entrepreneurs. It is unfortunate that there are no Japanese with such foresight."

FURUYA: "Because you say such things others charge you with attempting to take over the industry."

TSUTSUMI: "There's no need for me to talk about that on the plantations, but I have been thinking seriously about the issue. Basically, are foreigners forbidden to hold stock in Hawaiian sugar companies? The HSPA claims that this is a racial struggle, but isn't it racial when only the whites have the power over capital and don't let the other races even touch them with one finger?

"Ultimately labor struggles can't be resolved until workers hold some of the stock in their company, the capitalists involve themselves constantly in their businesses, and everyone connected to the company affirms that it is his company. Isn't it the recent trend for companies to say that distributing stock is better than giving cash bonuses, and isn't this beginning to be implemented?

"They are saying that the Federation headquarters is seizing control of the power over the industry, but an industry is not maintained and developed by capital alone. Because labor power is also necessary, labor and capital are like the wheels on a cart or like the two wings of a bird. They are both indispensable elements to industry. Consequently, capitalists should recognize the status and rights of laborers within industry. We are by no means asking for the power to control, but we will not hesitate to assert our rights as workers. To avoid misunderstandings I won't go further into this type of discussion at the moment, but I don't think that the capitalists' monopoly over industry is an auspicious thing for the industry."

These comments reveal Noboru Tsutsumi's theories on the labor movement, and he spoke to the striking workers in nearly the same manner. That was why the English-language newspapers accused Tsutsumi of being not only a Japanese government spy but also an IWW radical.

FURUYA: "So what is your opinion about the IWW issue?"

TSUTSUMI: "A walkout is the workers' last resort to bring the capitalists to their senses, so it's natural that they shut down factory operations and stop sugarcane cultivation in a legal manner. Who would go on strike if things were to go on as before? The IWW attempts to take over the control of industry by whatever means possible. Our movement is to achieve harmony between labor and capital by going out on strike only after all peaceful measures have been exhausted. The sun will legally wither the cane and the mills will legally stop because the workers are not there. Everyone would start working happily as soon as wages are increased. It will be obvious whether or not we are the IWW if by chance wages are increased."

The Federation of Japanese Labor had consistently emphasized that the essence of their movement was the "great ideal" of conciliation between labor and capital. Tsutsumi expressed this ideal by referring to the Japanese character: "Historically and socially the Japanese have a conciliatory and peaceful disposition. Since the founding of the nation, Japanese have based their society on feelings of affinity for kinship and on the family system, and since they do not insist on individual rights and duties this has naturally become their inherent character."

As his final question, Acting Consul General Furuya asked, "What about the issue of an Imperial warship coming to pick up the strikers?" What the English-language newspapers had questioned most about the Tsutsumi statement was that he allegedly said if the situation became dire, an Imperial warship would be sent in support of the workers. As it happened, the Japanese cruiser *Yakumo* was due to put in to port on March 8.

When the haole planters overthrew the Hawaiian monarchy, the Japanese government had quickly dispatched the warship *Naniwa*, ostensibly to protect the lives and property of resident Japanese immigrants. But a Japanese murderer who had escaped from prison sought refuge on the Japanese vessel. Captain Heihachirō Tōgō refused to hand over the man to the Hawaiian side, arguing that the ship was Japanese territory. The incident nearly caused an international incident between Japan and the United States, and many immigrants were so moved that they named their sons Heihachirō. Although this incident had occurred twenty-some years earlier, talk of a Japanese warship raised an issue that Hawaii's governing class could not easily ignore.

To Furuya's question, Tsutsumi replied, "During a sit-down strike you do not let workers come and go. We could not tell the workers not to move from their camps even if evicted, and then in the next breath tell them we were coming to pick them up in cars. So I certainly have not even thought about an Imperial Navy warship. And I doubt that we could carry on a serious strike if we resorted to such infantile foolery. The suggestion is so divorced from common sense that I can't take it seriously."

Kumazawa, the consulate secretary, blurted out, "This really is ridiculous. What made the papers write such things? It's even more extreme than the anti-Japanese feelings in California. Ha, ha, ha."

It is doubtful that Acting Consul General Furuya joined in the laughter. In a report to Foreign Minister Kōsai Uchida on March 1, Furuya observed that many strikers believed that a warship would certainly rescue them. "Regardless of whether Tsutsumi made such statements in his speeches," he wrote, "it is now necessary to sweep away the various rumors and misunderstandings." He urged issuing statements to the English- and Japanese-language newspapers clarifying that the visit of the cruiser *Yakumo* and the federation's strike were "entirely unrelated."

On February 13 the Japanese Consulate General issued an official notice denying any connection between the Japanese government and the wage increase movement and warning against such unfounded and inflammatory rumors. The visit of the *Yakumo*, the consulate explained, "had been planned as part of the itinerary set before its departure from Japan the previous November. Needless to say, there is no relation to the sugar plantation laborers' wage increase movement, and thus care should be given that there is no such misunderstanding."

After leaving the consulate, Tsutsumi issued his own statement to the newspapers: "Comments that I have been sent by the Japanese government or about the Imperial warship are entirely false. Why would I behave in a way so lacking in common sense? I can only think that this is the work of the planters' dogs seeking to benefit from the situation."

The Japanese newspapers carried daily warnings that anyone who undermined the solidarity of the Japanese was "a planters' dog" and urged people to beware of such a person. The papers continued to publish the names of "dirty traitors." The permanent domicile, the date of birth, and the actions of recalcitrant workers were also published in their hometown papers in Japan. The English-language press termed such disciplinary action a display of "fanatic nationalism." And they accused Tsutsumi of being a Japanese government spy on the grounds that he had gotten this information from family registers in Japanese local government offices.

On February 12, the day Tsutsumi was called into the consulate, an "emergency notice" issued by the federation disciplined seven people at Waipahu Plantation, all skilled workers in the mill who earned high wages, by exposing their alleged collaboration with the plantation management. Manpachi Ogata, a boilerman and a Waipahu delegate to the Oahu federation, was one of them. The February 12 *Hawaii hōchi* reported that Ogata's children, "feeling ashamed of their father's deed, cried aloud from morning on, and the betrayer's children refused to go to school." It is easy to imagine how bitter their parents must have felt. The HSPA not only gave money to the "planters' dogs," it cleverly exploited their hatred of the federation and used them to fabricate the so-called Tsutsumi statement.

The HSPA had made Noboru Tsutsumi, the de facto leader and a central figure of the federation, their main target. But when the HSPA claimed that their struggle against the strike was to protect "American democracy" from Japanese takeover, Tsutsumi made no concessions. He retorted that the strike was a struggle to bring American democracy to the Hawaiian cane fields. In Tsutsumi the HSPA faced a stout opponent the likes of which it had not encountered before.

The 1921 FBI report on the "strike leader T. Tsutsumi" observed, "He is a very fluent speaker, very radical in his views. The laborers at present worship him like a god and believe whatever he tells them."[6] Among those who heard Tsutsumi's speeches, impressions were mixed. Many agreed with the assessment of Tsuneichi Yamamoto, a former *Hawaii hōchi* reporter, who recalled, "Above all he was eloquent. He had presence, had no fear, and confidently fought with anyone."[7] Another former reporter thought that his appeal was intellectual: "Rather than being particularly eloquent, he had an exceptional intellect, and people couldn't help but heed his words."[8] Some, however, had the impression that Tsutsumi was a sentimental idealist. Takeshi Haga recalled, "His manner of speaking was one of waving his hands and appealing to the audience's emotions. Gradually he would become excited and even shed tears."[9]

Speeches printed in the Japanese-language newspapers suggest that Tsutsumi put things in a way that could be easily understood by the workers. But it is undeniable that he tended toward Japanese sentimentalism, and this may have given the HSPA the opportunity to fabricate the "Tsutsumi statement."

A 1921 FBI report indicated that Tsutsumi had made another inflammatory statement the year before: "Tsutsumi, in a speech, told the Japanese that if they did not win he would commit Hari Kari, that it would be an unpardonable sin if the Japanese did not win and that in that event he would suicide. He said that the Sumitomo Bank had agreed to advance $200,000 to the strikers in case of the emergency." This deepened the suspicion already created by Tsutsumi's alleged assurance that the Imperial Navy would rescue the strikers. Just as the HPSA had tried to sow dissension between the Japanese and Filipinos by entrapping Manlapit, it kept revealing alleged Tsutsumi statements in an attempt to establish the theory that the strike was a Japanese conspiracy.

This tactic had an immediate effect. A month after Manlapit spoke to the *Hawaii hōchi* about the "truth behind the back to work order," he reported to the Philippine Labor Bureau that "the attitude of the Federation of Japanese Labor" was the reason for his order to end the strike. "I found out," he wrote, "that, on the one hand, the Japanese are trying to strike a blow at the Hawaiian commercial circles, while on the other hand they are planning a general strike by all unions in an attempt to take over this Territory." Since the Philippines, like Hawaii, were an American territory, he said that he had put American interests ahead of everything else. "I opposed this shocking scheme of the Japanese who are attempting to occupy the Territory," he wrote. "I refused to become a tool used for Japan's interests." As a result, he felt no choice but to call off the strike. The report was obtained in Manila by Saburō Kurusu, later the special envoy to U.S.-Japan negotiations immediately before the Pearl Harbor attack, who sent it to Foreign Minister Uchida.[10]

In any case, whenever the HSPA or the English-language newspapers brought up the Japanese conspiracy, they invariably quoted Tsutsumi's alleged warship statement. With the passage of time the "Tsutsumi statement" came to be considered a historical fact—not only by the U.S. government but by the Japanese as well.

THE SPANISH INFLUENZA STRIKES

As he had done in the case of the Filipino workers, Acting Governor Iaukea asked the HSPA to postpone evicting striking Japanese workers from the plantations until the influenza epidemic was contained, and once again the planters refused. On February 18 the HSPA ordered that the striking workers be removed from plantation housing within forty-eight hours. At some plantations, such as Aiea, several dozen temporarily hired plantation police went from house to house throwing household goods on the street and nailing shut doors. The only workers permitted to stay at Ewa Plantation were two disabled men, who had lost limbs in accidents with cane knives and who were not participating in the strike. Even the sick, who had taken to bed heavily wrapped in clothes to ward off the chills of high fever, were mercilessly evicted. Children as well as adults, packing blankets, pots, pans, and basins on their backs, left their humble but comfortably familiar homes. The Japanese camps in all the plantations became ghost towns, where the voices of playing children and the cries of babies could no longer be heard.

"Striking Japanese were chased out of their houses," recalled Antone Camacho, a Portuguese luna at Kahuku Plantation who was twenty-six years old at the time. "Other people came to take chickens and other things which were left behind."[11] Some have testified, however, that it was not the plantation companies but the local Federation of Japanese Labor that forced the evictions. According to Seiichi Miyasaki, a junior in high school at Waialua at the time, "My father was head carpenter, earning $2 a day, he did not want to strike because I was little, and he thought I'd be in a bad situation thereafter. . . . [M]ore or less he was forced to go on strike. My father did not want to strike, but I distinctly remember four men came with the truck to load our stuff in the car."[12]

Though Hawaii is a land of eternal summer, February is the coolest month of the year, and on rainy evenings it can become quite chilly. The total number of workers and their families evicted was 13,393 (some 4,000 children among them). Many were forced to sleep outdoors near the railroad stations for several weeks after their expulsion. At Waipahu and Waialua plantations most evicted families took shelter in local Japanese-language schools and temples. But the majority of those at Aiea and Kahuku plantations headed for Honolulu in small trucks and rail cars arranged by the federation. Immediately after the expulsion order, 7,000 went to Honolulu, and the number continued to increase. This forced the federation to expend a vast sum of money. For the month of February lodging costs for evicted workers rose to $18,000 and transportation costs to $6,000.

Evacuation to Honolulu was only possible with the total cooperation of the supporters' association, which the federation had tried to keep at a distance. Since space was running out at all available inns, rental houses, churches, temples, shrines, and Japanese-language schools, the federation had to ask members of the Japanese community to open their warehouses for people to sleep in. It was only because the highly respected leaders of the supporters' association went around Honolulu with federation secretary Ichiji Gotō and others that the community agreed to help out.

At the newly rebuilt Honganji mission in Hawaii on Foat Street, supported by large donations from the worshipers, evacuees from Kahuku slept on bedding spread on the concrete floor of the great hall. Flush toilets had been installed a few months before, but children, familiar only with the more primitive nonflush public latrines on the plantation, kept throwing things into them even after being told not to do so many times. The plumbers' bills were sent to the federation.

Workers from Aiea Plantation were sheltered in a church on King Street. "We put wicker boxes and trunks in the wide hallway of the basement as partitions between families," recalled Violet Fujinaka. "Quite a few people were coughing and needed bed rest. I had come to Hawaii when I was one year old, and I was 22 years old at the time. I was working as a maid in a white military man's house, and I would go on my day off once a week to see my mother at that church." [13]

The Filipinos suffered much more than the Japanese after being evicted from the plantations. The Izumo Taisha shrine was the only place that took them in, and it was clearly not large enough. Hiroshi Miyazawa, the overworked federation staff member in charge of the Filipinos, finally arranged to use an abandoned sake brewery storehouse. The Filipinos slept on beds made from soap boxes placed on a dirt floor reeking of sour sake, and they had to dig holes in the dirt to use as latrines. Married and single workers were thrown in together, causing a great many problems.

The staff of the Honolulu Board of Health, on edge about the influenza epidemic, investigated conditions in each of the shelters. If they judged a place to be unclean, they ordered it to be closed immediately. For this reason, the presence of Filipinos in the sake storehouse was kept secret. Buying some time in this way, the federation started building shacks for the Filipinos on land it bought for $4,000.

The number of deaths attributed to the Spanish influenza in the United States from 1918 to 1921 was higher than all the American dead in World War I. In Japan there were some 130,000 deaths during the twelve months ending July 1920. The speedy imposition of a strict quarantine on ships arriving in Hawaiian ports kept down the number of flu patients, but even so the numbers were gradually rising. As Acting Governor Iaukea and the Board of Health had feared, with the migration of evicted workers from the plantations the numbers of patients rose dramatically.

The Honolulu Japanese Physicians' Association donated one thousand free consultation tickets to treat the evicted workers. The Japanese-language school, which became a temporary hospital for the striking workers, soon looked like a field hospital on a battlefront. Several young nisei women who worked as volunteer nurses at the public health section set up in the federation headquarters died from the disease. In February 1920 the causes of deaths recorded for Honolulu numbered 179 from influenza and 42 from pneumonia. But it is difficult to obtain an accurate count of Spanish influenza deaths. Doctors also listed acute pneumonia, respiratory infection, heart damage, and whooping cough on the death certificates.

Among the evicted Waialua Plantation worker families, forty-three people died just in the ten days after eviction. Many later recalled the epidemic in oral histories:

> I remember lot of Japanese died on that strike. And I had lot of school friends, too. Like, Nakatsu, Kamiyama and all that. I don't know whether they had some place down Haleiwa there, some church or something that . . . the place was so crowded. . . . [T]hat was a pretty bad strike influenza came in.[14]

> No doctor, doctor cannot. Everyday, so many guys are dying, so, you know, what they had to do was get a plantation truck and just dump the body. Put 'em in the graveyard. That's all. They cannot make a decent funeral. I notice

a place where mother and a son died together. They had to bury 'em together. So that epidemic was terrific.[15]

A person could get pains in the morning and be dead in the afternoon. My sister died too.[16]

(I went to Jōdo mission temple with my parents after eviction.) (There were) many people, I don't know how many, well, they all develop flu and original minister's wife passed away from the flu. Caught from the people. (Because of the strike), their sanitation was not as good as it should be then.[17]

Etsuta Inoue, the federation director from Maui, was one of those who died in the epidemic. Inoue had been trained as a Zen Buddhist priest and had also worked as a newspaper reporter. He was known to be passionate about his job with the federation. When he delivered a speech, using the strength of his entire body and his face flushing with emotion, it was like a "burst of flame." [18] He had returned from Maui on February 14 to make a report to the federation office, but for someone who was normally able to push himself hard, he seemed unusually lethargic. Another director, who had thought something might be wrong as he watched Inoue go off to the Kobayashi Inn, later found him shaking on his futon. He was immediately taken to the emergency hospital at the Japanese-language school.

The Japanese Hospital, originally called the Japanese Charity Hospital but renamed the Kuwakini Hospital during the Second World War, had been rebuilt two years before. It was a modern facility, but there were so many influenza patients that it was unable to handle them all. By the time Inoue was transferred to the Japanese Hospital from the dirt floor of the temporary ward two days later, he had contracted pneumonia and become delirious. A week later, half an hour after he was visited by the three federation secretaries, Tsutsumi, Miyazawa, and Gotō, and six directors, the thirty-two-year-old Inoue died. His last feverish words were, "Have the Filipinos gone back to work? Let's get all the islands. Oh, is that so? It's all right . . ." [19]

On Saturday, February 22, the day Inoue died, a grand Washington's Birthday parade was held in Honolulu. Marching schoolchildren were followed by members of the newly formed Hawaiian Post of the American Legion. A few days before, the local Legionnaires, following the policy of Americanism touted by the American Legion headquarters on the mainland, had issued a resolution stating that the Japanese-language schools and newspapers represented extreme anti-Americanism.

Determined to not let the death of Etsuta Inoue be futile, the federation turned his funeral at the Hawaii Honganji mission two days later into a major demonstration showing the renewed solidarity and determination of the striking workers. The funeral procession wound through the main streets of Honolulu, following Inoue's body from the Hosoi Funeral Home to the Honganji. First came a small marching band from the Waipahu Plantation youth group, quietly playing a song. Federation leaders walked on either side of the hearse, carrying a wreath of white and yellow flowers and a funerary banner of light yellow with the words "Mourning the spirit of Etsuta Inoue, director of the Federation" in black. The striking workers followed, grouped according to their plantations and walking in a silent, solemn procession. It was a clear day with blue skies. Along the funeral procession route, Japanese merchants pressed their palms together in prayer as they watched the coffin go by, and the large Hawaiian policeman who was directing traffic quietly gave a respectful salute.[20]

The mayor of Honolulu, Joseph James Fern, age forty-eight, who was already a patient in Queens Hospital, died two weeks later. Fern was of mixed white and Hawaiian parentage with the Hawaiian name Keo Kimo Pana. He had started out as a horse wagon driver at Kohala Plantation on Hawaii. From the start he had been sympathetic to the plantation workers. Indeed, he had declared that the success of the sugar industry in Hawaii was "due to the efforts of the Japanese workers,"[21] and like Curtis Iaukea, he had viewed the federation's actions with warmth. His lavish funeral was held in Hawaiian style, with colorful orchids.

THE PALMER MEDIATION PROPOSAL

Terasaki made no mention of Inoue's funeral. His diary for that day noted simply, "February 24 (Tuesday, fair): *Nippu* supports Palmer plan. *Hōchi* declares that if it is conditional then it cannot support it." Apparently he was much concerned about a strike mediation plan proposed by the Reverend Albert W. Palmer two days before. Palmer, the pastor of the Central Union Church, the most historic church in Hawaii, was a native of Kansas. After graduating from the University of California, he spent many years as a minister on the West Coast. He had come to the Union Church three years before at the age of forty-four. He had a doctorate in religious studies, was teaching at the University of Hawaii, and wrote a weekly column on religion for the *Honolulu Star Bulletin*. He had a warm personality, and despite having come to Hawaii relatively recently, he had gained the trust of the kamaaina. Perhaps because he was an outsider he was able to propose a bold mediation plan.

In testimony before Congress in 1921, Arthur F. Griffiths, the headmaster of Punahou School, an elite school for Caucasians in Hawaii, categorized the attitudes of the haoles of the time into three groups. The first group, the leaders of the sugar industry, were strongly anti-Japanese. "They regard [the Japanese] as a menace, they believe that the Japanese Government is seeking to control the local situation and that it will resort to any methods to accomplish its purpose." The second group, although "somewhat neutral," were "inclined to be opposed to the Oriental" and to "fear that [the] Japanese were getting out of hand." The third group, "the descendants of missionaries, *Kamaainas*, old timers, Christian workers and church members in general," advocated "broad friendly policies of Christianization and Americanization."[22]

Reverend Palmer belonged to the third group. Concerned about the effect on Hawaiian society of the confrontation between the HSPA and the Japanese immigrant workers, he approached not only other Caucasian leaders such as Arthur L. Dean, president of the University of Hawaii, who were concerned about the strike but also Japanese community leaders in the strike supporters' association to work out a solution. In the Japanese community, the Reverend Takie Okumura, Dr. Iga Moori, and Masao Kawahara, president of the Japanese Chamber of Commerce, responded to his appeal. Moori, a Christian and a physician, had been official physician in the Hawaiian kingdom's immigration bureau, and Kawahara was the owner of a local major store and the president of the Pacific Bank.

After meeting with these men, Reverend Palmer proposed his mediation plan in his Sunday sermon. The Big Five sugar planter families were all members of his congregation. Palmer warned them that half the population of Hawaii was Japanese and that misunderstandings could ensue if racial issues and nationalist suspicions intruded into labor-management relations. Reverend Palmer also cautioned the federation leaders about the danger of overly stressing their Japanese-ness for the sake of encouraging solidarity. He pointed out that the rising sun crossed with the hammer and sickle that appeared on the federation's flag and stationery exacerbated the misunderstandings on the part of the Americans, and so did publishing the names of "traitors" in their hometown newspapers in Japan.

Reverend Palmer proposed the following compromise:

To the Japanese Labor Federation, [we recommend] that it recognize the un-wisdom and peril of any such organization along national lines and that it therefore call off the present strike, abandon the field of plantation labor and thus leave that field clear for an organization of the employees within the sugar industry itself and so arrange as to be inter-racial in scope.

To the Planters' Association, we recommend that, as an expression of its progressive spirit and purpose to treat its employees in the most generous and enlightened fashion, it announce that it will arrange for an election by secret ballot on each plantation of an Employees' Committee to confer with the Plantation Manager in securing the utmost cooperation between the man-agement and the men. Such election to be held within one month of the date the men return to work.

Within the Japanese community, major organizations such as the doctors' association, the bankers' association, and the chamber of com-merce all announced their approval of Palmer's plan. Diplomatic docu-ments indicate that Acting Consul General Furuya also saw his plan as a way to end the strike and sent a memo to that effect to Foreign Min-ister Uchida.[23] The Terasaki diary notes that Sōga's *Nippu jiji* and Ha-tori's *Hawaii shinpō* both declared their overall support of the Palmer plan. But Makino's *Hawaii hōchi* dissented; on February 26 the news-paper characterized the Palmer plan as "a great insult to the workers, [which] throws the strike as a whole body into the jaws of death," and as a "disgraceful peace negotiation." It directly opposed the plan on the grounds that "a spoken promise cannot be trusted" and vehemently at-tacked the *Nippu jiji* for supporting it.

Among the haoles many in the religious and education community declared their support. So did Acting Governor Iaukea, who announced on February 25 that the planters had been "putting pressure" on him to use military force against the strikers just as they had used Americans to threaten the Hawaiians at the time of the 1893 "revolution."[24] "Under these circumstances," he said, "if the planters have evidence in their pos-session which proves the existence of Japanese conspiracy claims, if they have evidence other than agitated words, they should publish it."[25] In response to public opinion, which sought a resolution to the strike as soon as possible as apprehension about the influenza epidemic spread, the two English-language newspapers also declared the Palmer plan worthy of consideration.

On the evening of February 24, on their return from Inoue's funeral, the federation leaders argued animatedly over the Palmer plan. Once again a "Tsutsumi statement" became an issue. When the Palmer plan was announced, a Japanese reporter from the *Honolulu Advertiser* asked Tsutsumi his opinion. He responded, "It is excellent in terms of stressing harmony between labor and management, but realistically there are some problems. Most of all, I cannot accept the dissolution of the federation." The paper reported the story under the headline "Secretary Tsutsumi Is Firmly Against the Palmer Plan."

After a discussion at federation headquarters that lasted until dawn, Tsutsumi was called in the following morning by Acting Governor Iaukea, who asked him to explain the attitude of the federation. After meeting with Iaukea, Tsutsumi made the rounds of Japanese community leaders to explain his statement in the newspaper.

At 7:30 P.M. on February 27 the three federation secretaries, Tsutsumi, Miyazawa, and Gotō, and the five directors visited Reverend Palmer at the Central Union Church. Dean, Moori, Kawahara, and others were there as well. This discussion, which lasted five hours, focused on the dissolution of the federation. Tsutsumi and the other federation officials stubbornly opposed dissolution of the organization. Palmer and the other mediators suggested a compromise: "As long as the association is not limited racially to Japanese, we will not be concerned about the existence of a labor organization."

After reconfirming this point, Tsutsumi and his colleagues issued a statement dated February 27: "The directors and secretaries of the Federation of Japanese Labor accept the general principle laid down in Mr. Palmer's plan and stand ready to take the steps to put it in operation just as soon as it shall appear that the Hawaiian Sugar Planters' Association has accepted the general principles of the said plan and also stand ready to put it in operation." In other words, the Federation of Japanese Labor, trusting in the goodwill of the mediators who were known as men of good sense in Hawaiian society, was prepared to compromise. Since their stated goal was conciliation between labor and capital and harmony for Hawaii, the federation put harmony first. It was also a thoroughly Japanese way of dealing with the situation: showing respect to the mediators before discussing concrete plans for resolving the strike.

But the HSPA flatly refused to engage in collective bargaining with the workers. It refused to "consider any plan or suggestion involving even tentative relations, direct or indirect, of the nature of compromising the present strike situation through or in conjunction with the so-called Japanese Federation of Labor." It also rejected the humanitarian compromise that Reverend Palmer had proposed from the pulpit. And its attitude toward Tsutsumi remained unyielding. Calling Tsutsumi an agitator who was not a real worker, the HSPA insisted that cane field laborers were being intimidated and they would not permit that alien domination of the sugar industry.

The prospects for an early resolution of the strike evaporated.

THE PLANTERS' ASSOCIATION STRIKES BACK

In the midst of the uproar over the Palmer plan, the HSPA announced that the bonus rate for February would be 258.5 percent. This meant that the lowest-paid workers, who earned $20 a month, would receive a bonus of $38, or a total of $58. In actuality, the bonus was paid in two installments, so only half of the amount was to be paid in February, but the magic of this figure had a powerful effect on the workers.

The English-language newspapers pointed out that the strikers had lost $36 by listening to the labor agitators, and the Federation of Japanese Labor was obliged to warn strikers repeatedly not to be tricked by the amount of the bonus. Japanese plantation workers outside Oahu were laboring in the cane fields to raise support funds for the strike, but with the bonus increase they could save more money too. The workers on Oahu, the only ones on strike, could not hide their frustration.

One reason the HSPA firmly opposed the Palmer plan was an extraordinary rise in the price of sugar. Generally the sugar market was quite stable, but every few decades it went through a major fluctuation. The sudden price rise in 1920 was one of these exceptional shifts in the market. The wartime sugar price control law had been repealed in the United States the previous year. There was no immediate effect on the market price, which remained at 5 to 7 cents per pound. But as if in concert with the rising labor unrest in Hawaii, the price began to rise at year's end, jumping to 12.29 cents by January 5, 1920. It appeared to dip in late February, but then in March it reached 13 cents. The HSPA quickly calculated the bonus rate and once more announced it with great fanfare.

It was not only the sugar price that worked to the advantage of the HSPA. Rainfall in Hawaii was considerably less than that in Cuba, its main competitor. Hawaiian sugar growers had to invest heavily in irrigation, and the labor required was considerably greater than in Cuba. About the time the strike started, rain began to fall quite heavily even on Oahu, where rainfall was normally less than the other islands. The planters did not have to worry about irrigating the fields, and the sugarcane grew as expected. The striking workers felt that even the weather was in league against them.

The HSPA did not let this favorable opportunity pass. The planters began to recruit scabs who would work for $3 to $3.50 per day. Many were unemployed laborers. As one Waialua worker recalled, "Nobody tried to go out in the field to work, what I mean, to strike break, because it wasn't a safe thing to do. . . . [Strikebreakers] lot of them from Honolulu who did not have jobs [or] from other islands."[26] The *Hawaii hōchi* pointed out that many of scabs were Koreans and Chinese who harbored "national animosity" toward the Japanese. Since their homelands had experienced Japanese aggression, it was natural that they felt intense antipathy toward the Japanese. Indeed, many Chinese and Korean immigrants in Hawaii contributed funds to support independence or nationalist movements at home. And many of the Chinese scabs used their bonus money to take their families on long-postponed visits back to China.

Many Filipinos, who had ostensibly joined in the labor struggle with the Japanese, became scabs as well. In fact, HSPA president Waterhouse proposed a plan to import great numbers of Filipinos at the end of December 1919. By March they began arriving in Hawaii. In the HSPA's annual report after the conclusion of the strike, Waterhouse stated that during the strike 75 percent of the average monthly work had been accomplished.

CRITICISM OF THE FEDERATION

We don't like to strike
　But it can't be helped
　Because our wages aren't increased
Will you raise them, until you raise them
　Unless you raise them, we'll have to
Strike, *don don*
77 cents is cheap
　But we can't eat on it
　So it can't be helped
We'll launch our strike
　Until our cries can be heard above
Don don
　　　Strikers' *Don Don* Song

Until the greedy and cruel planters who are destroying Hawaii's industry
Wake up,
We'll go to the bitter end
Without quitting our united strike
Oya, Oya

Strikers' *Oya Oya* Song

As more and more scabs began working the fields, unrest spread among the Japanese laborers. The HSPA tactic of using monetary incentives to defeat the strikers had its effect, and a few Japanese became scabs as well. Late on March 1, for example, Noboru Tsutsumi rushed by car to Kahuku Plantation to deal with a laborer who had become an agent for the planters out of a grudge against the federation and was secretly stirring up a movement to return to work.

The number of federation rallies peaked in March: speeches at Waianae Plantation on March 1 and at Kahuku and Waipahu on March 2, the Pearl City striking workers meeting on March 3, and a lecture meeting sponsored by the supporters' association at Asahi Theater in Honolulu that night. All these rallies aimed at "planters' dogs," and often they were quite emotional. A newspaper reported that the audience at one rally was "an excited mob that heard speeches filled with tears, anger by the audience, crying by the orators—the entire house crazed." Unable to stay in the office and devote himself to reworking the federation's tactics, Tsutsumi raced from one plantation to another giving speeches nearly every day: March 4 at Waialua Plantation, March 7 at Ewa and Waipahu.

At the Oahu federation meeting on March 9, more than one thousand delegates from the federation branches at each of the plantations crowded into the garden of the Tokiwaen restaurant. The meeting moved indoors when it began to rain. Even with all the sliding doors open people spilled out into the hallway, so jammed they were unable to move. Yet no one left until the three rounds of "Banzai" signifying adjournment a little after midnight. Fifteen delegates from the various plantations rose to speak that night, wildly denouncing the "unforgivable traitors" who had gone back to work.

The number of Japanese laborers returning to work in early March was announced by the plantations as follows (figures in parentheses are those announced by the federation): Aiea Plantation, 8 workers (0); Waipahu Plantation, 25 workers (7); Ewa Plantation, 10 workers (0); Waialua

Plantation, 14 workers (9); Kahuku Plantation, 32 workers (21); Wai-manalo Plantation, 0 workers (0).

To deal with the strikebreakers, the federation devised the tactic "silent send-off." The idea was to put pressure on the scabs by mobilizing more than one thousand strikers to silently send off the trains carrying scabs to the cane fields. But the strikers had to leave Honolulu on street-cars departing at 4:00 A.M. to carry out this tactic. Initially approximately three hundred strikers turned out, but they became discouraged when it began to rain, and by the third day less than thirty showed up. The "silent send-off" tactic was soon abandoned.

The most effective way of disciplining the turncoats was to announce their expulsion from the union in the newspapers. Individuals disciplined for "acting on their own in violation of the rules of the federation" appeared with their photographs in the newspapers practically every day.

The influenza epidemic grew more severe. From the beginning of March the number of new patients averaged 120 daily. Federation expenditures on funerals rose to $965 in March. The amounts for the other months were $278 in February, $534 in April, $134 in May, $124 in June, and $67 in July.

Among the passengers on the *Siberia-maru,* which departed for Yokohama on March 5, were some three hundred Japanese immigrants returning to Japan. Many feared that the strike would last a long time and gave up the struggle, but many feared the spreading influenza. However, only those immigrants who had some savings were able to return to Japan at this time.

On March 12 the cruiser *Yakumo* entered the port of Honolulu. Since the alleged Tsutsumi statement about the dispatch of the *Yakumo* to rescue the strikers had become such a problem, Acting Consul General Eiichi Furuya had repeatedly issued warnings: "Needless to say, no connection or contact is to be made with the plantation workers' wage increase movement, take care so as not to incur any misunderstandings."[27] Japanese residents of Honolulu abstained from the usual welcoming reception. With special permission from the American military, the *Yakumo* put in to the naval port at Pearl Harbor. After replenishing water and other supplies, it quickly departed for Japan.

On March 15, the day the *Yakumo* left port, Terasaki noted in his diary, "(Monday, somewhat cloudy): The strike continues. Prospect seems unfavorable, but the workers believe the headquarters' statement that the outlook is favorable." In fact, by this time striking workers were voicing distrust of the federation leadership. Using Japanese agents, the HSPA intrigued to sow discord between the strikers and the federation leaders by skillful scandal-mongering. Responding both to threats and to gestures of conciliation, the number of laborers returning to work, although few in number, continued to increase.

Fliers of a cartoon depicting six federation leaders chomping on cigars and leaning back in a large model convertible decked out with small federation flags were widely distributed. Its captions read: "We are the lords (daimyo) of Hawaii." "If there wasn't a strike, I wouldn't be riding in a car." "I'm living in luxury." "Ten dollars an hour" [meaning this man was receiving compensation]. "The cigars of the Federation officers cost 50 cents each." "It would be great if the strike is prolonged."

The number of automobiles in Hawaii was increasing rapidly, but ordinary workers rode only trains and buses. Even the lowest-level staff at federation headquarters, however, used automobiles so as to respond promptly to any situation. The HSPA cleverly played on this point to promote estrangement within the federation ranks.

The HSPA pointed out that it was not clear how contributions to the strike were being used. Contributions were collected periodically, and a list of contributors to the wage increase movement support fund was published in the Japanese-language newspapers along with the amounts given. Contributing to the fund was regarded as evidence of loyalty to the striking workers. Naturally contributors who had donated funds from their own meager household budgets were interested in how the money was used. Among the slander and misinformation spread by the HSPA, references to the strike support fund were especially effective.

It was true that some federation headquarters members behaved in questionable ways. At a time when the typical laborer could scarcely afford a 10-cent bowl of noodles at a cheap eatery, federation staff members held meetings at restaurants. Ryōkin Toyohira, a reporter for the *Nippu jiji*, recalled, "I think Tsutsumi and the other leaders of the Federation were earnest, but it was a collection of many kinds of people and they had increased in number, so it can't be said for certain that there were no bad elements. The inn where the Federation leaders stayed included a restaurant where they held their meetings and consultations, so the *Hawaii hōchi* and others jibed at the drinking and eating."[28]

Tsuneichi Yamamoto, a reporter for the *Hawaii Hōchi* at the time, remembered that one day he was called in by the newspaper's president, Kinzaburō Makino, and editor-in-chief, Haga. Yamamoto was an old friend of Tsutsumi's who had taught him how to write articles when he had just started out at *Hawaii mainichi.* "Catch those guys in action when they are having a party at a restaurant with the money collected from workers," Makino told Yamamoto. And Haga added, "Yamamoto, I'll let you in on something. I hear they often use the detached room at Mochizuki. You should crawl under the room."

In Honolulu the Mochizuki Club was known as a first-class restaurant. It was located very close to the Japanese Hospital on Liliha Street on a quiet, cool hillside. There is a park there now, but the massive trees with jutting branches and the large pond in their shadow suggest the opulence of those days. In the middle of this pond, as if afloat, stood the detached room that Haga had mentioned. The directors of the federation held meetings there until late into the night. Since they were wearing cotton yukata kimonos, they may have appeared to be relaxing, and in Prohibition days, rumors were rife that they were breaking the law. Had they brought in illegal liquor to the meetings? Were they being serviced by geisha? Makino ordered Yamamoto to find out.

The detached room was connected to the main building by a long corridor with a railing. The small and nimble Yamamoto went along the corridor in the dark, holding onto the handrail, and somehow crept directly under it. Unaware that someone was hiding underneath them, the occupants spoke frankly. Yamamoto heard Tsutsumi's familiar voice. But no matter how long he crouched, he could not hear anything that might be improper. Neither did it sound like they were drinking sake. Mosquitoes were plentiful in Honolulu in those days. Out in the middle of the pond clutching the beam supporting the room, Yamamoto found himself being attacked. Unable to bear it any longer, he slapped at a mosquito. His other hand, which had gone numb, suddenly slipped, and he fell into the pond.

"What's that sound?!" a voice said. Yamamoto heard a shoji sliding open. If he were caught, he might face a beating. With only his head sticking out of the water, he waited silently. "It was probably a carp splashing," someone said. The shoji closed. His only suit soaked, Yamamoto returned to the office, but Makino was not angry, and the next morning he silently flung a newly bought suit at Yamamoto.

To respond to the suspicions about the support fund, the federation made its account balance public after the strike. For the month of March alone transportation expenses, including automobiles, amounted to $3,797. Other items such as special expenses and emergency expenses were unclear. The emergency expenses were $49,000, the highest expenditure for that month.

The strikers continued to show a brave face, attacking the plantation owners in song.

> While espousing Americanization on paper,
> They actually destroy Americanization
> Those English newspapers that don't even know Americanism,
> Let's defeat them
> *Oya*, defeat them, defeat them
> The planters rely on big money and power,
> We 25,000 laborers fight
> Our weapon for victory is to strike
> Until the planters increase our wage
> *Oya*, defeat them, defeat them
> To the oppressor planters
> We will show our working man's guts
> On this occasion at this time
> Until the planters take off their helmets in defeat
> Oya, defeat them, defeat them
> Strikers' Defeat Them Song (*Strike Yattsukero Bushi*)

As the strike dragged on, the federation planned various events to boost worker morale. On March 21 a sumo wrestling match sponsored by the Honolulu sumo fans' association was held in the garden of the Tokiwaen restaurant, and some two thousand workers gathered to watch. The following evening a large crowd attended a joint meeting at the Asahi Theater sponsored by the federation headquarters. With Ichiji Gotō as the master of ceremonies, representatives of the supporters' association, youth association, and newspapers gave speeches.

It was Torakichi Kimura, representing the supporters' association, who first brought up the Sakai $100-check incident in his speech. On the evening of March 5 a federation headquarters staff member went to Sumitomo Bank to deposit a $100 check contributed by the innkeepers' union along with other checks. Unable to reach the bank before closing time, he took the checks back to headquarters and handed them to the director in charge of finance, who put them into the inside breast pocket of his suit jacket and returned to Kyōrakukan where he was staying. The following morning he realized that the $100 check had disappeared. Several days later it was revealed that the check had been handed over to HSPA secretary Mead. It was said that a man named Sakai had picked it up and delivered it to the HSPA. In no time Mead used this incident to show how slipshod the federation was in handling contributions. It was not clear who this Sakai was, but from Mead's description the rumor started that it might have been Miyazawa of the federation.

Hawaii hōchi president Kinzaburō Makino stepped up on the stage after Kimura to belabor the federation leadership in his booming voice:

Federation headquarters should use its energies for propaganda, and listen to others. They should do something besides wearing leggings or feeding Filipinos. Not only did a $100 check get into the hands of the HSPA, it also appears that a man named Sakai reports the daily balance of accounts to them. There are other strange, peculiar, and inexcusable things going on. The fellows at headquarters have been sumo wrestling outside the ring, not inside it, so things remain unsettled. Then this becomes a problem for the Japanese-language schools and the Japanese-language newspapers. If this were simply a problem for 25,000 workers, we could leave it up to headquarters, but since it is a problem for our 110,000 comrades we cannot ignore it.[29]

Makino had often referred to himself as the "sumo grand champion of oration" among the Hawaiian Japanese. In response to his merciless criticism, the audience applauded, and showed its approval by stamping on the floor in unison. Noboru Tsutsumi, who spoke after Makino, began his remarks in a softer tone than usual.

I greatly appreciate President Makino's admonition. I would like to take this opportunity to clarify the Federation's stand. We have never ignored the opinions and guidance, whether verbal or written, from gentlemen in every quarter. Those who see our actions as arbitrary must, I think, be those who have not given us their suggestions.

Although he spoke politely, Tsutsumi was not about to yield anything to Makino.

It is because we wish to resolve the strike simply as a labor management issue that we emphasize solely the laborers so strongly. If the strike is treated as a problem of all 110,000 comrades, would it not by necessity become a Japan-United States problem and a race problem? We also often hear criticism about leaks of headquarters secrets. But it is a mystery to me what secrets are leaked and how these leaked secrets are spread to the world. A case like the $100 check incident simply means that at great pains someone took something from our office, then sent that one piece of paper to the HSPA as if he had obtained the head of a monster, and that secretary Mead put on a big act to upset our headquarters. If we fell for such a trick and engaged in mutual recriminations, Mead would be pleased, but we would appear ridiculous. At headquarters we are treating the case of the $100 check in a calm and collected manner so as not to create any opportunity for provocation. I am grateful that the issue has been raised this evening so that a headquarters member could state our position to our satisfaction.[30]

The audience responded to Tsutsumi's rebuttal by applauding after each phrase and finally by waving their hands and hats, in a display of support stronger than that given Makino. Makino, however, used his newspaper for a further reply. In the afternoon edition the next day the *Hawaii hōchi* ran as its headline, "Don't Let Secretary Tsutsumi Speak, the Pitfalls of Slipping the Rails Are Extremely Great." Tsutsumi had stated in his speech that since final federation account books were not available, no one could know the exact balance, but the newspaper reported him as saying that "there are no exact account books." It claimed that this was "slipping the rails."

KINZABURŌ MAKINO

Makino was so well known in Hawaii that it was said there was no one not acquainted with him. Tall and stocky, he attracted attention wherever he went. He sported a Panama hat, immaculate white suits, flashy bowties, and white shoes and always smoked a fat cigar. Unlike most Japanese, he drove to work each morning in a large Ford. With his thick neck, jutting jawline, and prominent fleshy nose, Makino looked more "foreign" than Japanese. Among Caucasians he was known as "Fred" Makino, but in the Japanese community he had a reputation as a rough-and-tumble character. In 1909 the Japanese consul general had described him as "of mixed blood, notorious for being irresponsible."[31]

Makino, who was born in Yokohama, was indeed a mixed-blood (or *hapa* as the Hawaiians said). His father was Joseph Higginbottom, a British woolen merchant, and his mother was Kin Makino, a Japanese woman. He had two older brothers, an older sister, and a younger brother. When he was four years old his father died in Shanghai from typhoid fever, and he was reared by his mother. Although Yokohama was a city with many foreign inhabitants, it is not difficult to conjecture what his memories of childhood as a child of mixed parentage with no father must have been. He finished school through the upper primary level. Whenever he could he went to the judo studio, and he was known on the street as a youngster quick to get into a fight. As he grew up he became a regular in the Motomaki pleasure quarter, and he was known among the geisha in Honolulu as "Kin-san," unequaled in his talent for singing Japanese ballads and ditties.

Although his mother had remarried, Kinzaburō and his stepfather never got along. So when Kinzaburō was twenty-two years old his second older brother, Eijirō, who had taken over their father's business, arranged for him to go to Hawaii. When he arrived, his eldest brother, Jō, was already successful as a merchant at Naalehu Plantation on the Big Island. After keeping the books at his brother's store for three years,

Kinzaburō opened the Makino Drug Store in Honolulu. The following year he married Michie, the daughter of an early government contract immigrants. Michie's parents had strongly opposed this marriage because Kinzaburō was of mixed blood, and not a few among the Japanese community called him a hapa behind his back. Despite this, Kinzaburō seemed to feel at home in Hawaii with its ethnically and racially diverse population. Except to return for his mother's funeral, he never again set foot in Japan.

In 1909, six years after Makino opened his drugstore, the first Oahu strike took place. The main instigators were Yasutarō Sōga of *Yamato shinbun* and Motoyuki Negoro, a recent graduate of a mainland law school. Upset by the conditions of the immigrant laborers, Sōga used his newspaper to fan worker demands for a wage increase. At the recommendation of the Honolulu merchants, Makino was named the chairman of the High Wage Association. The consul general criticized him for "gathering people like a low-class charlatan healer and holding lecture meetings to court popularity, just to make personal attacks and heap abuse and slander on the HSPA." [32] His charismatic presence at once turned him into a hero in the Japanese community. Arrested along with Sōga and others, he was convicted of inciting the strike, but he had become such a popular figure that each day during his four months in prison his supporters delivered more food than he could eat. Seeing how influential newspapers could be, Makino founded the *Hawaii hōchi* as a platform for his opinions. After the strike Makino and Sōga became estranged as a result of their disagreement on many issues. It can be said that Makino started his own newspaper out of his antagonism toward the "snobbish" Sōga.

Yasutarō Sōga, a native of Tokyo four years Makino's senior, had graduated from the English Law School (the predecessor of Chūō University) before going to Hawaii. After doing clerical work at a Japanese store on a plantation, he joined the *Yamato shinbun*, the oldest Japanese newspaper in Honolulu, and eventually became editor-in-chief and president. After the 1909 strike, the newspaper changed its name to *Nippu jiji*. Until the 1930s, the *Nippu jiji* was the only Japanese-language paper under special agreement with the Associated Press. Sōga, a soft-spoken intellectual, was known as a writer with sound judgment. Under the pen name Keihō, he wrote poems as well, and, a practicing Christian, he attended church on Sundays.

The personalities of Sōga and Makino were quite different. Seiei Wakikawa, a student at the University of Hawaii, went around to Japanese community leaders each month to seek contributions for the Japanese kindergarten. Sōga always handed him $2, saying, "Thank you for your efforts." But Makino would jangle his keys and open his safe as if Wakikawa were a nuisance, then toss a $1 coin to him. Wakikawa went on to study at Tokyo University and eventually became editor-in-chief of *Nippu jiji.*

After the 1909 strike Sōga deepened his association with the elite of Honolulu's Japanese community: the consuls general, the branch managers of Sumitomo Bank, and the branch managers of the Yokohama Specie Bank. He served as director on the boards of the Prince Fushimi Memorial Scholarship Association, the Japanese Chamber of Commerce, and the Rotary Club. The only Japanese whose names were listed in the English-language directory of prominent Hawaiians were Sōga and the Reverend Takie Okumura.

In stark contrast to Sōga, Makino did not frequent the consulate, and only once did he join a group greeting a Japanese warship when it put in to port. From its founding, the *Hawaii hōchi* vowed that it "would not bow to any power or pressure," and it regarded the *Nippu jiji* as its only competition.

Although the *Hawaii hōchi* and *Nippu jiji* were located just one block apart, Makino and Sōga did not acknowledge each other when they passed on the street. There was intense rivalry between the reporters on the two newspapers, and they clashed on nearly every issue: if the *Nippu jiji* called something white, the *Hawaii hōchi* would call it black. The catchphrase among the *Hawaii hōchi* staff was, "Don't lose out to *Nippu.*" By opposing the *Nippu* in its editorial stance, the *Hōchi* sought to cut into its rival's circulation.

Sōga penned articles as editor-in-chief, but Makino did not write a single sentence. Reading through newspapers from Japan and the English-language newspapers, Makino spat out his opinions each morning to "Fighting Haga," the editor-in-chief, who wrote them up as articles or editorials. Haga's poison pen turned Makino's thunderous shouts of "Those idiots!" into copy and established the *Hōchi* reputation as "Hawaii's ruffian."

Makino hired all types of people as reporters. Haga was said to have been an agent of the HSPA during the 1909 strike, but Makino turned this former enemy into his right-hand man. He also persuaded Teisuke Terasaki, a gentle teacher active in his church, to join the paper, and it was Terasaki, not Haga, that he welcomed into his private residence. Makino later hired Communist party members who were under official surveillance. "It's good to have a cause no matter what it is," he said. At the time of the 1920 strike the *Hōchi* was serializing *Chōbei Banzuiin*, a novel about a commoner ruffian who risked his life breaking into the mansions of the shogun's vassals. Makino, who called Chōbei "my hero," admired his manliness and chivalry. In the Japanese community, where others concerned themselves with what people thought about them and went along with the mainstream, Makino intended to be "a nail that stuck out." Indifferent to whether he was accused of sentimental romantic "heroism" behind his back, he confronted everything head-on. Freed from the restraints of Japanese society, his innate independent spirit flourished in the Hawaiian milieu.

After spending the morning expounding his views to Haga, Makino made the rounds of the community in the afternoon. He diligently visited various government offices, the courthouse, city hall, and even the police department next door to the *Hōchi,* and chatted casually with officials, lawyers, and policemen. Japanese immigrants usually addressed haoles as "Mr.," but Makino did not hesitate to call them by their first names. Using the English he had learned after arriving in Hawaii, Makino worked his way into haole society, and no other Japanese journalist was so quick to gather information. Wielding the *Hōchi* as his weapon, Fred Makino was a disruptive presence, jabbing at the haole leaders, including the HSPA.

The first time Makino helped out his fellow Japanese was on the issue of picture brides. When they arrived in Honolulu, picture brides were forced to take part in a mass marriage ceremony as they were not allowed to leave the immigration office unless they had husbands. The Japanese immigrant community had long deplored this practice as inhumane. Makino mounted a movement to change the law so that ceremonies presided over by a Shinto priest or a Christian minister could be held after the women left the immigration office.

When six Japanese-language teachers had been refused entry by the Honolulu immigration office the year before Tsutsumi arrived, Makino had also brought suit under American law, winning a decision in their favor. He was also a central figure in efforts to obtain citizenship for Japanese who enlisted in the American military during World War I, and he was active in the Japanese-language school debate. His hiring of a haole lawyer, Joseph B. Lightfoot, was unprecedented in the Japanese community.

At some point Makino had hung out a shingle advertising the Makino Law Office. He counseled Japanese immigrants who had no idea where to seek advice in this unfamiliar foreign land on everything from putting up their wives and daughters as collateral for loans, leasing land, and illicit sake brewing to prostitution, divorce, and renunciation of adoption agreements. When people came to seek advice, Makino swiftly invited them into his office. To avoid embarrassing them, he did not allow anyone else in, even the staff of the *Hōchi*. For legal problems, he referred them to his lawyer, Lightfoot, but took a fee for his intercession on their behalf. Since he had taken quickly to American-style give-and-take, he acquired a bad reputation as a petty shyster, some even calling him "Kinta the viper".

Makino's residence on the coast outside of Honolulu was an estate with a large Japanese-style garden, boasting a semicircular bridge and a rose garden, tended by his wife, Michie. Makino loved to fish. Whenever he was home he went on one of his fishing boats. The waters were shallow, and mahi mahi were plentiful. The Makinos had no children, but they were fond of their two German shepherds, Pīko and Kuro. According to Yoshimi Mizuno, who worked as one of their live-in maids for many years, "Uncle" may have been known as an irascible old man at work, but he did not yell at his wife or his domestic help.

The *Hōchi* finances were always tight, often making it uncertain when salaries could be paid. Many wondered how Makino was able to acquire his seaside mansion. A cloud of suspicion always followed him, but a clue to this mystery can be found in Foreign Ministry archival documents dealing with a lawsuit brought after the 1909 strike, when the HSPA used the local authorities to seize what were alleged to be secret union documents. The police had forced their way into Makino's drugstore without a search warrant, dynamited his safe, and carried off his account books and other items. When released from prison after serving his sentence for conviction on incitement charges, Makino sued the HSPA for unlawful seizure. Lightfoot was the only lawyer who was willing to take on this case against Hawaii's absolutely powerful HSPA. This was the beginning of the relationship between the two men.

Not wanting to stir up antagonism, the consul general pressed Makino not to aggravate the situation, but Makino refused to withdraw his charges. The HSPA, which complained that even the Japanese consul general could not control him, attacked him as a "Japanese anarchist" and called him "the worst element of Japanese." [33] Makino had quickly contacted Kumano Yamaguchi, an Imperial Diet member, through his eldest brother in Yokohama. During the contract labor days Yamaguchi had operated an immigration company and built up a political war chest with money wrung from the immigrants. When he heard about Makino's problem, Yamaguchi called for a formal official inquiry concerning the "illegal action inflicted upon a Japanese in Hawaii by the American authorities." He collected signatures from thirty-six Diet members, who protested the police seizure of Makino's records as an act of "brutality violating international goodwill" and contravening treaties between Japan and the United States.

The case became enough of an issue to require a secret report to Foreign Minister Jūtarō Komura from Yasuya Uchida, the ambassador in Washington. Documents expressing concern about the case were also sent several times from the U.S. secretary of state to the governor of the territory of Hawaii. In 1915, six years after the so-called case of illegal search, a delegation of senators and representatives from Washington, D.C., was slated to make an observation trip to Hawaii. Makino seized the opportunity to distribute a document describing the details of the case to each of its members. When the HSPA learned of this, it moved to settle out of court, and the case rapidly headed for settlement. Makino had sought $50,000 as compensation. In an obituary written at the time of Makino's death, his half-brother, Seiichi Tsuchiya, wrote, "He received some compensation money, but the amount is unknown." A report from Consul General Hachirō Arita to Foreign Minister Takaaki Katō at the time of the settlement noted that Makino had received about $10,000.[34]

It can be surmised that Makino, who had decided early on that Hawaii would be his permanent place of residence, invested the money in real estate. By the time he died Makino left pieces of land in various parts of Oahu besides his estate overlooking the ocean. It is unclear how much income Makino "the shyster" had accumulated, but according to Kumaiichi Kumazaki, the *Hōchi* accountant for forty-six years, no matter how financially straitened the newspaper was, no funds from the Makino Law Office were routed to it.

The 1920 strike took place eight years after the founding of the *Hawaii hōchi*. Along with the *Nippu jiji* it had become one of the two major Japanese-language newspapers in Honolulu. Compared to the *Nippu jiji*, however, its typeface was old-fashioned, and its readership smaller. On the plantations, however, the *Hawaii hōchi* was much more popular than in Honolulu proper. Among the striking workers its influence probably was no less than that of the *Nippu jiji*. It was easier for the plantation workers to comprehend articles appealing to their emotions than those based on reason.

The *Hōchi* had often criticized the federation for engaging in a "policy of secrecy." Its leadership shut out the Japanese-language newspaper that could most easily reach the workers, and they made no effort to consult its editor. Makino, who thought he had played a pivotal role in the 1909 strike, regarded himself as a Japanese community opinion leader, and from the start he intended to take a leadership position in the federation. When the federation was organized, the supporters' association had recommended him as a candidate for secretary general. But if a man with a past like Makino's were in a top post in the federation, it was obvious what the response of the HSPA would be. Tsutsumi and others quickly supported Seishi Masuda, who was popular with everyone.

Even so, Makino persisted in offering the benefit of his wisdom to the federation. When Governor McCarthy left for Washington to appeal to the federal government, Makino proposed that attorney Lightfoot be sent there as a federation director to state its case at the same time. He even suggested accompanying them himself, but the trip would require $5,000 in expenses. From the start the federation leadership did not know how to deal with Makino. The Oahu union was wary of Haga's attendance at federation meetings, for behind him loomed Makino.

In early March, when the federation was starting to worry about how to deal with scab workers, members of the U.S.-Japan relations committee arrived in Honolulu. This group, consisting of the president of the National Bank in New York, the president of the San Francisco Chamber of Commerce, and other business leaders, was stopping over in Honolulu on a goodwill mission to Tokyo with the goal of smoothing over tensions between the United States and Japan. Makino proposed showing these American business leaders the conditions in the Hawaiian sugar industry. The federation assented, but because the group was in port for such a short time, the opportunity was lost.

Makino was impatient with the federation. "They have solidarity and legality on their side, but they can't succeed in the strike with just those," he wrote in the March 5 issue of the *Hōchi*. "The HSPA is just waiting for us to give up and split apart as the strike drags on. As time goes on, we will lose to those with money. There is no chance of winning unless we resolve things quickly." He went on to say that he hoped "that putting someone in the Federation leadership merely because he knows English or has just graduated from school doesn't lead to defeat."

On March 10 Terasaki noted in his diary, "Somewhat chilly as the weather has not cleared up. Mr. Makino suggests attempting to mediate the strike." The next day he wrote, "Mr. Makino told Mr. Haga to suggest mediation by the acting governor." But Acting Governor Iaukea showed no interest because Governor McCarthy was to return on March 30. On March 18 he wrote, "Supporters' association holds its [regular] meeting, half of the members attend. [Illegible] discussed and decided on. Mr. Haga strikes Mr. Negoro."

THE 77-CENT FLAG PARADE

By late March federation tactics were lagging behind the HSPA's. An exception was the success of the 77-cent flag parade. The centennial anniversary of the arrival in Hawaii of the missionaries, the forefathers of the kamaaina planters, fell in April 1920. The Mission Centennial Celebration was to be in grand style, with leaders of the American religious community, academicians, politicians, and military men from the mainland invited as guests. The Prince of Wales (later King Edward VIII, who abdicated the throne) participated in this event, putting in to port on the cruiser *Renown.* Makino, who urged taking advantage of an opportunity when Hawaii would be the focus of the world's attention, suggested a demonstration. The federation asked the Hawaii Mission Board for permission to participate in the centennial celebration with a "period costume parade" showing the history of Japanese immigration to Hawaii. The centennial organizing committee, however, immediately rejected this application, concerned that their event might be used by an anti-American group.

The Federation of Japanese Labor decided to hold what it called a "77-cent flag parade" on April 3, the eve of the centennial ceremonies. The *Honolulu Advertiser,* anticipating that the union intended to upset the celebration, called for a roundup of the federation leaders, citing the same reasons as those for getting rid of the IWW and the Bolsheviks.[35] But the federation conducted its parade in a thoroughly American manner. At 1:00 P.M. Noboru Tsutsumi addressed more than three thousand workers who had gathered at Aala Park: "Ladies and gentlemen, it has been two months since the beginning of the strike. The obstinate HSPA had rejected our legitimate demands as workers and has attempted to mislead the public with false propaganda. Ladies and gentlemen, today's parade is to expose the obstinacy of the HSPA and to inform the general public about our plea for justice. I hope you will parade in an orderly and valiant manner." [36]

Divided into fourteen sections, one from each plantation, the demonstrators started to march, headed by a group of workers from Ewa Plantation carrying a large American flag. A group of Filipinos, too few to make up a separate group, marched with the Waipahu Plantation group. One section of demonstrators carried a hand-drawn likeness of Lincoln inscribed with the words "Hawaii's sugar plantation workers are still suffering under slave-like treatment. Free these slaves." The male demonstrators all held small white triangular flags with the words "77 cents a day," while the women waved small flags with the words "58 cents a day." Of the laborers on Oahu, 14 percent were women. The women workers marched in the clothes they normally wore to ward off dust when they raked leaves: skirtlike aprons worn around ikat (*kasuri*) work pants, hand coverings and leggings, wide-brimmed straw hats, and white scarves covering their cheeks. The children walking behind their parents waved small flags that said, "My Papa 77 cents a day" and "My Mama 58 cents a day."

Leaflets handed out to spectators expressed the workers' grievances: "77 cents a day, that's what we are paid for 10 hours of hard labor"; "We are not Reds, God forbid, but brown workers who produce white sugar"; "We simply requested $1.25 for a day—reasonable, don't you think? We are requesting living wages"; "There is a bonus, you will say, but it is a conditional bonus"; "If we fail to work over 20 days, we don't get any bonus"; "Can you support your family on 77 cents a day?" "We are sincerely wishing for the prosperity of Hawaii"; and "God created people to be equal." Any mention of being Japanese was avoided, nor was a red flag to be seen.

Acting Consul General Furuya quickly sent a report to Foreign Minister Uchida: "The participants in the parade observed the instructions of the Federation headquarters and behaved in an orderly manner from start to finish, with no threatening actions. They seem to have impressed some of the Americans." [37]

Many police officers had been dispatched in Honolulu, creating an imposing security force, but the parade leaders checked any break in the ranks. The demonstrators marched under a scorching noonday sun that radiated heat off the pavement, and most children walked barefoot just as they did on the plantations. The *Hōchi* noted, "Their pitiful figures made even the most cold-hearted people feel a sadness. Many Americans and Japanese watching from the barricades set up along the streets were seen with handkerchiefs pressing their faces at the sight of the marchers."[38] And the *Hawaii shinpō* reported, "American women, expressing their dislike of the planters' cold-heartedness, muttered, 'My what has happened to the planters.'"[39]

The Japanese along the parade route cheered encouragement to the demonstrators, often shouting "Banzai." According to the *Nippu jiji*, as the parade passed by the Honolulu fish market, a tearful middle-aged Japanese man called out, "Your demands are just. You're sure to win. Fight to the end." He was so overcome with feeling that he could not finish. When the demonstrators returned to Aala Park, the parade turned into a rally supporting the striking workers. They tried to use the raised bandstand in the park, but the police refused permission, so several men propped up a ladder and the speakers clambered up to give their speeches.

A voice was heard from the rear of the crowd: "Let me say something." It came from a tall Caucasian man in a sailor's uniform. Five destroyers from the U.S. Pacific fleet were in port in Honolulu for the centennial celebration, and many sailors were out on the town. Pushing through the suspicious crowd, the sailor made his way forward. Climbing onto the ladder, he took off his sailor's hat and gave his name as Smith. An innocent-faced youth, he showed no nervousness as he spoke to the workers from a land he had never seen: "I am a seaman and I earn $3 a day. Why is it that working under this scorching sun in Hawaii earns only 77 cents a day? It is a major embarrassment that there are such low wage earning workers in a leading civilized country like America. I think you should demand $5 a day, or even $10 a day."

Despite the warnings from FBI Director Hoover, on the mainland wildcat strikes by railway workers were spreading, stopping train service in many places. Although he may have looked like a carefree youth, the sailor probably had a background that made him sensitive to the rights of the Japanese immigrant workers. The demonstrators were deeply moved by this unanticipated encouragement from the sailor and responded with resounding applause.

The day after the demonstration there was a small furor over the portrait of Lincoln. The likeness had been drawn by workers staying at the Sōtō sect mission who had carried it to Aala Park. But someone at the residence of the Castle family, located near the mission, thought it had been brought from the Japanese Consulate General. William R. Castle, the head of the family, was not only president of Castle and Cook, one of the Big Five sugar planters, but also the chairman of the centennial celebration committee. The two English-language newspapers accepted this false report as fact. In its front page story, the *Star Bulletin* asked, "Will the Japanese Consul throw a little light on the subject? We rise to ask." [40] The paper accused the Japanese consulate of backing the demonstration from behind the scenes.

Acting Consul General Furuya's reported to Foreign Minister Uchida: "I immediately telephoned the same [Castle] and informed him of the misunderstanding, upon which he apologized deeply for his rashness." [41] Castle offered an apology in both English-language newspapers: "My information was mistaken. . . . This of course was a great surprise as well as a great relief." But the small story was buried in an inconspicuous part of the newspapers. It would not be surprising if guests invited from the mainland returned home thinking the Japanese government was behind the striking laborers.

The centennial celebration, which began on April 4, the day after the demonstration, continued for two weeks. The *Hawaiian Annual* for 1921 reported, "The commemorative season opened with religious services in all the federated churches, appropriate to the occasion, followed by conferences on the past, present and future on religious and educational lines." Each day there were different events: an industrial parade, a Hawaiian parade, a Hawaiian feast, and a recreation day with outrigger and regatta contests. Smiling hula dancers swayed to the strains of Hawaiian ukulele music. Hawaii seemed to have forgotten the labor-management confrontation that now rested like a sailing ship stranded in a dead calm. Hawaii was starting to attract attention as a tourist destination, and the centennial celebration was a major turning point in that direction. Large resort hotels and golf courses were planned, and within five years the number of mainland tourists had increased threefold.

In 1920 Japan still had troops in Siberia. Since America, Britain, and France had proclaimed a policy of nonintervention in the Soviet Union and withdrawn their forces from Siberia, world criticism focused anew on Japan. While the aloha spirit was flourishing in Hawaii during its centennial, disquieting anti-Japanese comments were being voiced in Washington. The secretary of the navy warned that since Japan was making preparations for war, viewing America as a threat, it was essential that the United States carry out new plans for military preparations, including the building of warships. In his April 12 statement to newspaper reporters the secretary made comparisons to the naval expansion programs in Britain, France, Japan, and Germany, but because it came on the heels of the Pan-American Association chairman's alarmist observation that Japan was America's strongest competitor in commerce and industry, it garnered attention.

In California the anti-Japanese movement had gathered momentum since the beginning of the year. Although Japanese ownership of land had been prohibited in California since 1913, Japanese immigrants had increased their agricultural holdings by buying land in the name of their American-born children. With the new census showing a considerable increase in nisei born to picture brides, there were calls to amend the 1913 Alien Land Law. The amendment proposed was harsh: those who did not have the right to citizenship were not allowed to manage their children's assets, nor would their leases be recognized.

To place the amendment on the November ballot, a petition had to be signed by one-tenth of the total number of voters in the previous gubernatorial election. It was difficult to collect the fifty thousand signatures needed. On March 10 Sen. James Phelan of California, a central figure in the anti-Japanese movement, made an ominous prediction of war between the United States and Japan. He said that unless a way for peaceful compromise was sought and reached, it would be difficult to avoid war since Japan had developed rapidly in the previous sixty years and now had the same technology to build warships as the Americans did.

THE EVE OF THE STOP STRIKE ORDER

After Palmer's raids in January 1920 strikes on the mainland were often crushed by violent counterattacks by police or thugs hired by the companies. The railway strike that the authorities had most feared was about to be broken, and the IWW and the Communist party were about to be outlawed.

Sen Katayama's name had been on the Palmer Raid list, but because he was not at home he avoided arrest and went into hiding in Atlantic City. Returning to New York when the situation calmed down, he distributed leaflets criticizing the "barbaric conduct" of Japanese troops in Siberia. Anti-Japanese agitation by the "Japanese radical faction" was more vexing to the Japanese government than to the American authorities. According to a leading daily in Japan, "[The radicals] attack Japan's imperialism and they predict that if the Russian Red Army is defeated,

Japan will become radicalized."[42] This article appeared on a Sunday, when the first Japanese May Day rally was held in Tokyo's Ueno Park. With the slump in stock prices in March, a postwar financial panic had spread, leading to unemployment, wage decreases, and factory closures. More than ten thousand members of fifteen labor unions gathered at Ueno to pass resolutions calling not only for improved labor conditions such as the eight-hour workday but also for the immediate withdrawal of troops from Siberia.

On April 29, 1920, Attorney General Palmer predicted, as he had the year before, that an assassination plot against federal and state officials and other prominent national figures with the aim of overthrowing the government might occur on May Day, and he threatened severe punishment for the perpetrators. However, nothing happened in any American city. The fact that "it passed without major disturbances"[43] made news in Japan.

On April 28 a report entitled "Facts about the Strike in Hawaii" was circulated to Home Minister Takejirō Tokonami, Foreign Minister Yasuya Uchida, and Education Minister Tokugorō Nakahashi: "There seems to be no hope for an easy solution; knowledge among Japanese laborers seems to be increasing considerably. The authorities, groundlessly concerned that in the future [the Japanese immigrants] will hold the governing power over all the islands, are using oppressive means in their plans to destroy the Federation of Japanese Labor from its foundations. This may result in efforts at exclusionary treatment toward the general Japanese populace."

The author of the report, Jūtarō Mabuchi, governor of Kyoto prefecture, based his comments on what Sakae Morita, leader of a tour group of Hawaiian immigrants visiting their homeland, told the Kyoto prefectural police department. Morita, a native of Ehime prefecture, operated a photography studio at Waipahu Plantation and was connected with the local federation early on. The Japanese authorities were interested in him as someone familiar with its activities.

As the report noted, in late April the Federation of Japanese Labor had changed its name to the Hawaii Laborers' Association. This was an attempt to counter the racial strategy of the HSPA, which touted the Japanese conspiracy theory. But in actuality, although the word "Japanese" was removed from the name of the organization, the federation headquarters personnel remained the same. There was no thought of including the Filipino Labor Union president, Manlapit, as an official.

Three days after the "77-cent flag parade," the U.S. attorney for the district of Hawaii, S. C. Huber, reported to Attorney General Palmer in Washington: "The Honolulu stock market during the past few days has shown considerable strength. This has been due to the favorable reports coming from the plantations in regard to production and also to mainland advices related to higher sugar price." The sugar price, which had been at 13 cents in March, continued to rise in April, reaching an unprecedented level of more than 20 cents in May. After the peak of 23.5 cents on May 19, it continued to stay above 20 cents.

On the mainland the national consumers' union had protested this extraordinary jump in price to Congress. As the sugar price rose, so did the price of all foods and canned goods using sugar. A national meeting of one hundred twenty agricultural associations pressed the federal government to investigate subterfuges by the major companies that monopolized the sugar industry. Even in Hawaii, a producer of sugar, the general populace could no longer afford the price of white sugar reimported from the mainland.

In mid-February 1920 the Justice Department had made a sweeping arrest of 875 food merchants for profiteering on the shortage of sugar. Of these, 28 were found guilty, 11 of them sugar dealers. The pursuit of improper profiteering was conducted in earnest after these arrests. Particular attention was paid to the actions of the California and Hawaiian Sugar Company (C&H Sugar). Despite the fact that cane production was the major industry in Hawaii, there was only one small sugar refinery on the islands, on Oahu. Most raw sugar from Hawaii was sent by ship to the C&H Sugar refinery outside San Francisco, where it was refined and then sent to markets on the mainland. The directors of the company included the Big Five Hawaiian plantation owners.

Hawaiian sugar had gained a much larger share of the American domestic market. Cuban sugar was being shipped to Europe, where postwar sugar production had dropped, and beet production on the U.S. mainland had been hit by successive poor harvests. In Washington there were suspicions that the HSPA had artificially engineered the unprecedented rise in sugar price under these circumstances.

When a representative of the Railroad Brotherhood asked the Washington HSPA representative about the rise in the sugar price, he replied that it was due to "the increase in the labor cost of producing sugar . . . in addition to [the higher labor costs for irrigation]. [F]or the past three months or more there has been a strike of the laborers . . . , [and] as a result strike breakers have been employed at a very heavy expense and only a portion of the crop is being harvested, and it is possible that they will not only have a loss of a considerable portion of this year's crop but an additional loss due to the failure to have planted and cared for the next crop."[44] While recognizing the slump in production, the Justice Department's suspicions deepened that the Hawaiian sugar companies were using it as an excuse to drive up the price of sugar.

Huber concluded his report to Attorney General Palmer by stating, "It is becoming increasingly evident that the strike is broken and it is just a question of time before the Japanese capitulate." The rapid price increase certainly favored the growers' position, but other circumstances were beginning to work against them in May. Pineapple production had already been targeted as the industry that would someday succeed the sugar industry. During the slack season, some pineapple field workers had been sent by the growers to work as scabs in the cane fields, but because harvest time was approaching, these workers were returning to the pineapple fields. The rainy season, which had brought unusually high rainfall to Oahu, was finally coming to a close too. The days turned into scorchers, and slowly the cane began to wither. It was obvious to anyone seeing the cane fields turning yellow that the strikers had their only chance to force a settlement in their favor.

The pent-up frustrations of the strikers were beginning to focus on the federation. Although released from the drudgery of hard labor, the workers were disappointed that their situation had dragged on for so long. Ennui caused fissures in their solidarity. With daily life uncertain, the problem of their children's education became increasingly worrisome as the days passed.

Among the Japanese community leaders, concern about the possible aftereffects on the Japanese community was growing stronger. Members of the strike supporters' association such as Masao Kawahara, president of the Japanese Chamber of Commerce, Dr. Iga Moori, and Reverend Takie Okumura, pastor of Makiki Church, who had been involved in Reverend Palmer's mediation plan, felt they could no longer leave things to the federation headquarters. In May they began to hold daily meetings to devise a proposal that would resolve the strike as soon as possible. By this time the federation leadership was willing to take a more conciliatory attitude toward the supporters' association. This was because of rising criticism among the striking workers that the federation, by insisting on a movement of true laborers, was neither heeding the warnings nor listening to the advice of local leaders.

Kawahara and his colleagues came up with a plan to have the haole president of the Oahu Railway and Land Company act as mediator. He was also president of the Honolulu Chamber of Commerce and was supposed to be a third party *with no connections* to the HSPA. Although he expressed interest, he was unavoidably called to the mainland for business and said he would consider the request again on his return. The *Hawaii hōchi* cautioned Kawahara's group against placing their hopes on the return of a Caucasian businessman or even asking a third party to find a solution to the strike. On May 8 the newspaper wrote, "Even though we believe in his [Kawahara's] sincerity, if this method of mediation should fail, his involvement would end up as a loss of face for the striking workers. . . . We must keep in mind that the strikers are tired, but the planters are also weakened substantially." The *Hōchi* warned the strikers to be "absolutely against a one-sided mediator."

The *Nippu jiji* supported the mediation plan of Kawahara's group, but on May 19 the *Hōchi* lampooned its position with a "Dokomademo bushi," or "Through thick and thin song":

Flattering the planters saying you want order through thick and thin
To your readers you show your dislike, that you don't care,
Proudly supporting the Palmer Plan through thick and thin
It's actually an empty sham, you show your dislike, that you don't care,
If you're going to mediate fairly through thick and thin,
It can't be settled unless conditions are attached, you show your dislike,
    that you don't care.

On May 21 Terasaki's diary noted, "Mr. Makino leaked word that he would be willing to mediate." Although Acting Governor Iaukea had refused to mediate a month earlier, Makino was now willing to do so, provided that he was requested to. This meant that either the federation or the supporters' association had to seek his help. By this time the group headed by Kawahara and other supporters' association leaders had disbanded, apparently stung by the May 22 *Hōchi* criticism that they had "no qualifications to resolve the strike which has become a major issue for all Japanese." The newspaper had labeled them "impure elements" for leaning toward workers' acceptance of the unconditional return to work demanded by the HSPA.

Makino went to work with Haga on a mediation plan. Even if Makino were to be the real mediator, they thought that the idea would be better accepted if it appeared that Governor McCarthy was involved. Since Lightfoot, the attorney for Makino's law office, was acting territorial chief prosecutor, they decided to have him approach the governor. But first it was necessary to get the private consent of the federation headquarters. Makino decided to have Tokuzō Shibayama approach Noboru Tsutsumi, likely to be the most difficult person to persuade. Shibayama, a coffee dealer with no previous direct or indirect connections to the federation, was from Gifu prefecture, next to Shiga prefecture, and had known Tsutsumi's father. Makino hoped the more senior Shibayama would bring Tsutsumi into his plan.

Shortly after 7:00 P.M. on May 23 Shibayama telephoned Tsutsumi as he was eating a delivered box supper with the other federation directors. After returning from his speaking tour on Maui, Tsutsumi had not been feeling well because of a cold. He told Shibayama that he wanted to go to bed early, but Shibayama insisted the matter could not wait until morning. Tsutsumi had no choice but to go to Shibayama's house in the Kalihi district at some distance by car from downtown Honolulu.

According to Tsutsumi's recollection, after showing him to an easy chair on his veranda, Shibayama began their conversation. "Tsutsumi, having the strike drag on must be a problem. How about trying to resolve the strike issue at a suitable time?" Then he continued, "As a method of mediation, Makino has said he would stake his life on having the governor mediate. For this mediation, we can have the governor take the surface role for appearances, while Makino, Haga, and you work behind the scene, and I'll act as your go-between. As you know, Haga is a wily tactician, Makino is trusted by Japanese and Americans, and you can take charge of the workers."[45]

When Tsutsumi expressed doubt that Governor McCarthy would agree, Shibayama answered, "Makino says he'll make sure by asking Lightfoot, so as his friend I want to bolster Makino's efforts." With words laced with emotion, Shibayama kept at Tsutsumi late into the night.

SHIBAYAMA: "It is your opinion that counts at Federation headquarters. If you think that mediation excluding the federation headquarters is disgraceful, then for the sake of the workers' welfare you should be prepared to give up and commit hara kiri. Now is the time when you must give me your head. I'm not telling you to die, but are you prepared to die?"

TSUTSUMI: "I have vowed to give my life to the workers, so if it will truly benefit the workers, I'm willing to give you my head or my life, but I don't want to die in vain."

SHIBAYAMA: "That's it. I knew your father, so when it comes time for you to commit hara kiri, I will commit hara kiri too. I promise I won't let you be killed alone. Please make up your mind."

Tsutsumi still would not agree to the plan, so Shibayama pressed him harder. "Won't you act like Kaishu Katsu did at the peaceful surrender of Edo Castle?" Tsutsumi avoided an answer. When he asked about the conditions for returning to work, Shibayama said he was not familiar with them, so he asked Tsutsumi to return the next evening to meet with Makino and Haga. As Tsutsumi departed, Shibayama reminded him that their discussion should be kept absolutely secret until the governor took action. But the meeting with Makino and Haga never took place. Shibayama told Tsutsumi that the meeting was postponed, and Tsutsumi did not hear from him after that.

On June 1 Terasaki noted in his diary, "Today at Mr. Makino's residence there was talk of [illegible: consultation?] about the strike problem, but hearing that Mott Smith intended to mediate, this was canceled." Like Iaukea, John Mott Smith was a Hawaiian with long service as a public official who had been acting governor as well. Mott Smith, in fact, was not active in mediation, but giving the rumor as his reason, Makino withdrew from involvement in mediating the strike.

Three days later, on June 4, Terasaki's diary noted, "Dole [company president] of Hawaiian Pineapple came [to *Hōchi*] and in a roundabout way sought help in recruiting laborers." The previous night a dynamite blast had exploded at the house of Jūzaburō Sakamaki at Olaa Plantation on Hawaii, but Terasaki made no mention of the incident in his diary. Indeed, the Terasaki diary made no reference to the strike or to Makino's interest in mediation for the rest of the month. But on July 1 one sentence suddenly appeared: "Federation headquarters issues stop strike order, several hundred return to plantations."

"WE ORDER RETURN TO WORK TODAY"

In a report sent to Foreign Minister Uchida the day after the order to end the strike, Furuya described the process of reaching "pau," or a conclusion, in greatest detail. It is clear from this report that Furuya, in whom neither labor nor management placed much faith, played a role behind the scenes in pulling the Japanese side together during the strike's final stages. According to Furuya, Hōsen Isobe, priest of the Sōtō sect Buddhist temple, told him that since Kawahara's group had disbanded, he had been negotiating secretly with the HSPA's chairman, Waterhouse, with "some possibility of achieving a solution." Furuya immediately called Tsutsumi, rumored to be the "most uncompromising" of the federation directors, to the consulate. "Continuing the strike any further," he told Tsutsumi, "is not only a disadvantage to the workers but also makes any resolution more difficult, so we should rapidly take measures to resolve the strike."

In his talk with Tsutsumi, Furuya had the strong impression that the federation preferred mediation by the president of the Honolulu Chamber of Commerce, as proposed by the strike supporters' association, to mediation through Isobe. Furuya urged Kawahara and Dr. Moori to move forward with their mediation plan, but the chamber of commerce president had changed his mind and refused to be involved in negotiations. "We have missed the opportunity and now it would be difficult to convince the planters," he said. Meanwhile, Isobe, accompanied by a pineapple dealer named Wakabayashi, had begun negotiations with Waterhouse.

The planters were under outside pressure to end the strike. The mainland was astir over the coming presidential election. It appeared that Attorney General Palmer, who had become a presidential candidate, wanted an issue to appeal to the delegates at the Democratic party convention on June 10. When Palmer received a report from Huber, the U.S. attorney, that sugar production would drop because of the strike in Hawaii (June 7), he fired off a telegram to Hawaii saying that any further decrease in sugar production would pose a grave problem to the entire country and urged the immediate resolution of the dispute.

While the HSPA was being pressed by the federal government to resolve the strike, Isobe, calling himself a "labor envoy," had approached Waterhouse, who took over from secretary Mead, the point man for negotiations until this time. The forty-seven-year-old Waterhouse was a member of the Baldwin clan, one of the Big Five families. Born in Hawaii as a kamaaina, after graduating from Princeton he joined the family business and held several positions as president or executive in the family-run companies. Tall and portly, he exuded a calm intelligence.

By contrast, the forty-three-year-old Isobe was short of stature, with a build as taut as a military man's. His long face was punctuated by narrow, defiant eyes and a bushy mustache. Isobe wore closed-collar jackets rather than priestly robes, so his military mien was even more pronounced. But a statement issued by the strike supporters' association indicated how little Japanese community leaders thought of Isobe's leap into the fray:

> We have great misgivings about Hōsen Isobe's involvement in mediation.
> Isobe has never attended any public undertakings in the Japanese community.
> Other than being a braggart, he is not especially a man of learning, nor does

he have any resources. Moreover, members of the strike supporters' association know well that he lacks good faith, causing us to feel misgivings about his efforts. If Isobe has a fragment of good faith, he should discuss with the Japanese in Honolulu how he expects to end the strike.

Hōsen Isobe was born into a large samurai family in Tokuyama, Yamaguchi prefecture, and was apprenticed to a temple at age seven. At seventeen he became priest of a series of dilapidated temples deep in the mountains. He would singlehandedly repair a temple and move on to another, becoming a well-known priest in the Sōtō sect. Sent to Korea to engage in mission work, he soon collected contributions from the Japanese community in Inchon to build a worship hall. It was rumored that while in Korea, Isobe had connections to the Japanese involved in the assassination of Queen Min (1895). In 1914, with his reputation as a man of action well established, Isobe was sent to Honolulu as the ninth pastor of the Sōtō sect mission. Since the Honganji sect had already put down deep roots in the Hawaiian Islands, the latecomer Sōtō sect found it difficult to expand its congregation. Even in Honolulu it had only a temporary mission. As he had in Inchon, Isobe made the rounds soliciting funds for a Sōtō sect branch temple in Honolulu, but with so few followers he found it impossible to make much headway.

By the time he volunteered to mediate in the strike, Isobe was finally ready to start construction on the main hall of the Honolulu Sōtō sect temporary branch temple. According to the sect's account, the mission was heavily in debt at the time:

> As the due date for repayment of a $5,000 loan from Honolulu Bank for the land in Palama for the temporary branch temple approached, the bank unfortunately closed. In addition, there were outstanding debts for land purchase and construction costs in the amounts of $4,000 to Hawaii Bank, and $1,000 to Mr. Kobayashi, and to three other public companies. We were forced to sell the land for the branch temple for $15,000 in order to repay these debts. As we had the fortune to have a surplus of $10,000 we were able to include this amount in the construction budget.[46]

It was at this juncture, according to the mission history, that Isobe decided to involve himself in efforts to resolve the strike. The money gained from selling the land for the temporary branch temple provided only a portion of the construction costs for the main hall. Substantial additional funds were needed. Thus at a time when he was desperately collecting funds for the temple, Isobe became interested in mediating the strike.

According to Furuya's report, Isobe told him on June 29: "Obtaining a *tacit agreement* from President Waterhouse that an increase in wages of *at least $2.50* (with the bonus rate reduced by a certain amount) would be *agreed* upon at this year end's annual meeting, it was settled that *outwardly there would be an unconditional* exchange of handshakes between the strikers' representative and the HSPA chairman allowing the strikers to return to work."[47] On the same day Furuya received a cable directing him to "immediately make efforts to end the Japanese labor strike." Furuya had immediately contacted Isobe and called in Tsutsumi.

Aware that criticism of the federation had sharpened among the Japanese community and among the strikers, the federation leadership was willing to listen to Furuya's recommendations. On June 30, at the Suigorō restaurant in Waiau, representatives of laborers from all the islands held an all-day meeting about ending the strike. That evening there was a heavy downpour, and the following day was unusually cloudy for the season. At 10:00 A.M. representatives of labor met with management at the Young Hotel. The labor representatives were impressed that Waterhouse himself had taken part in the negotiations. Counting on Waterhouse's integrity, they were willing to agree, at least on the surface, to the planters' insistence that no concessions would be made or terms considered while the laborers were still out on strike and that a return to work was the first condition for ending the dispute.

In the photograph commemorating the meeting, only HSPA president Waterhouse appeared from the management side. Indeed, he had been the only one from the HSPA to attend. Seated on either side of him were "labor envoy" Isobe in his closed-collar jacket, his assistant Wakabayashi, and the Japanese interpreter. Standing behind them were fifteen worker delegates, including two Filipinos, all darkly tanned. It was clear at first glance that they were pure laborers. Thus the commemorative photograph included no one from the federation headquarters, the central force behind the strike. Accepting HSPA insistence that it would "not recognize the federation as [its] negotiating partner, [but] talk only with those selected from the strikers,"[48] Tsutsumi and the other strike leaders agreed to show no outward involvement in the negotiations to end the strike.

The decision to end the strike was issued not under the name of Tsutsumi and the other federation headquarters secretaries but under that of Tsurunosuke Koyama, a delegate from Hawaii. At the strikers' rally held in Aala Park on June 31 just after the labor-management meeting, it was the Oahu federation chairman, Eijūrō Yokoo, who read the declaration to end the strike.

> The Hawaii Laborers' Association has the honor to announce this 1st day of July of the year 1920, to our twenty-five thousand members and the two hundred thousand residents of Hawaii that the great controversy between capital and labor on the sugar plantations of Hawaii, which has lasted for the past six months, has been completely settled by the mutual and confidential understanding between the magnanimous capitalists and the sincere laborers, and that it will henceforth endeavor to materialize the true spirit of capital-labor cooperation and bring about industrial advancement and prosperity of Hawaii.

Not one word explained the actual process by which the strike was concluded. It took less than an hour to read the declaration and an accompanying resolution:

> We therefore deem it proper and just to terminate the present strike, beginning July 1st, 1920 and to gently take steps along the line of capital-labor cooperation.[49]

Three choruses of "Banzai" were raised, and the rally came to an end. The workers headed impatiently for the Honolulu railroad station. Workers from Kahuku and Ewa boarded a special train at 11:00 A.M., immediately after the rally ended, and the train to Aiea departed at 11:10 A.M. After five months the workers returned to their plantations.

CRITICISM OF FEDERATION HEADQUARTERS

Nine days later, on July 9, the new Japanese consul general, Chōnosuke Yada, finally set foot on Hawaiian soil, arriving on the *Tenyō-maru*. Yada had returned to the ministry in Tokyo in late 1919 after leaving a previous post in New York. Despite a public announcement in late January that he was to be posted to Honolulu, as he watched the progress of the strike, he repeatedly postponed his departure and in the end arrived some seven months later. It was highly unusual for the consul general post to be vacant for so long. When Furuya received instructions from Foreign Minister Uchida to make efforts to end the strike, Yada was already on board the ship that brought him to Hawaii. As acting consul general, Furuya's actions were extremely risky. His role in ending the strike by consolidating the Japanese side under orders from Tokyo could have fueled the Japanese conspiracy theory of the HSPA. By delaying the arrival of the new consul general, the Japanese government could avoid becoming caught up in the strike and thus deflect the conspiracy theory.

Chōnosuke Yada, then forty-nine years old, was from Shimane prefecture. After graduating from Tokyo Higher Commercial School he worked for a company, then taught at the Kagoshima Commercial School, before passing the diplomatic examination. Yada was not on the same elite track as Imperial university graduates were, but unlike Furuya, he was a career diplomat. After postings to consulates in Vancouver and Ottawa, he spent three years as consul general in New York before going to Honolulu. As soon as he took up his new post, Yada publicly condemned the strike. At a welcome party arranged by the leaders of the Japanese community on July 18 at the Mochizuki Club, he told his audience,

> The fate of Japan will be determined by the friendship which she maintains with the United States. . . . The American-Japanese friendship is vital to the well-being of Japan and the people. . . . The Japanese nationals in Hawaii must remember that they are residing in an American territory and as residents of Hawaii they must trust and cooperate with the American people in all understanding. It would do well for Japanese to abandon old customs and conventional ideas, and keep in step with the world.

At a dinner party sponsored by the Japanese Chamber of Commerce, Yada noted, "Speaking frankly, there is plenty of room for the Chamber to grow." He urged the organization to target the buying power of all two hundred fifty thousand residents of Hawaii, not just the Japanese community.[50] His words clearly reflected a sensitivity to the islands' white elite. An avid golfer, Yada quickly made acquaintances not only within the Japanese community but among haole social circles as well.

The new consul general's comments were consistent with the new interest that the Japanese government was showing in Japanese immigrants in Hawaii. They were also a response to the increasingly vehement anti-Japanese movement on the West Coast.

A few days after Yada's arrival, a delegation of the Congressional Committee on Immigration, numbering nearly a hundred, arrived in Honolulu. One of the reasons that HSPA president Waterhouse participated in the resolution of the strike, it seems, was the group's imminent arrival. The delegation had first gone to California, where it appeared likely that the amendment to the Alien Land Law would be approved in the upcoming election. Since the Japanese government called it an "anti-Japanese land law," and had repeatedly objected to the American government, the law had become an issue in U.S.-Japan relations.

California's Governor Stephens urged the congressional committee to visit Hawaii after finishing its investigation of the Japanese immigration situation in California, so that they could see with their own eyes the developments California had to guard against. As the *Honolulu Star Bulletin* noted, "The Hawaiian islands, an American territory, are being conquered by the Japanese without opposition, and it is California's plea to the nation that this state shall not be conquered as Hawaii is being conquered by a foreign race."[51]

By the time the delegation arrived in Hawaii, the strike had just ended, but everywhere its members looked, they saw Japanese faces. They returned to the mainland shocked at what the *San Francisco Chronicle* called the "result of Japanese colonization." But among them were also those like Senator Lowell of California who, on his return home, insisted that California should look at Hawaii as a model, not as a warning. "Hawaii treats Japanese like southern states treat negroes," he said.[52]

On July 9, the day before the congressional delegation arrived in Honolulu, John Waterhouse was enjoying a round of golf at his country club. It had been some time since he had been able to relax on the well-maintained velvet-smooth greens of the club, whose membership was limited to the planter elite. His day on the links was suddenly interrupted by Hōsen Isobe, who pushed his way into the club accompanied by some of his parishioners. On several plantations posters had been put up detailing the discussion between Waterhouse and Isobe as they negotiated the strike settlement, and Isobe had come to persuade Waterhouse to take them down. Waterhouse refused. The Japanese labor leaders and Japanese newspapers, he said, had misinformed the strikers about what was said at their meeting, and he had decided to provide them a correct report, taken by a stenographer at the time, of every word uttered at the meeting. Isobe replied that revealing the details of the meeting to the laborers might result in a new strike. "Then let the new strike come," answered Waterhouse.[53]

At the daylong meeting of the labor delegates at the Suigorō restaurant on June 30, Ichiji Gotō, secretary of the federation headquarters reported the three "conditions" agreed on for the "unconditional return to work": first, the $2.50 minimum day wage increase would be presented as a voluntary action of the HSPA and announced at the HSPA annual meeting in a few months; second, the striking workers would be allowed to return to their previous jobs; and third, the specifics of the agreement would be worked out between management and the laborers. Isobe, as mediator, had reported to Furuya that he had extracted these conditions from Waterhouse, and Furuya had so informed the federation leadership. Waterhouse, however, stuck to his principle of refusing to recognize the collective bargaining rights of the federation. At the HSPA annual meeting in November, he insisted that "no concessions whatsoever, either direct or implied, were made and the men who returned to work were on the same basis which existed when the strike was called." [54]

Although Isobe had specifically told Furuya that he had exacted a "silent agreement" from Waterhouse on the $2.50 wage increase, the stenographic record of the meeting indicated that Waterhouse had said only that once the laborers returned to work "unconditionally," they could hold discussions with managers at each plantation's company to determine the details of what would happen. It was Isobe who had brought up the $2.50 wage increase. Waterhouse did not reject this, but he did not say "I'll make it a promise" or "I'll guarantee it." Indeed, he scrupulously avoided making specific promises.

Nevertheless, when Waterhouse's proposal for an unconditional return to work was conveyed to the federation, it was with the conditions stipulated by Gotō at the Suigorō. The federation leaders had interpreted it merely as the HSPA's outward policy of insisting on an unconditional return to work, and, because it had been communicated to them by Acting Consul General Furuya, they decided to return to work, "believing in the good will of the HSPA." The Japanese-language newspapers referred to it as a "gentlemen's agreement."

If there was one point on which labor and management agreed at the end of the strike, it was to refrain from talk about victory or defeat. Both the *Honolulu Advertiser* and the *Honolulu Star Bulletin* respected this and merely reported that the strike had come to an end. Even the *Hawaii hōchi,* usually quick to find fault, announced an "agreement reached between labor and management" without reflecting on which side had won. The *Nippu jiji,* however, in its extra about the "amicable resolution of the strike," happened to refer to the "victory" for the Japanese laborers. According to the *Hōchi,* "although it is unknown whether this was on purpose or an oversight," the *Nippu* extra, which disregarded the understanding among the press, led the striking workers to conclude that they had "won after all." This was clear when the workers began to negotiate with plantation managers after returning to their plantations. Convinced that the workers' sense of victory would make a settlement difficult, Waterhouse had posters distributed proclaiming the "truth about the negotiations to end the strike."

The laborers returned to their plantations full of bold energy but found management attitudes stiffer than they expected. It was not unusual for a skilled mill worker who had been earning $2 before the strike to be shifted to cane field work at 77 cents on his return. Non-Japanese workers who had moved into the strikers' quarters were in no hurry to move out. Strikers who returned to their plantations as soon as the strike ended immediately went to work to qualify for their bonuses, which required twenty days of work per month. In June the sugar price had fallen, but it was still holding at 18 cents, and the June bonus rate was 511 percent. But many plantation companies refused bonuses to workers who had participated in the strike even if they had worked the requisite number of days.

As the federation delegate from Aiea Plantation later reported, "Upon the strikers' return, the managers, lunas, and guards were all kind at first, but as the days passed their attitude changed, and when the Federation officers went to the plantations they were treated with contempt, and nearly fifty members were unable to return to the plantation." The strike leaders were blacklisted at the plantations, and one after another they were fired. Eijūrō Yokoo, the Ewa Plantation federation leader who had read the declaration ending the strike at the rally at Aala Park, was fired a month after he returned to work. "You said you would commit hara kiri if you allowed the strike to end in defeat," the workers chided him, "so now that we have lost the strike, you should commit hara kiri." [55]

The *Hawaii hōchi* began running a daily series of "Investigative Reports" that fanned the workers' discontent.

[August 12]: Circumstances leading to the resolution of the Labor Association strike: The facts should be probed by true laborers other than Federation headquarters officers, local branch organization officers, sycophantic newspapers, and the mediator Mr. Isobe; these laborers should also investigate the disgraceful behavior of the secretary and four or five other officers.

[August 13]: The malfeasance of bad elements in the Federation headquarters is considerable. They wasted $600,000 in expenditures and lost several million dollars in income to conduct a six-month-long strike, which could have been resolved to the benefit of the workers, but ended with no written contract, and put returning workers back in the same wretched conditions.

[August 17]: Did HSPA President Waterhouse deceive Isobe, did Isobe deceive the Federation headquarters secretary, or were the Federation headquarters secretary and Isobe in cahoots to deceive the workers? The truth of who duped whom will eventually be known, but there is no question that the workers were duped.

Consul General Yada reported to Tokyo that Isobe had started negotiations to resolve the strike on the spur of the moment because he feared the obstructive actions by ambitious men like *Hawaii hōchi* president Makino. The series in the *Hawaii hōchi* was Makino's retaliation against negotiations that had excluded him.

Rumors spread that another strike was in the offing. When Isobe, who continued to frequent the consulate secretly after Yada arrived, brought in such reports, Yada bypassed the federation headquarters. Instead, he immediately summoned laborer representatives from each of the Oahu plantations that had been on strike and instructed them to return to work quickly even if they had to put up with some worker discontent. It is not difficult to imagine their response. The plantations had returned to calm, but all the discontent and anger of the returned workers were now directed, not at the plantation owners, but at the federation headquarters. As if to pour fat on the fire, the *Hōchi* called for reform of the federation: "To establish an effective labor union, a restructuring of the federation headquarters is essential. We urge that an emergency meeting of delegates be held to allow the workers and the general public to be satisfied." [56]

In response to the *Hōchi*'s complaint, a special delegates meeting was held at the Suigorō restaurant at Waiau on August 19. The delegates assembled were the same ones who had gathered to discuss resolving the strike six weeks before. Once again federation headquarters secretary Noboru Tsutsumi was central to the discussions.

The first topic considered was the report of the Finance Committee, which had become the biggest issue after the end of the strike. Federation strike funds had amounted to a sum far beyond the imagination of ordinary workers, and the *Hōchi* had raised questions about federation accounts. The federation announced that its total revenue through July 31, 1920, had been $681,448.83. More than $670,000 came from membership fees and strike support funds paid by workers on all the islands. Donations from Japanese merchants and others amounted to only $6,000. It is not easy to calculate the current equivalent of $680,000. It might be more accurate to infer its value by comparing it to the capital of major Caucasian banks, which ranged from $500,000 to $1,000,000, or to the $25,000 capitalization of the Pacific Savings Support Corporation organized by Japanese immigrants in Hilo.

Chūhei Hoshino, the Finance Committee representative who gave the report, stated that only $30,000 remained. During its eight months of activities, the federation had spent a total of $650,344.82, half of which had gone to feed the workers evicted from the plantations. The next largest amount, $134,000, covered the Oahu federation's activities, and $60,000 was spent for lodging the evicted workers. According to the Finance Committee report, household goods purchased for the evicted workers were "mostly sold, at least the useful items," and so was the headquarters' truck and Ford automobile. Two hospitals for plantation workers in Kalihi had been purchased for $6,550, but after the strike one was appraised at $2,000 and the other at $2,400, so the federation directed the bank to take charge of their disposition. The relocation center that the federation had to buy for the Filipinos had cost $3,000, but the Oahu federation had offered to purchase it for $2,000. All other real estate, which had been appraised with the help of the strike supporters' association and carpenters, had been disposed of in the month since the end of the strike.

Although the Finance Committee report went into great detail even about the disposition of pots and pans from the nine centers for evicted workers, the evening edition of the *Hōchi* strongly urged a "clarification of the suspicions" about the use of federation funds. The next day, Tsutsumi, as federation representative, announced, "We wish to have an investigation and understanding of the facts of the matter." An audit committee, made up of members chosen from each island, focused on the federation headquarters' expenditures on negotiations, travel, and special expenses, all of which the *Hōchi* labeled "amusement expenses." The investigation, which took five days, resulted in a report approved at the August 25 delegates meeting. The report concluded, "We undertook this investigation of the accounts of the headquarters because of suspicions that there may have been questionable behavior on the part of headquarters staff or use of headquarters funds for personal entertainment at restaurants. We have come to the conclusion that there were no irregularities and no points of discrepancy between what was announced by headquarters as its final balance and what is contained in the ledgers of the headquarters." In short, the audit committee found that there were "no grounds for suspicion" in the federation's management of its accounts.

The investigators, who checked each restaurant mentioned in the accounts, determined that $800 was spent at Tsuboya and $400 at Sansuirō, but these could not be termed strictly "amusement expenses." "We heard that at Kikuzuki a headquarters staff had engaged in personal entertainment," the report said, "but this was not substantiated by information obtained from a geisha." The federation headquarters turned out to be innocent in this case too.

The Hōchi, which had insisted that it was sufficient to focus the investigation "on the content of the gentlemen's agreement and whether there was any entertainment involving geisha during the strike," found itself in a corner when the investigation results were announced. It swiftly turned its attack toward Hōsen Isobe, who had used restaurants ostensibly for the purpose of mediation negotiations. "A religious leader who engages in geisha entertainment," the paper fulminated, "isn't worth three cents." Isobe insisted that although he had never called a geisha, a fellow diner had. But Makino, who frequented the same restaurant, ascertained that Isobe had asked a geisha, as soon as she arrived, to play the *shamisen* accompaniment so that he could recite *jōruri* ballad dramas. The Hōchi even revealed the names of geisha Isobe specifically asked for.[57]

Since Prohibition was in force, perhaps out of consideration for the restaurant owners, liquor was not mentioned in these articles, but according to the current Sōtō sect mission priest, Gyokuei Matsuura, Isobe used to brag that "the only day that I didn't drink since coming to Hawaii was the night after I was in a car accident."[58]

The Hōchi also reported that Isobe had received $2,370 as a strike mediation fee from the HSPA which was paid in two installments: first $1,500 and the remaining amount a few days later. It was well known that Isobe had secured a piece of prime property near the Consulate General as a site to build the Sōtō Honolulu mission but had had trouble raising money for its construction. Shortly after the settlement of the strike, however, work began on the main hall of the mission.

After settling the issue of the federation's accounts, the delegates meeting finally moved on to the main topic, restructuring the federation headquarters. In anticipation of the debate Tsutsumi expressed his own view of the issue:

> Hawaiian society is too unenlightened to permit our headquarters to advance toward fulfilling the principles for which it has struggled. Even if we reshuffle, reorganize or change personnel, if we also refuse to abandon labor unionism, we will be oppressed by the capitalists and condemned by some elements in

the Japanese community. Are we to become a headquarters in name only because of this oppression and condemnation? Instead of turning into a den of power seekers, we ought to disband while we are still pure.

With no less vigor than it had criticized Isobe, the *Hawaii hōchi* had focused its attack on Tsutsumi, and his proposal to disband rather than restructure could be considered his response to the newspaper.

The *Hōchi* also brought up Makino's attempt at mediation in late May: "Since it may sound as if we are promoting ourselves, we had thought not to print this in the newspaper, but we have decided to announce the strike mediation plan we at the *Hōchi* proposed for the workers to use as reference." In his effort to bring in Governor McCarthy as strike mediator, Makino had asked Tokuzō Shibayama to persuade Tsutsumi to give the federation's informal consent before having Lightfoot, the acting territorial chief prosecutor, approach the governor. It is clear from the Terasaki diary that Makino cut short his efforts when he heard that Mott Smith might become mediator. The article in the *Hōchi*, however, made no mention of this and placed all the blame for the failure of the plan on Tsutsumi.

According to the *Hōchi*, Tsutsumi had promised Shibayama not to speak of the mediation matter until it was fully arranged. Despite this, Tsutsumi had brought it up at federation headquarters, allowing Isobe to hear of it, and as a result Isobe and Waterhouse worked out an unsatisfactory mediation. If Tsutsumi had kept his promise, and if Makino had been able to bring in the governor of Hawaii as mediator, the laborers would not have been made fools after returning to the plantations. In its effort to subvert Tsutsumi's standing as the central figure in the delegates meeting, the *Hōchi* ran articles calling him a liar who had betrayed his promise. To counter this charge, Tsutsumi responded with his own explanation:

> I am a secretary of the Federation headquarters, and our members have vowed on our lives to remain unified to the end. Even Mr. Shibayama has stated that he is prepared die [literally, slit his stomach] for the laborers. What is more, it is perfectly natural that privately I would inform the officers of the headquarters and the Oahu Union leaders, who are my comrades in this struggle, about this matter. If I had made an arbitrary decision without informing them, then I, Tsutsumi, would be an autocrat. There can be no room for secrecy or authoritarianism in a popular movement that is forthright and fair.

On August 26 the *Hōchi* responded to Tsutsumi's explanation with an article carrying the headline "False Points in Secretary Tsutsumi's Explanation; He Has Created His Own Provisions Here and There, Twisting the Facts and Daring to Engage in the Folly of Duping the Public." The next day an editorial ridiculed Tsutsumi's statement that he had risked his life in the struggle: "It is only a great genius who can thoroughly deride the public. He should realize that the schemes of ordinary mortals damage themselves as well as society." As the delegates discussed restructuring of the federation, they listened with one ear to the *Hōchi*'s clamor on the Tsutsumi issue.

In the following days the delegates held heated discussions on whether to restructure or disband. Although a decision to disband the federation headquarters was narrowly avoided, it was decided to get rid of Tsutsumi and the other federation officers who led the strike. As Consul General Yada reported to the Foreign Ministry,

> On the surface, the delegates meeting accepted the actions of the Federation headquarters and its staff and expressed its gratitude for the efforts and service of its members. In actuality, all the officers were retired [sic], and a socalled restructuring was accomplished, as the *Hawaii hōchi* faction insisted. At the same time, there are plans to soothe the hard feelings that arose from the federation's previous actions in dealing with the HSPA. From now on, at least until the annual HSPA meeting in November, it is thought that there will be no provocations such as [illegible].[59]

UNPRECEDENTED PROFITS FOR THE PLANTERS

On November 29 John Waterhouse opened the fortieth annual meeting of the HSPA with the comment, "The unprecedented and abnormal condition of the sugar market and the serious labor difficulties on the plantations mark the past year as the most stirring and eventful year in the history of the sugar industry. . . . 'Spectacular' and 'ruinous' seem to be the only words to use in describing the market conditions of 1920. One does not have to be much of a prophet to assert that there will be no repetition of the 1920 prices."[60]

At an extraordinary general meeting in October the HSPA had already decided to raise minimum wages for cane field laborers who worked at least twenty-six days per month to $30 for men and $22 for women. Four months after the strike ended the workers finally had obtained a daily wage increase from 77 cents to $1.15. Not only was this far less than the $2.50 that Isobe claimed was the silent gentlemen's agreement with HSPA president Waterhouse, it also fell below the $1.25 demanded during the strike. The bonus was set at a uniform rate of

10 percent, but workers still had to work at least twenty days per month to qualify for the bonus.

In fact, the planters had voted secretly during the extraordinary general meeting to gradually increase wages later on. Since the planters still publicly refused to recognize collective bargaining, wage increases were to be carried out cautiously so as not to give the laborers the impression that they had won the strike. The plantation workers had no way of knowing about this.

The *Nippu jiji* termed the $1.15 increase an improvement, and the *Hawaii shinpō* said that it should be taken under consideration. Only the *Hawaii hōchi* criticized it: "The planters did not increase the actual income of the laborers, and yet they apparently increased their own income to recover damages from the strike." The paper made an issue of the new method for calculating the bonus. "Although the daily wage has increased," it pointed out, "if the sugar price rises over 8 cents the laborers' income would be lower than the present amount."[61] If the monthly wage was more than $75, for example, there would be no bonus; thus the change amounted to an average decrease in the bonus rate of 0.5 percent.

In September, nine months after the start of the strike, consumer prices had increased further. Since the stock market slump in March, every time a ship from Japan arrived the prices of the rice, soy sauce, and miso imported for the Japanese laborers went higher and higher. Consumer goods from the mainland were also rising in price, and the fare for steamships between the islands rose in August, and the passage between Yokohama and Hawaii increased 20 percent in September.

Four months after his arrival, Consul General Yada expressed his opinion of the wage increase granted by the HPSA. "This revision does not significantly change the actual income of the workers compared to their current wage," he reported to Japan. "Their standard of living has not improved at all. . . . It could be considered a disciplinary revision against the strikers. Needless to say, it is a result of the planters' profit-first mentality."

Pablo Manlapit, chairman of the Filipino Federation of Labor, saw the HSPA announcement of a wage increase as a childish trick. Manlapit had strongly criticized the resolution of the strike. He said that it was difficult to believe that the Japanese leaders would end the strike merely by relying on the integrity of the planters' word without obtaining a firm wage increase. Changing the organization's name to Hawaii Laborers' Association to show that it transcended nationality had also been an empty sham. The reality was that the Japanese pushed the Filipinos to accept settlement after the strikers had returned to work. As a result, the Filipinos continued to harbor distrust toward the Japanese.

On September 10 the Hawaii Laborers' Association officers who had led the strike resigned en masse. The newly elected directors lacked the leadership of Tsutsumi and his colleagues. The association headquarters made no public comment or response when the HSPA announced the wage increase to $1.15. But once again the *Hōchi* took up the workers' cause: "This is not an improvement but a detriment; it is not a beneficial revision but a distortion." [62] As the days went by the *Hōchi* again made an issue of the "gentlemen's agreement." "The new bonus system clearly decreases income. Whose crime is this?" it asked. "Who declared the wage amount of $2.50?" [63]

Only a month later, on November 21, did the association react to the HSPA wage increase announcement. Complaining that the new scale still did not provide living wages, the association reiterated its "desire" for minimum wages of $40 for men and $30 for women. This was no more than the $1.50 per day demanded in the strike. The association also accepted the HSPA's bonus plan, and although the HPSA ignored demands for an eight-hour workday, the association said nothing about this.

The Filipinos were no longer acting with the Japanese, but under Manlapit's name, they voiced a demand for a $2.50 wage increase in exchange for ending the bonus system tied to the price of sugar and for establishing an eight-hour workday with half days on Saturday. The HSPA immediately rejected the renewed wage increase demands from both the Japanese and the Filipinos.

At the 1920 HSPA annual meeting, Waterhouse criticized the strikers' tactics:

> The cohesion and unity of action manifested by the Japanese was really wonderful when considered from a superficial viewpoint. An inside knowledge of the situation revealed a system of terrorism and intimidation most effectively adapted to the temperament of these people. An unswerving loyalty to their home country, to their hometowns and their home people is characteristic of the Japanese and influences their thoughts and actions. Relying on their loyalty, the labor leaders inserted in the articles of the Association of the Japanese Federation of Labor the following clause: "Should a member be found guilty of the act of contravening the interests of this Federation . . . he should be reported to several affiliated branches . . . and to the mayor of the offending member's permanent domicile in Japan."

Waterhouse concluded his remarks on the "eventful year" by invoking the Japanese conspiracy theory: "The Japanese newspapers were strong in their denials that the strike was anything but economic, but at times were incautious enough to state that it was racial and nationalistic, and in some instances the real feeling of the leaders along these lines were manifested." The 1920 *Hawaiian Annual* described the strike as "a movement for higher plantation wage demand [that] was launched by certain Japanese papers and Japanese language school principals." Although the workers were "already better paid than elsewhere," a "so-called laborers' committee" twice made arrogant demands.

According to the HSPA, losses from the 1920 strike in all the plantations on Oahu amounted to $10 million. At the annual meeting the HSPA decided that these losses would be underwritten by dividing them up among the plantations on the other islands. For example, the Olaa plantation, where the Sakamaki house dynamiting incident occurred, was apportioned liability for $470,000.

On January 21, 1921, a *Honolulu Advertiser* editorial crowed, "With the end of 1920 the most prosperous year in Hawaii's history comes to a close. . . . Virtually every business showed great growth during the twelve months. Probably the leading business barometer, as reflecting the material well-being of the Islands, is the story told by the bank deposits, commercial and savings." [64] HSPA president Waterhouse, however, had termed 1920 an unusually volatile year of "unbelievable price rises" and "ruinous price drops." In June, when an investigative committee directly under Attorney General Palmer began to investigate the abnormal surge in the sugar price, it began to fall, and by the HSPA annual meeting in November, it had dropped to 5.76 cents. Even so, the bank deposits in Hawaii reached the highest amount in a decade, 1.5 times that of the previous year. [65] Waterhouse's expression "ruinous" must be considered an exaggeration.

To take Olaa Plantation as an example, not only did the sugar price soar, but contrary to the pessimistic forecast at the start of the year, the cane fields yielded a good harvest in 1920. The plantation manager's annual report for 1920 stated, "Our crops are looking remarkably well, and with increased tariff protection and a reduction in Excess Profits Tax, we should make a very satisfactory showing for the year." The report concluded with an unusually bright outlook. Improvements to the mill and the warehouse had been completed, and expansion of the plantation railroad was progressing. The plantation was also improving the workers' welfare by building some thirty new housing units and by planning modernization improvements for the plantation hospital.

The "unprecedented profits" of 1920 not only enriched the plantation companies, they went into the pockets of ordinary laborers. The bonus rate had been 87 percent in 1919, but it averaged 279 percent in 1920. Wages paid to workers were also 3.2 times the amount paid the year before.

The labor contractors also enjoyed greater profits. The widow of Jirokichi Iwasaki, who had succeeded her husband's as the top contractor at Olaa Plantation, noted in her diary, "I was to receive $80,000. . . . This was the largest amount of money I made at one time in my life." [66] After paying back an advance from the company, the wages owed to the workers, and the huge debt her husband had left, she still kept $18,000 in profits.

Although the strike fund collected from the workers on islands other than Oahu reached the huge sum of $680,000, savings deposits by Japanese increased $200,000 over the previous year. To put it another way, what supported the strike for nearly half a year was the unprecedented rise in the price of sugar. The economy was enjoying such a boom that the English-language newspapers coined the term "bonus millionaire workers." Consul General Yada reported to his government that "these are the best conditions since Japanese have come to Hawaii." Ordinary people were indulging in "a spirit of luxury," and mutual loan associations had become popular. Not only were more and more immigrants taking trips back to their homeland, a growing number of plantation workers left the plantations to open businesses in towns with money they had earned. [67]

It was only on islands other than Oahu that "millionaire workers" emerged. On Oahu, where the strike took place, workers missed out on the chance to make the most profit in their lives. Although the association decided to compensate the Oahu workers for damages they suffered, the figure amounted to only $100 per striking laborer. This was one reason why support for the association cooled rapidly among the workers on Oahu. As one nisei said, "Laborer's money was small, after the strike the union was nothing, no more support." [68]

William Rego, a Portuguese who had been a luna for many years at Waialua Plantation, remembered how the attitude of the Japanese laborers changed after their return to the plantation. The experience of the long strike gave them a chance to think seriously about their future in Hawaii. The phrase that Tsutsumi repeated so often in his speeches—

"We are demanding a wage increase because we are determined to live here permanently"—lived on after the strike. "I saw a lot of difference in the camps," recalled Rego. "They [the Japanese] never planted any fruit trees, but when they came back, they planted avocados, mangos, oranges, tangerines, lemons, limes. They planted all kinds of fruit trees when they came back and they made the camps look nice, you know, with all those fruit trees growing in the yards."[69]

PRESIDENT HARDING'S PATRIOTISM

In late 1920, as the Japanese workers and all the residents of Hawaii were trying to get back to normal after their strike, America was reaching a major turning point. The administration of Woodrow Wilson, a Democrat who burned with the ideals of "the new freedom," had stumbled on its idealism and was coming to an end. The November election resulted in an overwhelming victory for the Republican candidate, Warren G. Harding. The American populace, tired of lofty idealism, had chosen the conservative policies of the Republican party.

Harding, a senator from Ohio, emerged as a compromise candidate when the votes at the Republican National Convention split among several leading candidates. At the Democratic convention Attorney General Palmer had made a strong showing in his effort to succeed Wilson, but ultimately he lost his bid for nomination. The Socialist leader, Eugene Debs, who ran for president from prison where he was serving a sentence for agitating, drew attention by garnering some one million votes. This was also the first election after American women won the right to vote. And in California the Alien Land Law, on the same ballot, was passed by a four to one margin.

The planters in Hawaii supported the Republican party, and their confidence at the HSPA annual meeting reflected the outcome of the presidential elections. Grand celebrations were held in Hawaii to welcome the new Republican president, and a phonograph of Harding's first election speech stirred patriotic feelings at victory parties. He had run his presidential campaign using the following patriotic slogans.

To safeguard America first.
To stabilize America first.
To prosper America first.
To think of America first.
To exalt America first.
To live for and revere America first.

The new president's slogans must have been reassuring to the planter elite, cloaking their fight to protect their rights from "the Japanese conspiracy" with the sanctity of Americanism.

In Hawaii anti-Japanese feelings were on the rise in the wake of the strike. A movement backing passage of the foreign language school control bill, which had narrowly been defeated the previous year, gained momentum. On November 25, a few days before the HSPA annual meeting, a special session of the territorial legislature passed the bill and set its enforcement to begin on July 1, 1921. Under its provisions, foreign-language schools were not to hold sessions before or during public school hours, and no pupil was to attend more than one hour a day, six hours a week, thirty-eight weeks a year. The Department of Public Instruction was authorized to prescribe the courses of study and the textbooks, and no one was allowed to conduct or teach in a foreign-language school without a permit from the department. Teachers moreover were required to demonstrate knowledge about democracy, American history and institutions, and the English language.

Four months later a foreign language press control bill was enacted. Its target was Japanese-language newspapers. As Consul General Yada observed, the *Hōchi*'s attack on the HSPA prevented "the reaching of a settlement between labor and capital and led to the antagonism of the general American public centered on the planters." Another factor behind the passage of the bill was the purchase of the *Hawaii shinpō* by the Hawaii Laborers' Association. The new law required the Japanese-language newspapers to submit in advance an English translation of any articles on law, politics, and social problems. "The burden of the difficulty and expense of English translation will lead to suppression of the freedom of speech," Yada predicted for the future.[70]

THE CONSPIRACY TRIAL

Honolulu: August 1921

By early 1921 the radical left on the American mainland was in retreat. The American Communist party, which had split in two soon after its formation, finally reunited in January 1921, with Sen Katayama elected to its central committee. By the end of the year Katayama had fled to the Soviet Union. A few months earlier Big Bill Haywood, the IWW leader, had defected there as well. Haywood was neither a communist nor a radical theorist, but he did not want to end his days in an American prison. Out on bail after the 1917 roundup of IWW leaders, he had been charged anew with attempting to overthrow the government and other crimes. The news that Haywood escaped abroad rather than fight to the end was an incalculable shock to his comrades in the labor movement. Not only was it the final blow to the IWW, it was a significant event in American labor history.

On May 31, just six weeks after the news of Haywood's defection, the trial of Sacco and Vanzetti finally began in Massachusetts. An anarchist group supporting the two defendants hired Fred Moore, a lawyer known for his struggle for civil rights, to head the defense team. Moore, who had just won acquittal of IWW members charged with dynamiting the residence of a Standard Oil Company executive in Oklahoma, headed for Boston, where he shocked conservative easterners with his long hair and cowboy hat.

The Massachusetts state attorney's office was treating this case differ-ent from a simple murder and robbery. It was attempting to make it a showcase for the crackdown on anarchists, communists, and other radi-cals. State troopers surrounded the courthouse, and, in accordance with

Massachusetts law, the trial began with the two defendants in a cage in the courtroom. The two sides faced off in a fierce struggle. The prosecution called fifty-nine witnesses, and the defense called ninety-nine. Several prosecution witnesses gave questionable testimony that was determined in later years to be perjury. Vanzetti, who was said to have been the driver of the car used in the crime, did not know how to drive; and the validation of the pistol that was to have been the key piece of evidence was inconclusive. But the case went to the jury with these and other points left in doubt.

In heavily accented broken English the two defendants each made statements in their self-defense. But in the eyes of the establishment Protestant Anglo-Saxons, these two Italian immigrants represented an alien culture, whose members belonged to a different religion and who produced too many children despite their poverty. Moreover, the image of the Mafia, which had started to insinuate itself in the United States, trailed Italian immigrants. The judge's final instructions to the jury appealed to their patriotism. He told them to deliberate on this case as if they were soldiers who had gone across the ocean to France to fight and die in the First World War to defend democracy. As if responding in that spirit, on July 14 the jury found the two foreign anarchists guilty. Massachusetts law decreed death by electric chair for the crime of murder and robbery. Sacco cried from his witness cage, "Sono innocente."

Wallace Farrington, the new territorial governor, had just returned to Honolulu from Washington, D.C. The fifty-year-old Farrington was a native of Maine who had gone to Hawaii twenty-five years earlier as a newspaper reporter. He worked at first for the *Honolulu Advertiser*, then for the *Honolulu Star Bulletin*, where he eventually became editor-in-chief and publisher. He was to serve as governor for two terms (eight years), establishing the "Farrington era" in Hawaiian history. But on August 1, 1921, less than one month after his appointment, and a few weeks after the guilty verdict in the Sacco and Vanzetti trial, the front pages of the English and Japanese newspapers carried similar headlines that shook Hawaiian society to the core. One announced, "Dynamiting Case, Indictments for Criminal Conspiracy in the First Degree."

A year and two months after the dynamiting of Jūzaburō Sakamaki's house at Olaa Plantation, the grand jury sent the case to trial. Since the dynamiting had been treated as a local incident, with only a few lines of reporting when it occurred, this was the first time that most people in Hawaii had heard of it. The *Honolulu Advertiser* summarized the indictment as follows: "On the night of June 3 a band of the 'assassination corps' forced an entrance into the house of a Japanese named Sakamaki, a plantation employee who had refused the join the strikers. While one member of the band stood guard with a drawn pistol, another deposited a quantity of dynamite under the house and then set off the fuse with a lighted cigaret, according to the evidence." [1]

Indicted in the case were twenty-one former leaders of the Federation of Japanese Labor, including Noboru Tsutsumi. It was the first time that so many Japanese had been charged at one time with a crime. In the *Honolulu Advertiser* report that sensationalized the charges by stating that those connected with the federation had organized an "assassination corps" to carry out "a campaign of terrorism," there was a half-page photograph of the Sakamaki house after the blast, together with insets of ten of the indicted, including Tsutsumi. The *Honolulu Star Bulletin* reported, "The round up of the indicted Japanese forms a dramatic climax to the series of outrages, cane-burnings, assaults, dynamitings, and other forms of violence which characterized the strike last year." [2] The Japanese-language newspapers also treated the defendants as guilty from the time of the indictment. The *Hawaii hōchi* already concluded, "Due to an internal quarrel within the federation headquarters . . . this shocking incident was divulged. . . . A crushing blow has been dealt, and the case will expand." [3]

The *Hawaii hōchi* reported that "the ringleaders," Miyazawa, Tsutsumi, Gotō, Takizawa, Kawamata, and Hoshino, had been placed in custody at 8:00 P.M. on August 1 and that bail had been set at $1,500. According to the trial records, the bail was later increased to $3,000 per person. The association could not come up with the money immediately, so Tsutsumi, Hoshino, and Fujitani remained in jail until the morning of August 3.

The caption under Tsutsumi's photograph in the *Honolulu Advertiser* identified him as a person "known among the Japanese as a radical socialist and the author of a voluminous history of the plantation strike written in the Japanese language." After he resigned from the federation, Tsutsumi wanted to edit the strike records. But because others were ineffective in collecting funds to compensate the strikers on Oahu, he had been going around to the other islands to solicit contributions. Although he had resigned after the strike, he had continued to lead the organization behind the scenes.

The Hawaii Laborers' Association had created the post of secretary-general after its restructuring, and Jirō Hayakawa, forty-one, a newspaper reporter, was chosen to fill it. Influenced as a youth by Toshihiko Sakai and Shūsui Kōtoku, he was interested in the labor movement, but he had been in Japan during the strike and had not been involved. Known as a serious writer in a Chinese classical style, he earned the sobriquet "the Sōhō Tokutomi of Hawaii," but he lacked Tsutsumi's charisma.

About a week after the indictment members of the haole elite were invited to a large party at the Moana Hotel, one of the top-ranked hotels in Honolulu. Hōsen Isobe, dressed in priest's robes, greeted guests at the entrance to the banquet room. His long-cherished dream of building the Honolulu mission main hall had been achieved, and this banquet was to celebrate that occasion in the presence of the head priest of the Sōtō sect who had come from Japan. Shortly after the event, Isobe left Hawaii for Los Angeles to build the first Sōtō temple on the U.S. mainland.

THE JUDGE, THE JURORS, THE PROSECUTOR, AND THE DEFENSE

The trial for conspiracy in the first degree began on Wednesday, February 1, 1922, in the First Circuit Court in Honolulu. The indictment read: "On 27th of May 1920, [the accused] did maliciously or fraudulently combine, or mutually undertake or consort together to commit a felony, to wit, to unlawfully use and cause to be exploded dynamite or other explosive chemicals of substance for the purpose of inflicting bodily injury upon one J. Sakamaki." Jury selection, which continued into the next day, took less than four hours. Challenges to rule out biases or prejudices of prospective jurors were raised once by the prosecution and nine times by the defense. All of the challenges were on racial grounds, to exclude people with names that were obviously Filipino, Portuguese, or Hawaiian. Indeed, the twelve jurors selected were all men with Anglo-Saxon names.

Judge James J. Banks, seated in the highest chair at the front of the room, instructed the jury not to read any newspaper accounts of the case and to consider only the testimony. To the press bench, he warned, "Newspapers kindly refrain from publishing anything. I don't want any expression of opinions from the newspapers about the case or any feature of the case." The judge also said that he would prohibit the attendance of anyone who published his opinions in editorials or articles during the course of the trial.

Banks, sixty-one years old, was a native of Alabama, a southern state with a history of discrimination against blacks, and had studied law at the University of Alabama. Four years had passed since he was appointed to the federal bench by the president, but his heavy, nasal southern accent could still be difficult to understand by those not used to it.

After jury selection was completed, the chief prosecutor, William H. Heen, made a twenty-minute opening statement for the prosecution. Heen was thirty-nine years old, young enough to be Judge Banks's son, yet he had already established a reputation in Hawaii's legal circles for his acumen. Although he had a haole name, he was dark-skinned, and his features were exotic, with a high forehead and piercing eyes that bulged slightly. His stiff dark hair was cut so short that it appeared to be standing on end. Heen's mother was from a distinguished Hawaiian family that had dominated Maui, and Heen was known as a man of wealth who owned prime property in Honolulu.

Heen returned to Hawaii after obtaining his law degree at the University of California. He was promoted two years later to deputy attorney general of the territory. In 1918 he was elected city and county attorney of Honolulu. At the Japan-U.S. friendship dinner sponsored by the strike supporters' association just before the strike began (January 23, 1920), Heen made a speech appealing for harmony. Yet four months later, when the Federation of Japanese Labor applied to participate in the Hawaii Mission Centennial Celebration, Heen expressed some of the strongest negative views among the committee members who opposed its participation. In addition to Heen, the prosecution side consisted of Harold E. Stafford and John W. Cathcart.

The defense team also consisted of three lawyers, all known in Hawaii's legal circles. The chief defense counsel, William B. Lymar, a forty-year-old native of Iowa, had graduated from Harvard Law School and come to Honolulu in 1909, the year of the first strike. After serving as assistant district attorney for the city and county, he set up his own law practice. The other defense counsels were Francis M. Brooks and Arthur M. Brown.

Of the twenty-one defendants charged in the indictment, fifteen appeared in court every day. Their names were called each morning at the start of each court session in this order:[4] Gotō, Miyazawa, Tsutsumi, Kawamata, Furushō, Hoshino, Takizawa, Baba, Tomota, Ishida, Koyama, Kondō, Sazō Satō, Fujitani, and Murakami. Each wore the only suit and necktie he owned. Although in Hawaii today casual aloha shirts are worn even in public offices, in those days, no matter how high the temperature, East Coast-style formality was still considered proper. From the first day of the trial oppressive clouds blanketed the sky above

Honolulu. At times the rainfall was so heavy that it was hard to hear the voices in the courtroom. The stone courthouse, with its narrow windows, was dark even when the weather was clear. The atmosphere was so solemn that the trial seemed to be taking place in a town somewhere in the eastern United States rather than in a tropical island called the "paradise of the Pacific."

SAKAMAKI TAKES THE WITNESS STAND

On Thursday, February 2, at 10:15 A.M., the first witness for the prosecution took his seat on the witness stand. It was the victim of the dynamiting case in the indictment, Jūzaburō Sakamaki, then fifty-one years old. Sakamaki had stowed away on a ship bound for America when he was fifteen. On learning that his mother was ill, he hastened to return to Japan, but when he reached Hawaii he discovered that she had already died. Instead of continuing his journey home, he took a job as an interpreter at the newly established Olaa Sugar Company on Hawaii. In the Honolulu courtroom twenty-three years later, his voice must have rung with pride as he identified himself: "I am just now assistant postmaster, Olaa post office, and official interpreter and clerk for Olaa Sugar Co." Not only was Sakamaki the sole pipeline connecting the sugar company to the Japanese laborers, as assistant postmaster he also handled administrative matters regarding family registration delegated to him by the Japanese Consulate General.

Sakamaki was known as a difficult man who constantly boasted of his family's samurai background. Yasuki Aragaki, a current resident at Olaa Plantation, remembered Sakamaki clearly as the man to whom his father, a tenant farmer from Okinawa, was always beholden. Even around the plantation, Sakamaki wore a good-quality three-piece suit. His thick mustache, which flared out at the edges, seemed to overwhelm his small stature, and his manner was arrogant. He often treated his fellow Japanese who worked in the cane fields with a lack of generosity that bordered on the malicious. On the witness stand Sakamaki was dressed neatly in a navy blue pin-striped suit with a maroon bowtie. As he glared at prosecuting attorney Heen, hardly blinking, he answered the questions put to him about the night of the explosion.

In a concise manner Sakamaki testified that shortly after 11:00 P.M. on the night of June 3, 1920, he was awakened by a deafening blast.[5] He ran to the plantation guard's house to inform him, but the guard had just left, thinking that something had happened at the mill. Sakamaki then ran to the company office and telephoned the plantation manager to find out how to handle the incident.[6]

Sakamaki finished his description of the night of the incident by stating that it was a "narrow escape" for his family. "We all think ourselves very fortunate," he said. Prosecutor Heen asked Sakamaki to give the names and ages of the six children whose lives had been spared, slowly and one at a time as if to impress them on the jury's memory.[7]

Then prosecutor Heen asked Sakamaki, "What is your religion?" "Christian," he answered.

At Olaa Nine Mile, now called Keaau, there is a shopping center of about ten Japanese stores anchored by a supermarket. In one corner stands the Olaa Japanese Christian Church, commonly called the "Japanese Church." The church is a small wooden structure painted yellow, with three spires rising from its dark green roof, and its denomination is the same as the most historic church in Hawaii, Honolulu's Central Union Church. Sakamaki had asked the Olaa Sugar Company for funds to build it, and the company had agreed. On the night of the explosion Sakamaki had gone out to a church meeting after supper and returned late. As head deacon of the church from its inception—a church he could be said to have founded—Sakamaki was in full charge of its administration.

Many Japanese who went to America to study at the turn of the century turned to the church or to the YMCA for help, and many American families who accepted Japanese students as houseboys or "school boys" were introduced through their churches. Not surprisingly, many Japanese students became Christians during their stay in America. Sakamaki, however, had been baptized only after becoming the interpreter at the Olaa Sugar Company. Conversion to "the Jesus religion" was a ticket into haole society, and even Japanese were more readily accepted by the Caucasians if they were Christian. It was rare for Japanese to take such a step. Most remained Buddhist. But Sakamaki, "the old fox," put the "Japanese Church" first, and he often took the side of the sugar company against the Buddhist temples on the plantation.

Many in the Japanese immigrant community succumbed to the temptations of gambling, prostitutes, and above all alcohol. To improve public morals, Sakamaki had organized the Olaa Japanese Temperance Union in 1911 and served as its chairman. This was several years in advance of the U.S. Prohibition Act, and it was unheard of at other plantations. Not surprisingly, the haole planters, descendants of missionaries, saw "Frank" Sakamaki as a man they could trust.

After confirming that Sakamaki was a Christian, prosecutor Heen concluded his questioning by asking, "During the strike and before your place was dynamited did you receive any threats of any kind?"

"No, sir," replied Sakamaki.

"Did not?"

"No, sir."

"Well, did you hear of any threats?"

Acting as though Sakamaki's reply was unexpected, Heen repeated his question, but defense attorney Lymar raised an objection and Judge Banks sustained it.

In the cross-examination Lymar focused solely Sakamaki's anti-strike activities. The prosecution was attempting to prove that the federation had attempted to get rid of Sakamaki by killing off the entire family with dynamite because he was an anti-strike leader. Lymar was trying to destroy the core of the facts of this indictment, and during direct questioning, Sakamaki had described his anti-strike activities:

> SAKAMAKI: "Most of the time they come to where I am. I am dealing with laborers daily, say ten to hundred, pretty near. Everyday I meet laborers, contractor; I come in contact personally all the time, morning and night. I meet different people, so, everybody come around. I have impressed upon them that it is not proper to do anything to support this strike just now."
>
> HEEN: "You at those times advised them against the strike?"
>
> SAKAMAKI: "Oh, yes."

Under Heen's questioning Sakamaki also testified that he had distributed *Kazan* (Volcano), a small anti-strike newspaper with a readership limited to Hilo and its surroundings run as a one-man operation by its publisher and editor, Kōhachi Yamamura. Yamamura, a native of Ehime who used the pen name Kainan, was known for his aggressiveness. When he was a road construction labor contractor in California, he lost a leg in a shootout with a Mexican contractor. In keeping with his violent character, he wrote pieces full of personal attacks. For some reason Yamamura, who also came from a samurai background, got along well with Sakamaki, and the two men were old friends, or *furen*.

Under cross-examination from defense attorney Lymar, Sakamaki testified that once or twice a week some 2,000 to 3,000 copies of *Kazan* were sent to his house. He placed piles of them where they would be easily seen. Lymar asked, "Isn't it true that, although you dispatched these papers by these different people, sent them out, that it was common knowledge that they were left undistributed at different places, large bundles of them each week were left at different points, undistributed and unread?"

Sakamaki made no attempt to deny this. "Might be," he replied, "but so far as I know if, maybe one or two read it that's all, sufficient; I don't expect all been read it, but as far as this paper get in some place, that's all I care for."

Sakamaki, the victim, was on the witness stand less than an hour, and he testified in English without an interpreter. In those days, even nisei interpreters spoke in pidgin English, mixed with some Japanese and Hawaiian, but Sakamaki had learned his English on the mainland when he was young, and he was said to speak English like a haole.[8] The trial transcript attests that he was fluent except for occasional misuse of the indefinite article or verb tense. Although his accent is not discernible from the transcript, his English was proficient enough for the plantation manager to listen to him without misunderstandings.

When questioned by Heen and Lymar, Sakamaki often replied "Yes, sir," or "No, sir." This was little different from the way southern blacks responded to their white employers. Despite his authority as the company's official interpreter and the fear with which he was regarded by Japanese laborers, Sakamaki's life of serving haole bosses left its mark.

Immediately after Sakamaki's cross-examination ended, one juror asked, "Please your honor, one question. One name I didn't get, the name of that man that . . . I want to see if it is the same as one of these names, the man that owned this newspaper." When Sakamaki, responded "Yamamura," another juror asked, "He is not one of the men named there?" The Caucasian jurors had trouble distinguishing the Japanese names, and this sort of question was repeated often throughout the trial. Some jurors never learned the names of the defendants, even though they were called out every morning when the defendants entered the courtroom.

"CO-CONSPIRATOR" MATSUMOTO'S TESTIMONY

The second witness for the prosecution gave his name as Junji Matsumoto. He wore frameless round thick-lensed glasses, but his physique was solid, indicating long years of physical labor. He answered prosecutor Heen's questions with short replies of two or three words in a low voice that was hard to hear. The thirty-three-year-old Matsumoto had lived in Hawaii for seventeen years. Starting as a cane field laborer at Ewa Plantation on Oahu, he worked at various plantations on several islands. When the strike began, he testified, he had been at Waialua Plantation on Oahu helping Honji Fujitani, who ran the *Nippu jiji* branch office on the plantation.

> HEEN: "That is H. Fujitani, one of the defendants in this case?"
>
> MATSUMOTO: "Yes." (Defendant Fujitani is asked to stand up.)
>
> HEEN: "Is that the man H. Fujitani?"
>
> MATSUMOTO: "That's the man."
>
> HEEN: "Have the record show that the witness identified H. Fujitani."

Honji Fujitani had organized the Waialua union, the first to engage in a wage increase movement on Oahu. After he became involved in the Oahu Federation of Japanese Labor, he was so busy that he hired Matsumoto to collect the subscription fees for the *Nippu jiji*. As secretary of the Waialua union, Fujitani was its actual organizer, but Tokuji Baba, who held a high position in the plantation mill, served as its president. In response to Heen, Matsumoto confirmed that Baba was one of the men sitting in the defendants' seats.

According to Matsumoto, in March 1920 the federation began to recruit special security or guard troops called pickets. Matsumoto was one of the pickets at the Wahiawa Plantation union. Their main work was to block scabs and to keep watch on the laborers who had returned to work. The pickets at Wahiawa were divided into several groups, and Matsumoto headed one of them.

Almost casually, Heen turned to his main line of questioning. "Now, in May, sometime, of 1920 did you have occasion to go to Waialua to see H. Fujitani?" Matsumoto replied that he had, on the night of May 21. Fujitani had been in bed with a cold at the time but had gotten up to talk with him. "When I went there he told me that he had some work for me, that I had to go to Hawaii. I was told that message come from Baba that I have to go to the federation office and for me to go tomorrow." Fujitani did not explain why he wanted Matsumoto to go to Hawaii, nor did Matsumoto ask. Fujitani handed him $75 for initial expenses.

On the morning of the next day, Matsumoto arrived by train in Honolulu at about 9:00. The station was near Aala Park, and Matsumoto headed directly for the Sumitomo Bank building, a five-minute walk. The headquarters of the Federation of Japanese Labor[9] was on the second floor of the building, along with the Oahu union office. The two offices were separated by a sitting room with newspapers and magazines.

Heen asked who the Oahu union officers were. Matsumoto responded, "E. Yokoo." Heen then asked, "Where is he now, do you think?" "In Japan," was the response.

Eijūrō Yokoo had been president of the Ewa union. When HSPA president Waterhouse refused to negotiate with Tsutsumi and the other federation leaders, Yokoo had been pressed into representing the laborers. During the turmoil after the strike, his fellow laborers turned against him, and the Ewa sugar company fired him as a dangerous person. According to his wife, Toyo, Yokoo then worked as a clerk in the Japanese Hospital in Honolulu. She came down with influenza and never fully recovered, so they returned to Yokoo's hometown, Chikushi-harada, Fukuoka prefecture, two months before the indictment.

In response to Heen, Matsumoto confirmed that of the defendants named in the indictment, Yōkichi Satō (Kahuku union) and Kaichi Miyamura (Hawaii Island union), had also returned to Japan and were not present in court. Heen then asked the Oahu union leaders—Waialua delegate Tokuji Baba, Waipahu delegates Shōshichirō Furushō, Fumio Kawamata, and Kan'ichi Takizawa, and Waimanalo delegate Shunji Tomota—to stand so that Matsumoto could affirm their identities. Although it was clear that Matsumoto knew nothing about those connected with the Federation of Japanese Labor, Heen had him confirm the identity of the three secretaries (Noboru Tsutsumi, Ichiji Gotō, and Hiroshi Miyazawa) as well as Chūhei Hoshino, who had come to federation headquarters from Hawaii, and Tsurunosuke Koyama and Chikao Ishida, who had come from the Hawaii Island union. As for Seigo Kondō and Tsunehiko Murakami, Matsumoto testified that he knew them well because they had also been pickets. Confirmation that the persons sitting in the defendants' seats were the same persons as those charged in the indictment was essential in establishing the indictment.

Heen asked Matsumoto to recall what happened on the morning of Saturday, May 22. When he went to see Tokuji Baba in the second floor office in the Sumitomo Bank building, Matsumoto said, "I was told [by Baba] that I had to go to Hawaii, that further details would be given to me by the directors of the Hawaii union when I got there." Six other defendants (Tsutsumi, Gotō, Miyazawa, Hoshino, Takizawa, and Kawamata) were also present, he said, and they told him the same thing. "First order was given to me by Baba, and while I was in that room every person that I met told me that 'you have to go to Hawaii, and when you go to Hawaii, the particulars and further orders will be given to you by the directors of the Hawaii union, and you must obey that orders.'"

Q: "Did you inquire of these men as to what you were to do over there?"

A: "I did."

Q: "What did they say?"

A: "I was told that further orders would be given me in Hawaii by the directors of the Hawaii union."

Q: "What else did these men who you have mentioned say to you outside of getting further details or particulars from the officers of the Hawaii union, do you recall?"

A: "Nothing else except those."

Q: "Well, do you recall whether or not they wished you good luck or something to that effect?"

A: "Takizawa, Kawamata, Tsutsumi, Miyazawa, Gotō, Hoshino, those people told me that 'you are going to Hawaii. On your work at Hawaii would be the success of this strike and I want you to do the best you can in Hawaii.'"

That afternoon Matsumoto returned to the federation office. Fujitani, who had arrived from Waialua, handed him a ticket for the evening steamship to Hilo. Defense attorney Lymar objected that the interpreter was not accurate: "The witness stated that at the time when these tickets were transferred there was one given to the witness and Fujitani held the other one, telling him, the witness, that he, Fujitani, was going to Hilo by the same boat for the purposes of making a speech."

The court interpreter, forty-five-year-old Kin'ichirō Maruyama, had come to Hawaii at the age of eight with his parents, who were part of the second group of government contract immigrants, and had graduated from a public high school in Honolulu. He had once caused an international incident by hiring a British ship to ferry twelve hundred Japanese workers to Vancouver, Canada, during the period when migration to the mainland was prohibited. Several years later he had been hired as a court interpreter, and by the time of the trial he had also opened up a law office. Maruyama had no legal credentials. His law office, like Makino's, probably handled procedures for immigrants who did not know English.

After high school Maruyama had returned to Niigata prefecture briefly for a conscription physical examination, but because he left his homeland at such a young age, Japan must have seemed like a foreign country to him. Maruyama had no problems speaking English, but his Japanese was a bit awkward. Compounding the problem, Japanese witnesses at the trial spoke in the dialects of the regions in which they were born. Reading the trial transcript, one cannot help feeling that he handled Japanese like a foreigner. In any case, only the Japanese defendants and several Japanese-language newspaper reporters listened to the testimony in Japanese. What Judge Banks, the prosecution, the defense attorneys, and the twelve jurors heard was Maruyama's interpretation, and the trial record itself was a transcript of Maruyama's English.

When Matsumoto boarded the *Maunakea,* a steamship that departed from Honolulu for Hilo at 3:00 P.M. on May 22, the passengers included Fujitani and a man named Taniguchi from the Aiea union who was also going to give speeches on the Big Island. When the ship docked at Hilo shortly after 7:00 A.M. the following morning (May 23), Matsumoto said that he went to stay at the Okino Hotel, a first-class Japanese establishment in the middle of Hilo, a short distance by foot from the Hawaii Island union office. Matsumoto went there at once to speak to Tsuruno-suke Koyama, Chikao Ishida, and Kaichi Miyamura, all of whom he was meeting for the first time.

After introducing himself and saying that he had come "by the orders of the federation of labor from Honolulu," they told him that because he was tired from the boat trip he should rest while waiting for their orders. Invited along by Fujitani, who was staying in the same hotel, Matsumoto spent a few days sightseeing at the erupting Kilauea volcano and other places with Taniguchi, I. Saitō, and Tsunehiko Murakami, another one of the defendants in the case.

On the evening of Thursday, May 27, his fifth night in Hilo, Matsumoto was chatting with Murakami and Saitō in his room at the Okino Hotel when a car from the Hawaii Island union came by to pick them up. By the time the three of them left the hotel, he said, it was dark outside. At this point in his testimony, Judge Banks adjourned the trial until the following morning. Throughout the trial Banks became impatient if the day's proceedings went one minute past noon, and he ended them even in the midst of important testimony. It might have been that he was simply a cranky old man (he was over sixty at the time), or he may have resented lunchtime being shortened.

As the *Honolulu Advertiser* pointed out, Matsumoto was the prosecution's "star witness." Indeed, he was the witness who could substantiate the charges in the indictment. Matsumoto had been indicted by the grand jury, but just before beginning interrogation of the prosecution witnesses, Heen had removed his name, along with that of I. Saitō, from the twenty-one defendants in the indictment. The prosecution had turned defendant Matsumoto into a state's witness.

On Friday, February 3, Matsumoto continued his testimony. The car sent from the Hawaii Island union, he said, drove along Hilo bay. On the coast about four miles from downtown Hilo was the annex of the Matano Hotel, called the Seaside Club. It once had been a club operated by Caucasians, and was used for receptions when the Imperial Navy training ships or the consul general visited from Honolulu and for local prefectural association gatherings. Nearby were several fresh seafood restaurants. One was a small teahouse diagonally across the street from the Seaside Club. (At the trial the name of this establishment was never raised. No one now remembers its name.) The car stopped here.

Matsumoto arrived at this teahouse between 8:00 and 9:00 P.M. on May 27. Four men were waiting for Matsumoto, Saitō, and Murakami in a private room. In addition to Miyamura, Koyama, and Ishida of the Hawaii Island union, there was a man named Yoshimura, who had come from Kahuku Plantation on Oahu. Under cross-examination, Matsumoto added that they had waited to hold their meeting until Yoshimura arrived in Hilo that day. (With so many Japanese names mentioned, the jurors became confused, and asked questions about who was in the car and whom they met.) After introducing themselves, the men sat around a table covered with a white cloth. After food was served and some general conversation, Kaichi Miyamura addressed the group, saying "that an order came from federation office as to what we were going to do, that 'you all here must keep this secret; that you must not tell this to anybody else. In case you do so, tell this thing to any outsider and to bring any damage to the cause of this strike, that the federation publicly suppression of my name and also the name of all the relatives.'" Then Miyamura asked, "Would you solemnly swear that you close the matter that will be discussed here?" After Matsumoto and the others swore to do so, Miyamura went to the heart of the matter.

"Then he told us that there is a man named Sakamaki who lives at Eight Miles, who is an interpreter who is obstructing the cause," Matsumoto testified. "He told us to kill this man with powder." After Matsumoto and the three others thought it over, Matsumoto testified, "I consented, all three consented." Miyamura rose from his seat and called each of the four men outside the room separately. To Matsumoto, Miyamura gave a $100 bill for expenses and told him to do his best. "I told him 'all right. I will consented,'" said Matsumoto. Leaving the others at the teahouse, Matsumoto, Murakami, and Saitō left for the Okino Hotel in the car that had picked them up. From conversation in the car, Matsumoto learned that Saitō and Murakami had also received $100 each from Miyamura. Back at the hotel, they retired to their rooms and went to sleep.

The *Honolulu Advertiser* reported Matsumoto's testimony under the headline "Dinner Party at the Tea House, Conspiracy Discussed." But Kaichi Miyamura, the defendant who had allegedly ordered the killing of Sakamaki, had returned to Japan, and he was in no position to refute Matsumoto's testimony. A contractor with several hundred workers under him at Wainaku Plantation near Hilo, Miyamura had also operated a large store at the plantation. The *Hawaii jinbutsu hyōron* described him as "a rustic man" but "quite well educated. . . . He is affable in the way he smiles as he deals with others. . . . He has an inborn dignity and is kind and courteous to his subordinates and is astute." [10] Of those active in the 1920 strike, some, like Tsutsumi, joined the movement of their own volition. But others, like Miyamura, were pressed into organizing locally and found themselves involved before they knew it.

At the time of the indictment the prosecution announced that it would request the Japanese government to extradite not only Kaichi Miyamura but also Eijūrō Yokoo and Yōkichi Satō, but it never made any formal request to do so. According to Yokoo's wife, Toyo, Yokoo was never investigated by the Japanese authorities.

Matsumoto testified that early the next morning (May 28), Miyamura arrived alone at the Okino Hotel, where he met with Matsumoto, Saitō, and Murakami in a large room on the second floor. He told them that he could not find Yoshimura, who had paid his bill at his hotel and left. (This Yoshimura was thought to have returned to Japan after the strike ended, and is referred to in the trial records with no first initial.) "[Miyamura] told us that he doesn't think that Yoshimura would disclose the conversation to any outsider but in case you fellows should run away, that [he] would notify the home government and publicly suppress your father's name and also your family that is living in Japan." Miyamura also reminded them of the need for secrecy. For the first time he mentioned compensation for killing Sakamaki. If they succeeded, each would be paid $5,000. "You came here for the cause of the twenty-five thousand laborers," Miyamura told the three men. "If you are going to help them I want you to succeed in this thing." Matsumoto testified that he and the other two vowed, "If the killing of Sakamaki with powder would help the cause of the twenty-five thousand laborers we would do so, and we consented to do so."

As soon as the conversation ended, Matsumoto went alone to Olaa Plantation, where he had lived for four years. He was familiar with the lay of the land, but he wanted to take a look at the Sakamaki house, the target of the attack, and he also intended to see what kind of anti-strike activities Sakamaki was engaged in. But Matsumoto was recovering from an operation for appendicitis and felt sick, he said, so as soon as he reached Olaa, he found lodging and took to bed. He spent several days there, only going out to a nearby eatery, Ikedaya, when he was hungry. It was there that he met Saitō, who arrived a few days later to make contact with him. Saitō informed him that Murakami had left for Oahu to see his wife and children and that he should do nothing until Murakami returned from Honolulu.

After Murakami came back to Hilo on the morning of June 3, said Matsumoto, Saitō at once contacted him with a message from Murakami to go to Hilo right away. Matsumoto, who was not feeling well, was still in bed, but he arose about noon and hired a car to take him to Hilo, where Murakami had taken a room at the Matano Hotel. It was already past 1:30 P.M. when Matsumoto arrived. "Murakami," he said, "told us that 'Everything is ready, that we will do the work tonight, that I am going to leave for Honolulu tomorrow.'" Still feeling unwell, Matsumoto asked a Dr. Takeda for an injection and went to rest until nightfall at his cousin's place on Waiakea Plantation, near Hilo.

As directed by Murakami, Matsumoto went to the Matano Hotel at 8:00 P.M. Murakami left the hotel soon thereafter to hire a car to drive to Olaa Plantation. Matsumoto waited at the corner, dressed in a suit and necktie and wearing a hunting cap, and Saitō waited at a different corner. Arriving in a large model Hudson (large enough to seat seven people) with a driver hailing from Okinawa, Murakami picked up the two men to drive to Olaa. Matsumoto recalled that Sakamaki often went to evening meetings at the Japanese Church, so he had the car stop there first. Peering through a window, Matsumoto did indeed see Sakamaki, who later came out and got in his car to go home. The Hudson carrying Matsumoto and the others followed him to railroad tracks near the Sakamaki house. Murakami had the car stop just before the tracks. He got out with Saitō, who was also riding in the backseat, and the two spoke in hushed tones in the dark for about thirty minutes, according to Matsumoto's testimony. Meanwhile Matsumoto sat waiting in the front passenger seat. When the two men returned to the car, Matsumoto said,

"Saitō told me that Murakami told him that he brought some powder from Honolulu; that he is going to set the powder tonight." This, Matsumoto said, was when he first found out that dynamite would be used to kill Sakamaki.

The Hudson moved on slowly. Murakami and Saitō jumped out just before Sakamaki's house and disappeared into the darkness. The car, carrying Matsumoto and the driver, drove on to Shipman Road to wait for the two men as arranged. After twenty or thirty minutes, Murakami and Saitō came running breathlessly. Jumping into the backseat, they told the driver "to start the machine and go fast." The driver pushed the accelerator to the floor and sped off toward Hilo. Matsumoto did not recall hearing the noise of dynamite exploding. He was dropped off near his cousin's house in Waiakea where he had spent the day.

The following morning, June 4, Matsumoto went to the office of the Hawaii Island union to pick up Murakami's travel expenses so that Murakami could return to Honolulu that afternoon. Miyamura welcomed Matsumoto in good spirits, telling him, "You did good. You done your work good." He gave Matsumoto $50.

When Matsumoto handed the money to Murakami, who was waiting at the Matano Hotel, Murakami told him that apart from his hotel expenses, he had used about $50 for hiring the car and other expenses. He showed Matsumoto a memo with his account. As there was little time before the ship's departure, Matsumoto advanced him $50 from his own pocket, and Murakami left on the *Maunakea* for Honolulu.

In those days the *Maunakea* was the only Inter Island Steamship Company ship sailing between Honolulu and Hilo. It departed Honolulu in the evening and arrived in Hilo the following morning, then returned to Honolulu the following afternoon. The next ship after Murakami's was not until Monday, June 7, at 3:00 P.M. Lying in bed all day, Matsumoto waited at the Matano Hotel. On the morning of June 7 he went to the Hawaii Island union office to pick up travel expenses for himself and Saitō. He spoke not only to Miyamura but also to Koyama and Ishida. "I said that Saitō suggested going back to Honolulu today and I think that's a good plan, Saitō told me that it's dangerous to stay here." Matsumoto continued his testimony: "He (Ishida) says, 'The officials are investigating very rigidly and it is not good for you fellows to stay here. You go back to the Matano Hotel and wait for me, I will bring the money.'"

Matsumoto was still feeling very tired, and as he waited in the hotel, he fell asleep. He could not recall how much time had passed, but when he woke up Ishida had not yet arrived. Impatient, Matsumoto looked out the hotel window and caught a glimpse of a police car. Saitō had already left the Matano Hotel that morning, so Matsumoto decided that it would be dangerous to wait any longer. Avoiding the front entrance, he left by the emergency stairs. As he cut through Mooheau Park on his way to the Hawaii Island union office, Matsumoto noticed Ishida sitting on a park bench. Ishida rushed up to him, saying that he heard that Matsumoto and Saitō had been arrested. Ishida went to get some money at the office and returned to give Matsumoto $100, half of which Matsumoto gave to Saitō, whom he met later. To be on the safe side, Matsumoto and Saitō boarded the ship separately, each buying his own ticket after boarding.

After arriving in Honolulu the following morning, Matsumoto went directly to the Federation of Japanese Labor headquarters. Although the dynamite exploded, Matsumoto and the others had failed to kill Sakamaki as ordered by the federation. But according to Matsumoto, Tsutsumi or Hoshino told him, "You made a success of your work in Hilo. We get the report from Hilo that all the spies up there are now afraid and this was a great success." The other defendants—Miyazawa, Gotō, Baba, Y. Satō, S. Satō, Yokoo, Kawamata, Takizawa, Tomota, Furushō, Kondō, and Fujitani—who were also at the office, thanked him for having "done well."

The *Honolulu Advertiser* described Matsumoto's testimony as substantiating the prosecution's charges. Matsumoto, an accomplice who knew the lay of the land so well that he had to participate in the alleged crime even though he was so ill that he should have been in bed, recalled the events of two years before as if they occurred the previous day. When Heen's questioning touched on details, Matsumoto replied while looking at notes in his hand. Defense attorney Lymar objected, but even after warnings from Judge Banks, he persisted in using notes to confirm his memory. The *Honolulu Advertiser* surmised, "It seems apparent that the defense will rely largely upon the impeachment of the witness for the testimony." But in fact, Lymar had raised objections on grounds of irrelevancy, leading the witness, no prima facie, and hearsay. Judge Banks summarily overruled 99 percent of his objections.

Before Matsumoto took the witness stand on Monday, February 6, the fifth day of the trial, Lymar objected that the conversation between Matsumoto and Saitō described in Matsumoto's testimony was not directly related to the crime of conspiracy. Sustaining this objection, Judge Banks told the jury not to consider that evidence at all, or any evidence of conversations between Matsumoto and Saitō after the alleged explosion about impending danger.

Resuming his direct examination, prosecutor Heen had Matsumoto repeat the names of each defendant who had congratulated him on dynamiting Sakamaki's house. Then he began questioning Matsumoto about his second trip to Hilo.

About five or six months after the night of the crime, Matsumoto said that he and Saitō boarded the ship for Hilo. Miyamura had told them that if all went well they would receive $5,000 from the Federation of Japanese Labor headquarters in Honolulu, but despite their repeated attempts the two men received nothing. Deciding they had no choice but to negotiate directly with Miyamura, Matsumoto and Saitō had once again headed for Hilo. At the Hawaii Island union office they met with Ishida and S. Sato and also appealed to Chūhei Hoshino, who had returned to Hilo from federation headquarters. Ishida and the others kept responding, "At that time, Miyamura and Koyama wasn't there. They will give me an answer later on." Two or three days later Matsumoto and Saitō talked in their room on the fourth floor of the Matano Hotel with the Hawaii Island union members Ishida, Hoshino, Sato, and Tomota (the latter was a leader in the Waimanalo Plantation union on Oahu, an obvious mistake on the part of Matsumoto).

"They told us," said Matsumoto, "that Miyamura [who had actually promised the $5,000] and Koyama [who was president of the Hawaii Island union] wasn't able to come." Instead Hoshino told them, "There's going to be a meeting of the representatives in Honolulu, that either I or Ishida would be one of those meeting and that they would put the thing at the meeting, and asked me to wait until that time." Hoshino also promised "that if the Oahu union refuses to pay this money, the Hawaii union would pay you." According to Matsumoto, he asked Fujitani, director of the Oahu union, to accompany him on this second trip to Hilo so as not to be manipulated.

The representatives' meeting that Hoshino said would settle the $5,000 issue was held November 23, 1920, to discuss measures to counter the wage increase announced by the HSPA. Hoshino, who came to Honolulu as a delegate from the Hawaii Island union, stayed at the Saikaiya Hotel, where Matsumoto and Saitō visited him and asked him to bring up the $5,000 issue at the meeting. Matsumoto also went to the

Kyōrakukan, where the meeting was being held, with a request to speak to the federation officers. He said this was because he was unable to comprehend the federation financial report in the *Hawaii hōchi* that detailed $6,300 in expenditures for newspaper printing and $500 for flyer advertisements.[11]

At Kyōrakukan he asked to talk with Tsutsumi, who was staying with Miyazawa and Gotō to attend the meeting as "advisers."

HEEN: "Did you have a talk with Tsutsumi at that time?"

MATSUMOTO: "I asked him, 'There is a big association in United States, headed by Mr. Gompers, and their expenses in newspapers and magazine is about $300 a month. This is a new organization and I can't see how you could spend over two thousand dollars a month, and I came to ask you how you spent that money.'"

Q: "All right. What else?"

A: "He told me that 'you are only a farmer, you better not say anything and go back and keep quiet.'"

A: "Then what happened?"

A: "I told him 'I don't know how educated you are, and even if you hold the head secretaryship of the association.' I said, 'I am doing what you are doing for these laborers, and what I am doing for the laborer doesn't make any difference,' and I told him 'and don't be so saucy.'"

Q: "Well, what happened then?"

A: "We had an altercation there; the doors came to be locked, when about twenty of them that were there came forward."

Q: "Well, who were these others?"

A: "Well, I had an altercation at this time and I could not remember all of them but I could remember four or five."

Q: "Well, who were these four or five, do you remember?"

A: "Tsutsumi, Miyazawa, Satō, Furusho."

Q: "Well, what sort of altercation did you have there?"

A: "While we were having this talk about 'you are fresh, go back and keep quiet,' etc., somebody says 'kill him.' Well, I got mad myself when I heard that. There were lots of people in back of me, in rear of me, and I struck Tsutsumi."

Whether or not Matsumoto used the Japanese words *Koroshite shimae!* (meaning "Kill him!") is a critical point in his testimony. When interpreting Matsumoto's testimony about Miyamura's order to kill Sakamaki, the court interpreter used the phrase "Kill him." But in the case of the Kyōrakukan altercation it would have been more natural for someone to use the expression *Yatte shimae* (Get him!) or *Noshite shimae* (Let him have it!). If Matsumoto did in fact testify that someone had said "Yatte shimae" or something similar, any murderous intent would have been ambiguous. The phrase could simply have meant "Beat him up!" rather than "Kill him!" However, when the court interpreter used the words "kill him" in English, that clearly showed intent to kill. The interpreter's use of "kill" in both cases raises lingering questions.

> HEEN: "Who struck Tsutsumi?"
>
> MATSUMOTO: "I struck Tsutsumi. Then everybody jumped me, and I and Tsutsumi grappled. While I was grappling with Tsutsumi, somebody from my left struck me in the head with a bottle. . . . I saw Satō with a broken bottle in his hand."

Matsumoto then heard something breaking. Furushō held a broken pitcher in his hands, about to attack Matsumoto. Matsumoto continued his testimony: "I know that I was going to be killed there so I was going to do my best; I struck the man who was in the rear of me with my elbow. I think I have knocked down two or three and did all I can at that place."

Matsumoto, who had injured his head, was so angered by this altercation that he finally went to the police to make a complaint of assault at the end of November 1920. Immediately afterward, Seigo Kondō visited him at the Tōhoku Hotel where he was staying. Matsumoto reported, "He told me that 'you already made complaint about this assault,' and he asked me if I am going to disclose the dynamiting matter. . . . I told him I am going to confess. I told him that 'some of the officials of the association is not right and I am going to fight them.' . . . He told me to wait. 'I am going to have talk with Baba and we will satisfy you,' and asked me to wait." After placating Matsumoto, Kondō left.

Among the defendants, the forty-three-year-old Seigo Kondō was particularly striking. With his intimidating thick neck and broad shoulders, he appeared larger than he in fact was. At the time of the grand jury indictment, the *Honolulu Star Bulletin* described him as "reputed to be the 'man Friday' of the real leaders of the federation." [12] Kondō's name was not once mentioned in documents related to the federation. He had no direct connection with the Federation of Japanese Labor, nor did he frequent its headquarters.

Kondō was the eldest son of a well-to-do family in Sanjō city, Niigata prefecture. When he was ten years old, his father, who had served on the town assembly for many years, drove out Kondō's mother and married a younger woman. Rebelling aginst his father, Kondō stopped going to school, and eventually he sailed to Hawaii as a coal stoker aboard a steamship. He worked at various jobs, starting with cane field labor, but by the time of the strike he was running a successful fishery in Pearl Harbor. He also owned a pool hall and other establishments in Pearl City. Some said he was a gambler, but it seems certain that he was a local boss. When striking workers evicted from plantations arrived in Pearl City, his chivalrous spirit prompted him to help them out, and eventually he and his followers joined in the strikers' patrols. According to Matsumoto, Kondō was a troubleshooter who stood between the strikers and the scabs.

With Baba in tow, Kondō visited Matsumoto once again at the Tōhoku Hotel. According to Matsumoto, Baba told him, "Even if the federation had ordered you to do this, you have gone and done this and you will go to jail for it." Matsumoto replied, "I don't care what will happen. Some of these officials are not good; bad officials, and they are causing all this trouble to the laborers, and I am going to put them away." Baba tried to placate him. "I am going to have a talk with headquarters," he said, "and we will satisfy you." Kondō gave Matsumoto $300 for lodging and for medicine for his head injury.

When Matsumoto again pressed Kondō about the $5,000 some time later, Kondō told him, "I did my best but I couldn't get the money for you." Accompanied by Saitō, Matsumoto then went to Ewa Plantation to see Murakami. In front of the Ewa Plantation company store, he told Murakami that since the promised money had not been paid he and Saitō were going to give themselves up. "As to yourself," he added, "why don't you come up like a man and give yourself up?" Murakami, who was in the middle of work, answered that he would meet with them that night.

That night when Murakami went to see Matsumoto in his new lodgings at the Kobayashi Hotel, Matsumoto was out, so Murakami was able to speak only to Saitō. The following night, when Murakami arrived at the hotel with Kondō, he saw Matsumoto lying on his bed. "You're a hell of a fellow," he said, complaining that he had come all the way from Ewa to see Matsumoto only to find that he was not in. "You are a friend of Saitō and you are open with Saitō," Matsumoto replied, "but you don't speak open with me and for that reason I left Saitō here and went to the movie picture show."

Suddenly Detective McDuffie from the Honolulu police poked his head in from the next room. "You have given this information—in connection with the putting powder on Sakamaki's house—to McDuffie to send us to jail," shouted Murakami. "Do you think that I could move McDuffie?" replied Matsumoto. "He came [so we could] give ourselves up."

In sum, Matsumoto's testimony suggested that he went to the authorities to get even with the federation leaders. After the dynamiting of the Sakamaki house, not only was Matsumoto unable to collect the $5,000 promised him by Miyamura, but the federation leaders derided him as a "farmer" and gave him such a beating that he barely escaped with his life. After Matsumoto filed assault charges against the federation headquarters leaders, Kondō and Baba tried to persuade him to withdraw them and to accept hush money for the Sakamaki incident. But the promised $5,000 never turned up, so Matsumoto made up his mind to turn himself in, accepting imprisonment for himself and taking along with him, and purging the movement of, the self-serving federation leaders who had squandered strike funds contributed by the hard-pressed laborers.

Heen ended his questioning of Matsumoto by asking about his relationship to Sakamaki.

> HEEN: "Did you have some misunderstanding with Sakamaki when you were working on Olaa?"
>
> MATSUMOTO: "I had some trouble with an old man that was there and this old man went and complained to Sakamaki and Sakamaki went and told the camp police about the trouble between myself and the old man. Then the plantation police came to my place and told me that I am not needed there, for me to get out. Without asking me anything and without investigation. I was told to get out. So I thought Sakamaki had something to do with it. There was a man by the name of Miyake was working in the (plantation) store. [He] and another old man came to me and said, 'it is not Sakamaki who had said anything bad about you and got you out.'"

The misunderstanding was resolved, and on the urging of Miyake and the others, Matsumoto and Sakamaki shook hands. All this had taken place some six or seven years before, Matsumoto said, and he did not want to harass Sakamaki because of a personal grudge against him. His only motive for involvement in the dynamiting incident, he answered Heen, was solely for the twenty-five thousand striking workers.

In later testimony Jūzaburō Sakamaki confirmed what Matsumoto said. The misunderstanding between the two men had been resolved, and they had shaken hands. In cross-examination by Lymar, Sakamaki characterized Matsumoto as "a man of high temper" who "was constantly getting into fights and brawls." But according to Sakamaki, he had not seen Matsumoto since they had shaken hands, until he unexpectedly bumped into him on the morning of his testimony. "He waited for me on the stairs of the county building," said Sakamaki, "as I come down he bowed to me and smiled and says, 'Well, very sorry to give you this trouble,' and shake hands with me."

"Mr. Sakamaki," asked Lymar, "after this explosion, did you make the statement that Matsumoto was a man who had had a grudge against you and that he might well be capable of having done that?" "No, sir," Sakamaki replied simply.

DEFENSE ATTORNEY LYMAR'S CROSS-EXAMINATION

The central figure on the defense team, William Lymar, was much taller than prosecutor Heen, and his features were sharper too. He had a full head of wavy, blond hair and deep-set, nearly transparent blue eyes. In his unaccented, midwestern monotone Lymar began his cross-examination by tenaciously extracting from the taciturn Matsumoto details of his life in Hawaii.

Matsumoto's father had immigrated to Hawaii when Matsumoto was a young child. When Matsumoto turned sixteen, his father, whom he had not seen for many years, brought him over to Hawaii. Shortly after his arrival, the father died suddenly, and Matsumoto had to go to work, moving from one sugar plantation to another. At Olaa, where he stayed several years, Matsumoto may have intended to marry and settle down, but his trouble there got him fired, and once again he shifted from one plantation to another every five or six months. In his cross-examination Lymar tried to establish Matsumoto's character as volatile, impatient, and short-tempered. The profile that emerged during the cross-examination was of the unhappy life of an immigrant forced to find his way in a foreign country at an early age.

After Matsumoto admitted that he had been involved in assaults at various plantations, Lymar asked, "You have allowed this ungovernable temper of yours to reach such a pitch that you have taken ant poison in chagrin. Haven't you?" Matsumoto admitted that he consumed pesticide in a suicide attempt and was taken to the Ewa hospital in November 1919. He had just turned thirty. Only a few weeks after his discharge Fujitani had hired him to collect subscription fees for *Nippu jiji* at Waialua.

According to the *Honolulu Advertiser,* on February 7, as Lymar was turning to questions about the charges of indictment, Matsumoto, who had been on the witness stand for three days, appeared nervous and complained throughout the morning of feeling ill. Lymar's cross-examination sought to undermine the indictment by demonstrating that Matsumoto was not acquainted with the majority of the defendants, the federation officers who, he claimed, had issued orders for the conspiracy. He questioned Matsumoto about when and where he had met each defendant and what conversations they had.

To be consistent with his answers to Heen on direct questioning, Matsumoto desperately repeated the same testimony. There were pauses as his answers to Lymar's forceful interrogation were translated, and he was able to gain time as prosecution lawyers came to his rescue by raising objections. On top of this, Matsumoto's repeated claims of feeling ill brought him frequent recesses.

Lymar spent an especially long time on his testimony about defendant Baba. Lymar asked, "What kind of tone did Baba use in speaking to you, was it a low whisper?" Matsumoto initially replied it was an "ordinary tone of voice." But when Lymar pointed out that Baba had contracted influenza at the start of the strike and had not come into the office even in late May, Matsumoto added, "He looked sick." Matsumoto, however, never repudiated his testimony that Baba had given the order to go to Hilo.

When asked what he talked about with the other defendants when he received his order from Baba, Matsumoto was evasive: "I couldn't remember exactly." "Some were going in and out of the place and some were attending to their business." "Some I talked with them standing up as they coming out of the place or coming into the office." "There's a long table in the center there with the pile of newspapers. We had conversation at that table." Yet he gave the name of each defendant, saying, "I remember distinctly the person—"as if reviewing to show his testimony was consistent. Lymar's cross-examination was persistent and detailed. Yet he kept asking about the same matters and was unable to get to the heart of the important points. He also had a habit of withdrawing his questions and rephrasing them. As these overlapped, the meaning of the questions became confusing even to others.

On February 9 Lymar began his cross-examination about the assault at the Kyōrakukan Hotel. He asked Matsumoto whether he had not asked Tsutsumi or any of those present "for money from the benefit fund of the labor union" before the altercation began. Matsumoto replied, "I couldn't say I needed any money at that time." When he discharged from the Ewa hospital after his suicide attempt, he said, he had "hundred to hundred & fifty dollars." But according to Matsumoto, he received no wages as a member of the picket troop but simply was reimbursed for expenses incurred. He was told that eventually they would be given reward money, but none was forthcoming after the strike ended. That was why he was so angry, he said, when he heard that large sums of money had been used by federation headquarters. The only sum he had tried to get from the federation was the $5,000 he had been promised for the Sakamaki incident, he insisted.

LYMAR: "About a week before this assault of Tsutsumi at the Kyōrakukan Hotel, you didn't meet Takizawa, one of these defendants, tell him that you were broke, and ask for the money?"

MATSUMOTO: "No, I had not."

LYMAR: "You didn't say to Takizawa on that occasion, 'I am broke, I hardly know how to get anything to eat. I have done much for the association and it ought to help me now,' you didn't say that?

MATSUMOTO: "It can't be, because I was working at that time for Sōma (Inn at Wahiawa) and I was not so hard up as that and I haven't made any demand of money upon Takizawa."

LYMAR: "And did you then not say to Takizawa, 'if the association does not help me, I will do them all kinds of harm'?"

MATSUMOTO: "No, I have not."

LYMAR: "And at the time of that assault, is it not true that you owed money, outstanding bills for auto hire at that time?"

MATSUMOTO: "I have no personal debt owing as auto hire, but while I was a picket, I had some auto hire that I had used, some automobile, and the bill has not been paid."

LYMAR: "Didn't you tell Kondō all of this about your outstanding bills for auto hire, your outstanding bill with Sōma, and other debts, didn't you tell Kondō that shortly before this assault?"

MATSUMOTO: "I remember having a talk with Kondō after the assault, when he came to me to—as a go-between to have this assault—have the matter settled up."

Matsumoto did admit that after he had received $300 from Kondō to treat his wound, he went to the Oahu union office to see Kawamata.

LYMAR: "Did you not go to Kawamata, one of these defendants, and ask him to pay your money so that you could get away to Japan?"

MATSUMOTO: "At the time I received three hundred dollars, I was asked not to tell."

He also said that Kawamata suggested that he leave for Japan. Kawamata assured him that since the federation ordered the dynamiting, he would be paid as promised and should keep his mouth shut. He continued, "The same day that I was assaulted, I made up my mind to give myself up. I asked Matsumura what is the best to be done, and he told me he thinks it best to give myself up."

This was the first time that the name Tamotsu Matsumura came up at the trial. In the FBI report of January 22, 1921, there are numerous mentions of Tamotsu Matsumura, who was thirty-six years old at the time of the trial. After graduating from middle school in Kumamoto, he worked as a minor clerk in the Taiwan colonial government and then left for Hawaii in 1909 to become secretary to Emō Imamura, the head of the Honganji Hawaii mission temple. Shortly after he arrived in Hawaii, he was arrested on suspicion of spying when he was discovered wandering near Diamond Head taking photographs of American military fortifications. After being released for lack of evidence, he became principal of the Kaawa Japanese-language school, where several years later he was fired on suspicion of embezzlement. When the school burned down, Matsumura was investigated on suspicion of arson, but the case was also dismissed for lack of evidence.

According to military intelligence, "He was a close friend of former Consul General Yada" and "was very prominently associated with the Japanese Federation of Labor, it being claimed that he was the silent head of that organization."[13] He was teaching at the Waialua Japanese-language school when the strike began. He was eager to give advice to the local union, and he also frequented federation headquarters. But Tsutsumi and the others, who considered him a dangerous opportunist, were wary of dealing with him.

Indeed, federation headquarters announced in the newspapers that Matsumura was a "planters' dog" who urged laborers at Waialua Plantation to return to work. The Military Intelligence report noted, "During the strike, he appeared to have had a break with the Hawaii Laborers' Association, and he went to work for the Hawaii Sugar Planters' Association. However, it was never believed that he was sincere in his efforts to aid the Hawaii Sugar Planters' Association, but that he did so for personal reasons."[14]

After the strike ended, Matsumura bought the *Hawaii chōhō* with remuneration received from the HSPA. Through the newspaper, he called for the restructuring of federation headquarters and made personal attacks on its leaders. In late December 1920 Terasaki reported in his diary, "Afternoon, Matsumura comes to the [*Hōchi*] company and says that there are improper funds of $_0,000 (illegible) issued secretly by the federation."[15] In other words, Matsumura was feeding information to Makino, who disliked the federation officers. Since the readership of the *Chōhō* was considerably smaller than that of the *Nippu* or *Hōchi*, Matsumura was fulfilling his aim by urging the *Hōchi* to make similar attacks on the federation.

Matsumoto testified that he had gone to Matsumura, known to be a "planters' dog," to seek advice on a legal matter. At first he did mention that it was his trouble with Sakamaki. Matsumura immediately took Matsumoto to see Frank Thompson, the HSPA lawyer who had duped Manlapit into issuing a stop strike order to the Filipino workers. Matsumoto talked with Thompson and with his partner John Cathcart, who was also an attorney for the HSPA. At the time of the trial, Cathcart was serving as special assistant prosecutor.

> LYMAR: "And that Matsumura told you, did he not, substantially this, 'You are in a tight place. One way to get immunity, to get out of this thing, is to go to Mr. Frank Thompson, the planters' attorney, and tell him that the labor union was responsible for blowing that thing up,' isn't that what he told you?"
>
> MATSUMOTO: "I have violated the law, I don't expect to get any remuneration."
>
> LYMAR: "Didn't Matsumura tell you it would be necessary to implicate all of these twelve men there on trial, it wasn't enough to implicate part of them, that every one of the twelve must be?"
>
> MATSUMOTO: "He told me to tell the truth, and I told the truth."
>
> LYMAR: "Between November, 1920, when the trouble took place and— between November of 1920 when this assault took place, and July or August, 1921, when the arrests were made, you were in Mr. Thompson's office over and over again, weren't you?"
>
> MATSUMOTO: "I did."

At the end of his four days of testimony, Matsumoto finally admitted that since the handing down of the indictment in August 1921, even when he was on the witness stand, he had been employed at Thompson's place on Tantalus. This meant that in the midst of the trial HSPA lawyer Thompson was taking care of, indeed providing a livelihood for, the most important territorial witness, the man who had confessed to attempted murder in the Sakamaki dynamiting case. Incidentally, no charges were filed on the complaint that Matsumoto had lodged concerning the Kyōrakukan assault, and the matter was not pursued further.

THE DRIVER ARAGAKI TESTIFIES

The third prosecution witness, Goichi Hamai, was the chief clerk at the Okino Hotel where Matsumoto had stayed in Hilo at the time the Sakamaki house was dynamited. Referring to a thick hotel register (prosecution exhibit E), he testified that the names Matsumoto, Saitō, and Murakami were entered as guests in rooms 19, 20, and 21 beginning on May 23, 1920; and that two days later they moved to rooms 12, 13, and 14. For some reason the prosecution did not submit the Matano Hotel guest register for the important night, June 3, when Murakami returned from Honolulu and the crime was committed.

The last witness of the day was I. Aragaki (the fourth prosecution witness), the driver hired by Murakami on the night of the crime whom Matsumoto had said was from Okinawa.[16] He testified that on the night of the crime one year and eight months before, after picking up three Japanese in Hilo, he first went to a stable near the Olaa church where he stopped the car for about thirty minutes. He was ordered to stop again near the railroad tracks for about fifteen minutes while the two passengers in the backseat stepped out to discuss something. He started the engine again and, shortly after passing the Olaa sugar company office, he was told to go slow. The two passengers in the back jumped out and disappeared, and he stopped the car at Shipman Road where he waited for about thirty minutes. The two men came running to the car and yelled at him to drive as fast as he could toward Hilo. Aragaki found out the following morning that the Sakamaki house had been dynamited. Aragaki testified, "A few days afterwards, I found a pistol, revolver, fully loaded on the right side pocket in the rear right door." According to Aragaki, he thought someone would come to pick it up, but in the summer of 1921, after a year had passed, he went to Chikao Ishida, the principal of the Japanese-language school at Wainaku Plantation, to ask his advice. (The trial records show that at this point prosecutor Heen pointed to one of the defendants to have Aragaki confirm that it was Ishida, the school principal. Even by the eighth day of the trial, Heen had not yet memorized the faces of the fifteen defendants seated in two rows on the defendants' bench and pointed to the wrong man. Even after Aragaki said, "He is a small man with eye-glasses," Heen was unable to pick him out. In the end Heen asked Aragaki to leave the stand and place his hand on Ishida's shoulder.)

According to Aragaki's testimony, when he asked Ishida about the revolver that was left in his car, Ishida said, "If you don't need that pistol wouldn't you give it to me?"

> HEEN: "I will ask you whether or not you recall any talk about the strike in 1920 and about the dynamiting of Sakamaki's house first and after that you mentioned about the finding of the pistol?"
>
> ARAGAKI: "No."

Heen was attempting to establish that Ishida asked for the revolver so that he could destroy the evidence, but even after Heen asked the question again in several different ways, Aragaki still replied in the negative. Finally the frustrated Heen asked, "Do you recall having a conversation with me at my office about two or three days ago? Do you recall saying at that time that you called on Ishida one night and you happened to talk about the strike and also about the dynamiting, and then you said, 'By the way, I remember taking three men up there that night of the dynamiting, and found the pistol, and he asked you for it'?"

Defense attorney Lymar objected, but finally Aragaki answered to Heen's satisfaction: "I went to Ishida's place and told him I found a pistol in my car and asked him what to do with it. He asked me when I found it. I told him that the day after that Sakamaki's house was powdered I found the revolver in my car. He asked me who that pistol belongs to. I told him, 'I don't know who it belongs to.' He says, 'If you don't need it, won't you give it to me?' I gave it to him."

In his cross-examination, Lymar pressed Aragaki on two important points: the time that Aragaki said he picked up the three men and confirmation of their facial features. Matsumoto had testified that he got into the Hudson after 8:00 P.M. Calculating backward from the time of the blast at shortly after 11:00 P.M., this time fits. But according to Ara-

gaki's recollection, it was about 6:30 P.M. Yet he also testified that because "it was dark" he could not make out Matsumoto's face, even
though it is still quite light at that hour in June. Even without bright
moonlight, it should have been possible to make out a passenger's face
in the reflection from the headlights. Matsumoto had sat next to the
driver, and at Shipman Road the two had waited together in the car.

> LYMAR: "Isn't this true, that you really are not at all sure whether this man
> Matsumoto was sitting in the front seat with you, but that he went down for
> the prosecution here a few months ago to Hilo and presented himself to you
> and told you, 'I am Matsumoto,' and that's the reason you are saying that he
> was Matsumoto?"
>
> ARAGAKI: "Yes."

Even in the middle of this important questioning, because it was after noon Judge Banks adjourned the court. Aragaki had been on the witness stand for fifty minutes or so, but he was not recalled to testify the
following day. Matsumoto had testified that he was in the car when he
was told for the first time that dynamite was to be used to kill Sakamaki.
Saitō said that "Murakami told him that he brought some powder from
Honolulu; that he is going to set the powder tonight." Aragaki could
have heard this conversation in the driver's seat, but Lymar did not give
him a chance to confirm this point in cross-examination.

ANOTHER KEY PROSECUTION WITNESS, I. SAITŌ

The fifth witness for the prosecution, I. Saitō, escorted to the witness
stand by interpreter Maruyama, hesitantly swore to tell only the truth.
Saitō, whose first name remains unknown, was the only other defendant
(besides Matsumoto) whose charges Heen dismissed before the trial.

In contrast to the rotund Matsumoto, Saitō was tall and thin. He
wore gold-rimmed glasses, and his eyes darted about nervously as he testified. The twenty-seven-year-old Saitō was five years younger than
Matsumoto. His brother had brought him over to Hawaii when he was
sixteen, and he worked on a sugar plantation doing the lowest-paid
holehole work. After a few years in the cane fields, he became a hand on
an interisland steamer and worked as a stevedore. Ten months before the
strike, he had started working at Waipahu Plantation as a *hapai,* loading
cut sugarcane. After being evicted as a striker, Saitō worked as a concrete
mixer at a military base. About two months later he was called back to
Waipahu Plantation by Shōshichirō Furushō, the president of the Wai-

pahu Plantation union. Furushō instructed him "to go and find out who is obstructing the strike and also to stop anybody going back to work on the plantation." He was put in charge of a picket troop at Waipahu Plantation at about the same time that Matsumoto became involved in the picket troop at Wahiawa.

The gist of Saitō's testimony was that on May 22, 1920, federation secretary Noboru Tsutsumi telephoned the Waipahu union picket troop leader, Takematsu, with orders to send Saitō to Hilo. Takematsu told him to get the details from Furushō at the Oahu union headquarters. He left Waipahu on the noon train. After he reached Honolulu, he went to the Oahu union office, arriving at about 2:00 P.M. Furushō told him that one person had been chosen from each Oahu plantation to go to Hilo. Saitō was to go as the representative from Waipahu, and he was to act on orders received from the Hawaii Island union officers.

Saitō testified that Takizawa and Kawamata, also from Waipahu, gave him the same orders. With $50 Furushō gave him, Saitō hurried to board the *Maunakea,* which was about to leave for Hilo. As it was close to departure time, Saitō purchased his ticket on the ship, and only after he had boarded did he notice that Murakami, whom he had known at Ewa, was also on board. He testified that he met Fujitani and Matsumoto for the first time after arriving in Hilo. Saitō also corroborated Matsumoto's testimony about the May 27 dinner when Miyamura ordered the killing of Sakamaki, about Miyamura's threat that they would be publicly labeled "planters' dogs" and would be ashamed to show themselves in public if they ran off as Yoshimura had, and about Miyamura's promise of a $5,000 reward.

To establish that the conspiracy presented in the indictment had taken place, it was legally necessary to have at least two witnesses. The prosecution clearly was attempting to establish the validity of the indictment by turning Matsumoto and Saitō into the prosecution's witnesses in return for a dismissal of charges against them.

Saitō's testimony about June 3, the night of the crime, neatly corroborated what Matsumoto said had happened up to the time the Hudson stopped at the railroad tracks, and he testified in more detail about what went on after that:

Myself and Murakami got off the car, to the side of the road. Murakami told me at that time that what he went to Honolulu for was to get some powder. He told me if I knew how to fix powder. I told him 'I haven't handled any powder before,' and I told him I don't know. Then he told me that he will fix the powder. 'Have you got a handkerchief?' Then I have got three strips from my handkerchief and handed that over to him. The powder that length of powder (indicating about a foot) was at three places . . . tied it three places.

Murakami had brought the dynamite wrapped in a black cloth. Using Matsumoto's flashlight, Murakami attached the fuses to the dynamite before wrapping the handkerchief around it. Their preparations completed, Saitō and Murakami returned to the car. After jumping out of the slowly moving vehicle just before Sakamaki's house, Saitō and Murakami crept under the floor of the house and set the dynamite under what they thought was the kitchen.

SAITō: "I had a pistol and Murakami told me to give it to him, so I gave it to him. I put the powder underneath that place. Murakami saw where I was putting the thing, and he told me to put it farther in. Then he gave me the pistol and he told me to watch, and he went and put the powder two foot farther than where I had put the powder before, farther in. He lighted the thing with a cigaret. We ran towards the automobile and get into the automobile."

At this point, Saitō's testimony differed from Matsumoto's. He said that it had not been decided where the car would pick the two men up. Saitō saw a black shadow ahead of him in the moonlight and, thinking it was the car, ran toward it. It was Saitō who shouted to the driver, "Start the car and drive fast," as soon as he jumped in the back. Saitō then added, "Afraid of being arrested by the police, the clothes that I wore at that time, it was working clothes, I threw that away."

Oddly, although the two men had taken so much care in planning and devising the dynamiting, Saitō had mistakenly left the revolver, the most traceable object, in the car.

The day after the crime, Murakami, who was returning to Honolulu, told Saitō that "the work has been done." Three days later Saitō left Hilo on the *Maunakea,* boarding separately from Matsumoto. As a precaution, he told Heen, on the trip to Hilo he used as an alias the name of an Okinawan acquaintance, A. Akamine, without permission, and he did the same on his return trip to Honolulu as well.

The passenger list of the *Maunakea* departing Honolulu for Hilo on May 22 (prosecution exhibit F) contained one hundred twenty names. "Akamine" was one of them. It immediately followed the names H. Fujitani, M. Taniguchi (an Oahu union member), H. Tabata (same), T. Murakami, and J. Matsumoto. Among the federation members only Saitō had used a pseudonym. From the passenger list it is clear that "Akamine" boarded with the other federation members, but this seems a careless act for someone cautious enough to use an alias.

The passenger list of the *Maunakea* departing Hilo for Honolulu on June 8 (prosecution exhibit G) also listed the name Akamine. Although both Saitō and Matsumoto testified that they were careful to board the ship separately, "A. Akamine" was listed directly after "J. Matsumoto" on the passenger list.

Matsumoto testified that on his return from Hilo he had gone immediately to federation headquarters, where Tsutsumi and the other defendants thanked him. Warned not to go near the office by Furushō, Saitō stayed away. It was only toward the end of June, when Furushō contacted him, that Saitō visited federation headquarters. Waiting for him were Waipahu union members Furushō, Kawamata, and Takizawa, who told him, "'You did a fine work, and all the spies of the plantation are afraid now.'"[17] Saitō told them that since he had violated the law and could not stay in Hawaii any longer, he wanted return fare to Japan. Kawamata promised that he would arrange for payment of the promised $5,000 at a special meeting to be held soon, but when nothing was forthcoming, he went with Matsumoto to Hilo to ask for the money.

In his testimony about the Kyōrakukan assault incident, Saitō said that it started when he, Matsumoto, J. Suzuki, and D. Suzuki were talking about the federation financial report one night at the Tōhoku Hotel. Saying "it is for us to go and investigate," Matsumoto stood up and ran off. Concerned, Saitō and Suzuki followed him twenty minutes later.

> SAITŌ: "As I put my foot on the steps, I heard the voice, 'kill him,' and as soon as I heard that, I jumped into the place to part them, with Suzuki."

On February 13, after a weekend recess, Heen probed Saitō's memory about the phrase "kill him."

> SAITŌ: "As I entered the place, they were grappling and Furushō was about to strike with a pitcher. I struck him on the ribs. Tsutsumi was knocked down, he was on the floor and holding Matsumoto's leg. Tsutsumi was about to get up and grapple with Matsumoto and I told him to stop, wait a minute. I think then Matsumoto ran away. . . . Then Miyazawa said that he was going to telephone to the police, and he went, he left the place."

Furushō was standing still, blood dripping from his nose.

According to Saitō, the next night Tsutsumi called him and Suzuki to the same room at the Kyōrakukan. Saitō testified, "He told Suzuki that 'if you bring this small thing up before the authorities, that the matter of Hawaii (the Sakamaki house dynamiting) would crop up, would become big,' and for Suzuki . . . for us to change our residence to some other island." Nevertheless, Saitō and the others continued to stay at the Tōhoku Hotel. Two or three days later, Kondō came by. Saitō continued: "He told me that if Matsumoto reports about this dynamite case other case may crop up, and 'it is no good for him to bring up a small matter like this now.' . . . He says, 'if you would hide and keep away that I would have everything settled up for you, go in hiding.'" About two weeks later Furushō, who came with a similar warning, left them $35.

After Saitō and Matsumoto moved to the Kobayashi Hotel, Murakami came with Kondō to visit them there. Saitō told Murakami that his conscience was not clear and that he "want to give [himself] up and confess to this crime." At that moment Detective McDuffie immediately burst in from the next room.

Saitō's testimony established that Oahu union member defendants Furushō, Kawamata, and Takizawa were implicated in the conspiracy to go to Hilo. This had hardly been mentioned in Matsumoto's testimony. At the end of his questioning, Heen returned to the time in Hilo when Miyamura ordered the dynamiting of Sakamaki's house. "Miyamura," said Saitō, "spoke about getting rid of Sakamaki and two or three others, Yamamura of the *Kazan* newspaper, Onodera of Eleven Miles (a contractor). . . . He told me, 'The quickest way to do this is to do them up by powder,' and for me to take the easiest party first and do him up." This was to give the jury the impression that federation leaders were planning other assassinations.

Defense attorney Lymar began his cross-examination by focusing on Saitō's character and attitude. Despite his initial denial, Saitō was forced to admit that he had gone into hiding from a month or so after the Kyōrakukan incident until March 1921. Under direct questioning by prosecutor Heen, Saitō had said that he had never been arrested, but in fact he had been arrested with two friends for distilling sake. One of the friends involved, "Mr. Jinbo," had been named in a grand jury indictment,[18] but happily Saitō slipped by under the name "Sato" because the police misspelled his name by omitting the "i." He had been released on bail when an older acquantance lent him $150. Taking advantage of the man's goodwill, he skipped town, hiding away in Wahiawa until a few weeks before the grand jury issued its indictment in the Sakamaki house dynamiting case. Although he had gone into hiding while on bail, Saitō was not sent back to jail. Indeed, at the time of the trial, like Matsumoto, he was employed by HSPA attorney Frank Thompson, living on his grounds and helping out as a gardener. He was earning $60 in wages, more than a skilled sugar mill worker.

LYMAR: "Mr. Thompson paid that $150 booze fine for you, didn't he?"

SAITŌ: "I paid that fine. I got fifty dollars from my elder brother and a hundred dollar was the money that I saved up from my work at Mr. Thompson."

Lymar pointed out that the fine had been paid with a check signed by Thompson. Saitō replied that he had given the money to a nisei clerk in Thompson's office named Noguchi to take care of and that he did not know who had signed the check. Despite repeated prosecution objections, Lymar continued to probe Saitō's background and character.

LYMAR: "You've had a good deal of trouble, haven't you, the last few years in connection with your work?"

HEEN: "We are going to object to that."

LYMAR: "Before the strike started, before you became a picket or detective, you were a professional gambler, weren't you?"

SAITŌ: "No, I am not a professional gambler."

LYMAR: "Weren't you discharged from Ewa plantation for gambling just before you went to Waipahu before the strike?"

SAITŌ: "No, I left of my own volition."

LYMAR: "Yet you and your fellow desperadoes gave yourselves up without any promises of immunity from punishment?"

SAITŌ: "I did, my conscience hurt me."

In fact, Saitō had been given immunity from prosecution. He answered questions just as Matsumoto had—as if he had rehearsed his testimony. Lymar's cross-examination tried to show that this key witness, who was essential to establishing the prosecution case, was not trustworthy, but Lymar was not able to refute specific points of testimony about the vital matters of the conspiracy and the crime. The *Honolulu Advertiser* noted that since Saitō's testimony matched Matsumoto's, the defense attorney was unable to overturn testimony that established the guilt of the fifteen defendants.[19]

The Japanese-language newspapers reported on the trial in a very simple manner, perhaps in keeping with Judge Banks's warning at the start of the trial. The English-language newspapers treated the trial as front page news, and the *Honolulu Advertiser,* in particular, added commentary in seeming disregard of Judge Banks's warning.

TESTIMONY OF A MYSTERIOUS
FORMER FEDERATION LEADER, SEIICHI SUZUKI

The sixth prosecution witness, Seiichi Suzuki, looked quite different from Matsumoto and Saitō, who looked like manual laborers. The *Honolulu Advertiser* described him as "dapper, excited and 'dressed to kill' in white flannels and a blue serge coat." The thirty-two-year-old Suzuki was a former comrade of the defendants. During the strike he had served at federation headquarters as an elected director from Maui. In a photograph of the federation directors, Suzuki is seated next to Tsutsumi wearing a wide necktie with a bold wavy pattern, one side of his mouth raised in a smile. Suzuki had succeeded Etsuta Inoue, who had died of influenza, as the Maui union representative in late February 1920. But by the end of April he quit. Suzuki had been at federation headquarters in Honolulu for only two months, but he testified that while there he had "organized the picket." It had been unclear so far in the trial by what organization and under whose responsibility the picket troop had been formed.

Suzuki testified, "We held a meeting at the Oahu union office and then had a special meeting at the Kyōrakukan, and at that place it was decided that each plantation was to supply me with a pickets and to report me. . . . It was after I became head of the picket, this talk about dynamite cropped up at the directors of the organization. [It was mid-April, shortly after the 77-cent demonstration march, that, Suzuki said, he had talked with Furushō and Kawamata about dynamite.] Furushō said there's lots of strike-breakers and want to use a place right on the top of Kipapa gulch [where the plantation train carrying laborers ran]. I had some sticks of dynamite."

Suzuki had "six sticks of dynamite" that he had brought from Maui. (Under cross-examination he said he carried the dynamite to Honolulu in a suitcase.) When Heen asked whether he had talked with the federation about the dynamite, Suzuki looked slowly over at the defendants and answered, "Yes, two or three amongst these defendants." Then, as if counting them out, he gave the names "Tsutsumi," "Hoshino," and "Sazō Satō." "I talked to Tsutsumi," he said, "and told I brought (from Maui) six sticks of dynamite. . . . There was no talk about how the giant powder to be used. It was soon after the strike and the strike was conducted peaceably at that time and there's no talk of dynamiting Sakamaki's house or anything improper was talked at that time."

As Heen continued to question him, however, Suzuki changed his answer: "I could not tell you who said this, but somebody said that until the strike proceeds farther, and in case there should be many strike-breakers, and then we may use it at that time. . . . I myself had said about scaring the strike-breakers, and Tsutsumi, Satō, Hoshino maybe said it too. . . . There was no talk of killing anybody with the powder at that time, just scare the strike-breakers with the powder."

It was in mid-April, shortly after the conversations with the federation directors, that Furushō came to inquire about getting dynamite. Suzuki testified: "He (Furushō) told me that one Filipino at Waipahu who is on the side of the plantation and that we were to knock him down, and he drew a plan and showed the plan."

Suzuki gave two sticks of dynamite to Furushō at federation headquarters. Kawamata was there at the time. Several weeks later, on May 5, Suzuki received orders from the federation to return to Maui.

> SUZUKI: "Before coming to Honolulu, I have made the powder into package and gave to my brother to have this package sent to me in Honolulu and, after I came back to Honolulu, I got the package."
>
> HEEN: "What did you get on Maui?"
>
> SUZUKI: "Giant powder."
>
> HEEN: "How many sticks?"
>
> SUZUKI: "My recollection is thirty sticks."

This was truly an explosive piece of testimony. The *Honolulu Advertiser* headline read: "Dynamite Sent by Mail Says Witness, Enough High Explosives to Destroy Steamer Brought from Maui to Honolulu." [20] Suzuki said that he had gotten these thirty sticks of dynamite from N. Fujii, a guard at the plantation equipment warehouse.

> SUZUKI: "Before I went to Maui, I have a talk with Tsutsumi and S. Satō at the Tokiwaen tea house. He told me that 'You are one of the picket and you are being watched by the police. Why don't you go to Maui and get your wife and live here in Honolulu?'"

It will be recalled that just before the strike began, during the first secret meeting of representatives, a director from Maui had stood guard with a loaded revolver watching for supporters of the planters. There was no gun control law, so it was easy to acquire a revolver on any island. Nevertheless, according to the testimony, Tsutsumi and the other federation leaders had gone to the trouble of sending Suzuki to Maui to obtain a revolver, even after Suzuki had quit the federation. According to Suzuki, he received $125 to $150 in cash as expense money for his trip to Maui. When he reported to Tsutsumi that the package of dynamite had arrived, Tsutsumi said, "Is that so?"

HEEN: "I will ask you whether or not he told you to distribute the giant powder among the picket men according to your best judgment."

SUZUKI: "He didn't say anything on our first meeting, when I first met him."

HEEN: "Did you meet him another time and spoke [sic] about the giant powder?"

SUZUKI: "No."

HEEN: "Did you meet him another time?"

SUZUKI: "Any business between the pickets and the federation office I could go down there and meet S. Sato, or Tsutsumi."

On Thursday, February 16, the next day of his testimony, however, Suzuki changed his story about Tsutsumi and the dynamite: "A few days after Tsutsumi said, 'Is that so?' he came to my house at Smith Lane and he told me in case of necessity, to supply them to the pickets. . . . I gave six sticks of dynamite [from Maui] to Yokoo."

Suddenly changing his line of questioning, Heen asked, "Did you have a talk with Murakami at any time about some dynamiting that was supposed to have occurred in Hawaii?" Suzuki responded, "I met him on Beretania and Nuuanu, opposite the Liberty Theater. I asked him, 'I didn't see you for some time, where did you go?' He told me he went to Hawaii. I asked him why did he go for? He told me that he went and had this done. We didn't have very much to talk about this secret, thought it wasn't good to talk on the street, so we left. . . . He told me that he did it."

Lymar began his cross-examination of Suzuki as he had with Matsumoto and Saitō—by asking how long he had been in this country. Suzuki had arrived from Japan at seventeen. He had spent most of his time on Maui, an island known for its many deep valleys. In fact, during the strike, HSPA president Waterhouse's daughter had died in an automobile accident on a precipitous mountain road. Suzuki had worked on a mountain tunnel, and dynamite was one of the tools of his trade. With help from a former fellow worker, Suzuki was able to obtain large amounts of dynamite. His friend assumed it was to be used in his work. Suzuki's testimony included information about some terrifying uses of dynamite, totally incongruous with his dapper, gentlemanly appearance.

During breaks from work on the tunnel, Suzuki was part of an acting troupe that traveled around Maui. A handsome man, he was a lead actor, popular especially among women. When the strike began Suzuki was working as a boilermaker at the sugar mill at Paia Plantation, Maui's largest cane field. His experience as a performer made him a forceful speaker and an activist in the plantation union. When Inoue died suddenly, he was sent to the Federation of Japanese Labor headquarters. Lymar asked him why he had resigned after only two months. "The regulation of the Paia Union calls that non-resident of the place could not be a director and for that reason, I resigned," he said.

But Lymar suggested another reason for his resignation: he had been relieved of his duties in a recall.

> LYMAR: "Didn't you ride around in an automobile a good deal, hire one, while you were a member of the federation?"
>
> SUZUKI: "Whenever I had any business, I would take an automobile and ride around but without any business, I haven't rode around."
>
> LYMAR: "Do you deny that you had trouble with Tsutsumi, particularly about an accounting for the amount of money that you claimed was due you in the car?"

Suzuki owned an automobile that, although used, would have cost more than a boilermaker's wage would allow. When he became a federation director, he took the car to Honolulu from Maui, and saying that he was lending it to the federation, he rode around in it.

> LYMAR: "Just before you resigned as director, wasn't there some trouble between you and the other officials of the Federation of Labor about an automobile charge that you had incurred, and wasn't there dissatisfaction about an accounting that was demanded of you and that was the reason you resigned? . . . Do you deny that you had trouble with Tsutsumi particularly about an accounting for the amount of money that you claimed was due you on the car?"
>
> SUZUKI: "No."
>
> LYMAR: "Did you not state repeatedly that you would get even with Tsutsumi for the treatment that had been accorded you in this automotive matter?"
>
> SUZUKI: "No."

Though pressed, Suzuki did not change his testimony that he had organized the picket troops on Tsutsumi's orders after he had quit federation headquarters. He said that he knew Matsumoto as a member of the picket troops, but he had not come to know Saitō, also a picket, until after the strike. It was only when he, Matsumoto, and Saitō stayed in the same hotel at the time of the Kyōrakukan assault that they "were a great deal together." Of Tamotsu Matsumura, who had taken Matsumoto and Saitō to Thompson's office, Suzuki said, "It was at the Federation office, Mr. Matsumura came in regard to Manlapit matter and at that time, Tsutsumi and myself met him."

Changing his line of questioning, Lymar threw out another question: "Didn't the manager of that plantation [Harry Baldwin, Paia Plantation] tell you to take dynamite down to Oahu and try to plant some around, distribute to some around the Japanese down here?" Lymar may have been trying to pump Suzuki for information, or he may have had some evidence to back up his question. In either case Lymar's questioning was persistent. "Didn't you report to the manager or to your superiors there at Paia what you were doing, every time you went back to Maui, report what you were doing in regard to getting dynamite down on Oahu? . . . Weren't you a plant or decoy duck,—whatever they say,— weren't you a 'plant' interjected into this strike by the plantation interests up there on Maui?" To all of these questions, Suzuki simply answered, "No."

Be that as it may, in September 1920, a month after the strike ended, Suzuki was hired by a leading haole-owned automobile dealership that sold expensive cars. (His dapper dress style was part of his job.) Although boilermakers were among the higher-paid workers on the plantations, Sazuki had been earning only about $40 a month. When he became a high-class car salesman, he earned a regular salary of $80 in addition to commissions. With some pride he told Lymar that he got to ride around in his favorite cars every day and that he earned more than $100 a month.

The lawyer for the automobile dealership was none other than Frank Thompson, the HSPA lawyer. Lymar asked whether Thompson had gotten him the job in return for his services as an informer during the strike. But Suzuki responded that he had talked with Thompson for other reasons: "I thought some day the police will ask questions about dynamite, so I went to ask advice from Mr. Thompson."

The following two witnesses confirmed Suzuki's testimony. One was N. Fujii, a young man in charge of the warehouse at Paia Plantation, who said that he gave Suzuki thirty-some sticks of dynamite, and the other was M. Morikawa, Suzuki's brother-in-law, who mailed the dynamite at Suzuki's request. Each was on the stand for less than ten minutes. At the end of their testimony at 10:50 A.M. on February 16, the prosecution rested its case of conspiracy in the first degree against nineteen members of the Federation of Japanese Labor.

DEFENDANT CHŪHEI HOSHINO'S ALIBI

On Friday, February 17, the thirteenth day of the trial, the case for the defense was begun not by Lymar but by Francis Brooks. The fifty-six-year-old Brooks, like Lymar a graduate of Harvard Law School, had lived for several years in Shanghai and Bangkok. In Hawaiian legal circles he was known to be knowledgeable about Asia. As a preamble to his presentation of the case for the defense, Brooks said that he did not intend to call all the defendants to the stand as that would take four or five weeks, but he did intend to put on four or five.

His first witnesses were two physicians. The first, Genshō Hasegawa, a native of Chiba prefecture, had practiced medicine in Honolulu for twenty years. The *Hawaii nihonjin meikan* also listed his son as a physician, so it can be surmised that Hasegawa was more than sixty years old. Perhaps because there were many unlicensed physicians in Hawaii, Brooks first confirmed Hasegawa's professional qualifications before questioning him about defendant Chūhei Hoshino, who had been his patient.

According to Dr. Hasegawa, the first time he diagnosed Hoshino, who had been sent to the Federation of Japanese Labor from the Hawaii Island union, was on February 12, shortly after the strike began. Hoshino had contracted influenza and was quite weak. Three months later, on May 22, the day that prosecution witnesses Matsumoto and Saitō said they had been ordered to go to Hilo by Hoshino and other defendants at the federation, the Kyōrakukan telephoned Hasegawa requesting a house call shortly after 9:00 A.M. Between 10:00 A.M. and noon Hasegawa went to Kyōrakukan to treat Hoshino, who was wrapped in his bedding and shivering intensely. He had a very high fever and severe cough, and his condition was so critical that unless he could be admitted to a hospital immediately, his life was in danger. But the Japanese Hospital was filled with influenza patients and had no beds available. Hasegawa was able, however, to make arrangements for Hoshino to go to the hospital from May 23 to May 28. In other words, on the morning of May 22, 1920, at precisely the time that Matsumoto and the others alleged they received orders to go to Hilo, according to Dr. Hasegawa's recollection and his notes, Hoshino was lying shivering from a high fever at Kyōrakukan.

(In questioning witnesses Brooks not only did not order his questions well but also sought information about several different things, making it difficult to understand what he was after. This was so trying that Judge Banks more than once made him clarify his questions.)

It was John W. Cathcart who stood to cross-examine Dr. Hasegawa from the prosecution side. Cathcart, a native of Minnesota, was sixty-two at the time. He had arrived in Honolulu when he was thirty-eight years old, and he had spent many years as city and county district attorney. Because they both hailed from the same state, Cathcart and Frank Thompson had been acquainted with each other. After retiring as district attorney, Cathcart went into a law partnership with Thompson. Shortly thereafter Thompson became the lawyer for the HSPA, and the Thompson Cathcart law firm was considered the most powerful in the islands. Cathcart alternated with Thompson as the president of the Hawaiian bar association.

As the testimony of Matsumoto and others made clear, at the time of the indictment Thompson was employing the key prosecution witnesses, Matsumoto, Saitō, and Suzuki. And now Thompson's partner, Cathcart, was assisting the prosecution as deputy attorney general.

In contrast to Brooks, Cathcart got to the core of things with short, succinct questions. He asked Dr. Hasegawa about Hoshino's condition by dividing it into diagnosis, house call, and medication. On May 22, Dr. Hasegawa testified, he gave Hoshino medication to reduce his fever and liquid medicine for his cough. After Hoshino was admitted to the hospital the following day he was given similar medication there. The status of Hoshino's illness on May 22, the crucial date, was obvious from this extremely detailed questioning. According to Hasegawa, Hoshino was so delirious from high fever and was racked with such strong coughs that he could not have stood to talk to others. Cathcart pressed him by asking, "If he wants to go he could go to the Federation Headquarter, didn't he?" Hasegawa responded that he could have gone had he been willing to risk his life. The interpreter phrased this so that the meaning was "if he could bear it," causing defense attorney Lymar to object and start another round of disputes on the interpreter's English.

The second defense witness, Hajime Fujimoto, a clerk in the Japanese Hospital, confirmed that Hoshino was first admitted as Dr. Hasegawa's patient on February 24 and released seven days later, then was readmitted at 9:30 A.M. on May 23 for influenza. Kazuo Kurusu, the third defense witness, was the Japanese Hospital physician who entered information about Hoshino on the patient's chart. He testified that "Hoshino was suffering from acute catarrh of the throat, and hypertrophy—

THE CONSPIRACY TRIAL / 181

a disease of the nose." Under Cathcart's cross-examination, Dr. Kurusu confirmed that Hoshino was in critical condition.

FEDERATION OFFICIAL HIROSHI MIYAZAWA'S TESTIMONY

The first of the defendants called to the witness stand was Hiroshi Miyazawa. The trial transcript indicates that his testimony was given "partly in English and partly through the special Japanese interpreter." As previously noted, Miyazawa, who was proficient in English, served as negotiator for federation headquarters with outside organizations, including the HSPA, and acted as liaison to the Filipino union.

After being sworn in in English, Miyazawa started out by answering defense attorney Brooks's questions in English. But Cathcart soon objected, "I don't understand." Judge Banks also said, "His English is broken, it is so broken that I don't get it. I don't know whether the jury understand it or not." As Miyazawa could understand questions in English, Brooks suggested, "If your Honor would prefer the Japanese interpreter, . . . I thought, may I suggest that just the answer be given through the interpreter."

The questioning of Miyazawa began on explanations of several federation documents (defense exhibits 4–7). The documents were federation bylaws, circulars to each island, and documents addressed to the HSPA and English-language newspapers during the strike translated by Miyazawa. These indicated that Miyazawa could write English, but it would not have been strange if his spoken English was difficult to understand. It appeared, however, that the prosecution was intent on casting doubt on Miyazawa's English-language ability.

In photographs of federation members, Miyazawa always appeared in a bowtie and wearing the boots he wore when he rode around the cane fields. His rimless glasses and high forehead gave him a very earnest look. Miyazawa, thirty-three years old when he stood trial, was the second son of a farm family living outside Ueda City in Nagano prefecture. At the age of eighteen he went to Hawaii to learn English. Since this was in 1906, just before transfers to the mainland were prohibited, he may have been influenced by Sen Katayama's *Tobei annai*.

After working in the cane fields for a few years, Miyazawa became a school boy and studied English. Like many school boys living with Caucasian families, Miyazawa converted to Christianity. But Miyazawa went one step farther and became a pastor. The only photograph of Miyazawa displayed at his family's home in Japan shows him when he was twenty-three, five years after he had gone to Hawaii. His expression suggests a gentle cheerfulness. Two other young Japanese are in the photograph, and on the back of it he had written in square characters, "Fellow volunteers who are my right-hand men and active in evangelism and studies." By then Miyazawa had finished his studies at a seminary.

As Miyazawa made the rounds of the plantations preaching and doing missionary work, Japanese labor contractors often asked him to interpret during negotiations with the sugar companies. Eventually the contractors began to pay him for his interpreting. Involvement in these negotiations familiarized him with plantation work and the need to improve the lives of the laborers. Miyazawa also taught Japanese at a school run by his church. It was through that connection that he must have become acquainted with Tsutsumi. The two men had organized cane worker unions in the Hilo area, and when the Federation of Japanese Labor was formed, Miyazawa went to Honolulu as Tsutsumi's right-hand man. Miyazawa had sent for a picture bride from his hometown. During the strike he had left his wife and children in Hilo and stayed in Honolulu alone. At the time of the trial he had a six-year-old daughter and a five-year-old son.

At federation headquarters Miyazawa was known for his genial personality. Though normally quiet, he was a man of action. During the "silent send-off" campaign to put psychological pressure on the scabs as they departed by train to work on the plantations, only a few strikers joined in, but Miyazawa was always there. And to find out about the scabs' labor conditions, Miyazawa frequented the plantations disguised as a Chinese, risking his life had he been discovered.

Miyazawa's defense of the Filipinos during the strike put him in a difficult position within the federation. He was the only federation official whom the Filipino Labor Union trusted. When he resigned from his position as federation secretary after the strike, Miyazawa planned to start a labor movement newspaper that would appeal to all the immigrant communities.[21] This project never materialized, perhaps because of HSPA interference.

Defense attorney Brooks began with questions about what happened at federation headquarters on May 22. Refuting Matsumoto's testimony, Miyazawa said, "Morning of May twenty two, I stopped at the office of Japanese Federation of Labor and soon went to check the Filipino strikers. I was not at the Federation office most of the time in the morning." He also testified that he had never seen Matsumoto until the Kyōraku-kan assault incident, nor had he met Saitō until then. (Regarding the

Kyōrakukan incident, Miyazawa said, "We were there all in that room when J. Matsumoto jumped into the place, and I told him it is not right to do that, and as I was going out to telephone to the police Saitō asked me not to do so.") According to Miyazawa, Tokuji Baba as well as Chūhei Hoshino was suffering from influenza during the strike and was in and out of bed. At the time Matsumoto and Saitō claimed that they received orders to go to Hilo, Baba had not been in the office. On the morning of May 22, when Miyazawa had dropped by Kyōrakukan to check on Hoshino, he was lying in bed, limp.

Although Matsumoto, Saitō, and the others testified that they had been ordered to kill Juzaburō Sakamaki, Miyazawa said,

[Sakamaki] is a good friend of mine, over ten years. . . . While I was in Hilo and while I was pastor of a church in Hilo and, as I have recollection, I think he became a Christian at that time, and there was a pastor by the name of Ban. I am a good friend of his. He became a good Christian after that, and sometimes he came to my place and slept in my house and, when his child died, I went up there at the funeral. . . . I was never present at any meeting at any time when these defendants were present, about Sakamaki was discussed, not a single time.

On his second day of testimony, Miyazawa testified that Tamotsu Matsurnura was an acquaintance of his. He had heard from Matsumura himself that he was doing work for the Thompson Cathcart law firm. About a month before the indictment, Matsumura had told him that he was helping in the investigation of the Sakamaki house dynamiting case and that he would be a witness at the grand jury proceedings.

BROOKS: "Well, you made no attempt to go to Japan or escape from the jurisdiction of this court while the grand jury were investigating this matter, did you?"

MIYAZAWA: "No."

The cross-examination was conducted by prosecutor Heen, who took over because Cathcart was ill. It took nearly two hours. Most of that time was focused on Miyazawa's qualifications as a pastor. Heen's first question was, "Have you got any certificate showing that you were ordained as a priest or minister of the Episcopal Church?" Miyazawa answered in English, "I was ordained as a catechist in Episcopal Church." Although this was a short exchange, Miyazawa did not speak in broken English, however problematic his accent may have been. But Judge Banks had insisted, "Give your answer in Japanese, I didn't understand you."

The previous day's *Honolulu Advertiser* had carried an article suggesting that Miyazawa was a bogus pastor. It reported that according to a Honolulu Episcopalian priest, Miyazawa was not a qualified priest but merely a lay reader.

> HEEN: "How much did you get at that time as lay reader, fourteen years ago?"
>
> MIYAZAWA: "At first twenty dollars, later on forty dollars. I haven't quit yet, but it is about five or six years that I haven't received any pay."

He said that as interpreter for the labor contractors, he earned about $70 a month and that he also interpreted for coffee growers, so he could make a living without a wage from the church.

Prosecutor Heen fired off questions as if he were representing the HSPA.

> Q: "What were the laborers getting before the strike?"
>
> A: "The pay was 77 cents a day."
>
> Q: "Were they getting bonus, too, at that time?"
>
> A: "I believe there was some bonus."
>
> Q: "Not much?"
>
> A: "Very little."
>
> Q: "Little bonus. In February of 1920 do you know what bonus the laborers were getting?"
>
> A: "I don't remember."
>
> Q: "About 200%, wasn't it, or more?"
>
> A: "The average of that year I think was over 200%."
>
> Q: "Over 200%. Do you remember when the bonus became very high, started to become very high?"
>
> A: "I think the highest was from May to July. . . ."
>
> Q: "No, no, when it started to rise, wasn't that in the latter part or the middle part of 1919?"
>
> A: "It was after the war started."
>
> Q: "After the war started, when sugar was selling around $125 a ton, the bonus went up, didn't it?"

Clearly Heen was trying to insinuate that even though the workers were doing well, the federation was organized and the strike was started to drive the Hawaiian sugar industry to the wall. He then turned his questioning to speeches made at various plantations by the federation directors during the strike.

Q: "Wasn't Fujitani one of the speechmakers?"

A: "Yes, he is a fine speaker."

Q: "How about Tsutsumi, he used to make speeches during the strike?"

A: "Yes, he is a fine speaker too."

Q: "You gave speeches, you urged the laborers to go on strike, didn't you? Because you thought they didn't get enough pay?"

A: "Yes."

Heen once more returned to questions that tried to show that the federation wage increase demands were unjustified, but Judge Banks issued a warning.

JUDGE BANKS: "I want to make this suggestion, gentlemen, that I am not going to permit any extensive inquiry into the merits or demerits of the strike, because I don't think we are concerned with that. I would permit any questions which show the activity of any one of the defendants in the strike, but whether the strike was a just one or unjust one, why I don't believe that we are concerned with that in this inquiry. . . . As far as this case is concerned it doesn't make any difference whether the strike was justified or whether it was not justified, and to bring that feature into the case might prejudice the jury one way or the other, you know. We must confine ourselves to the charge and the evidence must be limited to that."

After this warning, Heen turned to questions about the pickets. Prosecution witnesses Matsumoto and Saitō had said that they were members of the picket troop, and Seiichi Suzuki, a former federation director, had testified that he organized the picket troop, but Miyazawa stated, "As far as I know, each plantation had a watchman. If you called a watchman a picket, might have been a picket, that's all, as far as I know." Although he had been a federation headquarters secretary, Miyazawa said that he had never heard of "pickets," nor did he know whether the Oahu union or each plantation union paid the expenses of the pickets.

Appearing incredulous at Miyazama's answers, Heen repeated his questioning.

Q: "Did the Oahu union report about picketing to the Federation on its activities?"

A: "No."

Q: "Well, when the Federation paid money over to the Oahu union they didn't inquire what they wanted it for?"

A: "I don't know how the treasurer did that."

Suddenly, prosecutor Heen changed his line of questioning.

Q: "Did you have anything to do with the manufacturing of tools or implements at the Waipahu Japanese theater for setting fire to sugarcane?"

A: "I don't know."

Q: "Did you or the Federation have anything to do with setting fire to some cane at Waimanalo on May 7th, 1920?"

A: "Absolutely not." (in English)

Q: "Did you or the Federation have anything to do with setting fire to some cane near the cement bridge at Ewa on May 7th, 1920?"

A: "No."

Q: "Did you or the Federation or any officers of the Federation have anything to do with setting fire to some cane on field no. 2 and 13, on Waialua on May 12th, 1920?"

A: "No."

Q: "Did you or the Federation or any officers of the Federation have anything to do with setting fire to some cane at Waimanalo on May 14th, 1920?"

A: "No."

Q: "Did you or the Federation or any officers of the Federation have anything to do with setting fire to some cane at Waimanalo on June 7th, 1920?"

A: "No."

Q: "Did you or the Federation or any officers of the Federation have anything to do with setting fire to some cane at Waipahu, near Camp No. 10 on June 11th?"

A: "No."

Q: "1920?"

A: "No."

Q: "Did you or the Federation or any officers of the Federation have anything to do with setting fire to some cane at Ewa in the night time on June 11th, 1920?"

During the strike, after Reverend Palmer's attempts at mediation had broken down, incidents of arson occurred on various plantations. The planters insisted that they were the work of striking laborers, and they kept asking Acting Governor Iaukea to call out the territorial troops. But the federation made counterclaims that the planters had staged the incidents using "planters' dogs" to make it appear that the strikers were behind them. The *Hawaii hōchi* had reported, "It appears that the planters see a court trial as a way to break the resolve of the laborers and end the strike."[22] Indeed, union members on various plantations were arrested when the management accused them of being arsonists. Even those with airtight alibis were jailed for several days. On Kauai, the principal of the Japanese-language school, who had just made a statement supporting the local union, was arrested for arson even though a Filipino worker was later arrested as the actual culprit.

The *Hawaii hōchi* had frequently proposed countermeasures: "Seeing the recent rash of fires in cane fields, we propose that a guard team be organized by the striking laborers. By organizing a guard team and hiring special watchmen to guard against cane fires together (with the planters) the laborers could show that they are sincere about protecting the industry." To judge from Miyazawa's testimony that each plantation had a watchman and from when Matsumoto and the others became pickets, it seems likely that the the pickets referred to by the prosecution were security guards organized to prevent misunderstandings about the arson cases.[23]

In any event, Heen brought up the arson cases to give the impression that the Federation of Japanese Labor was behind them. Lymar raised obections to Heen's questions, but Judge Banks, despite his warning that no information not directly related to the dynamiting of the Sakamaki house was to be introduced in court, summarily overruled each of his objections. The jury therefore heard about the arson cases during the strike involving a director of Federation of Japanese Labor headquarters.

Heen continued to fire questions at Miyazawa on an even more unsettling line of examination.

> I will ask you whether or not you have anything to do with the placing of some dynamite under the house of one Hayaji Nakazawa at Ewa, in May, 1920, because he, Nakazawa, went back and worked for the plantation when the strike was on?
>
> Do you know anything about the placing of some dynamite by certain Japanese, the name being Y. Matsumoto, Z. Matsumoto and Miyake, under the house of a Filipino by the name of Alcara at Waipahu in the latter part of April or the first part of May, 1920, because this Filipino was working against the strike?
>
> Do you know anything about the assault and battery committed on Manpachi Ogata of Waipahu, on or about the 10th day of March, 1920, by the defendant Furushō, Fujita, Kobayashi, and a man by the name of Takematsu who used to be the head of Wahiawa picket?

Manpachi Ogata had served as a federation director until January 1920 when he and Hayaji Nakazawa were publicly denounced in the Japanese press as planters' dogs and informants for the HSPA. His son was so bullied at Japanese-language school that he refused to go, and Ogata was so upset at the federation that he went around urging the striking laborers to return to their jobs. When Shōshichirō Furushō, a leader of the Waipahu Plantation union, tried to stop him, the two men got into a fistfight. This was the assault and battery on Ogata that Heen referred to. A full year after the incident, on May 6, 1921, Furushō and the two other leaders of the Waipahu union were suddenly charged, tried, and sentenced to a year in prison. When indicted on conspiracy charges three months later, Furushō was already in prison.

The jury had heard Furushō's name several times from prosecution witnesses. Saitō had testified that Furushō had ordered him to go to the Oahu union office and given him travel expenses to board the *Maunakea*. After the Sakamaki house dynamiting, Saitō said Furushō had commended him for his action ("You did a fine work") and told him "some other things" might need to be done. The jury had also heard Furushō's name in connection with the Kyōrakukan assault incident, when Matsumoto said that Furushō attacked him with a pitcher and Saitō struck Furushō to protect Matsumoto. Saitō also stated that Furushō had come to his hotel and given him $35 to go into hiding, because if Saitō was caught the investigation would extend to the federation leaders.

Watching Furushō in the defendants' bench every day, jurors must have found that he drew their attention in a very different way from Kondō, the local boss. Not only was Furushō a large man, his posture was erect, his expression intense, and his gaze unusually steady. He was then thirty-seven years old. The eldest son of a farm family near Ōtsu City in Kumamoto prefecture, he graduated from agricultural school. At twenty-one he realized his dream of traveling abroad by going to work at the Waialua plantation on Oahu. The following year he had married his cousin, and at the time of the trial he had an 11-year-old daughter, an 8-year-old son, and a 4-year-old daughter.

Ten years before the strike, Furushō moved to Waipahu Plantation to become a contract cane grower. In the 1918 *Hawaii Nihonjin meikan* (Directory of Japanese in Hawaii), his profile stated, "The area he is in charge of has had good harvests for several years, and is among the highest producing in the plantation; this year's production is said to be greater than last year's." The directory said that Furushō had decided on permanent residence and had purchased land for a home.

As a contractor who employed several hundred workers at Waipahu, a major Oahu plantation, Furushō was a man trusted by the company. He was not a laborer who demanded higher wages, or one who could not make ends meet. If the strike had not taken place, he might have earned large profits as labor contractors on the other islands did when the sugar price soared in 1920. But because he had urged his workers to make Hawaii their permanent residence, he took the lead in demanding wage increases. After the strike ended, he helped to organize the Oahu Shōkai, a company to sell workers food and sundry goods. The sugar companies monopolized profits by deducting from wages the amounts workers and their families spent on essentials at company stores. The Oahu Shōkai, a new concept proposed by Furushō, was like a consumer cooperative that sold goods directly to the workers at low prices. Furushō served as the company's president, and Tsutsumi and other former federation leaders were on the board, but all were indicted before the company got off the ground and it soon went bankrupt.

Furushō was a man given to action, and as his granddaughter, Sachiko Ueda, recalled, "He was always yelling." This trait seemed to have become more pronounced as he grew older, but Furushō was already known for being short-tempered during his Waipahu days. Details of the Ogata assault and battery case are obscure as trial records no longer exist, but from contemporary newspaper accounts, it can be surmised that it was merely an argument that escalated when tempers flared on both sides, with Furushō striking the first blow.

Heen pressed Miyazawa about the Ogata case as if it were a crime committed by federation leaders. A Mr. Takematsu, who had been charged along with Furushō, Heen pointed out, was the man who prosecution witness Saitō said had given him the revolver he took to Hawaii. But Miyazawa told Heen that Takematsu had died after the strike, so the witness who could confirm or deny Saitō's testimony was no longer alive.

Lymar objected, saying, "Just a moment. If your honor please, counsel has stated something that was not in the question. The question was assault and battery, they were not convicted of assault with intent to commit murder."

But prosecutor Heen continued to ask Miyazawa similar questions: "Do you know anything about some assault and battery committed on T. Harada by a man named T. Hiroyama, Fujimura, and Matsumoto . . . ?"

Even Judge Banks thought he had gone too far. "I think you are getting beyond the limit," he told Heen.

In the redirect questioning, defense attorney Brooks asked just one question: "Did you or any of the officials of the Federation of Labor have anything to do with the dynamiting that occurred in Los Angeles, the McNamara dynamiting, or the blowing up of the *Lusitania,* or the Wall Street or the Mooney and Billings dynamiting in San Francisco, did you or any of the Federation have anything to do with that?"

Judge Banks seemed to be appalled: "Mr. Brooks, I hardly think you can be propounding that seriously." Brooks replied, "I consider it just as relevant as the questions of [Mr.] Heen."

AN ALIBI CONFIRMED

Tokuji Baba, the defendant who took the witness stand after Miyazawa, was thirty-three years old. He wore rimless glasses similar to Miyazawa's but was much shorter and thinner. As the eldest son of a wealthy farm family near Shibata City in Niigata prefecture, he might have inherited the family lands, but when he was fifteen years old he went to Hawaii where his uncle lived.

Aside from Tsutsumi, Baba and Ichiji Gotō were the only Federation of Japanese Labor officers mentioned in the FBI files. According to one FBI report, "Upon his arrival [in Hawaii], Baba went directly to Waialua plantation where he worked for four years and then returned to Japan. He stayed in Japan about one year and then again he came to the territory and obtained work at Waialua plantation where he has been up to the time of last strike. He was active as the head of Buddhist Youth Association and he wrote to Buddhist magazines and short stories etc. He likes to write and contributes to Japanese newspapers occasionally."[24]

At the time of the strike Baba worked at the Waialua sugar company mill and was one of the higher wage earners. Along with H. Fujitani, he became involved early on in the local wage increase movement. When the Waialua union was organized, he was named its chairman. According to the FBI report, "At first Baba was very conservative in his views and actions, but gradually through his association with Tsutsumi, Miyazawa and others, became more or less radical in his views and actions."[25]

Defense attorney Brooks started his direct examination of Baba by focusing on his health on May 22, 1920. Baba testified that after coming down with influenza on February 18, he had been ill all during the strike. He denied giving orders to Matsumoto to go to Hawaii on May 20. "I was not in the office that day," he said. He recalled seeing Matsumoto at Fujitani's home "for a little while," but he did not talk to him. And the first time he saw Saitō, he said, "was when he came here and was on the witness stand."

Brooks completed these direct examination questions in about fifteen minutes. His method of operation was to present his witnesses quickly; then, after allowing Heen to press them during his cross-examination, he tried to overturn those points during his redirect questioning.

In response to Heen's cross-examination, Baba provided further details of his illness. After coming down with influenza after a speaking tour of Maui, Baba remained in bed at the hotel housing workers evicted from Waialua, but so many people were staying in the same room that he could not rest. Both Hoshino and his doctor, Genshō Hasegawa, feared that his life was in danger if he stayed there. Indeed, Hasegawa took Baba home to stay with him in Honolulu.

BABA: "I went to Dr. Hasegawa's place and stayed there. On the third of April I came with Dr. Hasegawa in his automobile to see the flag parade.[26] My health was not very good and my friends thought that I could not do any business as an official so they telephoned me one day and wanted to know if I would go back to Japan. I told him if they are going to send me back to Japan I want to go back to Japan. It was about the 17th of May."

The following day, May 18, Baba returned to Waialua Plantation, where he stayed for eight days. It was May 26 when he returned to Dr. Hasegawa's house. On May 22, the day that Matsumoto said Baba had issued the order to go to Hilo, Baba was still in Waialua.

The cross-examination brought out details of Baba's movements around the crucial date of May 21. When Baba returned to Waialua, he sent a resignation letter dated May 20 to the Oahu union, giving poor health as his reason. (The May 25, 1920, *Hawaii shinpō* suggested that Fujitani might take Baba's place as Waialua delegate.) His fellow workers objected to his resignation because they felt the strike would soon end, so his offer to resign was deferred. "It was about the time the strike was to end," he said, "that I was asked by Tsutsumi to come to Honolulu to confer with him as to the settlement of the strike. He said, 'we want to have some laborers to be connected with this settlement.'" Despite his illness, Baba had to attend the final negotiations with HSPA president Waterhouse at the Young Hotel.

Heen asked Baba, as he had asked Miyazawa, about the daily wage of the workers at the time of the strike, making it seem that their wage increase demands were unjustified. He also sought to show how much Baba (and the other defendants) were being paid by the federation or the unions during the strike. Baba said that he received no pay, only expenses, when he served as a federation director. His monthly salary of $85 began only in August, after the strike ended, and continued for about six months until he returned to Niigata in January 1921.

An FBI report of January 22, 1921, stated, "[Baba is] among the Japanese returning to Japan by the Shunyo Maru tomorrow morning. He is returning to his native land for recuperation." Heeding Dr. Hasegawa's advice, Baba returned to Japan for a time to recover his health. He also married a local woman, who came back with him to Hawaii, and he turned his family home over to his younger sister and her husband. It was clear that he intended to make Hawaii his permanent residence. About two months after he got back to Waialua Plantation he was indicted. Although Baba had resigned as Waialua union chairman, when he returned from Japan he agreed to take on the job again.

Changing his line of questioning, Heen asked Baba in conclusion, "Isn't it a fact that the Federation or the Hawaiian Laborer's Association is paying nine thousand dollars for the defense of all of you in this case?" To this, Brooks interjected, "Not to me."

The first female witness to take the stand was Sajo (Sayo?) Inoguchi, a middle-aged woman whose face reflected a difficult life. According to her testimony, she had worked in the cane fields with her husband on Ewa Plantation until they were evicted during the strike. After going to Honolulu she worked at Kyōrakukan from February 28 until the beginning of June doing cleaning and washing. At that time, about ten federation leaders were staying at Kyōrakukan, among them Hoshino, who was in bed most of the time she worked there. It was witness Inoguchi who had seen that Hoshino's condition was dire on May 22 and had telephoned Dr. Hasegawa.

INOGUCHI: "As he was unable to eat normal meals, I had made him rice gruel, but he could no longer eat that. His fever was very high, and I cooled his forehead with ice. He couldn't even make it to the lavatory across the hall, so I had to take him by the arm and lead him there. I think it was just before noon that Dr. Hasegawa arrived. The next day, Mr. Hoshino was admitted to the hospital. I took his arm and led him to the car. The night before he went to the hospital, I was at his side all night, changing the ice to cool his head. No, he was in no condition to leave his room at Kyōrakukan during that day (May 22) and go to the Federation office. . . .

There were many people connected to the Federation who came and went, but I remember well Mr. Hoshino from his condition. His high fever and serious cough continued particularly seriously for four or five days before the doctor came to see him. Mr. Hoshino took the medicine the doctor gave him, but just when his fever seemed to go down, it would go up again. This situation was repeated, and he gradually got worse.

In his last question to Inoguchi, Heen asked, "Did they tell you what you are to testify of?" She replied, "He told me not to tell lie, to tell *pololei* [the truth]," Inoguchi replied. "I also became ill with influenza about the time of the strike's end, and I'm still not back to normal health even after a year and a half." Inoguchi left the witness stand with unsure steps.

The *Honolulu Advertiser* noted that Inoguchi's testimony established Hoshino's alibi for May 22.

The seventh defense witness was thirty-four-year-old Yasuyuki Mizutari. His face was almost too delicate for a man, but his firm mouth expressed the strength of his will. Mizutari came from Mashiki County in Kumamoto prefecture. His father was a spear-fighting teacher, and his family had served the Hosokawa clan for generations. Until the strike Mizutari had worked in the mill at Pioneer Plantation in Lahaina on Maui. Mizutari and Inoue, who died of influenza, were the only two federation headquarters directors from Maui. It was Mizutari who, armed with a revolver, stood guard at the first meeting of delegates from all the islands at which the issue of whether to strike was discussed. At federation headquarters, Mizutari at first dealt with finances, but after the increase in influenza patients, he was active in the health department. After the strike, at the end of October 1920, Mizutari left the federation and returned to Kumamoto with his wife and three children. He came back to Hawaii two months later, on Christmas Eve, went to work at the Oahu Railway. Perhaps it was for these reasons that he was not indicted with the other federation leaders eight months later.

In response to Brooks's direct examination, Mizutari said that he went to Maui on business several times during the strike. In May, however, he went only once to Maui. Mizutari remembered this trip well because it was the only time that he went with Tsutsumi. In cross-examination he stated, "I am a laborer, I couldn't talk very well, and I asked

Mr. Tsutsumi to go along and have this explained." The two men went to Maui on May 19 and returned to Honolulu on May 22.

On May 22, after their ship from Maui arrived in Honolulu at 6:30 A.M., Mizutari and Tsutsumi walked to federation headquarters. Tsutsumi telephoned Umemoto, another director, asking him to come in. Umemoto arrived with *Nippu jiji* reporter Gen'ichi Ōkubo at about 7:00 A.M. They talked until after 8:00, then Mizutari and Tsutsumi headed by car for Suigorō in Waiau. (The driver of this car later died of influenza.) On the way they stopped off to see Mizutari's family, which was renting a house in Honolulu. It was only after 9:00 A.M. that the two arrived at Suigorō. As they had a meeting scheduled for 7:00 that evening at federation headquarters, they spent the time until then at Suigorō, ate an early supper, and returned to Honolulu.

In other words, Mizutari's testimony directly conflicted with that of Matsumoto and Saitō, both of whom had stated that they received orders from Tsutsumi at the federation headquarters office during the day on May 22. Mizutari confirmed Tsutsumi's alibi. The Suigorō was located near Waiau station, standing alone on a narrow road facing Pearl Harbor. It was some distance from Honolulu, but it was beyond the reach of bothersome newspaper reporters and there was no chance for planters' dogs to enter there. Federation leaders often gathered there, including the meeting that decided on the strike's end, because it was possible to maintain confidentiality.

In response to Heen's cross-examination, Mizutari spoke in detail about the day at Suigorō: "I was hungry, I had some rolled rice and, while we were eating, the nine o'clock train passed. Well, we went in the boat to crab fishing and we took some food along with us and, while we were eating the food in the boat, that a train that passed there a little after nine o'clock."

The Oahu Railway schedule for that year shows a train leaving Honolulu at 9:15 A.M., the only one around the time Mizutari heard a train pass by. This train arrived in Waiau at 9:45 A.M.

When Mizutari and Tsutsumi reached Suigorō, they changed into cotton kimonos. It seemed that they were hit by the accumulated fatigue from four months of rushing around night and day since the strike started. The two men relaxed to prepare for the struggles ahead. Pearl Harbor was calm as usual that day. No doubt they were able to see several U.S. warships in the distance as the construction of the naval base was in progress. Then they fished until after 2:00 P.M. After returning to the Suigorō, they asked that the crab they had caught be cooked, played some go in a room overlooking Pearl Harbor, and left at about 6:30 P.M. to attend the meeting.

Take Hamamoto, the manager of the Suigorō, confirmed Mizutari's account. Her husband was a fisherman who went out to sea every day. While caring for her four children, Take had operated the Suigorō on her own since its opening seven years before. Her testimony was summarized as follows:

> Many Federation members came, but I remember Mr. Tsutsumi well. I think it was Mr. Mizutari who first started to come. The first time that Mr. Tsutsumi came a while later, he said he had a cold and wasn't feeling well. He slept in for a couple of days. After that, I think he came about three times other than when there were meetings.
>
> It was just once that he and Mr. Mizutari came together. I can't give the exact date, but it was in the middle of May and I know it was a Saturday.
>
> When they came they says, "Well, fix up something for us, we want something to eat, we have just come back from Maui." I was making sushi, that is rolled rice, and my husband was not there, and I told them, "Why not take some of this sushi?" and they says, "Well, if you have that we don't need anything else." And they took that sushi and went to the pier, eating sushi.
>
> I remember distinctly the time that they came together they took these two rolls of sushi and went out, eating, and looked funny to me and, for that reason, I remember the time.
>
> I think they were in their suits [this is the only point on which her memory differed from Mizutari's], and they went off with the towels I lent them draped around their necks.

Take Hamamoto's testimony, devoid of extraneous emotions, seemed very solid. The *Honolulu Advertiser* noted, "The cross-examination of [Mizutari and Hamamoto] by Judge William H. Heen for the Territory, failed to bring out any contradictory testimony each holding to the fact as stated in direct examination."

NOBORU TSUTSUMI TAKES THE STAND

The trial went into recess on February 22, Washington's birthday, a national holiday. Late that night Cathcart, the special deputy attorney general, died of a sudden heart attack, and when the court began its session the next day at 9:00 A.M., at the suggestion of defense attorney Lymar, it was adjourned out of respect for his memory. Just twelve days earlier it had been announced publicly that the Republican party convention unanimously recommended that Cathcart be appointed judge of the U.S. district court, the highest post in the territory's judiciary. Naturally, it was only possible with the backing of the HSPA. At the time the sixty-two-year-old Cathcart stood at the pinnacle of his nearly forty-year career.

On the morning of Friday, February 25, the seventeenth day of the trial, defense attorney Brooks noticed Tamotsu Matsumura in the courtroom gallery. Brooks raised an objection. He said that he intended to call Matsumura, who had taken Matsumoto and other prosecution witnesses to the Thompson law office and had helped the prosecution gather evidence for the charges, as a witness. Judge Banks ordered Matsumura to leave the courtroom and then defendant Chūhei Hoshino took the stand.

The facts of Hoshino's background are sketchy. He came from a farm family in Chiba prefecture, and he worked for a time at a shipyard in Japan. After coming to Hawaii when he was twenty-eight years old, he worked at the Papala sugar mill in Kau County on Hawaii. At the time of the trial he was forty-three years old. In photographs Hoshino has a long jaw and a languid expression. During the strike the Japanese-language newspapers often described him as "moderate" (*onken*). Yet on his card in the immigration directory at the Japanese consulate in Honolulu there was a notation in thick red ink: "Warning: dangerous person who attempted to bring charges against Consul General Yada."

The consulate's notation was dated 1921, indicating that Hoshino had some altercation with the consul general concerning federation activities after the strike. As no charge was filed, it is unclear what it was about. Had some pressure or accusation by the consulate pushed the normally moderate Hoshino beyond his limits? Or might someone have informed on Hoshino for commenting that he would be willing to take legal action to settle some point?

The jury had already heard testimony from several witnesses that Hoshino was ill during the strike. Now the jury heard directly from Hoshino about his condition at that time. As the *Honolulu Advertiser* observed under the headline "Testimony Unshaken," "Hoshino's testimony proved to be more or less bullet-proof on cross-examination." Under prosecutor Heen's questioning he affirmed that he had been delirious on the day Matsumoto claimed to have received orders from him.

Hoshino said that he had met Matsumoto and Saitō just once. In the latter half of October, one month after Hoshino had returned to Hilo, the two men suddenly visited him at the Hawaii Island union office asking for a hearing. According to Hoshino, Matsumoto said, "I have done my best and for that the Oahu union is not rewarding us for the work we have done." Because he was not able to procure any work, Matsumoto wanted to go back to Japan. He asked that the Hawaii union pay his and Saitō's expenses for the trip. Along with Chikao Ishida and Sazō Satō, who were in the office at the same time, Hoshino listened to their story. Explaining to them that they needed to talk to the Oahu union about Oahu matters, and that the Hawaii union couldn't take care of matters related to other islands, he sent them away. Hoshino stated flatly, "They have not claim to us any money for any alleged blowing up of Sakamaki's place."

At 11:08 A.M. on Friday, February 25, Lymar, who relieved Brooks, called the tenth defense witness to the stand. Instantly, the courtroom stirred.[27] It was "N. Tsutsumi," the strike leader who had been the eye of the storm for nearly half a year and the troublemaker whom the FBI files designated "the most dangerous radical in Hawaii." The atmosphere in the courtroom was tense.

Lymar began his questioning by asking whether his name was Noboru or Takashi, then asked his age. Tsutsumi answered, "Thirty-one and ten months." It must have been evident to the jury that this witness was clearly different from the other Japanese witnesses who had come before. Tsutsumi, thinner since the strike, seemed taller than he really was. Although it had been four years since he arrived in Hawaii, his face was pale, not tanned by the sun. His responses were given through the interpreter, Maruyama, but he faced Lymar squarely and answered in a firm voice.[28]

Tsutsumi testified that he found out about the dynamiting of the Sakamaki house from reading the *Nippu jiji* on June 4, the day after it occurred. He had met Jūzaburō Sakamaki when he was the principal of the Japanese-language school in Hilo, and he said that he knew that Sakamaki was opposed to the strike. "Mr. Sakamaki is an interpreter for the plantation," he said. "It's no surprise his position at the strike. But his opposition was no influence at all."

LYMAR: "Had you ever discussed with anyone or heard anyone else discuss a plot or a project of a possible trip down to Olaa for the purpose of doing injury to Sakamaki or his premises?"

TSUTSUMI: "I had not."

Regarding his activities on May 22, the date that Matsumoto and Saitō said they were ordered to Hawaii to dynamite Sakamaki's house, his testimony was the same as Mizutari's: the two men had returned from Maui that morning and spent the day at Suigorō. The only additional points were (1) that he had telephoned the *Nippu, Hōchi,* and *Shinpō* to let them know he had returned from Maui (the only reporter who came to get the story was Ōkubo from the *Nippu*) and (2) that the house rented by the Mizutari family was near a pineapple factory. (As defense exhibit, the passenger list of the *Maunakea* with the names Tsutsumi and Mizutari included was presented.) As for Matsumoto and Saitō, Tsutsumi said that he had not met them until the trouble at Kyōrakukan. He categorically denied the testimony of Matsumoto and others that he had issued orders on May 22 to kill Sakamaki on Hawaii.

Lymar then gave Tsutsumi the chance to give testimony about the Kyōrakukan assault incident.

TSUTSUMI: "I think that evening I was playing go with Miyazawa, a kind of Japanese chess, and I was called by the servant that somebody wants to see me. I went towards the parlor and I saw a big man walking, coming into the parlor. He says, 'Well, I am Matsumoto from Waialua,' he says, 'You know me?' I says, 'Are you Matsumoto?' I said, 'Do you have any business with me?' He says, 'The meeting of the delegates is not satisfactory to me.' So I says, 'What's the matter?' He says, 'You know everything,' he says, 'You know everything in your heart.' I told him it is sudden, I says, 'Don't make so much noise, why don't you be quiet and talk this thing over?' and he stood up, he slapped the table. I told him he looked intoxicated, 'You are excited. Why not talk a little more quietly?' He says, 'You are fresh.' I told him that night, at this time, 'I have no interest in the Federation and if you have any business, why don't you go to the person who is now attending to this business?' "

Judge Banks interrupted his testimony to adjourn the court, but Tsutsumi continued the next day, Monday, February 27.

TSUTSUMI: "As I stated before, the conversation took place in the parlor and the man was intoxicated, so I left the place and went to my room, I went back to the room to continue the game with Miyazawa. The man was standing on the verandah at that time, he called out, 'Tsutsumi, come out, come out.' 'I have no reason to be called by you and go out.' I heard steps and a person calling 'Fix him,' and the person came into the room, S. [Seiichi] Suzuki walked into the room. He had a pistol in his left hand pointed toward me. I stood up. As he was going to press the trigger, Miyazawa hit him on the elbow. The result of Miyazawa hitting this man's elbow the gun flew away from his hands and struck the bureau on the other side room, breaking the glass.

Matsumoto came in at this time, between Suzuki and Miyazawa, and struck me on the eye. Then I grappled with Matsumoto and kicked him on the foot and he fell down. At the time he fell there was a big chess board, he struck his head on this board and he cut himself. When he fell down I held him down, I says 'What you do?' Then Saito came out and asked me to wait."

Matsumoto, known for being quick to fight, was confident of his physical strength. And yet he had been knocked down by a pale intellectual and injured so badly that his head was bleeding. Out of spite at having been embarrassed in front of onlookers, it seems, Matsumoto had gone to the police to report the incident as a case of assault. This was the nature of the Kyōrakukan incident that the defense attempted to prove.

Tsutsumi also testified in detail about Seiichi Suzuki, the prosecution witness whom he said had pointed a pistol at him. When Suzuki had faced a recall, Tsutsumi had accompanied him to Maui. Lymar asked whether the real reason for Suzuki's recall was not that he no longer resided in Maui (as Suzuki had testified) but that he had been involved in money problems in Maui. The prosecution objected to this line of questioning, and Tsutsumi was not allowed to answer. He was, however, given the opportunity to deny that he had spoken to Suzuki about acquiring dynamite or ordering Suzuki to bring firearms from Maui.

Lymar ended the direct examination of his most important witness with the following question. "Mr. Tsutsumi, you had quite a little influence in the organization of the strike, and I want to ask you whether, throughout the strike, you were ever present at any meeting of any Japanese interested in that strike when violent acts were discussed to be used against obstructers of the strike?"

Tsutsumi's response was unequivocal. "As to that," he said, "we have discussed, not what we would use violence against the others but violence has been used against us. At one time, it occurred at Waialua plantation—police have pointed a gun at the strikers, and we discussed what actions to take on that."

PROSECUTOR HEEN'S CROSS-EXAMINATION

At 9:20 A.M. Heen began his cross-examination of Tsutsumi by asking about Seiichi Suzuki: "Wasn't he a picket, or the head of the picket in Honolulu during the strike?"

All of Tsutsumi's answers regarding the picket troops were interpreted with a different nuance, causing defense attorney Lymar to raise objections. The answers quoted here are those that interpreter Maruyama rephrased.

There is no picket organization in the Federation.

I don't know as to Oahu union except what they report to the Federation, we don't know anything outside of that.

Whatever that would come into our attention we would investigate.

We investigated the watchmen at Waipahu. I don't know whether the strikers put watchman at Waipahu or the plantation put a watchman at that place. The Federation didn't have any picket at all. I was informed that they organized these picket gangs by themselves.

I don't know a picket gang at Aiea. I didn't see it at Aiea.

We hired special police at Waialua, I know that. Watchman is men waiting at street corners to keep away the laborers from going to work. I made inquiries and they said they are doing that for themselves.

Heen then changed his line of questioning. "Now, the other day you stated that you were a professor of ethics, is that it, of biology?" he said. When Lymar had asked him about his educational background during direct examination, Tsutsumi must have answered, "After graduating from Shiga Normal School, I studied agriculture at Hiroshima Higher Normal School, and at the Education Department of Kyoto Imperial University I studied philosophy, biology, and education." Yet what the courtroom heard was Maruyama's English interpretation. It merely strung words together into the answer, "I obtained degrees of higher philosophy, normal school, educational, ethics, natural history." Maruyama obviously was not familiar with the Japanese educational system. Where he should have interpreted that Tsutsumi had qualifications to be a schoolteacher (*kyōshi*), Maruyama instead had said "professor." This was why prosecutor Heen seized this English interpretation of the direct examination and asked Tsutsumi whether he was a professor of agriculture. During the questioning the interpreter must have used the word "teacher" (*sensei*) in Japanese, so it was natural that Tsutsumi's answer was "Yes."

Heen then asked if Tsutsumi was a "professor of elocution." Not noticing Heen's sarcasm in using a word similar in pronunciation to "education," interpreter Maruyama took it for a mistake by Heen, and speaking for Tsutsumi, said that it was "education." Heen once again asked whether Tsutumi wasn't a professor of elocution.

By making Maruyama repeat over and over that Tsutsumi was a "professor" in a variety of disciplines, from the humanities to science,

Heen was obviously trying to give the impression that Tsutsumi was misrepresenting his educational background, in an effort to show the jury that Tsutsumi was a charlatan. And Heen added, "You are a professional agitator, too, aren't you?"

In responding to questions about his source of income since arriving in Hawaii, Tsutsumi said that he had left Japan with the promise of receiving $75 as Japanese-language school principal, but once on the job he was told that the school could only pay $65.

> HEEN: "When you were secretary of the Federation, how much were you getting?"
>
> TSUTSUMI: "Never got any. They asked me to wait until the meeting of the delegates to decide the salary of the secretary (which was after the strike). But my board and lodging were paid."
>
> HEEN: "Have you received any money at all from the Federation?"
>
> TSUTSUMI: "I had my money at that time."
>
> HEEN: "When you went down to Waiau and had a crab dinner down there, did you pay that out of your pocket?"
>
> TSUTSUMI: "I paid myself."
>
> HEEN: "Have you ever been refunded for the money you advanced?"
>
> TSUTSUMI: "No."

During the strike, in late April, when delegates met immediately after the Federation of Japanese Labor was renamed the Hawaii Labor Association, the *Hawaii hōchi* reported,

> Director Katō proposed that "salaries be set for secretaries Tsutsumi and Miyazawa." Director Inoguchi explained that secretaries Tsutsumi and Miyazawa had not taken salaries but were only being paid their lodging expenses. The island delegates agreed that salaries should be set. Secretary Tsutsumi, however, declined, stating, "At this time when we have yet to fulfill our promise to the Oahu laborers, and as I have stated to my direct assistant, I will not accept a salary until the problems have been resolved. If you insist on giving me a salary, I will immediately donate it to headquarters." Thus, the Katō proposal was referred to the board of directors.[29]

It was evident from this article that Tsutsumi and Miyazawa had not received a salary from the federation.

> HEEN: "How are you making a living?"
>
> TSUTSUMI: "I have spent all the money I had with me (from Japan and earned as Japanese language school principal) and I am a little hard up for my living at this present time."

No doubt it was due to the circumstances reported in the *Hawaii hōchi* that at the first delegates' meeting after the strike Tsutsumi's salary was set at an extraordinary $450. The amount was clearly meant to compensate him for not taking a salary during the strike. But Tsutsumi was actually paid that amount only during the month and a half before he resigned. In his testimony, Tsutsumi added that because he was finding it difficult to make ends meet, he intended to return to Japan as soon as the trial was over.

Heen then turned to the secret meetings the federation held frequently during the strike. According to Tsutsumi, when the federation discussed measures that it did not wish to reveal to the HSPA through newspaper reports, it excluded reporters. That was why the newspapers refered to them as "secret meetings." But he added, "There's records and minutes of every meeting. I kept the minutes myself, except ones Mr. Gotō kept."

Prosecutor Heen was not satisfied. As if to suggest that the "secret meetings" not only discussed measures against strikebreakers or picketing but also conspired to carry out illegal strike tactics like the Sakamaki house dynamiting, he kept pursuing the issue in his questions. But Tsutsumi did not waver in his insistence that everything that happened in the meetings was in the minutes. When Heen asked where the meeting minutes were, Tsutsumi answered, "They were taken to the grand jury. All the records were taken . . . by a police officer in a canvas bag to the grand jury. . . . There were a number of books that I couldn't count. I think the treasury department book alone was about twenty. There might have been several hundreds of books in that bag."

When Heen expressed doubt that Tsutsumi had seen this happen, Tsutsumi once again answered firmly: "Automobile came here and as I looked into the automobile I saw a number of books. I said, 'What's the matter?' He said all the books of the Federation is brought here and as I looked into the automobile, there were books there that I remember was in the automobile." (The loss of these records was no doubt the reason that Tsutsumi did not write a sequel to his volume covering the history of the strike up to April.)

Heen's cross-examination ended without making significant inroads into Tsutsumi's testimony. Even the *Honolulu Advertiser* concluded that the testimony of this "star witness" was not shaken. In particular, it noted that he "told a radically different story of the now-famous 'ruckus' at the Kyōrakukan teahouse."

THE TESTIMONY OF KAN'ICHI TAKIZAWA AND FUMIO KAWAMATA

The eleventh witness for the defense, Kan'ichi Takizawa, the federation director representing the Waipahu union, was the second son of a farm family outside Komagane City in Nagano prefecture. Since his older brother was adopted through marriage into another family, Takizawa was to have succeeded as head of the family, but when he was seventeen years old a friend who dreamed of going to America enticed him to run away from home and go to Hawaii. Only thirty-two, Takizawa was short, fat, and balding and looked considerably older than Tsutsumi and Miyazawa, who were the same age. He was a good-natured man who liked to compose Japanese *waka*-style poems and write essays, even though he was not much good at it. The card on Takizawa in the immigration directory at the Honolulu Japanese consulate bore the same red-ink notation as Hoshino's: he was marked as a "dangerous person who attempted to bring charges against Consul General Yada."

According to Matsumoto's testimony, when he was ordered to go to Hawaii on May 22, Kan'ichi Takizawa told him that the quickest way to get rid of someone was to use dynamite, and afterward Takizawa shouted at him that he had done the job for their twenty-five thousand comrades so he should not demand payment for it. Not only did Takizawa deny Matsumoto's testimony, he said that he had never met or talked to him. "I only saw him at the office of the Waipahu union, talking to somebody else," he testified. "I never talk to him." The only time he had seen Saitō was on or about June 12 or 13. "There was going to be a [sumo] wrestling tournament at Waipahu," he said. "Before the wrestling tournament took place, everybody practiced in front of the union office. A tall and lean man was there and he was the next, and I asked them who he was and I was told that that was Saitō." But he had never spoken to Saitō.

Prosecutor Heen's prefunctory cross-examination prompted only one significant response from Takizawa, who said that Ogata, Nakazawa, and other planters' dogs at Waipahu had stirred up trouble throughout the strike and that the plantation had been the site of the greatest number of clashes with scabs. Tsutsumi and Miyazawa had already testified that the strikers on various plantations had organized security groups on their own and that federation headquarters had not known the details. But Takizawa testified, "There were twelve hundred members [striking at Waipahu] and it was divided into several departments and somebody named one department as picket." At the very least this was an admission that there had been a picket troop at Waipahu Plantation. Heen had tried to establish that prosecution witnesses Matsumoto and Saitō had been pickets and that because they were engaged in "dirty work" during the strike, federation headquarters leaders had ordered them to kill Sakamaki. That was why he had persistently asked the defendants about the existence of picket troops. Nevertheless, when he finally obtained a response confirming the existence of the pickets, he failed to pursue the matter.

Fumio Kawamata, the twelfth witness for the defense, faced direct examination for twenty minutes, cross-examination for another twenty minutes, then redirect for about five minutes. Kawamata, a native of Ibaragi prefecture, had experience as a technician in the shipping industry. He had arrived in Hawaii ten years earlier, and when the strike began he was working at the Waipahu Plantation company store.

Together with Takizawa, Kawamata participated in the Oahu union as a delegate from Waipahu Plantation. About one month before the strike ended, he was selected as Waipahu delegate to the federation, replacing a predecessor who had died of influenza. Kawamata was in the "internal affairs" department of the organization. After the strike, Kawamata was elected the Oahu union secretary. When Tsutsumi and others resigned from the Hawaii Laborer's Association (formerly the Federation of Japanese Labor), Kawamata was elected association headquarters secretary.

In late December 1920, around Christmas time, Honji Fujitani of Waialua Plantation, who had remained at association headquarters after the strike, had gotten into a heated argument with Kinzaburō Makino, president of the *Hawaii hōchi,* at a public meeting. The *Hōchi* had been ridiculing the new leaders of the association, but there were rumors that Makino had demanded $110,000 from the HSPA to act as mediator in the strike. The commotion occurred when Fujitani confronted Makino about this directly.

Since the association had bought the *Hawaii shinpō* as its mouthpiece, the debate raged on in the pages of the *Hōchi* and the *Shinpō.* But instead of confronting Fujitani, the *Hōchi* made personal attacks against Kawamata. For example, the *Hōchi* ran a front page headline saying that Kawamata was blacklisted for having duped "the Consulate General of the Empire of Japan." In large type, it printed a "notice" issued by the Consulate General two years before the strike.

Notice:
Fumio Kawamata:

For giving untrue statements regarding the existence of a previous wife in the guarantee for proof of sending for a wife submitted to this consulate by Ryōsaku Koike on January 25, 1918, we hereby prohibit you from acting as guarantor for applications to this consulate for the next six months, according to Notice No. 1 of January this year.[30]

Kawamata may have been unaware of Koike's bigamy and merely guaranteed him as he was requested to do, but the *Hōchi* cited this document as proof that Kawamata was a "smooth talker." "It would be a simple matter for Fumio Kawamata, who attempted to deceive the Consulate General of the Empire of Japan, to deceive laborers," the newspaper declared. "If the laborers think of the self-serving articles he has published in the *Hawaii shinpō*, they will certainly realize what he is up to."[31]

Kawamata, who had a long face with even features, rarely expressed his emotions. His gaze was aloof, but his "nihilistic" manner was attractive to women. His common-law wife was an older woman who managed a hotel, where he lived with her during his release after the indictment. For this reason, the *Hōchi* called Kawamata a "gigolo."

It was because of the articles in the *Hōchi* that Heen abruptly asked Kawamata during his cross-examination, "Are you married?" When Kawamata answered that he was not, Heen pursued the point: "You are living with a woman, are you not?"

Although Lymar instructed Kawamata that it was his constitutional right not to answer a question about whether or not he was living with a woman, Kawamata answered Heen with composure. "I would not answer how many years, but I am living with a certain woman."

In spite of the tropical climate, the Puritan ethic of the missionaries had taken root, so there was a prudishness about relations between men and women in Hawaii. Hoping to appeal to the moral sentiments of the jury, prosecutor Heen continued to focus on Kawamata's character.

HEEN: "Isn't it a fact that Japanese Federation of Labor gave you certain money to pay to the strikers at the rate of $25 and that, instead of paying the strikers the $25 allotted, you paid the strikers $20 each and embezzled five dollars out of each sum?"

KAWAMATA: "No. I could give a reason to that if you wish to hear . . ." (Heen stopped him.)

Heen stopped this testimony, then peppered Kawamata with questions about his involvement in violence during the strike. "Isn't it a fact that during the strike, you attempted to dynamite the house of one Alcara at Waipahu?" "Isn't it a fact that, during the strike, you committed assault and battery on Y. Saito at Waipio?" "Isn't it a fact that during the strike, you attempted to dynamite the house of T. Fukunaga on Kauai?"

The prosecution was seeking to paint Fumio Kawamata, Tsutsumi's successor at association headquarters, as a womanizer lacking in morals. Heen did not ask a single question related to the charges in the indictment.

The next witness for the defense was Ichiji Gotō, who was sitting with the other defendants. As noted before, when he was sixteen Gotō had been brought to Hawaii by his father and had gone to work on a sugar plantation. Before the strike he was a reporter for the *Nippu jiji*. His friends regarded him as a very serious and quiet person.

In contrast to Tsutsumi and Miyazawa, Gotō's strength was his ability to work quietly in the background. But at public meetings he displayed a passion that seemed wholly uncharacteristic. On the speaker's platform he would recall the unforgettable experience of seeing his father whipped by a Portuguese luna for some minor infraction. Gotō reached Hawaii the same year that Sen Katayama's *Tobei annai* was published. On its back cover was an advertisement for the journal *Rōdō sekai*: "*Rōdō sekai* sympathizes in particular with the weak in present-day society." Gotō may have been one of those who took these words to heart.

After the strike, Gotō wrote:

> Numerous struggles awaited the Japanese immigrants, who lived under countless unfavorable conditions, when they sought decent treatment as human beings. Confronting them were strong enemies: oppression by the planters who saw them as cattle; public officials who backed the capitalists in their quest for profits first; unfairness of political power; and deep-seated racial discrimination against foreign communities. . . . Harmony and friendly relations can be realized only when both sides are on equal footing; it is utterly impossible when one side acts like the king and the other is treated like beasts of burden.

In responding to Lymar's short direct examination, Gotō said that he had first seen Matsumoto and Saitō in the courtroom, and he denied having heard about Matsumoto and the others going to Hawaii on May 22. Prosecutor Heen's cross-examination was simple.

HEEN: "As secretary in the Federation how much were you getting?"

GOTŌ: "At first I received a salary of $85 and, in meeting of delegates in June [1920], the salary was fixed at $150."

Gotō was an only child who looked after his elderly parents. That was why Gotō was the only federation secretary who had received a wage from the start.

HEEN: "During the strike, did you go around and find out whether anybody was obstructing the strike?"

GOTŌ: "No, I didn't make any investigation. I had in mind that capitalists would object, and interfere with the strike."

HEEN: "Well, isn't it a fact that officials of the Federation made it their business to find out who among the Japanese were obstructing the strike?"

GOTŌ: "In my opinion, everybody thought that our strike was *pololei* [true] and everybody was in favor of it."

HEEN: "These speeches that you made during the strike were for what purpose?"

GOTŌ: "My intention was to keep these strikers quiet, to have them use a peaceful method and, being there's lots of number, I was afraid these strikers may go astray."

HEEN: "And you continued to make those speeches throughout the strike?"

GOTŌ: "Not only that, but I was making speech to strikers to bind themselves with each other and not go back to work until final instruction is given for them to go back to work, and that, of course, has been continued right to the end of the strike."

Gotō was the only defendant to use the term "capitalists" or to assert that the workers had a legitimate right to strike. While working as a school boy, Gotō had sought solace in the Bible. He was a deeply religious Christian believer throughout his life, and his testimony fully revealed his simple but innate sense of justice.

THE EXAMINATION OF WITNESSES ENDS

On February 28 the fair weather that Honolulu had enjoyed for several days turned to gray skies and strong winds. The direct examination of the day's first witness, Tsurunosuke Koyama, was conducted by Charles Davis, Brown's law partner, who served as attorney for Koyama and Ishiyama, the two defendants from Hawaii. The thirty-three-year-old Davis had studied law at Stanford University, then served as prosecutor for the city and county of Honolulu.

Davis's questioning of his witness, whom he always addressed as "Mr. Koyama," was orderly and easy to follow. Koyama, who was forty-two years old at the time, gave his answers succinctly, with no extraneous information. Like Kondō and Hoshino, both forty-three, he was one of the older defendants. On August 2, 1921, at the time of the indictment, the *Honolulu Advertiser* reported that Koyama was "an active radical agitator among the strikers," but nothing could be further from the truth. In contrast to the other defendants, he was a calming personality.

Koyama was born and raised in Shinonoi, Nagano prefecture. The hill behind his family home, now owned by his nephew, is an apple orchard. Koyama's father had moved to Shinonoi from Kyoto to open a one-room school in a temple. Koyama, the fourth son, was registered as Tazurunosuke, but he disliked this name, which sounded like that of a Kabuki actor specializing in female roles, so he went by the name of Tsurunosuke. After graduating from the Nagano normal school, he hoped to study in the United States. As a first step he emigrated to Hawaii, only to find that he could not cross to the mainland owing to the legal ban on immigration. He worked as a school boy for a Caucasian teacher in Olaa, then worked in the cane fields and used his savings to open a store at Waiakea Plantation. By the time of the strike eight years later, he had succeeded at raising chickens and managed to acquire some land.

Koyama and his wife, Teru, were known to be a very close couple. They had no children of their own but raised a family of five orphaned children. Koyama was a taciturn and placid man who did not mind helping others. Japanese laborers sought him out to discuss their troubles, including those related to women and gambling. He was skilled at calligraphy, and almost every day someone asked him to write a letter or a document.

When the Waiakea Plantation union was formed in November 1919, Koyama was unable to turn down its chairmanship, and soon thereafter he was elected chairman of the Hawaii Island union. As delegate from Hawaii he attended the January 1920 meeting to determine whether to hold the strike, the April delegates' meeting, and the June delegates' meeting, which voted to end the strike. Koyama was chosen to chair these meetings, which had to reach agreement on key issues. Koyama always managed to calm the excited debate with great skill. Because he came down with influenza, he had declined to chair the poststrike delegates' meeting that discussed the restructuring of the federation, but he was finally pressured into service and brought the contentious meeting to an agreement. When Tsutsumi and the others resigned their duties, Koyama also resigned from the Hawaii Island union.

Koyama testified that he had visited Olaa Plantation several times during the strike to make speeches, but he had never seen Jūzaburō Sakamaki at these lecture meetings, nor had he heard anything about Sakamaki's activities to obstruct the strike. This was important testimony. If Sakamaki's efforts at obstructing the strike were so negligible to be of little concern to the Hawaii Island union, then the territory's indictment was considerably weakened. He also said that he had seen Matsumoto and Saitō for the first time in the courtroom. And he denied the allegations of Matsumoto and Saitō about the conspiracy forged at the teahouse outside Hilo and orders to dynamite the Sakamaki house.

In his cross-examination prosecutor Heen asked Koyama how responsibilities were distributed at federation headquarters, but Koyama answered that he saw the officers only when he went to Honolulu for meetings and did not even know their names very well.

To Heen's question, "Where were you on the 23rd of May, 1920?" Koyama answered, "I was at (Hawaii Island union) headquarters." When asked whether Ishida and Miyamura had been there, he answered, "I think he was there" and "I think everybody was there." For some reason Heen did not ask Koyama if Matsumoto, who allegedly had been given orders in Honolulu, had visited the office, but he did ask Koyama who had been at the office on May 27, when Miyamura allegedly ordered the Sakamaki house to be dynamited. Once again, Koyama said he had been, and Heen merely confirmed that Ishida and Miyamura had been there as well. Heen did not question Koyama about the crucial secret meeting at the teahouse. He simply treated Koyama's response as establishing the fact of the secret meeting at the teahouse.

The next witness, Sazō Satō, thirty-three years old, also from the Hawaii Island union, was the only defendant whose place of origin and background I was unable to trace. His testimony revealed that at the time of the strike he was working at the Laupahoehoe Plantation sugar mill and was elected its union chairman. As director from the Hawaii Island union, he was at federation headquarters in Honolulu from the end of February on. Plantation company guards tried to force his wife and child, who had remained at Laupahoehoe, to move out of plantation housing because Satō was not there. Deciding to return to Hawaii to settle the matter, Satō submitted his resignation to federation headquarters on May 20.

Before leaving for Hawaii, Satō visited a friend by the name of Hamano in Kailua. In those days there was no highway cutting through Nuuanupali gorge, so he had to travel along the coastline. Satō left Honolulu on May 21 and stayed two nights at Hamano's house in Kailua. Although prosecution witnesses Matsumoto and Saitō had said that he was at federation headquarters on May 22, Satō asserted in his testimony that he was still in Kailua that day. Only on May 23 did he return to Honolulu.

Satō was unable to reach agreement with Laupahoehoe Plantation about his family, so he took his wife and child to Honolulu, where he was in charge of the federation headquarters' warehouse from June to September. His work consisted of managing everything from distributing foods and sundries to the evicted workers to the use of automobiles by federation headquarters. He testified that there was "trouble" between Seiichi Suzuki, a former director of the federation, and federation headquarters.

> [Suzuki] brought an automobile from Maui; that was with the proposition of the Federation buying that automobile. We bought the automobile. . . . The agreement was that the Federation was to buy automobile, in case the Federation would become unnecessary with the automobile that they would re-sell this to Suzuki. He came to the place where I was staying on Nuuanu Street, and he broached this proposition to me, he says, "I have sold this automobile to the Federation. I want to be clear of that sale. Would you pay me $300? and that you could do with the automobile just as you please." I told him the automobile is not worth that much and I offered him a hundred dollars and notified him to that effect. I paid him $150 and had the thing settled up. He was dissatisfied and he says that "the Federation had this automobile for a long time and now to just give me $150 for it is not right." He says, "I am hard up for my living and I couldn't go back to Maui for reasons that I was dismissed from the place that I came from," and he said that he was not treated right.

In his cross-examination, Heen made no reference to this trouble between Suzuki and the federation. He focused instead on trying to shake Satō's alibi that he was not at federation headquarters in Honolulu on May 22, but Satō did not change his story. With Satō's testimony, Lymar completed the case for the defense. Fifteen witnesses had been called for the defense, including nine of the defendants, and ten exhibits had been submitted into evidence.

On Wednesday, March 1, when the court opened, Harold Stafford, an attorney for the prosecution, asked the judge, "If your honor please, at this time we would ask to reopen the case for the purpose of putting on the testimony of a certain witness that we discovered. This information was discovered last night between eight and nine o'clock." Defense attorney Lymar immediately objected because he had not been notified of this request in advance. After forty-five minutes of argument between the prosecution and defense attorneys, the newly discovered key witness for the prosecution was finally called.

Very nervously, the witness gave his name as Bunkichi Tsuda.

I work at the wireless station at Koko Head now, but was working at Ewa plantation until the strike. After being evicted and going to Honolulu, I worked as a crew member of the inter-island steam ship. But the work was too hard, and I only worked there for a short time. I lived at Katō shrine which was a camp for evicted strikers. One day I was contacted by Ewa plantation union chairman Yokoo to become a picket.

The headquarters of the pickets was . . . behind Tokiwaen. I met Mr. Tsutsumi and Mr. Furushō there. I don't remember the exact date and time. It may have been about a month after the dynamiting [about mid-July]. I was with two other pickets, Y. Matsumoto and J. Matsumoto [different person from prosecution witness Junji Matsumoto].

Mr. Tsutsumi said he was on his way to visit a friend nearby, and I hardly spoke to him. He may have said something like, things must be hard for you. Mr. Tsutsumi had just dropped by.

Becoming impatient, Judge Banks interjected that he did not think the testimony offered was material, but Heen asked for the court's indulgence.

[TSUDA]: "[About mid-August] I went to the federation office with Y. Matsumoto and told Tsutsumi if he would not give us five dollars a week for our expenses. Tsutsumi said 'I think that could be done,' and says, 'I wish you to act as you were acting up to this present time,' and then we left the place.

"I also talked to Mr. Tsutsumi and Mr. Furushō about Nakazawa. It was also at the Federation headquarters office."

HEEN: "Do you remember you had a talk with Furushō and Tsutsumi after the dynamiting at Olaa?"

TSUDA: "No."

HEEN: "Did you have a conversation with me last night, through the interpreter, about some conversation you had with Furushō and Tsutsumi?"

Lymar objected to the question: "We object to this as an attempt to impeach his own witness, without any showing of hospitality."

Heen then asked Tsuda whether he had not said the night before that Tsutsumi and Furushō had ordered the dynamiting of Nakazawa's house in Ewa and that they had told him he should do the same thing that Matsumoto, Saitō, and Murayama had done in dynamiting Sakamaki's house in Olaa. Lymar objected again, and arguments between the lawyers continued for a while. Finally, Heen produced a summary of the statement the witness had written for him the night before.

HEEN (to the witness): "Read this over and see if that will refresh your recollection as to the facts stated in it."

TSUDA: "Yes."

HEEN: "Now, when you had this talk with Tsutsumi and Furushō about Nakazawa, was that before or after the dynamiting of Sakamaki's house?"

TSUDA: "Before the dynamiting."

If Tsuda insisted that the talk had taken place before the Sakamaki dynamiting incident, then the prosecution could not show that Tsutsumi and others had ordered that Nakazawa be dealt with in the same way. Heen, taken aback by Tsuda's answer, asked to have the jury removed and to put on testimony to show that his witness was adverse. After the jury left the courtroom, Judge Banks told Heen that he had a right to withdraw his witness if he wished. Heen replied that he wished to do so, but Lymar was not satisfied. So Tsuda was called again to the witness stand for cross-examination by the defense.

Lymar was about to begin when Heen called out for the judge to wait.

HEEN: "Now I object to the defendant's talking to him, if the Court please. Tsutsumi and this man here, Kawamata, were just talking to him when they were asking that counsel talk to him. That is not right."

JUDGE BANKS: "Just a moment gentlemen."

HEEN: "Furthermore, we have got evidence that Tsutsumi talked to him before he was brought in this morning, that's our trouble. Tsutsumi is still talking to him, right at this moment."

The judge permitted prosecutor Heen to question Tsuda again.

HEEN: "Do you wish to make any change in the testimony that you gave this morning? Tell him to answer the question yes or no [to the interpreter]."

TSUDA: "No, I do not."

HEEN: "Were you advised by anyone not to make any statement this morning?"

Turning to Judge Banks, Heen asked to withdraw the witness, closing the curtain that he himself had raised on this little drama. The *Honolulu Advertiser* headlined, "New Witness in Bomb Case Is Surprise," that the prosecution was disappointed in Tsuda's testimony. The prosecution, however, had readied a final move. Heen recalled Seiichi Suzuki to the stand. The dapper Suzuki was dressed in white flannels, but in contrast to his earlier appearance on the witness stand, he gave the impression of being a professional killer in his answers to Heen's questions.

Yes, first part of April, 1920, Kawamata and Furushō gave me instructions about this Filipino Alcara, at the Federation headquarter office. They told me that this man Alcara is for the plantation and working against the cause, and wanted me to go and kill him.

Yes, at that time Furushō told me to blow up the bridge at Kipapa Valley. It was this bridge, on the main road, in plantation as it was a bridge where plantation railroad runs.

Yes, I talked with Murakami about T. Harada, a contractor. Harada is the man that tried to get laborers back to the plantation, and we had to fix him up. We talked about beating him up. I talked with Tsutsumi after the assault. He was very happy when I made the report to him. He says, "You did fine," and he gave me some money to be paid to parties working under me.

Yes, sometimes afterwards (after talked about Alcara), it was either Togashi or Sakurai who was returned to work and, for that reason, I received a telephone message and I went to Waiapahu branch. Furushō asked me to kill them.

In contrast to his earlier testimony, Suzuki repeatedly used the word "kill," as Heen had expected he would. Judge Banks ordered Suzuki to stop his testimony at 12:15. He adjourned the court by stating, "Gentlemen, I want to get through with this case this week, I have other matters in court that need my attention and I am very anxious to get through this case this week." So Seiichi Suzuki continued his sinister testimony the next day.

Yes, I knew Sumizawa at Kahuku. I was sent there by Tsutsumi, he told me he got a telephone message from Y. Sato, for me to go there, there's some trouble up there.

I went to Honganji (Honganji Temple where strikers from Kahuku stayed) and talked to Y. Sato and others. I went to the Federation hospital at Kalihi with Y. Sato and others by automobile. We took Sumizawa into stable near the hospital and Y. Sato was telling Sumizawa to go back to the plantation. Sumizawa was asked by N. Baku to come to Honolulu to get the laborers back. Sato was telling Sumizawa to telephone to these two persons Tokimatsu and N. Baku that the laborers are ready and for them to come into Honolulu, but for them not to come by way of Waipahu because it is dangerous but come from outside.

It was a few days after that. I drove Sumizawa from Sato's house to Dr. Hasegawa's place in Alewa Heights. We met T. Baba at Doctor's place. Sumizawa requested that he wanted to work and he asked us to send him somewhere to work. Dr. Hasegawa said he could not keep him at his place but he would telephone to a man named Okazaki, who had a pineapple field, and he would find out whether he is home or not. After telephoning Okazaki, he wasn't there. Dr. Hasegawa said that there's a man by name of Seikan Saitō at Leilehua and he said, "I think that's the best place to go." And we decided to send him there. Then we all went there.

I was afraid that in case the police get hold of him that everything would come out, and to hide him away by supplying him with some work.

The testimony was cut off when Lymar objected, so it is not clear what they were afraid might come out. Then Heen continued his questioning.

HEEN: "Mr. Suzuki, when you came back from Maui and brought thirty sticks of dynamite, you told us before that you saw Tsutsumi after you got back. Do you recall that?"

SUZUKI: "I did."

HEEN: "Now what did Tsutsumi tell you about the dynamite that you brought back, if anything?"

The court never heard his answer because Lymar raised another objection. Having managed to link Tsutsumi's name to dynamite and to suggest to the jury the connection between the two, Heen ended his questions to Suzuki. Perhaps because Suzuki's testimony was not relevant, defense attorney Lymar did not cross-examine him.

CLOSING ARGUMENTS

On Friday, March 3, closing arguments were presented. It was to turn out to be a long day for all in the courtroom. The prosecution's arguments were opened by Harold Stafford, whom Judge Banks referred to in court as "Captain." An infantry captain in World War I, Harold Stafford had been a central figure in the American Legion in Hawaii. When the legion had presented the Hawaiian legislature with a bill to regulate the foreign-language press, it was Stafford who had drafted it. Although his closing argument and that of the defense do not exist in the trial transcript, the *Honolulu Advertiser* reported them in detail.

According to the newspaper, although Stafford's argument consumed the entire morning session and stretched well into the afternoon, "it can be truthfully said that there was 'not a dull moment' during the time he was addressing the jury. Even while the prosecutor painted prosaic word pictures of the less dramatic situations of the alleged conspiracy, he commanded the close attention of every person in the courtroom. On the occasions when he rose to oratorical flights, the entire assemblage was, figuratively speaking, on its tip toes."[32]

"Gentlemen of the jury," Stafford began, "the Territory was in no way concerned with the strike itself—whether or not it was justified, or even properly conducted. Every man has a right to a fair return for the labor and a right to strike in order to get it. Show me a man who is ashamed of a hard spot on his hand put there by honest labor and I will show you a man who has a soft spot in his head." But, he continued, the Japanese Federation of Labor needed money to carry on the strike.

> Any man who stood in the way of their raising that money might well have been considered an enemy, and his eliminating a blessing. . . .
> Even though [the defendants] had no intention of ordering the three alleged dynamiters to commit an unlawful act when they dispatched them from Honolulu to Hilo with the instructions to see the officials of the Hawaii Union for further details, the mere facts that they were thus dispatched and that they did subsequently dynamite Sakamaki's house, if proven, bound the defendants to pay the penalty in company with the actual perpetrators of the atrocity.

After designating the key prosecution witnesses, Matsumoto, Saitō, and Murakami, as "perpetrators," Stafford said that he did not claim that all defendants had knowledge that the three men were promised rewards: "In our opinion, the offer was probably made by Miyamura without authority. It was a big 'sack of oats' held out to Matsumoto, Saitō and Murakami after Yoshimura (who was to have aided in the Sakamaki bombing) had vanished. However these defendants did not dare repudiate the offers because they knew what the three men had done. Consequently, they passed the buck from one to the other until the men got tired and told their story."

In commenting on the defendants who claimed to have alibis for May 22, when the order was said to have been issued, Stafford said, "If the defense had been at all satisfied with any of these alibis, . . . I defy them to say that what they have proves that they had no faith in any of them, nor have we." For example, Stafford termed Hiroshi Miyazawa a liar for claiming that he was a pastor when he had no such qualifications at all. Indeed, Stafford attempted to give the impression that all of those with firm alibis were also suspect. By contrast, Stafford praised prosecution witnesses Matsumoto and Saitō, whom he had called "perpetrators": "They could not have stood the long grilling of Judge Lymar, in cross-examination for the defense, had they not been telling the truth." Concluding his lengthy closing argument, he urged that "for the sake of the peaceful and law abiding citizens of the Territory, no matter what their nationality," a guilty verdict be returned.

After an hour's recess for lunch, defense attorney Brooks spoke first for the defense. "His remarks," the *Honolulu Advertiser* reported, "were surcharged with forensic vitriol." He characterized Matsumoto and Saitō "as conscienceless rogues and bastards, cold-blooded as snakes, who would just as soon blow up women and little children as eat their dinner." He continued, "The Territory has known for months just who dynamited Sakamaki's house, but they don't care about that. They have deliberately stepped aside, and allowed private interest to intervene. They have dismissed the case against Matsumoto and Saitō in order that private interests might break up the Japanese Federation of Labor."

When Brooks finished, the chief defense attorney, Lymar, began his closing argument with the observation that never before in his experience as an attorney had he listened to "a supposed argument of facts in which had crept so much intolerance and prejudice as had characterized the attitude of the prosecution in this case." For the next two hours, he stoutly proclaimed the innocence of the defendants. The prosecution's charges, he said were like "the tale of a thousand and one Arabian nights." As for the key prosecution witnesses, he characterized Matsumoto as "a desperado and a crook"; Saitō as "the wrestler who tells anything for money"; and Suzuki as a "fire brand 'fitted in every way for desperate business'—a man who should by all rights be deported." The prosecution, he suggested, had suborned the three witnesses and had fabricated evidence to fit the objective of the investigation. Heen and his colleagues, he said, had mounted "one of the flimsiest cases ever presented by a group of public prosecutors in the Territory."

In concluding, Lymar pleaded with the jury to disregard the nationality of the accused men. Because they were not familiar with the English language, he said, they should be given the same benefit of the doubt that the jurors would give any "underdog" in the interests of the American ideal of fair play.

At 8:15 P.M., Judge Banks addressed the jury, "If you have any feelings in this case, any prejudice either for the defendants or against them, you must subordinate that to the one great purpose of arriving at a just verdict which, in all the future years, will meet the approval of your conscience." It was after 9:10 P.M. when the twelve members of the jury withdrew from the courtroom to begin deliberations on the case. They no doubt looked very tired after the long day in court. Two hours later, at 11:21 P.M., they announced their inability to arrive at a decision and repaired to a nearby hotel for the night.

In selecting the jury, both the prosecution and the defense attorneys challenged everyone with names sounding like those of people of color. The twelve jurors had Anglo-Saxon names. If any were of partly Hawaiian heritage, given the Hawaiian social structure, they would have been close to the white governing class. And one must wonder how many of the jurors would have been able to connect the names and faces of the fifteen Japanese defendants as they deliberated on the verdict.

All of the witnesses had been Japanese, and most of the names mentioned in their testimony were Japanese. Throughout the trial the jury complained that they were confused about the names and that it was difficult for them to grasp the gist of the testimony. The judge and the prosecutors had raised similar questions. Even the trial transcript often erred in reporting names. It referred to Sutsumi (for Tsutsumi), Konda (for Kondō), Mujazawa (for Miyazawa), Hashino (for Hoshino), making it seem as if they were entirely different people. Since laborers on the plantations were identified with numbers, it is perhaps understandable that haoles had trouble remembering Japanese names, no matter how many times they heard them. One cannot help but be disturbed at the thought that this linguistic barrier may have affected the verdict.

Indifference to getting Japanese names right was echoed in the failure of either the prosection or the defense to address witnesses with the normal courtesies. Jūzaburō Sakamaki was the only one who both the prosecution and the defense addressed as "Mister."

With the exception of Sakamaki's testimony and part of Miyazawa's, the jury heard the Japanese witnesses only through the filter of the court interpreter, Kin'ichirō Maruyama. But the crux of the problem may have been the way that Japanese was spoken at the trial. Even in spoken English the meaning is unclear unless a subject is named. By contrast, in spoken Japanese it is easier and smoother to omit the subject. Even if a Japanese speaker does not use the first-person singular or the first-person plural, or even the second- and third-person, his meaning can be discerned from the context.

In English, it is also necessary always to clarify the affirmative or the negative. But in Japanese, the conversation often proceeds by using expressions that can be taken as either affirmative or negative, and there is a tendency to use very few words in expectation that the listener will divine the meaning. If Japanese spoken in this way is converted directly into English, a language that stresses clarity, then the result may be not only misunderstandings but also even a reversal of the nuances of the words used.

Naturally, this characteristic of the Japanese language reflects the psychological structure of a homogeneous society. To outsiders, tacit understanding among those sharing the same history, customs, and traditions as an ethnic group can appear as mutual indulgence, and avoiding verbal confrontations can be seen as evading responsibility. By contrast, in the United States, a heterogeneous nation made up of immigrants from very different cultures, people face many internal social boundaries, so perhaps it is natural that they expect clarity in daily conversational exchanges.

In any case, Maruyama's job at the trial was not easy. That said, however, the English interpretation appearing in the trial transcript raises doubts about how much of the testimony the jurors, who were ignorant of Japanese culture and customs, really understood.

WHAT WAS JUDGED?

The more one rereads the trial transcript, the more doubts arise about the testimony. The prosecution case was based on the testimony of Matsumoto and Saitō, the two accomplices who had "confessed" to dynamiting the Sakamaki house. While their testimony was extremely specific, most of it did not agree with objective facts or material evidence. Odd and illogical statements crop up everywhere.

The prosecution had not established the facts as charged as solidly as Heen claimed. It should have been easy for the prosecution to substantiate the whereabouts of various witnesses through hotel registration records, yet the only one entered as an exhibit was a guest registry of the Okino Hotel. And this merely confirmed the names of Matsumoto, Murakami, and Akamine (not the name Saitō) for the night of May 23 when they arrived in Hilo. The hotel in Olaa, where Matsumoto said he stayed after leaving the Okino Hotel until the night of the crime, June 3, was not named in the testimony, nor was its guest register submitted. The accomplice Murakami was said to have arrived in Hilo on the morning of the crime, June 3, secretly carrying dynamite, and to have returned to Honolulu the following day, but a guest register for the night of the crime, when Murakami stayed at the Matano Hotel, was not submitted. Nor was a passenger list submitted for the interisland steamer that Murakami used to travel between Honolulu and Hilo. Instead the prosecution submitted the passenger list for the *Maunakea* of May 22, the day Matsumoto and others allegedly received their orders to go to Hilo. This list included the names Matsumoto and "Akamine," the alias that Saitō allegedly used. Matsumoto and Saitō both testified that they had boarded the ship separately and had not met until they were in Hilo. But the passenger list notes the names Fujitani, Murakami, Matsumoto, and Akamine in that order. And although both key prosecution witnesses stated that on the way back to Honolulu they had boarded separately so as not to be noticed, the names Matsumoto and Akamine were together on that passenger list too.

If Matsumoto and the others boarded using their real names, it should have been obvious that eventually they would be found listed together. That made it meaningless for only Saitō to use an alias. Saitō said that he had "borrowed" the name of his acquaintance, but it makes more sense to conclude that it was Akamine himself who boarded the ship for Hilo. The prosecution needed a second witness to corroborate Matsumoto's testimony, so it was not inconceivable that the prosecution had Saitō state that he used the alias "Akamine."

The trump card in the prosecution's case was the testimony of Matsumoto and Saitō. It was indispensable for establishing the crime of conspiracy. But the testimony of the two men lacked consistency, raising a suspicion that they perjured themselves. If so, then there must have been a reason why they did so. Matsumoto may have wanted revenge against the federation leaders for the humiliation he received in the Kyōrakukan assault incident, and perhaps for a life so failed that he had attempted suicide. Saitō had been arrested for illegally distilling liquor and gambling, and he was also guilty of jumping bail. And it is possible that the district attorney's office had some other things on both men.

Matsumoto and Saitō were clearly in weak positions. Each had reached a dead end in life. What if the HSPA had secretly assured them that their slates would be wiped clean and they would receive money to return to Japan? If one recalls the trap that HSPA lawyer Frank Thompson set for the Filipino union president Manlapit to force him to issue a stop strike order, this does not seem far-fetched. There are no clues as to what happened to Matsumoto and Saitō after the trial, and there is a strong possibility that Saitō was using an alias.

The motive for the conspiracy charged by the territory of Hawaii may appear plausible at first glance. But Jūzaburō Sakamaki himself admitted in court that his attempts to obstruct the strike were limited to Olaa Plantation and merely consisted of placing the newspaper *Kazan* (Volcano) where the laborers would see it. If, as the prosecution asserted, the motive for the conspiracy was to serve as a lesson to other "planters' dogs" who were resisting the federation, doing away with Sakamaki would not have had much impact. In fact, the names of several "dogs" working for the planters on Oahu in opposition to the federation were raised more than once in the trial. If the purpose of the "conspiracy" was to restrain anti-strike activities, it would have made more sense to take action on Oahu than on Hawaii where the laborers were still at work.

The aims of the territory in bringing the indictment can be understood if we divide the twenty-one defendants into four groups. In the first group were the three federation secretaries, Noboru Tsutsumi, Ichiji Gotō, and Hiroshi Miyazawa, who led the strike. Clearly these men were children of their time, influenced by the reverberations of the Russian revolution. All three were moved by a clear consciousness that they were reforming the world. Though their actions may not have been tied to an ideology, to the power elite in Hawaii, they were committing threatening crimes of conscience.

Of the three, Tsutsumi, who had resigned his position after the resolution of the strike, remained the brains behind association headquarters. As late as 1921 he traveled around the islands raising money to compensate the laborers who had joined the Oahu strike. Tsutsumi also urged collective action by the cane field workers and the pineapple field workers to demand higher wages. Since the majority of the latter were also Japanese immigrants, from the vantage point of the territorial authorities, a labor struggle involving both of these major industries would have posed the danger of a Japanese takeover of Hawaii. An FBI report issued six months before the indictment reflected such fears: "The Japanese Federation was a weapon in Japan's strategy to take over Hawaii. The Japanese engaged in a radical labor movement as a means and weapon of national and racial policies to dominate the Hawaiian islands economically and politically. The Federation was an example of the frightening unity and teamwork of the Japanese." [33]

In the second group were the officers of the Oahu union that had gone on strike in 1920: Fumio Kawamata (Waipahu), Kan'ichi Takizawa (Waipahu), Shunji Tomota (Waianae), Honji Fujitani (Waialua), Tokuji Baba (Waialua), Yōkichi Satō (Kahuku), and Eijūrō Yokoo (Ewa). After the strike, when Tsutsumi and the others resigned, they became the core leaders of federation headquarters, directing the labor movement until the indictment.

The third group consisted of those at the location where the crime took place: Tsurunosuke Koyama, Kaichi Miyamura, Chikao Ishida, Chūhei Hoshino, and Sazō Satō of the Hawaii Island union. The prosecution claimed that they were the main actors in the Sakamaki house dynamiting incident.

The fourth group was made up of two men connected with the workers' security organizations, Shōshichirō Furushō and Seigo Kondō. These defendants formed a supporting cast to corroborate the testimony of Matsumoto and Saitō. According to the prosecution, both were semi-outlaw local bosses.

It is also possible to divide the defendants into those able to defend themselves on the witness stand and those who were not given that opportunity. To review, of the twenty-one defendants named in the indictment, fifteen actually appeared in court, and nine of these took the witness stand: the three federation secretaries, Tsutsumi, Miyazawa, and Gotō; the federation directors, Baba, Hoshino, Takizawa, Kawamata, and Satō; and Koyama of the Hawaii Island union.

At the outset, the defense attorney stated that in the interests of time, and taking into consideration Judge Banks's desire to complete the case as soon as possible, he would not call each defendant to the witness stand. One of those who did not testify was Shunji Tomota, twenty-seven years old, who worked as a mill hand after he arrived in Hawaii from Hiroshima at fifteen and who represented Waimanalo Plantation at the Oahu union during the strike. After the strike and the resignation of Tsutsumi and others, he joined federation headquarters. As his position was similar to that of Kawamata and Takizawa, it is understandable that he would not need to testify.

In the case of Ishida, however, the defense may not have pursued the best strategy. The testimony about Ishida given by the prosecution witness was not sufficiently countered by the testimony of Koyama, who

222 / THE CONSPIRACY TRIAL

was also from the Hawaii Island union. The driver of the car Matsumoto and the other perpetrators allegedly used on the night of the crime testified that he had handed over to Ishida the gun he had found in his car. This was crucial testimony that the prosecution used to insinuate that Ishida had wanted the gun so as to destroy the evidence. Yet Ishida was not afforded the opportunity to explain or deny the assertions made. The revolver was not presented as evidence in the trial, nor was any mention made during the trial as to what had happened to it.

Although Honji Fujitani, the Waialua delegate, was not called to the witness stand, Matsumoto testified that not only had he hired Matsumoto to collect subscription fees for *Nippu jiji,* he had also told Matsumoto to go to Honolulu and receive orders from Baba about going to Hilo. On May 22 Fujitani also boarded the same ship for Hilo with Matsumoto on his way to raise strike support funds in Hawaii. Fujitani appears on the passenger list along with Matsumoto and the others. Matsumoto did not give Fujitani's name as one of the conspirators at the teahouse in Hilo, but he did testify that he asked Fujitani to accompany him the second time he went to Hilo to seek the promised $5,000 from the Hawaii Island union. It would seem that the defense could have clarified many of the facts claimed by calling Fujitani to testify.

But defense attorney Lymar might well have wanted to avoid questioning Seigo Kondō and Shōshichirō Furushō. One of Kondō's sidelines was operating a pool hall, and the *Honolulu Advertiser* hinted at his involvement in gambling. Furushō had been convicted of assault and battery on Manpachi Ogata.

The other defendant who did not take the witness stand was Tsunehiko Murakami. Thirty-seven years old at the time, Murakami was from Kumamoto prefecture. During the strike he was the delegate from Ewa Plantation at the Oahu union, but not much more is known about him. The prosecution witnesses testified that Murakami was ordered, along with Matsumoto and Saitō, to dynamite Sakamaki's house and that he obeyed the order. Murakami allegedly was the one who set the dynamite, secretly brought in from Honolulu, under the floor of Sakamaki's house and actually lit the fuse.

Murakami's actions were described only in the testimony of Matsumoto and Saitō. Although Murakami was said to have arrived from Honolulu on the day the crime took place, the prosecution showed no physical evidence to support this, not even, as noted earlier, the passenger list of the *Maunakea.* Yet Lymar never gave Murakami the opportunity to counter the testimony. If Murakami associated with Matsumoto and

Saitō after the strike, was there something besides the Sakamaki incident that the defense did not want the prosecution to question Murakami about?

It is also possible to consider as a group the defendants who had already returned to Japan and were tried in absentia.

Eijūrō Yokoo, the Ewa Plantation union chairman, came from Tsukushi-gun, Fukuoka prefecture. After graduating from middle school he became a local primary school teacher, but he went to Hawaii to work on Ewa Plantation to pay off family debts. His wife, who had accompanied him, died two years after their arrival. According to his second wife, Toyo, Yokoo became a staff member of the Japanese Hospital after the strike ended, but since members of the Ewa union frequently went to his place of work, the Japanese doctor who got him the job told him to cut his ties with the labor movement. Two months before the indictment, he returned to his hometown in Fukuoka, for what he intended as a temporary stay. (Yokoo died in an accident five years later.)

Yōkichi Satō, the Kahuku Plantation union president (33 years old) was a graduate of an agricultural school in Miyagi prefecture. Two years earlier he had been sent from Miyagi prefecture to Kahuku to conduct research on crop practices. Satō won the trust of the Japanese at Kahuku, and as the local Honganji-affiliated school representative he attended the Hawaii education meeting that Tsutsumi participated in. He had been asked to join the movement for a wage increase and had been a central figure among the Japanese at the plantation after the strike. Matsumoto had accused Satō of striking his head with a bottle in the Kyōrakukan incident, and according to Seiichi Suzuki, Satō had assaulted Sumizawa in the stable near the makeshift hospital for evicted workers. But Satō had returned to Japan seven months before the indictment.

It was Kaichi Miyamura whose importance to the case outweighed that of the other defendants who had gone back to Japan. Indeed his return to Japan might have been convenient for the prosecution. Like Koyama and Satō, Miyamura, a contractor at Wainaku Plantation outside Hilo, had been pressured to join the local union movement. The jury heard that Miyamura ordered Matsumoto, Saitō, and Murayama to dynamite Sakamaki's house when they met at the teahouse in Hilo. Miyamura was, in effect, the main alleged perpetrator of the crime behind the scenes. Matsumoto and Saitō had testified that Miyamura had forced them into committing the crime by threatening them: "In case you do so, tell this thing to any outsider and to bring any damage to the cause of this strike, that the Federation publicly suppression of my name and also the name of all the relatives." As if to impress this fact on the jurors, the prosecution had Matsumoto and Saitō repeat this several times. Hidden in their testimony was what the territory really sought to bring to judgment in the trial.

In the first stage of the strike, the Federation of Japanese Labor had made public its regulations for disciplining turncoats. Punishment by ostracism, in the eyes not only of the HSPA, the direct enemies of the federation, but also of other immigrant communities in the territory, was a peculiarly Japanese practice that was difficult to comprehend.

Though Japanese immigrants constituted nearly half the population of the islands and were the largest ethnic group, Hawaii was unmistakably an American territory, part of a country that was founded on respect for individual thought and dignity. Though there may have been a gap between reality and ideal, America as a country and society taught that democracy assures the right to opposition on any occasion. Using ostracism to punish those who disobeyed the collective action of the Federation of Japanese Labor, including even their families, seemed reactionary to Americans.

Within the narrow framework of national consciousness in a relatively homogeneous society like Japan, it was reasonable to bundle everyone together in the name of unity. To use ostracism as a punishment to protect an organization in Hawaii, as if it were operating in Japan, underscored just how insular the Japanese immigrant community was. The alarm felt by the Hawaiian elite rapidly transformed itself into the Japanese conspiracy theory.

Judge Banks had warned the prosecution and defense, "I am not going to permit any extensive inquiry into the merits or demerits of the strike, because I don't think we are concerned with that." While not going so far as to accuse Judge Banks of dissimulation, it could be said that what the territory wanted to pass judgment on was the "threat and pressure" (such as that attributed to Miyamura) that lay at the heart of the prosecution's charges.

THE VERDICT

As the jury deliberated on the morning of Saturday, March 4, rain fell steadily outside. At 9:30 A.M., Frank James, the jury foreman, told Judge

Banks that the jury wanted to ask about "extenuating circumstances." The request indicated that the deliberations were going in the prosecution's favor. At 11:10 A.M., the jury foreman again asked Judge Banks about specifics in the extenuating circumstances provision. Fifteen minutes later, the jury returned to the courtroom to report that they had reached a unanimous verdict. All the defendants were found "guilty as charged." However, they recommended "leniency for all the above defendants with the exception of Murakami."

It took the jury less than five hours to reach a verdict on the fifteen defendants. The *Honolulu Advertiser* reported that the jury had voted a total of twenty-five times. It was obvious that the jury had reached its conclusion during two hours of deliberation on the previous evening and during the morning had been discussing whether to grant leniency.

In his instructions, Judge Banks told the jury,

> You are not bound to believe anything to be a fact simply because a witness has stated it to be so, providing you believe from the testimony and evidence that such witness was mistaken or has testified falsely, and if you believe that any witness has willfully testified falsely as to any material fact you have a right to disregard his entire evidence except insofar as it may be corroborated by other credible evidence, facts or circumstances in evidence in this case.[34]

Thus in finding all the defendants guilty the jury decided that the testimonies of Noboru Tsutsumi, who said that when the orders to commit the crime were allegedly issued on May 22, 1920, he spent the day crab fishing at Suigorō; of Yasuyuki Mizutari, who testified that he was with Tsutsumi that day; and of the woman who managed the Suigorō, who testified that she remembered that Tsutsumi and Mizutari had come that day, were not believable. And they also decided that the physicians who testified as to the illness of Tokuji Baba and Chōhei Hoshino and the maid who took care of them at Kyōrakukan were unbelievable as well.

What the twelve members of the jury had taken to be the truth was the testimony of Matsumoto and Saitō, accomplices who had been compromised by the authorities and who had turned state's witness for the territory. They decided to believe the testimony of two men who repeated themselves, as rehearsed, while looking down at their notes, and claimed that the defendants ordered them to go to Hawaii to kill Sakamaki.

The March 5 *Honolulu Advertiser* headline proclaimed, "Fifteen Japanese Found Guilty of Conspiracy." The paper praised Judge W. H. Heen, city attorney, and H. E. Stafford, deputy city attorney, "both of whom handled the case with exceptional brilliancy."

Six days after the guilty verdict, on Sunday, March 10, the participants in the trial met again in court at 2:00 P.M. Before issuing the sentences, as was customary, Judge Banks asked each defendant if he had anything to say. All except Tsutsumi, who was last, stated through the interpreter, Maruyama, that they had nothing to say. Standing at the defendants' bench, Tsutsumi looked up directly at Judge Banks. There was no longer any reason for him to remain in Hawaii, he said, and he wished to return to Japan if possible. Judge Banks then sentenced all the defendants to "be imprisoned in Oahu prison at hard labor for the term of not less than four years nor more than ten years."

On the mainland, Sacco and Vanzetti were awaiting their death sentences in prison. Petitions for a retrial were circulated, and support funds were raised not only from anarchists and labor union members but also from academics and intellectuals. European labor unions and leftist groups, starting with those in Italy, the two defendants' native land, sent telegrams to President Harding requesting that he overturn the death penalty. Demonstrations opposing the death sentence took place outside American embassies.

In contrast to the Sacco and Vanzetti trial, the trial of Japanese defendants in the Sakamaki dynamite case attracted no attention either from mainland labor organizations or from the defendants' home country. Nor were any voices raised among the Japanese cane field workers who had demanded wage increases under the leadership of the defendants. Perhaps they believed the territory's indictment, but whatever the reason, the workers did not rally to the support of the former federation officers. They flatly abandoned them as criminals charged with the crimes of dynamiting and attempted murder.

The Japanese workers who returned to the plantations after the strike wanted to start their lives anew, determined to become permanent residents in the islands. At a turning point in their lives, they wanted to avoid at all costs anything that might complicate their relations with the sugar companies. The authorities were clearly connected to the sugar companies, and the authorities had determined the defendants to be criminals.

The indifference of the Japanese laborers to the trial also reflected the way the Japanese-language newspapers treated it. Throughout the trial, none of these newspapers carried more than short notices about its progress, almost as if they were indifferent. Even the *Hawaii hōchi,* which proclaimed its support for the underdog, remained quiet. Kin-zaburō Makino, the president of the *Hōchi*, had constantly feuded with the federation leaders, and the reports in the paper were cold and un-sympathetic, treating the defendants as guilty from the time they were charged.

No one in the Japanese immigrant community protested that the trial was intended to teach a lesson to those who opposed the HSPA. This coldhearted indifference was obvious from Teisuke Terasaki's diary. As a newspaper reporter, Terasaki should have had a deeper interest in the trial than did the general public, yet he mentioned it in his diary only three times: February 1, a simple entry, "the trial begins"; February 17, "Miyazawa takes the stand"; and February 22, "a top ranked law-yer who can achieve the conviction of the Federation headquarters Mr. Cathcart died suddenly this evening of a a heart attack." No entry was made the day the defendants were found guilty.

The main concern reflected in Terasaki's diary was the difficulties of the *Hawaii hōchi*. Finances had been strained since the newspaper's office had moved and expanded. Debts were so high that no money was available to repair a broken printing press motor. At the end of 1921, Makino had sought a $5,000 loan from the Bank of Hawaii, offering his house as collateral, but the bank turned him down. Terasaki thought this was due to intervention by the sugar planters, but in his diary he did not speculate that the HSPA might have been behind the trial.

During the period of the trial, Terasaki also referred several times to the departure of Consul General Chōnosuke Yada. Socializing on the golf course may have helped to give the impression to the haole govern-ing elite that Yada was cooperative. In any case, leaving this reputation behind, Yada departed for Japan on the afternoon of February 27, the day Noboru Tsutsumi took the witness stand. His successor, Keiichi Ya-mazaki, arrived to take up his post in Honolulu one month later.

The FBI report issued during the trial noted,

The reason for the delay in the arrival of the new Consul-General is to give Consul Yada an opportunity to meet him in Tokyo to discuss the situation in the Hawaiian Islands. A confidential agent informs this office that M. Kuro-kawa, a secretary of the Japanese consulate, who has been stationed in Hawaii for a number of years, is the "mischief maker" at the consulate. Agent claims that ordinarily when a new Consul-General arrives, he immediately comes under the influence of Kurokawa, who endeavors to influence him from the viewpoint of the old radical Japanistic idea. Informant claims that this is one of the main reasons for the recent Consul General going to Tokyo to meet his successor so that the former will be able to give him a correct estimate of conditions in Hawaii.[35]

If this is true, then what kinds of activities had Kurokawa been engaged in during the strike while Acting Consul General Furuya occupied the post, waiting for Yada? Might the shadow cast by Kurokawa be one reason that the HSPA asserted emphatically that the strike was a Japanese conspiracy? The FBI report concluded by stating, "Kurokawa is a reserve Lieutenant of the Japanese Army."

Seven months after the guilty verdict, FBI headquarters in Washington, D.C., issued a report on the activities of the Federation of Japanese Labor in Hawaii.

> It has previously been reported in the pages of this summary that the Hawaii Laborers' Association, formerly known as the Japanese Federation of Labor [sic], was steadily disintegrating. The *Hawaii Hochi*, in an editorial published this week, makes the statement that the Japanese Federation of Labor has become a "meaningless organization," and that although the Federation still maintains an office in Honolulu, the officials have no work to do and furthermore they have no real desire to help the laborers. The *Hochi* advocates a complete reorganization of the Japanese Federation of Labor. . . . The *Hyoron-no Hyoron* (Review of Review), a Japanese monthly magazine published in Honolulu, stated, in an editorial, that a group of Japanese labor leaders were planning to inaugurate a new labor union, which would have no connection with already established Hawaii Laborers' Association.[36]

The new labor union never saw the light of day, and the already existing Hawaii Laborers' Association barely maintained itself in form. The U.S. Military Intelligence Office Pacific Region Weekly Report noted, "According to confidential informants, one of the reasons to indict the officials of the Japanese Labor Federation is to destroy the Federation financially."[37] In fact, the federation was in dire financial straits because it had to pay bail for the indicted defendants and defense expenses. "The depleted treasury of the Japanese labor organizations," the report continued, "indicates that the labor leaders are losing their hold upon the laborers." The federation was no longer able to collect union fees. The energy of the Japanese laborers that had surged in the 1920 strike suddenly dissipated, just as the rice riots in Japan had. The six-month strike did not provide a firm base for a new labor movement.

In early December 1921, two months before the start of the trial, the HSPA, on the grounds that sugar prices had fallen to 3 cents, reduced minimum wages for sugarcane field workers from the $30 per month paid just the year before to the prestrike level of $26. The weakness of the Hawaii Laborers' Association is evident from the fact that it did not issue a single statement of protest about this wage decrease. (The HSPA annual meeting report for 1921 clearly showed that even though wages had been decreased, the HSPA suffered no budget deficit that year.)

SIX

REOPENING CHINESE IMMIGRATION

Washington, D.C.: June 1922

GOVERNOR MCCARTHY AND THE "JAPANESE THREAT"

On the morning of May 4, 1921, three months before the indictment of the Federation of Japanese Labor leaders, members of the Hawaiian economic and political elite gathered at the Honolulu pier to send off the *Matsonia,* departing for San Francisco. Three men in linen suits—Walter Francis Dillingham, Charles F. Chillingworth, and Albert Horner—smiled and waved from the ship. They were members of the Hawaii Emergency Labor Commission on their way to Washington, D.C., to attend hearings of the Immigration and Naturalization Committee of the House of Representatives on the "labor problem" in Hawaii. The May 4 *Honolulu Advertiser* praised Governor McCarthy for his selection of the three: "There are not three other men in the whole territory better posted in regard to the labor situation."

After spending six days in San Francisco to lay the groundwork for their efforts, the group boarded the transcontinental train headed for Washington, D.C. It was late May, and the banks of the Potomac River were bright green when they arrived. A month later, on June 21, the House Immigration and Naturalization Committee began its hearings on the emergency labor issue in Hawaii. In advance of the hearings, a summary statement, "The Sugar Industry of Hawaii and the Labor Shortage—What it means to the United States and Hawaii," had been distributed to the committee. The cover was stamped Top Secret to prevent leaks.

"Hawaii has always been American," the summary statement began.

From the days of 1820 when the brig Thaddeus brought to the shores of "the Cross Roads of the Pacific" a hardy band of New England missionaries—the advance guard of civilization—American thought, institutions, and ideals have predominated in these islands. A century ago was laid the foundation of the sturdy American citizenship that today signifies the Paradise of the Pacific as the outpost of Uncle Sam in the Pacific. . . . The seeds sown by those earnest missionaries have yielded fruit in abundance. . . . It was the dollars of Americans that financed the sugar plantations which were the earliest industry, and which have been the chief basis of Hawaii's development, and it was the indomitable spirit of the American pioneers that tided the sugar industry over distressing periods when agricultural industry was at its lowest ebb. . . . Hawaii has won the right to be recognized as an integral part of the American union; has won the right to generous consideration at the hands of the American people of the mainland. For Hawaii has demonstrated her Americanism beyond peradventure of a doubt. And today, Hawaii is seeking the help of America in solving the greatest problem that has yet confronted her. [The problem, it seemed, was a looming industrial paralysis, unless additional labor was brought to the island.]

Many thousand acres of luxuriant cane will soon lie fallow unless relief is provided through the instrumentality of the Congress at Washington. Also, it is but good judgement from a national standpoint to allow Hawaii to diversify the alien population within her borders, instead of permitting the continued domination of the nationals of one race. . . . If you would preserve Hawaii to Uncle Sam, help her. Otherwise, Hawaii cannot answer for consequences that loom darkly menacing on the horizon.

REMEMBER, HAWAII IS THE OUTPOST OF AMERICA IN THE PA-CIFIC, EVER STANDING GUARD TO INTERCEPT ANY UNFRIENDLY HAND THAT MAY STRIKE.

The summary, which repeated the words "America" and "Uncle Sam" over and over again, appealed to congressional patriotism, and it blamed Hawaii's problems on its "Asiatic" plantation field workers. It continued:

The labor shortage is due, in effect, to the generosity of the sugar plantations to their employees. This sounds paradoxical but the truth of the statement is evidenced by the fact that, over and above regular wages, the plantations in 1920 paid to the laborers an enormous sum as a bonus. When the final installment of the bonus was paid at the end of the grinding season of 1920, the laborers, their pockets lined with gold, had more wealth than they had pictured was ever possible. Immediately began an exodus of plantation hands, principally Japanese and Filipinos migrating. In 1920, 5,386 Japanese left Hawaii for Japan according to the figures of the Toyo Kisen Kaisha.[1]

In 1921, when the summary was written, the total number of plantation laborers in Hawaii was 39,502. Of these, 45.5 percent were Japanese (17,981), and 31 percent were Filipinos. Compared to the plantation labor force in 1919, before the strike, the number of Japanese laborers had decreased by more than 6,000, but the number of Filipinos had increased by 2,000. The exodus of the Japanese laborers, in other words, was the cause of the labor shortage. As the summary noted, "The Japanese through racial cohesion and nationalistic bonds are a preponderant power in the industrial life of the islands. In the immediate past, this solidarity has been evidenced in an attempt at dictatorship and control to the great embarrassment of the American industry." To solve its labor shortage and to break up the national solidarity of the Japanese, the summary statement called for the importation of Chinese laborers: "The Chinese are wonderful agricultural pacemakers. Experience has proved that they make splendid American citizens. No more desirable offshoot of an alien race is to be found in Hawaii today than the generation of Chinese born here in Hawaii. There is no racial solidarity among them that breeds hostility to the government under which they live."

The problem was that after annexation the laws excluding Chinese immigration had applied to Hawaii. "Bear in mind that not Hawaii but the United States government is responsible for the preponderance of an alien race in Hawaii," the statement averred, "for while the republic of Hawaii had, just prior to annexation, taken steps to limit Japanese immigration, its prerogative of action was lost with annexation, by which it automatically came under the laws of the United States." In fact, at the time there had been strident criticism of Chinese immigrants in Hawaii because it was believed they were impossible to assimilate, and Japanese laborers were recruited aggressively to replace them because Japanese immigrants allegedly became accustomed to Hawaiian customs more quickly. But circumstances had changed, and now it was the Chinese once again who seemed preferable.

Four years earlier the movement to relax the Chinese Exclusion Act began to gain momentum in Hawaii, just about the time that the Japanese-language schools question was being debated. Behind the scenes the Chinese merchant community in Honolulu, who saw the Japanese aggressively intervening in their homeland, lobbied to resume the importing of Chinese laborers. The Chinese population of Hawaii in 1921 was 22,000, a mere fifth of the Japanese population. The desire of the HSPA to rein in the Japanese laborers, the largest segment of the plantation labor force, meshed with the hope of the Chinese to increase their influence in Hawaii. Both supported a push for revision of the Chinese exclusion legislation.

At the end of 1917, when a congressional delegation visited Hawaii, Consul General Rokurō Moroi had reported to the Japanese Foreign Ministry that territorial leaders had brought up not only the "issue of the various problems related to Japanese" but also the issue of a "special clause in the immigration law related to the importation of Chinese." According to Moroi, some congressmen "agreed with this, while others expressed disagreement." [2] Given this response, the HSPA, which wanted Hawaii to be made an exception to the law, decided to put off efforts to seek liberalization of the Chinese exclusion law. But when the Japanese laborers organized a union movement to demand higher wages, they raised the issue anew.

The first voice was raised in an editorial in the *Honolulu Advertiser* on January 12, 1920, when it became clear that a strike was unavoidable: "The importation of a large number of Chinese laborers into Hawaii would not only solve our labor problem but would help solve some of our other problems." Two weeks later, under the headline "Hawaii Should Work for Chinese Labor," it urged that revision of the law be considered by the U.S. Congress.[3]

On February 3, 1920, three days after the Federation of Japanese Labor decided to strike, a request to resume importing of Chinese labor was put forward in the U.S. Senate by the representative from the territory of Hawaii. Despite the rising tension between labor and management on the islands, on New Year's Eve of 1919, McCarthy, the territorial governor, departed for the capital to lobby for a revision of land laws protecting native Hawaiians and for the granting of statehood to Hawaii. While in Washington, McCarthy made important statements, not on land law or statehood, but on the issues concerning U.S.-Japan relations. In effect, he launched a campaign to reopen consideration of the Chinese exclusion law. On February 28, 1920, the very day that the HSPA rejected the effort at mediation by Reverend Palmer, members of the Senate Committee on Immigration and Naturalization met with the Hawaiian governor and five territorial legislators. The minutes of this informal discussion were treated as top secret to prevent leaks to the press. The topic was "The Japanese in Hawaii."

Governor McCarthy began by stating, "I have lived in the islands for 39 years, and the Japanese began to be imported about 8 years after I first went there, and I have seen the Japanese population increase from nothing to the present number 120,000."[4] McCarthy, a Bostonian who went to Honolulu at the age of twenty as a salesman for a fruit wholesale company in San Francisco, had married a Caucasian woman born in Hawaii and settled down. His wife, however, was not a kamaaina or a descendant of missionaries. McCarthy was a haole outsider, but he soon acquired a reputation as a man of ability while he was a territorial legislator. He promoted the development of Waikiki, then an uninhabited swamp, into a prime residential area. He was appointed governor in 1918 with the backing of the HSPA. When he arrived in Washington, McCarthy was fifty-nine years old. His blond hair was thin, and his mustache was noticeably gray, but he was a voluble man, who spoke with enthusiasm, opening his large blue eyes wide with a surprised look.

The meeting with the Senate subcommittee lasted three hours, most of it an exchange between McCarthy and Sen. James D. Phelan of California. Governor McCarthy argued that when the Chinese exclusion law was applied to Hawaii after annexation, the planters were compelled to bring in Japanese as a cane field labor force. When one senator from Idaho asked whether "Japanese coolies" had been brought to the Hawaiian Islands before the Chinese were excluded, Senator Phelan promptly suggested that "we did not then know the character of the Japanese coolies." And when Governor McCarthy touched on the unusually high birthrate of the Japanese picture brides, three times that of Caucasian women, Senator Phelan added that in California one in three births was Japanese.

The senators were particularly interested in the Hawaii-born nisei. Governor McCarthy brought up the problem of dual citizenship: "You are aware of the fact that Japanese born in Hawaii, of course, he is a citizen of the United States: but his father can register him at the Japanese consulate at any time before he is 16 years of age, which makes him a Japanese citizen."

McCarthy emphasized the point that issei parents pushed their nisei children to be educated in Japanese-language schools. These schools, he said, prevented second-generation "Japs" from assimilating into American culture. When Phelan noted that "a Japanese source" indicated "that in less than 14 years they would control the politics of the island," McCarthy replied, "We have a suspicion—we do not know whether it is so or not—but we have a suspicion that the Japanese in Hawaii, even though they be citizens of the United States, are acting under instructions from their own Government, and therefore not exercising the right of suffrage. There is something that is holding them back, because we are satisfied that there are at least a thousand of them that are eligible and there is something that is holding them back." (The governor did not suggest that the low voting rate among the nisei may have been due to their exceedingly low political and social consciousness.) He went on to argue, "What it is we do not know, and if it is the policy of the Japanese Government that very few of them exercise the franchise, and that policy of their Government could change, and they were all instructed to register and vote, we might be swamped." By contrast, he said, the voting rate among the second-generation Chinese was always high. "The Chinese voter down there is not looking to China at all, he is looking to America. There is nothing back in China that is drawing him at all."

Senator Phelan had no interest in the Chinese Americans but wanted to know more about suspicions about the nisei. He asked the governor, "You spoke of control by their consuls, is it not a fact that they have some agents in every settlement of Japanese on the several islands?" Robert Shingle, a territorial senator who had accompanied the governor, replied that as the director of the war bond and stamp campaign during World War I, he had negotiated with the Japanese consul general, who had been cooperative but had insisted that rather than have the territory go directly to the Japanese immigrants to seek contributions, the consulate would make all the contacts through the agents it had in various local areas. The "agents of the consulate" that Phelan referred to were the individuals on each plantation, like Jūzaburō Sakamaki on Olaa Plantation, who were designated to handle tasks such as birth and death notifications in the family registers. They were unpaid, honorary agents chosen to represent their plantations. The Japanese bought a large number of war stamps, Shingle said, but in contrast to the Filipinos, who cashed them when hard up for money, the Japanese held onto them. "The Japanese have not cashed them, they have held them, as a rule," he said, "The Japanese are very shrewd and seem to know the value of these stamps."

At this point Senator Phelan brought up the pending strike for the first time:

I have read in the *Hawaiian Pacific Commercial Advertiser* that there is a great strike going on now in the islands, and that the Japanese have formed unions, and that in order to coerce the men to join the union and engage in the strike, that they have threatened to report their names to the burgomasters of their cantonment at home in Japan, which probably would entail severe penalties on their families. . . . That seems to be a favorite method with the oriental, to punish the family of the man doing wrong.

Phelan asked McCarthy whether the fact that the consulate condoned this method of discipline meant that the Japanese government was behind the Federation of Japanese Labor, urging the Japanese workers to join the organization and inciting them to strike. McCarthy replied that a report from the acting governor indicated that the acting Japanese consul denied this, and he added that the strike was confined to the island of Oahu.

But Senator Phelan pressed on: "I see that there was a Japanese warship came into the harbor out there the other day, was there not?" McCarthy replied that he had learned of the arrival of the Japanese warship *Yakumo* from the Washington newspapers as well, but he could not say why the ship had put in to port. Phelan responded in irritation, "I understood it came in to take off the Japanese. . . ." The chairman interrupted Phelan to call a recess, perhaps because he felt that Phelan was talking too much about U.S.-Japan relations.

When the meeting resumed ten minutes later, Phelan made no further reference to the warship. Instead, he brought up the Japanese-language schools control law and wanted to know why it had not passed the Hawaiian legislature. Governor McCarthy explained that at the time President Wilson was proposing the racial equality plan at the Paris Peace Conference and Secretary of State Robert Lansing had strongly urged the governor of California to postpone the Alien Land Law, known to Japanese as "the Japanese exclusion land law." When this news reached Hawaii, the territorial authorities decided that passage of the Japanese-language school control law would damage the goals of the federal government.

The meeting finally turned to the expansion of the American army and navy bases in Hawaii. When Governor McCarthy observed that 90 percent of the construction workers on these bases were Japanese, the senators were shocked. "Are they employed in simple construction work or are they employed in gun emplacement?" asked Phelan. McCarthy responded that Japanese laborers were needed to build "actual fortifications, gun emplacement, etc.," but that the responsibility lay with the U.S. Engineer's Office.

"You say that [the Japanese] were employed in the building of the first Pearl Harbor dry dock?" asked Phelan.

"Yes sir."

"Well, is it not a fact that the dry dock collapsed?"

"Well, that was through the fault of the specifications."

"You think so?"

When other members of the Hawaiian delegation raised doubts about whether Japanese laborers had worked on gun emplacements, Phelan cut them off. "Well, it is immaterial who builds the fortifications, so long as we have 120,000 aliens owing foreign allegiance—in case of trouble with Japan they could take the fortifications and massacre the native population without trouble, could they not?"

Sen. James Phelan, a contemporary of Governor McCarthy, had been an attorney in San Francisco during his youth, then had taken over the real estate and banking interests left him by his father. Known as a patron of young Bohemian artists, this handsome and wealthy man remained single all his life. After serving a term as mayor of San Francisco, from 1897 to 1901, he was elected to the Senate. As mayor he was well known for his opposition to Asian immigration, and he played a leading role in the movement to strengthen the anti-Japanese land law passed by the California legislature in 1913. The law prohibited land ownership by "immigrants without the right to become naturalized" (i.e., Asians), but it left other ways open for Japanese to acquire land: by giving title of the land to their nisei children who had citizenship or by becoming their guardians. To plug these loopholes, Republican state senator J. M. Inman had proposed a revision of the law in 1920, and Phelan supported it from the Democratic side. Not to be outdone by Inman, Phelan affirmed his reputation as a staunchly anti-Japanese by backing a voter initiative to put the revision into law.

Absent from the meeting with the Hawaii delegation was Sen. Hiram W. Johnson, chairman of the California Japanese Exclusion League. Together with Inman and Phelan he was at the center of the anti-Japanese movement. Five years earlier, when Bunji Suzuki of the Yūaikai participated in the AFL annual convention in California, the three men protested to Paul Scharrenberg, the California AFL representative. Though he had a deep interest in the "Japanese problem in Hawaii," Johnson was mentioned as a serious candidate for the Republican presidential nomination and was unable to attend the meeting with Governor McCarthy because he was campaigning around the country.

Phelan himself was facing a reelection campaign in six months, under the slogan "Keep California White." In March 1920 a ban on picture brides, "who bred like rabbits," was instituted under his leadership. For Phelan, who had helped to place the new anti-Japanese land legislation on the ballot, the opportunity to hear how Japanese immigrants were putting Hawaii in harm's way was a political windfall. He now had a new slogan: "Keep California from going the way of Hawaii."[5]

In November 1920 the revised Alien Land Law on the California ballot passed with a margin of three to one. This did not necessarily mean that the voters of California supported anti-Japanese politicians. Phelan lost the election and his seat in the Senate. As for Hiram Johnson, after a split vote, he lost the Republican presidential nomination, and Warren Harding walked off with the presidency in the 1920 election.

But anti-Japanese sentiments were kept alive in California by the Hearst newspaper chain. In March 1921, for example, the *Los Angeles Examiner* began a six-part series on the Japanese in Hawaii with the headline "Jap Menace Lies Black on Pacific!" "Hawaii," the paper proclaimed, "is a menacing outpost of Japan ruled invisibly by a carefully organized government that functions noiselessly and whose mainspring is in Tokio."[6] A political cartoon accompanying the article showed the black shadow of a Japanese soldier with a sword spreading across the Pacific Ocean. His military cap nearly touches the West Coast, and the words "Hawaiian Islands" are etched where his heart would be. The *Los Angeles Examiner* boasted the largest newspaper circulation in California.

The series was written by a Caucasian reporter who had gone to Hawaii to investigate the "astounding situation" there. The third in the series was entitled "Hawaii's Jap Peril—Jap Anti-Americanism Blazes Out in Strike." Not only did it charge that Hawaii was a "vast incubator for American Japs" and that "Hawaii Japs" held alien ideas dear, it also reported on the dubious morality of the "Japs."

> The sordid facts are that geishas are prostitutes and tea-houses are houses of assignations. . . . This popularity of the geisha and tea-house institution is symbolic of the character of the Japanese population of the islands. . . . As in Japan, pleasuring and politics and business revolve around the geisha. Banquets are held in the tea-houses. Geishas, not the wives, are the companions of the banqueters. . . . Two thousand nine hundred geishas and helpers are listed in the Japanese Consul General's tables of occupations of Japanese in the Hawaiian islands in 1919. . . . When labor delegates came into Honolulu from the other islands last year, disposed in part to oppose the strike, they were banqueted and given over to the seductive charms of the geishas. The geishas promptly brought them into line.[7]

REVEREND TAKIE OKUMURA'S AMERICANIZATION MOVEMENT

In early 1920, when the Japanese plantation workers went out on strike, tensions had risen between the United States and Japan on a host of issues: the failure of the Japanese to withdraw military forces from Siberia; the granting of the Japanese mandate over the island of Yap; the issue of independence for Korea; and the continuing Japanese occupation of the Shantung peninsula in China. The *Mainichi nenkan* (Mainichi Yearbook) painted the prospects for Japanese relations with the United States in 1920 in uncertain colors: "The re-occurrence of the Japanese exclusion issue in California has plunged relations between the two nations into greater instability. Unless the citizens of both nations awaken to the problems and remove the root of evil that will affect the future, the relations between Japan and the U.S. will likely face an unmanageable danger in days to come."

At the end of September 1920 Kijūrō Shidehara, Japanese ambassador to the United States, met with Roland Morris, U.S. ambassador to Japan, in Washington to discuss the problem of anti-Japanese movements in the United States. The two ambassadors met twenty-two times between September and late January 1921.

Time and time again, the federal government in Washington had been at wit's end about how to deal with anti-Japanese activities in California. Whenever problems over Japanese immigrants arose in California, they turned into diplomatic problems. The two ambassadors met to minimize diplomatic damage at a time when anti-Japanese feelings were aggravated by the debate over the anti-Japanese land initiative in California, but they engaged in informal discussions to allow a frank exchange of opinions without binding either government.

When Ambassador Morris's ship docked in San Francisco, the Democratic National Convention was being held in the city. At the suggestion of Secretary of State Charles Evans Hughes, Morris met with Senator Phelan and state senator Inman to hear their views. As a prelude to his meeting with Shidehara, Morris wanted an accurate understanding of the viewpoints of these anti-Japanese politicians.

The Shidehara-Morris conferences focused on abolition and prevention of discrimination against Japanese and revision of the Gentlemen's Agreement. The two men agreed that the key to resolving the anti-Japanese problem was the assimilation of Japanese immigrants into America, but they differed on how to accomplish this. For example, when Ambassador Morris pointed out that the dual citizenship of the nisei fueled anti-Japanese arguments, Shidehara observed that as this issue touched on the Japanese Nationality Act itself and that unless Congress revised U.S. immigration laws in a thoroughgoing manner, eliminating dual nationality for the nisei was not possible.

The Japanese had ceased issuing visas to picture brides at the end of February 1920, but the U.S. side sought to go one step further by having the Japanese stop issuing passports to all except those returning to America. Shidehara disagreed, asserting the need for Japanese immigrants to be able to send for wives and children left in Japan, for immigrants to return to the United States with wives they had married on temporary visits to Japan, and for them to bring over those adopted into the family.

The "Japanese problem in Hawaii" was taken up on October 23 at the eighth of these meetings. The second Oahu strike had ended just three months before, and Ambassador Morris pointed out that since the strike, "relations between the Japanese laborers and the plantation owners have not been smooth and this has given rise to the development of anti-Japanese sentiments." To stamp out the roots of anti-Japanese and anti-immigrant feelings in the future, he said that he would strongly urge a revision of the Gentlemen's Agreement so that Hawaii would be treated on the same basis as the mainland. Ambassador Shidehara refused to yield on this point too. "The labor conditions in Hawaii are entirely different from those on the American mainland," he said, "and Japan is already strongly restricting immigration to Hawaii on the same basis as to the U.S. mainland."[8]

In the end the two ambassadors agreed on a compromise proposal. In principle the restrictions on immigration would be applied to Hawaii. The United States would allow Japanese immigrants in Hawaii to send for their wives and children, but this practice would be prohibited on the mainland. The Shidehara-Morris conference can be considered a history-making attempt by both sides to approach the immigration problem, a constant source of friction in U.S.-Japan relations, from every angle and in good faith. Although there were many differences of opinion, or, rather because of these differences, the differing perspectives of the two nations were brought into clear relief. For this reason the conference was of no small import.

While these meetings were in progress, however, the Republican party ousted the incumbent Democrat from the White House in November. Because of the change in administration, the results of the Shidehara-

Morris conference did not become a formal declaration of the two governments and the matter was deferred. In his autobiography, Shidehara wrote that the Shidehara-Morris talks "served only the role of temporarily calming the domestic moods in both nations." [9]

On January 22, 1921, two days before the last of the Shidehara-Morris meetings, FBI headquarters issued a report, "The Japanese Problem in the United States." The bureau's first overall summary concerning Japanese immigrants relied heavily on military intelligence reports on the Pacific region. Its analysis of the reasons for Japanese immigration was, to say the least, unique. "The Japanese are physically a peculiarly constituted people," it reported. "It is known that they cannot stand either the extreme cold climate or the extreme hot climate. Therefore, it is not possible to extensively colonize the Japanese in Siberia or in northern China, neither is the colonization of Formosa or other equatorial land feasible." Hence the Japanese tried to emigrate to California, where the climate was ideal. "This peaceful penetration finally became obnoxious to California, who saw that ultimately if the Japanese were permitted to emigrate to the United States, the white race in no long space of time would be driven from the state, and California eventually become a province of Japan, as the Hawaiian islands are, practically, today until the entire Pacific Coast region would be controlled by Japanese." [10]

This extremely pessimistic prediction echoed comments Governor McCarthy had made the year before. At the end of January 1921, immediately after this overview was issued, the FBI began to make weekly reports on Japanese affairs in Hawaii. The first of these reports, focusing on the "problem of Japanese laborers in Hawaii," provided detailed information about Tsutsumi and other Japanese labor leaders. Of particular interest in this report was a two-page document asserting that the Japanese community had come to feel that it was "misled in [the] strike." It quoted Reverend Takie Okumura of the Makiki Japanese Church when he was invited by Reverend Palmer of the historic Union Church to preach to the kamaaina congregation. "Many Japanese of Hawaii," he said, "are coming to realize that during the 1920 strike they were bulldozed by agitators and that the difficulties did not constitute an industrial strike, but between two nationalities which should not have been." The report stated that Reverend Okumura's pronouncement, made as it was by a Japanese, was of great interest to the kamaaina elite.

Unusual for a Japanese, Takie Okumura was listed in the Hawaii *Who's Who,* which noted that he came from a long line of samurai. He was one of the few Japanese close to the center of haole power, and he was recognized by the *Who's Who* as a leader of the movement for the Americanization of Japanese. Indeed, in January 1921, when the FBI report mentioned above was issued, Okumura, appealing to second-generation Japanese, or "new Americans," began his "anti-Japanese prevention and edification movement."

In his small booklet, "An Americanization Primer: Preparing Our Hawaiian Compatriots," Okumura urged the Japanese immigrants to settle permanently in Hawaii. Beginning a five-year campaign to promote assimilation, he traveled to all the Hawaiian Islands preaching his ideas. Okumura was already over sixty years old, so he had not undertaken this task lightly. As the vast majority of the Japanese immigrants were Buddhist, Reverend Okumura was often denounced as a traitor in his travels to the plantations. Undaunted, Okumura was not hesitant to counterattack. In one speech he criticized the Japanese immigrants for trying to "reestablish idolatrous practices" in "this Hawaii which became Christian after strenuous efforts of its [kamaaina] forefathers." Not only did they build shrines and temples, they also built "images of the Inari, the god of harvests, stone sarcophaguses, and worship halls." Of all the Japanese religious groups, Reverend Okumura viewed the Honganji, the most powerful sect in the Japanese community in Hawaii, with particular enmity. "Buddhism is the greatest obstacle to assimilation," he proclaimed. This assertion may have been correct from the perspective of Americanization, but it leaned so far toward the viewpoint of the Caucasian elite that one can see the limitations of Okumura's Americanization movement. When he boasted of his samurai origins, acting as though he had exchanged his sword for the Bible, many were offended by his authoritarian righteousness.

Rumors about the source of funds for Reverend Okumura's Americanization movement constantly floated around the Japanese community. Despite the small number of Christians in the Japanese community, Okumura had built the Makiki Church, an elaborate rendition of the donjon of the castle in Kōchi, his hometown, in an expensive neighborhood of Honolulu. He also operated a dormitory for promising nisei from other islands who came to study in Honolulu, yet his own son was the first Japanese to go to Punahou School, attended by the children of kamaaina. What is more, this appeared to be due to Okumura's close association with Frank C. Atherton, one of the powerful kamaaina sugar planters. Okumura was a frequent guest at the Atherton house, and through Atherton he had made connections with other members of the haole elite.

Reverend Okumura often went to Japan on what he called goodwill visits to improve U.S.-Japan relations. He departed on such a trip on July 14, 1920, shortly after the strike ended. "Adverse feelings between Japan and America being on the rise," he recalled, "the situation was such that if things were left alone, anti-Japanese movements such as in California might erupt. After consultations with the Japanese Consul General and a few Americans [Atherton, Castle, and Cook among the Big Five], I went to Japan to obtain support from Hitoshi Asano to start a movement to prevent anti-Japanese actions."

Three days after his arrival in Yokohama, Okumura visited Viscount Eiichi Shibusawa, with whom he was acquainted. Not only did Shibusawa arrange for Okumura to meet with Foreign Minister Uchida and other government officials, he also threw a banquet for the Japan-U.S. Friendship Committee, whose members included the top executives from major business conglomerates such as Mitsui, Mitsubishi, and Sumitomo so that Okumura could inform them about the conditions of Japanese in Hawaii. These economic leaders unanimously agreed with Okumura's anti-Japanese movement prevention idea and promised financial support. Shibusawa twice sent to Okumura 1,000 yen as his personal contribution. It was such contributions from capitalists in Japan and Hawaii that funded his campaign to Americanize the Hawaiian nisei.

Reverend Okumura was one of the few Japanese who had been strongly opposed to the 1920 strike from the start. Throughout the strike he publicly criticized the Federation of Japanese Labor, and at every opportunity he spoke of Tsutsumi and the other federation leaders as being enemies of friendly relations between the United States and Japan and the Americanization movement.

At the Sakamaki dynamiting trial the prosecution claimed that the motive for the conspiracy of the federation leaders was to teach turncoats a lesson and to crush the anti-strike movement. If this was so, then the federation overlooked Okumura, a major figure in the Japanese community who denounced the federation head-on. But rather than deal with Okumura, which would have drawn the greatest attention, the federation had, according to the prosecution, plotted the assassination of Sakamaki, whose anti-strike activities were limited to distributing the anti-strike newspaper *Kazan* on a plantation where no strike was taking place.

Even after the strike ended, Okumura denounced it and the Federation of Japanese Labor that had led it. "It is true," he said, "that the attitude of the Americans toward us had changed substantially due to the effect of the anti-Japanese movement in California reaching Hawaii as well as the occurrences of the Korean incident and the Shantung incident. But what clearly brought out the anti-Japanese feelings here has been the problem of the Japanese language schools and the strike."

According to Okumura, both the aloha spirit and the Christian spirit of the missionaries' descendants had put a brake on anti-Japanese feelings and preserved harmony in Hawaiian society, but the strike had destroyed this social balance. Just as "a cloud spread over U.S.-Japan relations" when the English-language press took up the anti-Japanese cry in the debate over the Japanese-language school problem, "the strike darkened the clouds. It is nature's course that when clouds thicken rain will fall." After the strike, he said, "even pro-Japanese Caucasians began to feel strong doubt and apprehension." The surfacing of the movement to renew Chinese immigration and the enormous sums and great effort the territory expended on the issue, he pointed out, came in the main from the strike. The result of the strike was "loss of faith in Japanese laborers and the arousal of misgivings in Americans."

DILLINGHAM JOINS THE DEBATE

The Hawaii Emergency Labor Commission was organized on April 12, 1921, to work for the importation of Chinese laborers, banned under the Chinese Exclusion Act, to work in the sugarcane fields in Hawaii. It came into existence a mere three weeks before its members left for Washington to begin lobbying Congress. It seems clear that the commission was put together through the careful work of the HSPA.

Royal Mead, secretary of the HSPA, had been posted to the capital in November of the previous year as the organization's special labor relations representative. Publicly it was stated that Mead was working to recruit laborers from Puerto Rico, but his main effort in the capital was to lay the groundwork for an appeal to Congress to renew the immigration of Chinese.

Not everyone in Hawaii was in favor of once again allowing Chinese laborers to come in for a fixed period. Opposition was heard from Reverend Palmer and other religious leaders and academics as well as from some planters themselves. Opponents of the measure took the position that letting the Chinese immigrants in again was a step backward to the old contract immigration system and that this would contradict the goal of Americanization, which had been the major reason for opposing the Japanese-language schools. Despite this opposition, the Hawaii Emergency Labor Commission took shape under the direction of Governor McCarthy, a Democrat who was about to retire and be replaced by a Republican appointed by the new president, Warren Harding.

Explaining to the territorial legislators that Noboru Tsutsumi was agitating for a general strike on the sugar plantations and pineapple fields of the islands, Governor McCarthy on April 27, the last day of the legislative session, guided the passage of an appropriation of $15,000 to send the commission to Washington to represent Hawaii "upon this important and vital mission." In effect, the HSPA was attempting to deal with labor problems in the sugarcane fields with territorial funds.

The three members of the Hawaii Emergency Labor Commission appointed by Governor McCarthy were influential men among the Hawaiian elite. Charles F. Chillingworth, a politician of mixed Hawaiian heritage, was a suitable person to represent the territorial legislature. His heavy physique, typical for a Hawaiian, made him look older than his forty-four years. Chillingworth had been a central figure in the passage of the foreign-language schools control act, which had been drafted by the American Legion under the leadership of Captain Stafford, who later served as a prosecutor in the Sakamaki dynamiting trial.

Fifty-eight-year-old Albert Horner, the second member, was a head shorter than Chillingworth and thinner, and his sunken eyes made him look almost gloomily cautious. After arriving in Hawaii at the age of sixteen, he worked his way up at several sugar companies. He went to Washington as a representative of the Pineapple Association, but for many years he had been known in the territorial legislature as an expert on sugar cultivation. Horner was an avid supporter of the plan to bring in Chinese immigrants from the start.

But the most important member of the commission was its chairman, Walter Francis Dillingham. On learning of the Dillingham appointment, The *Hawaii hōchi* predicted, "It is not difficult to surmise that the movement to re-import Chinese immigrants will proceed fiercely." [11]

Still lining the streets of downtown Honolulu today are wooden Japanese and Chinese shops that look like they could easily go up in flames. But across a boundary marked by the Honolulu police station lies an entirely different world of three- and four-story solid-looking buildings with stone-faced exteriors in shades of gray and cream, red-tiled roofs, and decorated window frames. Pushing open the heavy door of one of these buildings, one enters into a cool interior where thick walls block the outside sunlight. Even now when tall skyscrapers cast shadows over them, these old stone buildings are impressive. This was the world inhabited by Walter Dillingham.

Six years after he published *Treasure Island,* the British novelist Robert Louis Stevenson visited Hawaii. In a photograph taken at the luau held to welcome him appears the face of fourteen-year-old Dillingham standing amid the Hawaiian royalty. No account of Dillingham would be complete without touching on the host of the luau, his father, Frank. Frank (formally Benjamin Franklin) Dillingham, a merchant seaman from New England, was injured when his ship put in to Honolulu to replenish food and water. His life took an unforeseen turn when the ship departed, leaving him behind. After starting a successful general store in downtown Honolulu, he married the daughter of a leading missionary, and as he rapidly expanded his business, he began to buy land for sugar plantations. In fact, Olaa Plantation, where the Sakamaki house was dynamited, had been owned by Dillingham.

Indeed, the history of Olaa Plantation traces the life of Frank Dillingham. The land at Olaa was originally owned by Hawaiian royalty. At the suggestion of Lorrin A. Thurston, a cabinet minister in the Hawaiian monarchy and later the publisher of the *Honolulu Advertiser,* Dillingham joined in investing in development of the land into a sugarcane plantation. It was the largest plantation planned in Hawaii. When Olaa company stock was offered publicly, investors were so confident of Dillingham's ability to succeed in any business that it sold out immediately. But the price of sugar began to fall, and soon the operation of the plantation was in trouble. The harvest was no worse than on other plantations, but the plantation was so large that production costs were enormous. Even an entrepreneur like Dillingham found himself in a tight spot.

To raise new capital Dillingham turned to San Francisco. East Coast capitalists were not inclined to invest in the Hawaiian sugar industry, even when they had extra money, because they saw Hawaii as an unstable land, an "exotic" place populated by lots of yellow-skinned people. Dillingham tried to raise funds from the general public by selling Olaa company bonds in California, the first time a Hawaiian sugar industry had ever done so. But the bonds were extremely slow to sell. One reason was the burning down of buildings in Honolulu to prevent the spread of the bubonic plague some six months earlier (1900). Using the plague as an excuse, the authorities set fire to congested buildings in

Chinatown and expelled their inhabitants. Overnight the assets of the Chinese merchants, who had been expanding their economic power independently, were turned to ashes. (The fires also spread to the neighboring Japanese shopping district, where 177 buildings belonging to Japanese were destroyed.) The incident was reported widely on the mainland, reinforcing the impression that Hawaii was uncivilized territory. Coupled with concern about labor shortages in the sugarcane fields owing to the migration of Japanese workers to the mainland, California stockholders panicked, sending the Honolulu stock market into a tailspin. The Olaa fiasco caused Dillingham to have a nervous breakdown, and he secretly admitted himself to a sanatarium in San Francisco. Thirty-five years of constant work to expand and finance his businesses had taken its psychological toll. He had changed so much that he was hardly recognizable as the man who had hosted General Arthur MacArthur (Douglas MacArthur's father) the year before on a visit to study the feasibility of constructing American military facilities in Hawaii.

Dillingham's second son, Walter, then took over his father's businesses. As his older brother had died early, Walter was for all intents and purposes the family heir. He had dropped out of Harvard a few years before to help his father, who was already showing symptoms of psychological distress. Though only twenty-nine years old when he took over for his father, he had already had a reputation as a man of ability, and he quickly cut company employees and began to tighten control over the Dillingham companies. At Olaa Plantation the Caucasian manager was fired for being too lenient with the Japanese contract labor bosses. Two years before the 1920 strike, Frank Dillingham died of cancer, and leadership of the Dillingham interests passed to the next generation in name and reality. Walter was not merely his father's successor; the kamaaina heritage from his mother made him a legitimate member of Hawaii's elite, as his father had not been. Making good use of his prerogatives of birth, he was able to achieve plans for the future far greater than his father's.

Dillingham was eminently suited to represent the Hawaii business community. He was president and director of ten companies, including Oahu Railway and Land Company, Hawaiian Dredging Company, Ltd., Hawaiian Hume Concrete Pipe Company, Honolulu Bond and Mortgage Company, Haleiwa Hotel Company, Realty Syndicate, Mokuleia Ranch and Land Company, and Woodlawn Stock and Dairy Company. He was also vice president and director of the Bishop Trust Company,

Hawaii Macadamia Nut Company, Honolulu Rapid Transit Company, Oahu Sugar Company, Olaa Sugar Company, Waipahu Sugar Company, and Waikiki Water Company. He was director of the B. F. Dillingham Company, Bank of Hawaii, the Advertiser Publishing Company, and other corporations. And he was not merely a figurehead. His voice was influential in all these companies.

One of them was American Factors, Ltd., formerly a German sales agency engaged in a wide range of businesses. During the First World War its assets had been frozen as enemy property, and the Big Five collectively bought the company from the U.S. government for a fraction of its actual worth. Reorganized under its patriotic new name, the company became the largest of those that handled sales and office management for sugar plantations and also recruited workers and procured seeds and fertilizer. The top executives of the Big Five held major posts in the firm. Although Dillingham was listed simply as a director, his voice was one of the most powerful in the company's operations.

On the island of Hawaii Dillingham was best known as the president of Oahu Railway and Land Company, which was founded by his father, who had foreseen the need to transport sugarcane from the plantations to Honolulu. Walter bought up land around the railway to expand the company's holdings and make it the most important transportation agency on Oahu.

In May 1920 it was this powerful haole businessman that the strike support group formed by Masao Kawahara, president of the Japanese Chamber of Commerce, and Dr. Iga Moori, thought would be the best person to mediate the strike. Kawahara had explained to Acting Consul General Furuya that Dillingham would be suitable because he was a third party, not involved in the sugar industry. This decision shows how little the leaders of the Japanese community knew about Hawaii's business circles, for Dillingham was a major stockholder of the Ewa and Waipahu sugar companies, both of which had been struck. According to Kawahara, Dillingham expressed interest but had to leave on business for the mainland and promised that he would hear them out when he returned a month and a half later. But, for some reason, after his return his attitude changed and he refused to negotiate.[12]

Dillingham had gone to the mainland on business for the Hawaiian Dredging Company, which he had started on his own and which served as the contractor for construction of the Pearl Harbor dry dock, the largest of the American navy. As Senator Phelan had mentioned in the informal hearing with Governor McCarthy, many technical problems had plagued the project, but after ten years of construction the Pearl Harbor dry dock finally opened one month after the strike ended. On August 11, 1920, the territory celebrated by welcoming the first visit to Hawaii of a secretary of the navy with a public holiday for schools and government offices. The *Honolulu Advertiser* proclaimed the dry dock's contribution to world progress, and Congress appropriated additional funds to expand it under contract with Dillingham's firm.

The large Dillingham estate overlooking the ocean near Diamond Head was constructed of marble in the style of a Florentine palace where Dillingham and his wife, Louise, had spent their honeymoon. It was a social gathering place for Honolulu's elite. Dillingham also owned a weekend country house in northwestern Oahu. On its vast land were a pool, tennis court, polo field, and stables for polo horses. Polo was Dillingham's favorite sport, and he was said to be Hawaii's best polo player. Dillingham married at age thirty-five after he had brought his businesses under control. He had four sons and one daughter. A photograph taken at the country house six months before his trip to Washington shows him standing in a one-piece bathing suit with his legs apart and arms outstretched. Hanging on his arms are his four sons, the oldest ten years old.

When Dillingham became chairman of the Hawaii Emergency Labor Commission, he was forty-six, two years older than territorial senator Chillingworth, but in photographs of the three commission members, his physique, trim from polo and sailing, gives him the appearance of a man in his twenties. With chest out and posture upright, he looked even taller than the heavyset Chillingworth, and his gentle facial features expressed intellect and character. Though he never went to the front, Dillingham served in the military during the First World War and became one of the organizers of the American Legion in Hawaii.

On his trip to Washington as chairman of the Hawaii Emergency Labor Commission, Dillingham used his title as president of the chamber of commerce of Honolulu, the most powerful group of businessmen in Hawaii. At the time of the 1920 strike the chamber voted "unanimous support of the Hawaiian Sugar Planters' Association in its fight against the control of the sugar industry of Hawaii by an alien race." But even before the strike, in 1918, it had petitioned, under the name of Dillingham as president, the secretary of the interior in Washington to allow the renewal of importing Chinese indentured labor.

One of his father's legacies was the great importance Dillingham placed on his relations with the mainland. From his youth, he had worked hard to build business connections in California and Washington. In particular, through the construction of the Pearl Harbor dry dock, Dillingham had cultivated goodwill among the military leaders in the capital. According to Albert Horner, lobbying for the importation of Chinese labor was Dillingham's "one man show." [13]

In a nine-page document addressed to President Harding the commission placed the blame for the labor shortage in Hawaii's sugarcane fields on Japanese immigrant laborers. Its conclusion summarized the issue as they saw it:

> To sum up the foregoing, our problem is definitely to conserve the prosperity of the Territory through its industries. We believe that it is vital that steps be taken immediately looking to supplying the shortage with labor which is suitable for the requirements of our tropical industries, which will neutralize, as far as possible, the effect of the preponderance of any one alien nationality, and which, further, will stimulate higher efficiency among the labor in the Territory.

On May 22, 1921, three days after their arrival in Washington, the commissioners visited the White House with their petition in hand. According to the *Honolulu Advertiser,* the newly inaugurated president promised them that he would do what he could.[14]

As a senator from Ohio, Warren Harding, fifty-six, had been chairman of the Committee on the Philippines, and he had been involved in bringing Filipino laborers into Hawaii. Whether or not this was the reason, for many years Harding was known as a politician willing to lend a hand to the territory of Hawaii, which could send no representatives to the U.S. Congress. In Congress he made statements defending the interests of the Hawaiian sugar industry. Two weeks before the 1920 presidential election, John Waterhouse, the president of the HSPA, observed that "if Harding is elected, he has guaranteed that he would increase tariffs on sugar imported from foreign countries in order to protect the Hawaiian sugar industry." [15] It seems likely that the HSPA contributed to Harding's presidential campaign.

This may have been why the new president, despite his busy schedule, took time to meet with the Hawaii Emergency Labor Commission. Reporting on this "good news," a *Honolulu Advertiser* editorial observed, "President Harding knows Hawaii and he has always been known as a friend of the Islands and their people. There are other men in the administration also who know us, and are friendly toward our interests." [16] An effort to invite President Harding to Honolulu for the Pan-Pacific Commercial Conference planned for the summer of 1922 was already under way in Hawaii.

As a politician Harding was poles apart from his predecessor, Woodrow Wilson, who was known as a man of principle. In contrast to Wilson, the former college president who entered politics burning with ideals, Harding started his career as a reporter on a local newspaper and turned to politics after becoming its publisher. Rather than a master of compromise, Harding was a conservative politician with an opportunistic streak. In his presidential campaign speeches in California, Harding expressed his support of the revised Alien Land Law to the governor, Senator Phelan, and other state representatives. "Orientals" had a bright history of contribution to world civilization, he said, but their national character and their style of life were vastly different from Americans. It was obvious that it would be impossible for them to become Americanized. To prevent problems with the Orientals from spreading to the eastern United States, he said that it was perhaps necessary to enact laws permitting immigration of only those foreigners able to assimilate and to limit the immigration of Orientals.

The Shidehara-Morris meetings were beginning at the time, and Ambassador Shidehara criticized Harding's statement: "I must say that Americanization is possible to proceed only when there is an atmosphere of amicable goodwill; antipathy and persecution are its great obstacles." Morris, who had been appointed ambassador to Japan by President Wilson, stated that he agreed entirely. Harding's statement became an issue in Japan too. When Harding was elected, the press in Japan reported it alongside news about the passage of the revised anti-Japanese land law in California. For example, under the headline "New U.S. President Mr. H. Is Anti-Japanese," the *Kokumin shinbun* warned, "We must be prepared for the worsening of Japan-U.S. relations." [17] Immediately after the election, the Japanese consul general in Honolulu, Chōnosuke Yada, reported to the Foreign Ministry, "With the Republican victory, the sugar companies are placed in an even more favorable position." [18] He had already predicted that the HSPA would make concrete moves in Washington to lobby for bringing in Chinese laborers.

THE HOUSE HEARINGS ON "LABOR PROBLEMS IN HAWAII"

To most people living on the U.S. mainland Hawaii was an unfamiliar place. The *Honolulu Advertiser* was astonished that a major publisher in New York had mailed a letter to the newspaper addressed to "Honolulu City, Hawaii Island, the Philippines."[19] Dillingham began his work as chairman of the Hawaii Emergency Labor Commission by visiting each member of the Immigration and Naturalization Committee before the hearings, explaining to them Hawaii's geographic location. Harding helped to arrange interviews with high-ranking government officials. As there was only one month to lay the groundwork, Dillingham was extremely busy in Washington.

The House Committee on Immigration and Naturalization consisted of fifteen representatives, ten of whom were Republicans. The chairman, Albert Johnson, fifty-two, from the state of Washington, had been a newspaper reporter. He entered politics after he became a leader of a citizens' movement to quell a paralyzing IWW-led strike against the Washington State lumber industry. During his twenty years in Congress he had been involved in immigration issues, and it was said that no one in Congress stood to the right of him on the issue. Indeed, he was so conservative that even within the Republican party he was called a nationalist. When the revised Alien Land Law was being debated in California in 1920, Johnson had taken members of the House Immigration and Naturalization Committee there to inspect the situation of the Japanese immigrants. The conclusion he reached was that Californians were not overreacting in their concern about the "invasion" of their state. Before the hearing began Dillingham reported home that chairman Johnson was extremely sympathetic to Hawaii's position.[20]

The House Committee on Immigration and Naturalization began its hearings on labor problems in Hawaii at 10:30 A.M. on Tuesday, June 21, 1921, with Dillingham as its first witness. From the first day committee members focused their questions not on the main issue of whether to renew importation of Chinese laborers but rather on the 1920 Oahu strike that had been led by "frightening Japanese agitators."

A few minutes into the hearing, Rep. Robert S. Maloney from Massachusetts asked whether the strikers were American-born or foreign-born or mixed. Dillingham replied, "Very, very few Hawaiian-born Japanese . . . will do work in the cane fields." Of the six thousand who went on strike, he said, probably very few were American citizens or American-born. But he then introduced Royal Mead, representative of the HSPA, as a person more familiar with the strike. Mead had dealt directly with Federation of Japanese Labor during the strike, so he must have known that there had been no nisei among the federation leadership. But Mead quickly asserted, "Oh, yes, some of the very worst agitators among the Japanese strikers were American-born Japanese young men. In very many instances, they were the heads of the unions on the plantations which created a great deal of trouble . . . and, while we had no direct evidence, we had good reason to believe that they were the ones that were firing cane fields."[21]

Rep. Guy L. Shaw of Illinois then asked Dillingham, "Is it not a fact that the Japanese are organizing and endeavoring to get control of nearly every line of business in the islands, building trades and everything else where they can—stores and all that sort of thing?"

Dillingham replied, "That is correct, whether they are organizing to do it or not, we do not know; that they are doing it, we do know."

The reply must have come as a surprise to Keiichi Yamazaki, who had succeeded Chōnosuke Yada as consul general in Honolulu. In reports to the Foreign Ministry, he had appraised Dillingham as "a person who has been considered pro-Japanese all along." As Dillingham was not a man to reveal his emotions and behaved in an even manner at all times, he may well have given Yamazaki this impression. His well-bred self-control made others trust him. He seemed to keep people at a certain distance, but this was no disadvantage for it projected an air of dignity. With his calm gaze fixed directly on the congressmen in front of him, he spoke in measured tones about the "fearsome Japanese conspiracy."

On the second day of the hearings, Wallace R. Farrington, the newly appointed territorial governor, spoke as a witness. The fifty-year-old Farrington, a native of Maine, had gone to Honolulu twenty-five years before as a newspaper reporter. Eventually he had become publisher of the *Honolulu Star Bulletin* and one of the founders of the Republican party in Hawaii. He hit it off well with President Harding, a former newspaper publisher, whom he had known since Harding visited Hawaii as a senator. The Hawaiian sugar planters had probably recommended Farrington for governor because it would be easy for him to approach the new president.

Like Albert Horner, Governor Farrington was an early advocate of the plan to renew the importation of Chinese workers. Freely sprinkling his testimony with the words "Japs" and "Chinamen," the new governor supported the plan from the perspective of the Japanese conspiracy theory. "The strike of last year opened the eyes of a good many of us to a condition which has become more acute as time has gone on," he said. "It stands to reason, and I think that it appeals to all of us, that the main industry in any part of our country should not be in the hands of, or subject to the dictates of, an alien element, regardless of the origin of that people."

When the *Los Angeles Examiner* ran its sensationalist series about the Japanese problem in Hawaii, some in Hawaii objected that the territory was being portrayed against its will as a negative example of the yellow peril in order to underpin the anti-Japanese cause in California. During the strike the two Honolulu English-language newspapers fanned the flames of the Japanese takeover theory, but they were exceedingly critical of the anti-Japanese movement in California. The *Honolulu Advertiser* denounced California as "playing with fire," and Farrington's *Honolulu Star Bulletin* remonstrated against the hysteria in California.[22]

The Hawaiian elite felt that Hawaii's labor problem differed from the anti-Japanese problem in California, and they did not want to bring California's exclusionary policy to Hawaii. Waving the banner of "aloha spirit," these descendants of missionaries wanted to resolve the problem through paternalism. Although it may go too far to call their position hypocritical, it was clearly two-faced. Nevertheless, a year after his paper proclaimed Hawaii different from California, Farrington tried to focus attention on the Japanese at the hearings on the renewal of Chinese immigration, and so did Royal Mead of the HSPA, whose testimony followed Farrington's.

"I have had to do with the two different strikes we have had out there of the Japanese," Mead said, "and I have never had any delusions in regard to Americanizing them—without doubt, as a race, the absolute coherence and solidarity of the Japanese is marvelous." In response to Rep. John F. Raker of California, he said this was true whether they were born in Hawaii or not.

On June 30, the last day of his testimony, after the press was excluded from the room, Mead read with deliberation the special petition entitled "Hawaii and the Japanese," whose contents dealt with the Japanese government. The document began by stating the need to trace the Japanese problem and the history of Japanese immigration in order to achieve an accurate understanding of Hawaii's labor shortage. After citing the problem of the schools and the control of Buddhism over all aspects of the lives of Japanese immigrants, it described the 1920 strike as follows:

> The intractability and hostility of the Japanese as a class toward the American community was forcefully demonstrated during a strike of Japanese plantation laborers on the island of Oahu during 1920. The strike, it has been sufficiently proved, was planned and fomented by the Japanese language

press, the principals and heads of Japanese language schools, and the Buddhist priests. . . .

There is no proof of charges that were frequently made during the strike that it had been called in obedience to orders from Tokio, but it is certain that some of the strike leaders led their followers to believe that such was the case. Many Japanese laborers were reluctant to strike, probably on account of the large wages and bonuses they were then receiving, and some few of them actually refused to strike. These latter were persecuted, abused, maltreated, even beaten and kidnapped by the strike leaders and their fundamental love of and respect for home, family and country were played upon to keep them in sympathy with the strike. During this strike, there appeared in the Japanese language newspapers, statements and advertisements to the effect that those recreant laborers who refused to go on strike would be reported to the municipal heads of their native towns in Japan so that their relatives living there might be ostracized and otherwise punished. In pursuance of this policy of intimidation, there appeared in the Japanese press lists of names of Japanese who had defied the strike leaders.[23]

After reading the document, Mead stated that the real purpose of the second strike was not wage increases but a Japanese conspiracy to establish a "Little Japan" in Hawaii. As proof he brought up a plan by Japanese to purchase the Olaa sugar plantation. "Within the past several months," he said, "Japanese or persons representing them have made two actual offers to purchase outright, or to purchase the control of, Olaa Sugar Company." During the rest of the hearings no further details were given, nor were the names of these Japanese mentioned. Since Dillingham was the major stockholder in Olaa Plantation, could he have been the source of this information? However, Japanese knowledgeable about the situation at the time, including Tazuko Iwasaki, the widow of Olaa's major contract boss, Jirokichi Iwasaki, did not recall hearing of any such overtures by Japanese.

It is true that in 1920, the year of the strike, Tomekichi Konno, a labor contractor on Hawaii, attempted to raise capital from Japanese businessmen to buy undeveloped Lanai and grow sugar for direct export to Japan. Four years before, Konno had operated a small sugar refinery at Kona on Hawaii, the first such effort by a Japanese. The Yokohama Specie Bank, acting as its agent, sold stock in Japan to finance the operation, but it went bankrupt in a few years. It was after this that Konno tried to develop land on Lanai, but it was clear from the start that the HSPA would not sit idly by, and that probably doomed the project.

Consul General Yamazaki later speculated on the real reason that the territory of Hawaii brought up the "Japanese threat" in its petition to Congress. "Shortage of labor alone was too weak a reason to import

Chinese coolies and it would not draw the attention of the congress-men," he reported to Tokyo. "It is clear that, as the congressmen were generally ignorant about the situation in Hawaii, the plan is to focus the attention of the congressmen on declamations of the Japanese peril in or-der to seek passage of the resolution."[24]

Some committee members at the hearings sensed that this was the ter-ritory's aim. Raker pressed Governor Farrington on the point: "The real truth of the matter is that this resolution while generally drawn, is some-what uniquely drawn, with a good deal of ingenuity and with a good deal of handling of the language—the purpose really is to bring in Chi-nese?" Raker, fifty-eight, had served many years as a judge in Califor-nia. He had worked hard on labor issues after being elected to Congress and had the overwhelming support of the AFL. Referring to the circum-stances on the West Coast that had led to the Chinese Exclusion Act, he probed Farrington about the implications of importing Chinese inden-tured labor once again.

> Was it right to bring in an alien race, hold them in bondage for five years, and then send them back, breaking up their families if they have married Chinese-American women? . . . But if they gave birth to a child, that child would be an American citizen. Now you would send the husband back home, leaving a wife on the island with an American citizen as a child. That does not look very good, does it, to our country? . . . Do you think the American people would submit to a law that would permit people to be brought in here to work and would deny them the right to have a family? . . . If you brought these Chinamen there and their wages were not satisfactory and they struck and refused to work, they would be a perfect drag on the market—They just absolutely refused to work. What would you do with them?

To such questions, Governor Farrington's replied that Hawaii had had very few troubles with Chinese workers but would send them home if it did.

Although the committee members showed inordinate interest in the "Japanese conspiracy," that did not necessarily mean they would ap-prove the Hawaiian plan to renew Chinese immigration. But Dillingham remained calm. On June 28, when the hearings entered their second week, Dillingham sent the HSPA his assessment of the committee: "I think that all of the members are convinced that our situation is serious and that we must have relief. Unfortunately, however, several members of the Committee are from labor sections of the country and are afraid of their jobs."[25]

THE AFL ERECTS A WALL

There were others at the hearings who suggested that the Hawaiian representatives were using the Japanese as an excuse to obtain a source of cheap labor. Around the time of the hearings America's largest labor organization, the AFL, was holding its national meeting in Denver, Colorado. On June 21 the AFL executive council was instructed to prevent revision of the Chinese Exclusion Act that would reinstate contract labor immigration. The AFL further declared the "gentlemen's agreement" negotiated by Shidehara and Morris a failure. Asserting that the Japanese had cunningly outwitted the intent of the California anti-alien law, the AFL convention voted in favor of the total exclusion of the Japanese and other Orientals from the United States.

The AFL, which had a membership of more than 5 million, was an organization that politicians could not ignore. On June 3, shortly after arriving in Washington, Dillingham and his colleagues, through the good offices of the secretary of labor, met AFL president Samuel Gompers for three hours. Dillingham came away from the meeting optimistic. As he told former governor McCarthy, "Gompers and the officials next to him are not hostile themselves to the Chinese labor plan." But Gompers's craftiness may have given such an impression. "Sam" Gompers was a small-statured man of sixty-seven when he met the members of the Hawaii Emergency Labor Commission, but he exuded an obstinacy that brooked no deceit. He gauged his opponents as he puffed on the cigar constantly in his mouth or dropped ashes from it. He was known for never showing his true feelings and controlling the pace of his conversations. The people he most despised were those born with silver spoons in their mouths, privileged from birth, like Walter Dillingham.

Gompers emigrated from London when he was thirteen years old and became active in the labor movement as a cigar maker. He was the founding president of the AFL, a post he held until his death in 1924. Under Gompers, the AFL pursued a course of harmony between labor and management. Clearly distancing itself from radical socialist groups like the IWW, the AFL avoided direct involvement of labor unions in political struggles. During the First World War, Gompers was on the advisory board of the Council of National Defense, and he aligned organized labor with national policy. It was his multifaceted flexibility that allowed him to bear the burden of preserving his large organization.

Gompers's name was known in Japan from the early days of its labor movement. Fusatarō Takano, who organized the first labor union in Japan, was awakened to the labor movement after witnessing the activities of the AFL when he was a struggling student in San Francisco. Indeed, he directly sought advice from Gompers about starting a labor movement in Japan. Impressed by Takano's enthusiasm, Gompers appointed him the AFL agent in Japan, and after he returned home he sent dispatches to the AFL journal on labor issues there. At times this was his main source of livelihood. In 1897 he established the Society for Formation of Labor Unions (Rōdō Kumiai Kiseikai) with others who had also recently returned from America, including Sen Katayama.

From the beginning the AFL worked to raise living standards for skilled workers but did not concern itself with organizing unskilled laborers. It also denied membership to African American laborers, and it maintained a policy of racial discrimination toward the alien laborers from Asia. One of the AFL's first activities was to support the passage of the anti-Chinese immigration legislation in the 1880s.

Interestingly, while the American Congress was passing anti-Chinese immigration laws, the issue of immigrant Chinese laborers also arose in Japan. The Rōdō Kumiai Kiseikai led by Takano and his colleagues, taking an anti-foreign stance, called on Japanese workers to unite against letting in Western capitalists who might exploit Japanese workers or Chinese laborers who would work for cheaper wages than Japanese. In short, rather than confront the AFL's policy of racial discrimination, the early leaders of Japan's labor movement followed the same line.

In 1905, when the increase in Japanese laborers migrating to the mainland from Hawaii was becoming an issue, Gompers proclaimed, "The Caucasians are not going to let their standard of living be destroyed by Negroes, Chinamen, Japs or any others."[26] After Congress passed anti-Chinese immigration laws, the AFL turned to targeting Japanese laborers, who, like the Chinese, worked for low wages, sent their savings back to Japan, and had no intention to settle in America.

Japanese business leaders like Eiichi Shibusawa were apprehensive about the anti-Japanese problem on the West Coast. They regarded the Japanese immigrant laborers as the cause of anti-Japanese sentiments and concluded that anti-Japanese sentiments were casting a dark shadow over U.S.-Japan relations. To alleviate that condition, in 1915 Bunji Suzuki and other members of the Yūaikai attended the AFL convention held in California, in the heart of the anti-Japanese exclusion movement. Ignoring the objections of Phelan and other anti-Japanese legislators, the AFL gave Suzuki the opportunity to make a speech declaring that no national borders divided the common interests of workers. Suzuki attended the following year's AFL meeting, but its anti-Japanese policy did not change. During the 1920 referendum in California on the revision of the Alien Land Act, an AFL resolution supporting it swayed the outcome of the ballot. The California state AFL was the strongest branch within the organization.

On June 25, the fifth day of the hearings, Paul Scharrenberg, secretary of the California AFL, testified as a representative of mainland laborers. He cited the "Japanese problem" in Hawaii as a bad example that should not be repeated in California and made it clear that the AFL was strongly opposed to permitting Chinese immigration. Two days later an AFL representative read a telegram from George W. Wright, president of the Honolulu Central Labor Union, the Caucasian workers' organization in Hawaii, declaring opposition to the renewal of Chinese immigration. "Hawaii's emergency commission misrepresenting conditions," it began. "Statistics in our possession indicate no actual labor shortage in Territory. . . . Japanese here striving for American ideals and standards. Strike purely economic. No nationalistic issues involved." It called the HSPA's charges of Japanese conspiracy to control industry "a ridiculous falsehood." Another statement was presented by the Iron Molders' Union in Honolulu: "To-day we are competing with the Jap, which is bad enough, and if the planters are allowed to flood this territory with cheap foreign labor we Americans will be compelled to leave here." [27]

The AFL mounted the strongest opposition to the Hawaii Emergency Labor Commission's efforts. After the AFL convention in Colorado, Gompers directed local branches throughout the United States to send telegrams opposing renewal of Chinese labor immigration to Albert Johnson, chairman of the Committee on Immigration and Naturalization. At a press conference in Washington on July 11, Gompers denounced the Hawaiian sugar planters for hiring the most easily exploited workers. Now, he said, they were targeting Chinese coolies who were used to exploitation and unmerciful conditions. He characterized the touting of a "Japanese conspiracy to take over Hawaii's sugar industry" in the commission's petition as "a Hawaiian conspiracy." [28]

The first round of the hearings closed on July 8 for a two-week recess. Washington had already entered its hot, humid summer season. In Honolulu the evening trade winds bring cooler temperatures, but in Washington the summer temperature changes little between day and night, offering no relief while people sleep. Dillingham had been living in a hotel for two months, but he was undaunted by the AFL's firm opposition. On the contrary, he was determined to overcome this challenge.

When Scharrenberg testified against the renewal of Chinese immigration, Dillingham sent a telegram to Frank Thompson, the HSPA attorney: "One of the Gompers crowd has tipped me off twice that our bill would be half won if we could pull off or split the opposition from home. I hope that work to that end is going on." He also directed that a petition campaign be mounted to show general public support in Hawaii for the renewal of Chinese immigration. The campaign was so widespread and intensive that the Iron Molders' Union of Honolulu complained to the secretary of the interior, "We, the Molders of Honolulu, as taxpayers, object to the office that has been created by the Planters Association and the Chamber of Commerce for the sending of telegrams, letters and wireless messages to congressmen and influential friends in the states at the expense of the taxpayers of Honolulu."

On June 28 Dillingham had wired George M. Rolph, general manager of C&H Sugar in San Francisco to request an introduction to Secretary of Commerce Herbert Hoover. Just before the hearings recessed, on July 8, Dillingham wired his thanks to Rolph, saying that he had a "satisfactory meeting." He also contacted former Senator Phelan for advice on how to handle the AFL representative from California.

THE EXQUISITE TIMING OF THE SAKAMAKI CASE INDICTMENT

When the hearings resumed on July 24, the first witness was Henry T. Oxnard of the American Beet Sugar Company, the man who had started the beet industry in California. He proclaimed his firm opposition to Chinese immigration for reasons quite different from the AFL's. He saw it as a scheme by his competitors, the Hawaii sugar planters, to import cheap labor. According to Oxnard, it cost 4 cents to produce sugar in Cuba, 6 cents in Puerto Rico, 7 cents for mainland beet sugar, and 7 cents for cane sugar in Louisiana. So Hawaii's production cost of 5 cents was not especially high. "We oppose Chinese immigration," he said, "but we want the same deal for our interests as the Hawaiians got, either no Chinese for Hawaii or Chinese for the mainland as well."

While admitting frankly his demand was a selfish one to protect his own industry, Oxnard accused the Hawaii planters of being selfish as well and of putting the blame on the Japanese. "If you will say that they are patriotic, then put me in the patriotic list," he said. "I do not think the Hawaiian planters are asking for Chinamen to help the Government.

They asked for them ten years ago, and they have always asked for what they believed would get the cheapest and best labor." When a Hawaiian delegate countered that the mainland beet sugar growers had used cheap labor from Mexico, Oxnard replied, "We pay them current American wages and we are perfectly willing for the Hawaiians to use Mexicans." He suggested to the Hawaiian representatives that if there really was a labor shortage in Hawaii, they should solve it by bringing in laborers from the Philippines, which was also American territory.

John M. Rogers of Louisiana, representing the American Cane Growers Association, echoed Oxnard's views. He was "strongly opposed to any man coming to America unless he had the uniform traits essential to full-fledged American citizenship." The majority of the labor force in Louisiana was made up of African American laborers, however, so the southern cane growers were no different from the Hawaiian in seeking workers at the bottom of the economic ladder to protect their profits. U.S. mainland sugar industry representatives testified against the renewal of the importation of Chinese labor for two days.

On the morning of Friday, July 29, AFL president Samuel Gompers, accompanied by several aides, made his first appearance at the hearings. Tension ran through the hearing room, making onlookers forget the humidity for a moment. Seated next to Gompers were George W. Wright, president of the Honolulu Central Labor Council, and Wilmot Chilton, the organization's financial officer. The two men had arrived just three days before from Honolulu.

Before the Hawaii Emergency Labor Commission left for Washington, two of its members, Albert Horner and Charles Chillingworth, had paid a call on George Wright. The forty-four-year-old Wright was younger than Walter Dillingham, but his wind-ruffled hair was already speckled with gray. He looked like a man used to physical labor, but he had a degree in physical chemistry, a subject he was said to have taught at his alma mater in Pennsylvania. After working in mining, in 1917 he went to Hawaii as an engineer on the construction of the military facilities at Pearl Harbor. He was a civilian employee of the U.S. military, not an employee of Dillingham's construction company.

In August 1920, after the second Oahu strike was over, Wright was elected to the Honolulu Central Labor Council. An effective writer, he had contributed to the council newsletter. The council's membership was limited to Caucasian and Hawaiian skilled workers who had American citizenship. Since it claimed only some one hundred fifty members, it was not a powerful group, but it did represent Hawaii's Caucasian labor unions. Although under the umbrella of the AFL, it was not recognized as its official Honolulu chapter. After meeting with Wright, Chillingworth and Horner left with the impression that he would not be easily persuaded to their cause. Jack Butler, the new executive secretary of the HSPA, who succeeded Royal Mead, sent Dillingham a letter from Honolulu during the hearing recess. It stated in part, "Wright is the real leader from all information I can get. He claims not to lead at all and gets more strength by such claim. In his presence, those who desire to take our side, remain silent."[29] Dillingham was rather sanguine, thinking that Wright was far away in Hawaii, but now Wright and Chilton had arrived in the capital.

On July 29, betraying no hint of fatigue from his lengthy trip, Wright read a long statement opposing the importation of Chinese indentured labor. Representative Raker questioned him about the relationship between the Hawaiian sugar industry and the territorial authorities.

RAKER: "Is it your intent to convey to this committee that the president of the Hawaiian Sugar Association went to the governor to get this matter started?"

WRIGHT: "Absolutely. That is the explanation that Mr. Bishop (HSPA president) himself gave us in a conference at which I was present."

RAKER: "In other words, instead of taking it up themselves personally, they started through the governor to make it an official act?"

WRIGHT: "Yes. That's right."

Walter Dillingham surely wished to avoid this testimony about the close connection between the sugar planters and the Hawaiian political-economic circles that controlled the territorial administration and legislature. Kuhio Kalanianaole, the elected delegate to Congress from the territory of Hawaii, raised frequent objections during the exchange between Raker and Wright.

On Monday, August 1, an outburst by Kuhio brought the hearings back to the issue of the Japanese laborers. He attacked Gompers for calling the territory's petition for the importation of Chinese labor "a Hawaiian conspiracy" a few weeks earlier. "My impression is that we were not discussing Japanese," said Gompers, "but Chinese." But Kuhio continued his diatribe. He shouted at the congressmen on the Immigration and Naturalization Committee: "You sent there shiploads of Japanese and put them in the Territory of Hawaii. The people there had nothing to do with the dumping of those Japanese into the islands, and we are coming to you, who dumped them in there, to solve the problem that they make today for Hawaii. We did not bring them into Hawaii, you did it!" Dumbfounded by this historically inaccurate charge, the hearings fell into a momentary silence. Kuhio's outburst would have been easier to understand if it had been directed at the kamaaina sugar planters rather than congressmen.

Known in Washington as a "prince," Kuhio was more directly connected to the Hawaiian royal family than was Acting Governor Iaukea. His wife came from a branch of the Hawaiian royal family that had ruled Maui. Prince Kuhio, who had studied in England, was known for his dignified British-style manners. With his title, a rarity in America, he was an ideal person to advocate the territory's position on various issues to the Congress. He had been at his post for eighteen years. Suffering from rheumatism since going to Washington, he left the capital each year when the cold winds began to blow and spent the winter months at his residence in Waikiki. It had been rumored for about two years that his heart was weak as well.

An important part of his job as the Hawaiian delegate to Congress was to protect the profits of the Hawaiian sugar planters. In other words, Prince Kuhio was serving the interests of the new Hawaiian governing class, who had overthrown the Hawaiian monarchy of his ancestors. For this reason Kuhio's feelings toward his job must have been ambivalent. This was clear from his passionate effort to petition for the return of lands to Hawaiian natives.

Did the emotions that had built up subconsciously under the burden of defending the Caucasian sugar planters' policies prompt his sudden outburst at the hearings? Or was it the cloying heat of the capital that made him lose his princely dignity? It must have been more than the heat—his face was flushed and his breathing heavy. Resting his corpulent body on the table, perspiration poured from his forehead. The emotional excitement must have put a burden on his weakened heart.

Taking this to be a bad turn of events, Dillingham quickly attempted to change the direction of the dialogue: "One fact must come to the fore, and that is that the people of Hawaii for 40 years have realized that the only way to secure American control of that country was to keep the races in balance." But Representative Raker was disturbed by Kuhio's charge. Noting that Chinese and Japanese immigrants entered Hawaii under the Hawaiian monarchy, he said, "This was the first time that an official request had been made to have Japanese immigration stopped." When Gompers agreed, Kuhio became more agitated. He shouted,

If you do not believe in the solution we are presenting to you, for God's sake give us something else, but do not condemn us for coming over here and trying to save ourselves. It seems as though you think we are a bunch of damned crooks and that we are trying to sneak something through Congress—I tell you that you must solve our problem and not let it continue until a condition arises in Hawaii similar to the condition that arose in the South, and let lynch law solve it.

The charge made by the obviously upset prince cannot be treated as mere hysterics if we assume that his words were meant for the kamaaina sugar planters, that is, for Dillingham.

The hearings finally quieted down when Chairman Johnson said, "We will suspend this line of debate." George Wright continued his testimony by suggesting that while there was a labor shortage at the sugarcane plantations, the number of laborers needed was 2,000 to 3,000 rather than 5,000 to 6,000, as Dillingham and the Hawaii Emergency Labor Commission had asserted. The main reason for the labor shortage, he said, was that despite soaring sugar prices that put more money in their pockets than they had dreamed, Japanese laborers had left the sugarcane fields because labor conditions on the plantations were so bad that they could not bear to live there.

Wright was by no means protective of the Japanese. "Our efforts have been directed with this point of view, of keeping the Japanese on the plantations as far as possible," he said.

> Our fear, our menace, has been the upward crowding of the Japanese, and we have believed that any means that could be devised to keep the Japanese on the plantations where he was originally brought to do his work, would be the solution of the problem. If Chinese were imported, the Japanese would yield to the pressure from below of this lower grade of Orientals—and absolutely, they would crowd out those at the top, and we who consider ourselves on the top level would be the ones crowded off the islands.

In other words, keeping the Japanese on the plantations was a way of protecting Caucasian workers.

Representative Shaw, citing the *Honolulu Advertiser* article about Tsutsumi's statement that the warship *Yakumo* had come to pick up striking Japanese, asked Wright, "Do you still believe that the strike of 1920 was purely economic and that no national issues were involved?" Wright responded, "I certainly do."

Representative Free of California took up the questioning. "Do you believe the Japanese are loyal to this country as against Japan? Do you not believe they all pledge their first loyalty to Japan?" "No, I would not say they all do," Wright answered. "Of course, I have no use for the Japs any more than the rest of you have, but I know that some of them are Americans, and probably just as good Americans as lots of the rest of us. But that does not touch upon the question of this strike that the gentleman has just brought up." Wright, as he later testified, had no Japanese acquaintances except for one or two school boys who were high school classmates of his sons.

The next day, after testifying that neither the mainland AFL nor the Honolulu Central Labor Council had anything to do with the strike, Wright observed, "The strike was not nationalistic, even if all the American papers in Hawaii had called it so for the evident purpose of discrediting the strikers." At this, Free, repeating a question asked earlier by Johnson, asked Wright, "You are on pretty friendly terms with the Japanese, are you not?"

As if on a signal, Chairman Johnson jumped in. "Mr. Wright, I want to ask you if you visited any Japanese before you came on here from Honolulu?"

"I have talked on the street with a part Jap, who is the editor of a Japanese paper, namely Fred Makino."

"Had the Japanese labor association offered you support in any way, financial support in particular?"

"No, sir."

Charging impatiently into this interchange, Representative Free threw out an explosive accusation.

"Is it not a fact that some Japanese put up at least $500 for the expenses of either yourself or your associate, Mr. Chilton?"

"I say that they offered me no support. Now, I will make this thing absolutely clear to this committee, because there are certain things in connection with . . ."

Cutting Wright off, as if he were a prosecuting attorney in court, Representative Free said, "Let us have an answer, yes or no, to the question." Wright responded, "As I told you, personally I do not know. Money has been raised from individual contributions who absolutely do not want to go on record. . . . As to that, we do not consider that it is anybody's business as to who did or who did not contribute."

"We consider it our business," replied Free. "I will tell you right now that I consider it my business, as a member of this committee, to know whether Japanese contributed to the expense of you coming here."

Chairman Johnson pressed Wright for an answer: "How much money did the Japanese contribute to your expense fund?" When Wright said,

"I am not in a position to say," Representative Free asked Chilton the same question. Chilton answered that since the Honolulu Central Labor Council was a small organization, it could not come up with the travel expenses so he went to ask Japanese merchants for contributions. It was suggested that he clear the request with Tokuji Onodera, secretary of the Japanese Chamber of Commerce. But Onodera refused to make a contribution, since it would be unwise to incur the enmity of Dillingham's Honolulu Chamber of Commerce. However, Onodera said, he did not mind if individual Japanese merchants contributed on their own. Calculating that the expenses for himself and Wright to travel to Washington would be $1,500, Chilton sought contributions for that amount. Donations by Caucasian workers in the Honolulu Central Labor Council amounted to only $170, and the rest came from Japanese contributors.

Representative Free resumed his attack on Wright, "You knew that some of the money you came here on, came from the Japanese, did you not?"

"I knew that some of the money did come from the Japanese, yes."

"Why did you not say that when I asked you before?"

"Because I was told I was not at liberty, that this money was collected confidentially."

"You had been in pretty close touch with them on the matter before you came, had you not?"

"Not particularly, no. I have not been in close touch with them."

"You have had their views, you have discussed it with them, and what you would testify to before the committee?"

"No, sir. We did not expect to come before this committee. They knew the purposes for which we wanted to come, and, as Mr. Chilton has just said, they contributed."

One week earlier, in a letter dated July 20, Prince Kuhio had written to HSPA attorney Thompson, "Chilton and Wright appear before the Committee Friday when we hope to have some startling exposure." The Hawaiian side had chosen Representative Free as the person to leak this startling information. A newly elected member of the House, Free was eager for a chance to play to the stands. The other congressman from California, Raker, was skeptical of the hearings from the start. He was an experienced congressman known for his analytical abilities, and he was not someone whom the Hawaiians could easily manipulate. Moreover, he was close to the AFL, which expressed its strong opposition to the petition from Hawaii.

The Dillingham group had targeted Free to use him to destroy the credibility of Wright and the labor representatives from Honolulu as well as the AFL. Toward the end of the first hearings at the end of June, Dillingham, through Thompson, had directed HSPA secretary Butler to try to block opposition by the Honolulu Central Labor Council and to foment internal discord in the organization. When AFL opposition turned out to be far stronger than expected, Dillingham sent an SOS message to Thompson: "Prominent Federation official advises work on Honolulu local council withdraw or split protest against our bill. Urge your best endeavor accomplish this." Two days after receiving this telegram, Butler had invited Wright and others to the HSPA. Wright had refused to withdraw the council's opposition to the importation of Chinese labor. In fact, however, opinion was split within the Honolulu Central Labor Council. Some thought it a bad idea to make an enemy of the all-powerful HSPA. But Wright, who had seized the issue to strengthen ties with the AFL so that the council would be formally recognized as its local branch, overcame the opposition and decided to go to Washington. At that point, however, it was clear that the Honolulu Central Labor Council would not be able to come up with travel expenses.

Just after this Wright had his chance meeting with Kinzaburō Makino, president of the *Hawaii hōchi.* Only about two weeks earlier Wright had first met Makino and other Japanese-language newspapermen at a meeting sponsored by the Federation of Japanese Labor to sound out the intentions of the Honolulu Central Labor Council. When he met Makino on the street, Wright said that he had decided to go to Washington to express his opposition to the renewal but was having difficulty gathering the necessary funds. Displaying his usual magnanimity, Makino not only suggested having the Japanese merchants contribute but also provided Wright with several introductions.

When the council's fund-raising effort became known to the HSPA, it was just the opportunity they had sought. After Wright and Chilton departed for Washington on the *Siberia,* Governor Farrington's *Honolulu Star Bulletin* ran a scoop sensationalizing the ties between the Honolulu Central Labor Council and the Federation of Japanese Labor. "The 'Labor' delegates who went on to Washington for the avowed purpose of defeating the Hawaiian emergency labor bill stand convicted of having been financed in their mischievous errand by Japanese money!" The paper reported that the federation had donated $500 to Wright to help the Japanese cause in Washington.

After this "startling exposure" at the hearings, at a press conference

Prince Kuhio issued a statement that for many years the Japanese had plotted to take over Hawaii. Since the story involved the AFL, newspapers throughout the country carried the testimony of the AFL, Wright, and Chilton. In California the *Los Angeles Examiner* and the *San Francisco Chronicle* fanned anti-Japanese sentiments with headlines like "Japanese Pay Whites to Fight Chinese Labor." The *Boston Globe* ran the headline "Say Japs Paid Their Way"; the *Philadelphia Record,* "Honolulu Japanese Behind Fight Against Coolie Labor"; and the *Albany Knickerbocker Press,* "Hawaii Labor Row Financed by Japs."

By August 2 the two major English-language newspapers in Hawaii ran exceptionally large headlines: "Chilton Admits on Stand that He and Wright Took $1,500 in Contributions," suggesting that the Japanese federation had bought the Caucasian labor group's leaders. The *Honolulu Advertiser* noted in a sarcastic subheading "Labor's Fight Is Helping, Not Hurting Hawaii." [30]

Alongside the articles on the hearings in Washington, however, came reports that twenty-one Japanese were under indictment for dynamiting the Sakamaki house at Olaa Plantation. The August 2 *Honolulu Star Bulletin*'s headline screamed: "'Assassination Corps' of Labor Federation Carried Out Campaign Terrorism." The timing of the indictment was exquisite.

In an editorial sending off Dillingham's Hawaii Emergency Labor Commission, the *Honolulu Advertiser* had pledged that those remaining in Hawaii would do their utmost to support the commission in its life-and-death struggle for the territory of Hawaii. It can be said that those remaining in Hawaii kept their promise. The timing of the hurried indictment of the leaders of the Federation of Japanese Labor more than a year after the Sakamaki dynamiting incident coincided well with the timing of Dillingham's June 25 telegram to HSPA secretary Thompson. According to their trial testimony, Matsumoto and Saitō had confessed to the crime in late November 1920, after the Kyōrakukan incident, yet the territory took no specific action for seven months after the confessions, until things seemed to be going badly for the commission in Washington.

The exquisite timing that connected Washington, D.C., and Honolulu was the real reason that charges were brought on the Sakamaki dynamiting incident. To shore up its efforts to renew the importation of Chinese labor, the territory of Hawaii charged Noboru Tsutsumi and other leaders of the federation with conspiracy in the first degree to perpetuate a "shocking crime of conspiracy." With the indictment, the territory of Hawaii had already accomplished its real purpose.

SAMUEL GOMPERS'S COUNTERARGUMENT

Because of the difference in time zones, news of the indictment of the leaders of the Federation of Japanese Labor was reported on the mainland with headlines such as "Japanese Accused of Inciting Sugar Riots!" a day later than articles about Japanese contributions to the white labor representatives. Yet it was treated by the papers across the country as a continuation of the previous day's articles. Many newspapers exaggerated the violence of the 1920 strike. The *San Francisco Chronicle,* for example, reported, "The culminating act of violence during the strike occurred June 3, 1920, when the house of the Japanese who refused to join the strikers was dynamited."[31] West Coast newspapers, especially in California where the anti-Japanese movement was strong, played up the story with sensational phrases—"violent incident in the strike," "criminal conspiracy," "dynamiting," "attempted murder,"—and emphasized that these acts were perpetrated by Japanese. At the trial Judge Banks had said that "the Territory was in no way concerned with the strike itself—whether or not it was justified, or even properly conducted." In direct contrast to his words, the mainland press exposed the true intentions of the Hawaiian authorities by emphasizing the connection between the strike and the dynamiting.

Thirty-five years earlier, when dynamite was thrown into a rally of striking laborers in Chicago, the authorities quickly punished labor leaders whom they accused of being under the influence of anarchists. The "Hay Market Massacre" was notorious in American labor history. Subsequently, no matter what the actual circumstances, the radical left-wing labor activists, anarchists, and IWW members were labeled "bomb throwers." The newspapers used "dynamite" as a synonym for such labor activists. The Palmer Raids of early 1920 were the most extreme example of playing on public fears in that way.

The petition of the territory of Hawaii to renew the importation of Chinese labor had not attracted much attention in Washington because it was a problem affecting a far-off territory in the Pacific. But when the issue became entangled with the AFL, the largest union organization in the country, it suddenly became news all over the country. And the articles about it were replete with the word "dynamite," a word that unmistakably drew readers' attention. Walter Dillingham must have read the news that morning as he took his customary breakfast in the hotel restaurant. His face no doubt exuded more easy confidence than ever before.

The hearings on August 3 included the testimony of Wilmot Chilton, who had come to Washington with George Wright. He was a member of a unique minority in Hawaii, white laborers. He was born and raised in a class sandwiched between the rich haoles and the Japanese immigrants, who were the majority in the labor force. He had grown up thinking of Japanese as economic competitors, so his perspective differed from that of Wright, who had come to Hawaii from the mainland. In response to questions, Chilton said, "[The Japanese] were prolific, clannish, patronized only their own industries, were masterful in attitude, and were giving the Americans a hard run in all sorts of business." And he added, "They work like a ratchet." By this, he meant that their sole goal in life was getting ahead and that they used any means to achieve success.

In direct opposition to Wright, Chilton characterized the 1920 strike as a conspiracy "wound up on a nationalistic basis." His testimony seemed to show that he had shifted his allegiance to the Dillingham side. Before he had departed for Washington, Chilton had engaged in some strange behavior. Later it was rumored that Frank Thompson, the HSPA lawyer, had bought off Chilton, and his testimony at the hearings seemed to substantiate that rumor.

The AFL did not know that Wright and Chilton traveled to Washington on funds donated by Japanese. Samuel Gompers was particularly incensed that the organization had been embarrassed at the hearings and, even worse, in the press. When Gompers testified on August 4, the day after Chilton, he appeared to be very displeased, his lined face hardened. He sharply criticized the Honolulu Central Labor Council. While he admitted that they may have been "driven to desperation in an effort to help in a just cause," he distanced the AFL from their actions. "I do not exculpate these men, I do not stand for any such procedure, nor do those with whom I am associated in the American Labor Movement," he said. "I regard it as an almost inexcusable blunder on the part of the organization at Honolulu, or the men themselves, to seek contributions from Japanese. I can understand their straits."

Chairman Albert Johnson, however, was intent on treating the AFL president as a surrogate for Wright, who was no longer present. Pointing out that Wright had denied twice that the 1920 strike arose from Japanese nationalistic ambitions, Johnson asserted that his testimony could not be trusted as it was clear that he had received money from Japanese. Gompers responded,

> The fundamental principle for which I and my associates were contending was the principle of Americanism. Whether Japanese movement in Hawaii was nationalistic or not did not make a jot of difference. . . . The testimony they have given would show clearly that the Japanese have not received value for their money. They have shown the Japanese in their true colors, and yet I can understand how men so far away would grasp at almost anything in order to carry out an honest and high purpose.

Dillingham, who had been on the listening side for several days, tried to return attention to the Hawaiian petition for renewal of the importation of Chinese labor. Dillingham had sent Honolulu a telegram the day before that victory was 99 percent certain, but Representative Raker had thrown cold water on his confidence on this matter. Gompers was happy to return to the main purpose of the hearing, for it permitted him to launch an even more forceful attack: "Intellectually [the Chinese] are living in the year 1921 but industrially they are 400 years behind the times and imagine that the people of the United States will consent to the introduction of a feudal system, or peonage, or a bondman system." Warming up to his topic, Gompers spoke of his memories about how moved he was when he heard of the freeing of the black slaves in America when he was a youth working in a cigar factory in London: "I am a protestant against injustice or a reversion to the old reaction and the old-time conditions of the life of labor . . ." But in his guise as a champion against racial discrimination, Gompers ignored the fact that for many years the AFL did not permit those very blacks he spoke of to become members. No one at the hearings countered Gompers, however. He concluded by proclaiming:

> America's workers were not going to stand idly by and see Hawaii "Chinaized" as a remedy for Japanese evils. This resolution would be an entering wedge for greedy profiteers, to bring Chinese to the mainland. The proposal would arouse the ire not only of the Japanese in Hawaii—who could not be deported—but of their government as well. How could Congress on the one hand pass a Japanese exclusion act and on the other a law to admit Chinese coolies?

One week later, on August 12, the House Committee on Immigration and Naturalization hearing entered its final day, calling Walter Dillingham as a witness once again. After another series of heated exchanges with Representative Raker, Dillingham renewed his appeal to the congressmen:

> Judge Raker, we have sat here for six weeks with an open resolution which would give the Secretary of Labor the power to bring in any alien otherwise inadmissible to meet the situation in Honolulu. Has any constructive plan or suggestion been developed in the six weeks by this body or any one else by which we could meet the situation, which you yourself describe as being deplorable?

Prince Kuhio seconded his protests, but the committe chairman, Johnson, without referring to the validity of the Chinese labor plan, gaveled the two-month hearing to a close with the simple comment, "I think the committee was wise in carrying the Japanese phase of the Hawaiian situation into this matter."

THE SENATE HEARINGS

The Senate hearing on the Hawaiian petition started the following day, August 13, at 10:30 A.M. The chairman of the Senate Committee on Immigration and Naturalization was LeBaron Colt of Rhode Island, but the hearing on immigration into Hawaii was chaired by Sen. William P. Dillingham. At seventy-eight, Dillingham, formerly governor of Vermont, was in his fourth Senate term. His twenty-one years in the Senate made him a veteran legislator. Like Albert Johnson in the House, he had been a member of the Immigration and Naturalization Committee from the start and had served as its chairman for many years. Senator Dillingham was actually a relative of Walter Dillingham of Hawaii.

Perhaps because of this connection, Walter Dillingham appeared quite optimistic as he began his testimony, comfortably choosing his words to maximum effect.

> Up until a year ago this spring, I was one of those who believed that the work of Americanizing the Japanese in Hawaii was meeting with success.
>
> A year ago, when 6,000 Japanese laborers, headed by a group of men not from the laboring community, but a group of organizers and agitators, struck and left their jobs, it developed that every Japanese in the country was on the side of the Japanese strikers, and that those who were closely affiliated with the American business interests—meaning by that the large Japanese business interests, banking interests, and the professional interests; that is, the men who were following professions—were all on the side of the Japanese strikers. While they admitted, as a number of the superior Japanese admitted, that the strike was wrong, that it was nationalistic, and that it should not be,

it was not for five or six months that it was possible to get a statement out of any one of these prominent Japanese to the effect that the strike was wrong, that the principle was wrong, or that it was the duty of these people to return to work, although they freely admitted these facts in private conversations. Then, it seemed, and from publications which we will put before you here, it is demonstrated clearly, that when it comes to any big question the solidarity of the Japanese is perfect, regardless of where they were born.[32]

Dillingham also deployed God and theories of pigmentation to substantiate the theory that Japanese were plotting to take over Hawaii. Anti-Japanese activists on the mainland argued that Japanese aimed to invade California because their physical makeup could not tolerate severe cold or heat, but Dillingham's opinion was entirely the opposite. The Japanese were more persevering than Americans and hardworking in the sugarcane fields, he claimed, and they were suited to working in tropical conditions. As Dillingham continued, however, the senators must have been appalled: "When you are asked to go out in the sun and work in the canebrake, away from the tropical breeze, you are subjecting the white man to something that the good Lord did not create him to do. If He had, the people of the world, I think, would have had a white pigment in the skin and not variegated colors." The senator from South Dakota challenged Dillingham's theory of God's intentions, citing as an example the brutally humid heat of the southern United States.

Following Dillingham, Prince Kuhio brought up the issue of dual nationalities as solid proof that the nisei were under orders from the government of Japan. At the close of the day's hearings, Kuhio issued a statement declaring, "The control of Hawaii has been Japan's objective for many, many years."

The Senate hearings were suspended after two days because Congress was due to recess for the summer in one week. Dillingham and the two other members of the Hawaii Emergency Labor Commission were forced to stay in Washington until the Senate reconvened in the fall, but Dillingham's attitude was positive. He wrote to Governor Farrington in Honolulu that the majority of the senators should be leaning toward the Hawaiian side when the hearings resumed.

However, on September 29, the day before the scheduled resumption of the Senate hearings, Dillingham was suddenly called in to meet with Henry P. Fletcher, undersecretary of state, who told him that the State Department was extremely concerned about upsetting the Japanese government. The following day, September 30, Secretary of State Hughes met with Dillingham for thirty minutes to explain the importance of an international conference about to be held in Washington. He asked Dillingham's cooperation in postponing the hearings on the importation of Chinese labor until the conference was safely over.

THE WASHINGTON CONFERENCE AND JAPANESE IMMIGRATION

Four days later, in a letter to Dillingham, Hughes explained the Washington Conference.

> It would be most unfortunate if, while the coming Conference were holding its sessions, this legislation should come up for debate in Congress. The Bill, in essence, relates to the immigration of Orientals and it would be impossible to avoid in its consideration a general discussion of our Far Eastern policies. It is quite within the range of possibilities that the Conference itself might in this connection become the subject of debate. . . . The hopes of many nations of the earth for future peace are centered on this Conference and it is felt that nothing should be permitted to mar its deliberations or cause embarrassment or uneasiness to any connected with its work.[33]

The three members of the Hawaii Emergency Labor Commission had already concluded that they would have to postpone consideration of their petition by the Senate. There was no advantage in defying the secretary of state. Chillingworth and Horner immediately left the capital, where chilly winds had begun to blow, for the ever-summery Hawaii, while Dillingham continued to make the rounds of congressmen. He finally left Washington on October 28, three days after the other two men had arrived in Hawaii. On the way home he attended the national meeting of the American Legion in Kansas, to seek their help in speaking to their congressmen. On November 15, just before he boarded the ship bound for Honolulu, he told local newspaper reporters in San Francisco why Hawaii was petitioning Congress for the renewal of the importation of Chinese labor: "It has been a case of bringing Congress to see that America needs a colonial policy, that the conditions and requirements of Hawaii, the Philippine Islands and Puerto Rico cannot be judged by the mainland standards."[34]

The Washington Conference, the success of which had so concerned Secretary of State Hughes, had begun four days earlier, on November 12. The purpose of the conference was to put a brake on an incipient naval arms race that had escalated after the First World War. Already on its first day, Secretary Hughes had proposed a naval disarmament plan establishing the ratio of capital ship tonnage among Great Britain, the United States, and Japan at 5:5:3. Behind the proposal for naval arms reduction were Anglo-American concerns about Japan. Not only was Japan stretching its reach on the Asian continent as China was riven with internal strife, it also was extending its influence to the western Pacific, where it had acquired League of Nations mandates over islands in Micronesia.

The Japanese delegation arrived just after Prime Minister Takashi Hara was assassinated. The only Japanese-language newspaper reporter from Hawaii to cover the Washington Conference, Yasutarō Sōga, president and editor-in-chief of the *Nippu jiji,* reported,

> It was fruitful just to have been able easily to read the countenances of the galaxy of powerful men of various nations who gathered this conference to discuss disarmament, so significant an issue in the world. From Japan alone, there were Ietatsu Tokugawa, Tomosaburō Katō, Kijūrō Shidehara, Masanao Hanihara, and other plenipotentiaries, as well as advisors in various fields. With a group of over fifty reporters, the stately Japanese Embassy on Massachusetts Avenue seemed practically like a little Japan.

Hughes's proposal for naval arms reduction was enthusiastically supported not only by the American press but also by foreign reporters. The Japanese plenipotentiary, Navy Minister Tomosaburō Katō (later Prime Minister), indicated his support of the Hughes proposal, but he disagreed about the ratio. Britain, the United States, and others refused to budge, and in the end the Japanese negotiated the maintenance of the status quo of military presence in the Pacific in return for the 5:5:3 ratio of capital ships.

The Washington Conference also discussed Pacific and Far East issues, including Japan's special interests on the Chinese continent and its Siberian intervention, and it reached agreement on such issues as the territorial integrity of China, the Open Door policy, and equal economic opportunity. At the same time, the Anglo-Japanese Alliance, which had restricted America's expansion into Asia, was allowed to lapse.

The four-month Washington Conference ended on February 6, 1922, with a treaty signed by the nine participating nations, just as Matsumoto was testifying in Honolulu about the Japanese conspiracy. This conference was clearly a way for the United States to consolidate its Far Eastern policy. The reaffirmation of the open door principle, which guaranteed the territorial integrity of China, also opened the way to future contention between Japan and the United States. For Japan, the capital ship ratio decided on at the Washington Conference relieved Japan of the heavy financial burden imposed by naval expansion, and given relative national strengths the ratio could be considered fair. Within Japan, however, the treaty agitated the expansionist nationalists who wanted Japan to dominate Asia, and it invited criticism that accepting an inferior level of naval strength was a "national disgrace."

The Japanese community in Hawaii responded to the arms reduction agreement in a way that was no less emotional. It is true that the second Oahu strike was a labor-capital struggle based on economic issues, as Noboru Tsutsumi and the other federation leaders had claimed, but it is undeniable that what allowed the Japanese laborers to endure their half-year struggle was a conviction that their own country was a first-class nation, as strong militarily as the United States or Britain. Perhaps because they suffered racial discrimination by white capitalists, the patriotism of the Japanese in Hawaii became more intense.

This can be easily surmised from the warm welcome the Japanese community accorded Imperial Navy ships when they made port calls in Hawaii. The 1920 announcement of Japan's plan to build an "Eight Eight Fleet" (Hachi Hachi Kantai)—eight battleships and eight battle cruisers—just after the end of the strike was greeted especially warmly by the Japanese community in Hawaii. When a training ship made a port call in Honolulu during the Washington Conference, they turned out in full force, lining the streets and waving small rising sun flags, displaying their patriotism in an unprecedented show of welcome at a time when military disarmament was under discussion.

Over many years the Japanese community had witnessed the expansion of naval base construction at Pearl Harbor. To them, the agreement on naval arms reduction was something real and something significant. It meant not only that Japan's ratio was lower than that of the United States and Britain but also that the Eight Eight Fleet plan would be curtailed and that the construction of large warships in Japan would have to be abandoned midway. It was a disappointment. It was not strange that many Japanese immigrants saw the construction of the Pearl Harbor base as a symbol of American intentions to thwart the development of their homeland. The reaction to the Washington Conference agreement was so vehement that the *Myōjō*, a monthly of the Jōdo sect of Buddhism, urged, "Britain should abandon its foreign outpost at Gibraltar and the U.S. should abandon its military port at Pearl Harbor."

Before Walter Dillingham left Washington, he received a communication from the Japanese ambassador, Kijūrō Shidehara. According to Dillingham, Shidehara had sounded him out on the proposal to renew Chinese labor immigration: "If assurances of no more labor troubles in Hawaii, would you aid in defeating the planter's bill?" No documents remain indicating Dillingham's response. How was Ambassador Shidehara intending to "assure" that the Japanese immigrants would not engage in further labor struggles? Such a comment by the Japanese ambassador was bound to give weight to the Japanese conspiracy theory propounded by the Hawaiian authorities, who argued that the 1920 strike involved the Japanese government.

Two weeks after the Washington Naval Treaty was signed, the U.S. Military Intelligence Report on the Pacific area took note of the statement made by Eiichi Shibusawa, an observer at the historic conference, that it was regrettable that the immigration issue, which was at the core of the misunderstanding between Japan and the United States, was not on the agenda at the Washington Conference.[35] But Ambassador Shidehara, one of the Japanese plenipotentiaries at the conference, advised the Foreign Ministry that because it was a bilateral issue between the United States and Japan it was not likely to make much headway:

> Letting the immigration issue be decided by this international conference will not be something the U.S. will favor. Even if the U.S. agrees to allow the issue to be discussed, Britain will not oppose the position of the U.S. because of her position of possessing colonies. Many of the other nations will choose not to oppose the position of the U.S. on the whole. We must be prepared to face the fact that, should this issue be discussed at this conference, it will be much more disadvantageous for us than our position was at the Paris Conference and at the League of Nations.

When Shidehara met with Secretary of State Hughes on September 15, two months before the Washington Conference, Hughes had expressed his conviction that although he was concerned about the Japanese immigrants' problem, negotiations on the question should wait for an opportune time so as not to incite public opinion in a detrimental way in both nations. A few weeks later Hughes called in Dillingham to request the postponement of the hearings on the petition for renewal of the importation of Chinese labor.

On October 18, a month after his meeting with Secretary Hughes, Ambassador Shidehara received a telegram from Foreign Minister Uchida: "It is not desirable that we attend the Washington Conference ignoring the immigration issue. Therefore, I instruct you to find out if the U.S. is ready to give us some sort of guarantee or, in the case of the opening of a new round of negotiations, the approximate position of the U.S." As Uchida noted at the outset,

> On this issue we have respected the U.S. intentions by concluding the Gentle-men's Agreement, prohibiting transfers from Hawaii, prohibiting picture brides, etc. Putting that aside, the informal discussions conducted between you and Ambassador Morris have achieved a general agreement. Even with this result, the current U.S. administration, despite having been in office more than half a year, has not initiated any effort to resolve our differences. This is in great contrast to the Imperial government which has been making steady efforts based on the spirit of mutual compromise. This impasse is of great re-gret to our government.

Referring to the situation within Japan, he continued,

> As a matter of reality, the situation in California is so urgent that the resident Japanese report feeling threatened and are concerned about their own well-being. The stubborn course of action pursued in California and other regions perturbs public sentiment in Japan in no small way. . . . With the Washing-ton Conference about to begin, arguments are running rampant as the Diet session approaches. At this critical time, we cannot possibly accept the U.S. side's position that it will consider negotiations on this issue after the end of the Washington Conference. To attend the Washington Conference while keeping the status quo is undesirable for us. I direct you to explain our posi-tion to the Secretary of State.

As to the time frame of the negotiations on immigration, he emphasized the importance of the success of the Washington Conference.

> The Imperial government wishes the U.S. government to agree on negotia-tions to be based on the "Shidehara-Morris" draft. Should the U.S. govern-ment guarantee this to the Japanese government, we will consider holding these discussions after the Washington Conference is concluded.

As the man most directly involved in the U.S.-Japan negotiations on immigration matters, Shidehara was called back to Japan after the Wash-ington Conference. At a meeting with Secretary Hughes before his de-parture, Shidehara touched on the immigration problem, sounding him out again on issuing the Shidehara-Morris agreement as an official state-ment by the two countries. Hughes expressed concern that bringing up the immigration problem at a time when hawkish elements in Congress, angered by the gentle treatment of Japan at the Washington Conference, were "arguing in a thoughtless manner with no concern about offend-ing a friendly nation," might bring a further eruption of anti-Japanese sentiment on the West Coast. Shidehara suggested, "We look forward with anticipation toward the coming of an opportune time to resolve this issue after the Washington Conference when emotions in both countries are improved and calmed." [36]

As mentioned earlier the Japanese consul general in Honolulu, Chō-nosuke Yada, had departed for Japan on February 21, 1922, during the Sakamaki dynamiting trial. On board the *Taiyō-maru* bound for Yokohama were a group of the plenipotentiaries from Japan, including Admiral Tomosaburō Katō and Vice Foreign Minister Masanao Hanihara, on their way back from the Washington Conference. It is not difficult to imagine that Yada told these high-ranking Japanese officials about the territory's petition efforts in Washington, about the Hawaiian authorities' attempt to label the 1920 Oahu strike a Japanese conspiracy at the hearings, and about the trial of Tsutsumi and other federation strike leaders.

Eiichi Shibusawa had stopped off in Honolulu on his return to Japan about a month before the Japanese plenipotentiaries arrived there. The FBI report noted that Viscount Shibusawa, the "grand old man of Japan," was "probably one of the most sincere Japanese who has ever visited the United States." [37] During his four-day stay in Hawaii, it continued, Shibusawa had made a special effort to investigate the Hawaii Laborers' Association and conditions affecting the Japanese laborers in Hawaii. Before arriving in Honolulu, he had met in California with pro-Japanese elements about the anti-Japanese problem in California. Shibusawa was one of the few key Japanese leaders who had shown an early interest in the U.S.-Japan friction over the Japanese immigrant labor problem. Indeed, he had sent Bunji Suzuki, president of the Yūaikai, to attend the AFL convention and had supported efforts to achieve harmony between labor and capital at home.

Even so, according to the FBI report, for the first several days of his visit he made no effort to get in touch directly with the Japanese labor leaders. Instead he confined his activities to obtaining information from the Japanese consul and influential members of the Japanese community. Just before he departed for Japan, Shibusawa reluctantly agreed to meet with a few federation representatives for a short time. It is known that the federation secretary general, Jirō Hayakawa, met with him, but it is not clear whether Tsutsumi and the other former federation leaders, who were free on bail, did so too. After listening to the federation representatives, Shibusawa suggested to the labor leaders "that they should appoint several prominent Japanese to act as go-betweens, between the labor federation and the capitalists." Leaders of the Japanese community in Honolulu, such as Reverend Takie Okumura, Dr. Iga Moori, and Assistant Professor Harada (Japanese studies, University of Hawaii) also attended the meeting, and Shibusawa hoped that they would act as the go-betweens.

According to the FBI report, the federation members opposed this suggestion because they thought that "any prominent Japanese in the community, who might be called upon to act as a go-between, would in all probability become pro-capitalist, as such had been in the past." They pointed out that the recent attitude of Consul General Yada was a good example of how "the capitalists might influence any go-between that may appear among the conservative Japanese." [38]

It is clear that Shibusawa was upset with the federation leaders. After they had left, according to the FBI report, he suggested to another prominent Japanese that the Japanese labor federation should be broken up. Reverend Okumura, who had met Shibusawa several times before, agreed. Among the Japanese in Hawaii, Okumura was closest to Shibusawa. Six months earlier, while in Japan seeking contributions for his "anti-Japanese prevention movement," Okumura had been supported by Shibusawa. He now asked Shibusawa "to take steps to have the Japanese Labor Federation broken up when he arrived in Japan." [39] The discussion at this meeting among Japanese was known to the Hawaiian territorial authorities before the day was over.

As the result of his visit, Shibusawa concluded that the causes of the Japanese problem in Hawaii were "labor union, Japanese language schools, dual citizenship, Buddhist activities." When his ship docked at Yokohama, Shibusawa told a group of reporters: "As a member of the Japan-U.S. relations committee I see the need for solving the problem of labor organizers in California and Hawaii. . . . The immigration issue is one that always casts a deep shadow on Japan-U.S. relations." [40]

THE BAPTISM OF NOBORU TSUTSUMI

A month after the conclusion of the Washington Conference, Noboru Tsutsumi and the other federation leaders were convicted in the Sakamaki house dynamiting case. Of the fifteen defendants found guilty of conspiracy in the first degree, thirteen appealed immediately after Judge Banks had sentenced them to imprisonment for not less than four years or more than ten years and raised their bail from $3,000 to $5,000. On March 10, the *Hawaii hōchi* reporter Teisuke Terasaki noted in his diary that because Noboru Tsutsumi and five others were unable to come up with bond money, they were placed in detention at 2:00 P.M.

Even had the Federation of Japanese Labor headquarters been so inclined, it had no financial resources to pay bail for its former leaders. It left the responsibility up to the local unions on the plantations where each defendant resided by having them raise bail using reserves of funds contributed by laborers. As a result, many local unions announced their dissolution. The tactics employed by the territory of Hawaii to force the dissolution of the federation by assaulting it financially were finally succeeding.

As if to make doubly sure, the territory of Hawaii indicted four of the Sakamaki house dynamiting case defendants—Fumio Kawamata, Honji Fujitani, Shunji Tomota, and Kan'ichi Takizawa—on charges of conspiracy to bomb the house of Hayaji Nakazawa, a "planters' dog" on Ewa Plantation. Kawamata and others, who had served as federation leaders after Tsutsumi and others resigned, were free on bail paid by the Waipahu Plantation union, but they were immediately required to post another $2,500 in bail per person. The Waipahu union was the largest on Oahu, and it had survived even after the other unions disbanded, but with this additional expense it announced its intention to dissolve. The indictment for bombing of the Nakazawa house was never brought to trial; it was later withdrawn by the territory as not a worthwhile use of the taxpayers' money.

On May 21, some two months after Judge Banks handed down his sentence, Terasaki noted in his diary that Noboru Tsutsumi had been baptized that day at 4:00 P.M. at the Japanese Hospital. And on a fair Sunday two weeks later, he met Mr. Tsutsumi at church "after not having seen him for a long time." An ardent Christian, Terasaki was a member of the Nuuanu Union Church in Honolulu. An English record of Tsutsumi's baptism by Reverend Teikichi Hori still remains in the church's archives.

Of the three secretaries of the Federation of Japanese Labor who led the strike, Hiroshi Miyazawa was a pastor and Ichiji Gotō was known to be a fervent Christian. Could their religious piety have piqued Tsutsumi's intellectual curiosity when they were in jail together, unable to make bail? Or had Tsutsumi resigned himself to dying in Hawaii? Tsutsumi suffered complications resulting from influenza contracted during the strike, and he was still not well at the time of the trial. Immediately after the strike he had been admitted to the Japanese Hospital where he was baptized. Yet Tsutsumi's family never knew of his baptism. According to family members, from his youth he had been a romantic, prone to enthusiasm. That he was baptized as a Christian, even though born and raised in a family that had been Buddhist priests for generations, may substantiate this aspect of his character.

Thirteen of the fifteen convicted defendants appealed the guilty verdicts, but neither Noboru Tsutsumi nor Chūhei Hoshino was among them. While Tsutsumi was in Hawaii, his wife, Chiyo, lined up their two children once a year for photographs to send to their father far across the Pacific. When he had left for Hawaii, Tsutsumi had promised Chiyo that he would send for her, but he had never shown any inclination to do so. Hawaii was a stepping-stone to meet with his brother Ekan on the American mainland, not a place where he intended to settle. As he told Judge Banks before sentencing, "I have no reason to be in Hawaii any more." He wanted to go home.

American labor leaders such as Samuel Gompers of the AFL and Big Bill Haywood of the IWW were all men who experienced "work that calloused one's hands," as HSPA secretary Mead put it. The determination and the urgency with which they plunged into the struggles for labor were vastly different from Tsutsumi's. For Tsutsumi, it was a case of having become too involved before he realized it. Kinzaburō Makino, president of the *Hawaii hōchi*, who had decided to settle in Hawaii, must have detected in Tsutsumi the behavior of someone merely passing through. His thorough distaste for Tsutsumi could not have arisen merely from self-interest.

Along with the thirteen defendants, including Gotō, who insisted on their innocence and appealed, Tsutsumi got out of detention on bail. (It is unknown which union organization put up his bail.) In mid-June, one month after his baptism, Tsutsumi and Hoshino entered the Oahu prison to start serving their sentences. Even though it might seem that he acknowledged his guilt, Tsutsumi simply wished to complete his sentence as soon as possible and return to Japan.[41]

THE HEARINGS END

On February 8, 1922, two days after the signing of the Nine-Party Treaty at the Washington Conference, Walter Dillingham left Honolulu once again for Washington. A February 1922 survey by the territory showed that with the entry of many Filipino laborers into the sugarcane fields, the total size of the plantation workforce was larger than that immediately before the strike. Despite this, Dillingham still insisted on seeking the passage of the renewal of the importation of Chinese labor in the U.S. Congress.

On January 9, 1922, at the age of fifty-one, Prince Kuhio had died of a heart attack in Honolulu where he was spending the winter. The Sakamaki house dynamiting trial took place in the midst of an election to choose his successor as delegate to Congress. Several major political figures had declared their candidacies. Votes were split among the native Hawaiian candidates, but the winner was Harry A. Baldwin, a kamaaina and one of the Big Five, owner of a large plantation on Maui. Baldwin left immediately for the capital, but because he was new in Washington, he was not able to help the Hawaii Emergency Labor Commission as Kuhio had. After Dillingham had returned to Honolulu, it had fallen to Charles McCarthy, the former governor of the territory, to continue lobbying for the petition, as special representative of the Honolulu Chamber of Commerce with a substantial annual compensation of $15,000. With the Washington Conference over, Dillingham and the Hawaii Emergency Labor Commission felt that it was their crucial chance to have Congress approve their petition for Chinese labor. They mounted a campaign to influence Congress by arousing public opinion throughout the mainland.

Most kamaaina planters had graduated from elite colleges on the mainland. Drawing up a list of fellow classmates in powerful positions, they urged these classmates to lobby their local congressmen. In the state of Washington, where House Immigration and Naturalization Committee chairman Albert Johnson had his election district, they held an elaborate banquet for the press to publicize the Japanese problem in Hawaii. At the capital, more than five hundred high-level government officials and congressmen were invited to a Hawaiian Night party on March 27 to kick off the campaign. The banquet room was festooned with palm trees, American flags, and Hawaiian flags, and hula dancers brought over from Hawaii swayed to Hawaiian music. The main event of the evening was a film of Prince Kuhio's funeral, which, befitting a member of the Hawaiian royal family, was gloriously decorated with colorful orchids. To the audience in Washington, it was an exotic glimpse of Hawaii. In reporting on plans for this party, which cost the territory a considerable amount, Dillingham wrote to Governor Farrington, "We cannot expect to catch all of the fish with the same bait, but everything that contributes towards bringing a few more into harmony and sympathy with Hawaii will help in the general sum-up."

On April 13, a few weeks after the Hawaiian Night, a document en-

titled "The Hawaiian Situation," prepared by James Phelan, former senator from California, was read into the *Congressional Record*. On his
way back to Hawaii the previous fall, Dillingham had invited the central
figures in the anti-Japanese movement in California, Phelan, and Virgil
S. McClatchy, the owner of the *Sacramento Bee,* who was better known
as president of the Oriental Exclusion League of California, to invite
them to Hawaii.

A few weeks later McClatchy visited Hawaii to attend a world newspaper reporters' meeting in Honolulu. At a Rotary Club gathering arranged by Dillingham and attended by Hawaii's leading figures, Mc-
Clatchy stated that the Japanese could not be assimilated and that it was
suicidal for the United States to attempt to assimilate them. Phelan also
stopped over in Honolulu at the end of 1921 during a trip around the
world.

Phelan's report was a summary of his observations in Hawaii addressed to Dillingham. It began, "In Hawaii, the Japanese, inassimilable,
indigestible, creating economic disturbance and labor distress . . . steal
between the meshes of the law and breed with alarming rapidity. . . .
Hawaii has been abandoned to the Japanese by the blundering policy of
our government."[42] While urging the federal government to formulate a
policy on Japanese immigration he also recommended the renewed importation of Chinese workers: "The expedient proposed to gain time,
namely to admit a limited number of Chinese for five years, might give
our government a chance to turn around, like the strategic move of a
general confronted with stubborn facts and an agile enemy." Acting
Ambassador Sadao Saburi, filling in for Shidehara, who had been called
back to Japan, reported to the Foreign Ministry that Phelan "had made
exaggerated expressions that Hawaii was under Japan's economic and
political domination."[43]

On June 7, 1922, four months after Dillingham went to Washington,
the Senate hearings were reconvened. The hearings were a repeat of the
previous year's and focused on the "Japanese problem." Not to be outdone by his predecessor, Harry Baldwin emphasized that the 1920 strike
was a "Japanese conspiracy." He described the Japanese nisei in strident
terms: "A great many of the Japanese who are born in the islands go
back to Japan to be educated. After they get their education, they come
back to Hawaii, which they can do, being American citizens. Their feeling is Japanese, they do not assimilate with the Americans."[44]

Sen. Hiram Johnson seconded this sentiment. "Once Japanese, always
Japanese, and you can make all the four-power agreements and all the

alliances you want to, and they will remain Japanese to the end." It was public statements like this that Secretary of State Hughes had wished to avoid during the Washington Conference. Johnson, who had lost the 1920 Republican presidential nomination to Warren Harding, was known as a progressive Republican who supported social and political reform. However, while he was governor of California, Johnson, ignoring President Wilson's intervention, had backed passage of the Alien Land Law.

When Gen. John DeWitt, head of the Western Defense Command area, who supervised the dispatch of Japanese Americans on the West Coast to relocation camps after the attack on Pearl Harbor, made his remark, "Once a Jap always a Jap," he was merely repeating the words that Senator Johnson spat out twenty years before at the Senate Immigration and Naturalization Committee hearings.

Dillingham continued his testimony by citing the Oahu Ice and Cold Storage Company's complaint about "the silent penetration by the Japanese" into Hawaiian industries. "Individual Japanese who did not purchase ice from the Japanese company," he said, "were being called traitors to their race." Here was a specific example of the Japanese conspiracy. But the reconvened Senate hearings ended without any testimony more explosive than this—or than testimony the year before that the Federation of Japanese Labor had used Caucasians affiliated with the AFL to oppose Chinese immigration.

DILLINGHAM'S BITTER FIGHT

The July 28, 1922, entry in Terasaki's diary was a single sentence: "Mr. Dillingham, who spoke irresponsibly in Washington, returned." The Hawaii Emergency Labor Commission had spent another six months working hard in Washington on the territory's vital mission, but what awaiting them on their return was criticism that they had not encountered before. In particular, Baldwin's statements about the second-generation Japanese Americans became an issue. As a June 30 Nippu jiji headline reported, "Leading Americans oppose Baldwin's slander of American citizens of Japanese descent."

"Local people of sound judgment," as the Japanese-language newspapers called them, had decided that they could no longer keep silent about the anti-Japanese statements the territory's representatives made in Washington. The previous year's hearings had not been reported in detail other than the incident involving George Wright. Dillingham had suppressed coverage for fear that a negative reaction to the activities of the Hawaii Emergency Labor Commission would create obstacles to its efforts in Washington. It was only when "people of sound judgment" heard with their own ears McClatchy's declaration at the Rotary Club that Japanese were incapable of assimilation that they felt that the commission might be heading in an unexpected direction. Their doubts deepened when former Senator Phelan's statement in the Senate was reported in detail.

Baldwin's statement about the Hawaiian nisei was the decisive factor in confirming these doubts. The Japanese-language newspapers, beginning with the *Hawaii hōchi*, raised a furor when they learned of his statement through the English-language mainland press, and prominent haole leaders did their best to mend the damage it did. Twenty days after Baldwin's testimony in Washington, the English and Japanese newspapers in Hawaii printed an open letter to Japanese Americans.

> Young Friends,
> Recent reports from Washington made in disparagement of our young American citizens of Japanese ancestry prompt us to send a message to you declaring our emphatic dissent from such statements as reported.
> In the last few years, while you were approaching young manhood and young womanhood distracted between two conflicting environments, all eyes have been upon you, wondering how you would meet the test. We have seen you, on reaching the age when you must decide for yourself, coming into realization that the land of your ancestors is not your land; that its traditions and customs are incompatible with the education and environment in which you have been growing up, and so your American training and your point of view has often brought you into estrangement in your own homes. In these circumstances you have had our genuine sympathy.
> Again, as you have been brought to understand that by reason of your Hawaiian birth you are American citizens, we have been pleased to see you, in increasing numbers, endeavoring at much trouble and expense to establish proof of Hawaiian birth and preparing yourselves with the characteristic idealism and enthusiasm of youth, for the responsibilities of citizenship. . . .
> The true-hearted can always afford to wait, knowing that "time will tell." And meantime you can rest assured of the steadfast confidence of those who have come to know and trust you. We strongly deplore always and anywhere statements which minimize your loyalty and capacity for useful citizenship.

The letter was signed by thirteen of the pastors of the major Christian denominations starting with Reverend Albert Palmer. From the academic circles were five professors at the University of Hawaii, including the university president, Arthur L. Dean, who was active in the Palmer mediation attempt during the strike. Among the others were Prescott F.

Jernegan, principal of McKinley High School, where the majority of students were Japanese Americans; Reverend John Hopwood, president
of the Mid-Pacific Institute; and even Vaughan MacCaughley, superin-
tendent of the Department of Public Instruction. Business leaders who
signed included Clarence H. Cooke, president of the Bank of Hawaii
and a major sugar planter, who had just that spring succeeded Walter
Dillingham as president of the Honolulu Chamber of Commerce. Of the
Big Five families, Arthur C. Alexander, department manager of American Factors, also signed the letter. Most notable were members of Dillingham's family: attorney Walter F. Frear, the husband of Walter Dillingham's older sister who had served as governor ten years before; and
Reverend John P. Endman, field secretary of the Hawaiian Evangelical
Association, the husband of Dillingham's younger sister, who had spent
a few years in Japan as a missionary.

Many among the haole elite, although involved in the sugar industry,
still believed strongly in Christian charity and the aloha spirit. They did
not want Hawaii to become like California, and their signatures on the
open letter was proof of this.

It should be noted that "Captain" Harold F. Stafford, first deputy city
and county attorney during the Sakamaki house dynamiting case trial,
also signed. It may have been in the hope of assimilating the nisei that he
had submitted a resolution supporting the foreign-language press control bill as a member of the American Legion. Honolulu Mayor J. Wilson had maintained neutrality throughout the labor struggle, but in response to the Baldwin statement, he told the *Nippu jiji,* "Those who say
that the Japanese are a threat are *popole* (crazy)." [45]

On June 13, while Dillingham and the other commission members were
still in Washington, Paul Scharrenberg, chief of the Pacific Coast AFL,
arrived in Honolulu. At that year's AFL convention Gompers had reiterated his opposition to renewing the importation of Chinese labor
in words that showed his position was firmer than it had been the year
before. He had not even replied to a letter from Dillingham expressing
willingness to find points of compromise and modify the bill. Gompers
sent Scharrenberg to Hawaii to investigate the local circumstances in order to discover the true intentions of the Hawaiian capitalists. During
Scharrenberg's monthlong stay in Hawaii the HSPA tried to accommo-
date him by having its secretary, John Butler, guide him through the
plantations on each island. After finding out that Scharrenberg was fond
of drink, Butler made sure that liquor was available at each plantation,

even though arrests for bootlegging were reported daily in the papers. Scharrenberg freely accepted the welcome he received at the plantations, but he felt no constraints about meeting with George Wright and other representatives of the Caucasian laborers, Filipino Labor Union president Pablo Manlapit, and Federation of Japanese Labor secretary general Jirō Hayakawa.

After returning from the hearings in Washington, Wright realized that the only means to establish workers' rights in Hawaii was a federation of unions that transcended racial lines. Manlapit took part in his effort to build such an organization, and so did Hayakawa of the federation, which was just barely surviving. In January 1922 the United Workers of Hawaii (UWH) was organized with Wright as a central figure. The HSPA immediately attacked the new union in the English-language press, suggesting that Wright was plotting revenge for having been embarrassed at the Washington hearings. The press made a succession of charges against Wright, including allegations that he was connected to the mainland communists who were even more radical than the IWW. Just after the verdict was reached in the Sakamaki house dynamiting case, Governor Farrington rejected the new union's application for official recognition.

Though the UWH claimed to transcend racial boundaries, it did in fact limit Japanese participation. By restricting the number of Japanese workers, who were in the majority in Hawaii, the UWH leadership planned to keep control of the union in the hands of the Caucasians. Even so, Scharrenberg indicated his opposition to the UWH's permitting any Japanese participation at all. Taking advantage of Scharrenberg's visit to Hawaii, Wright sought official participation of the UWH in the AFL, but in the end Scharrenberg did not give his support.

Scharrenberg's report on conditions in Hawaii appeared two months later in the September issue of the AFL magazine *American Federationist* under the title "Does Hawaii Need Chinese?" He began by asserting that the importation of Filipinos had alleviated the labor shortage in the past year. It was only because the Hawaiian sugar planters had been frightened by the "racial cohesiveness" of the Japanese during the 1920 strike that they wanted bring in Chinese labor. "The expressed hope of the sugar planters to stabilize conditions in the islands by the importation of more Chinamen is based upon topsy-turvy logic," he wrote. "And the prospect of Americanizing the islands in this manner is as brilliant as the idea that petroleum will extinguish a fire."

Scharrenberg also attacked Dillingham's argument that the Hawaiian climate was unsuited for Caucasian manual labor. "With a superb climate," he said, "bracing trade winds ten months of the year, Hawaii could be made a paradise for workers no less than for tourists." Noting that the problem was the mentality of the white governing class, who thought plantation labor unsuitable for Caucasians, he proposed that labor conditions be improved and that a workforce of Hawaiian-born Caucasians be developed. He concluded by observing that unless the policy of seeking cheap labor from abroad was ended, there was no hope of a positive solution.

In the October issue of the *American Federationist,* Scharrenberg wrote a ten-page article entitled "The Japanese in Hawaii." His argument was simple: "Hawaii is the most complete and convincing object lesson to the mainland as to what would have happened to California if the workers of that state, and the people generally, had not been so determined to hold the state as a heritage to the white race." Scharrenberg was in Honolulu on July 9, when the Imperial Navy training fleet (the *Iwate, Izumo,* and *Asama*) put in to port, welcomed by the Japanese consul general and local Japanese community leaders dressed in tailcoats. Japanese immigrants crowded into the port as if it was a public holiday, singing the Japanese national anthem and waving small rising sun flags. It is not difficult to imagine how this frenzied welcome must have appeared to the AFL representative from California.

Scharrenberg also criticized the Gentlemen's Agreement between the U.S. and Japan, which had failed to curb immigration of Japanese.

> In addition to these picture brides, thousands of male laborers came over during the ten years with passports. They obtained passports because of peculiar family relations. Under the regulations, a Japanese in Hawaii may bring over his wife, his father and mother, his children. . . . There should be an early abrogation of the "Gentlemen's Agreement" and the enactment of a law denying admission, as immigrants and permanent residents, to all aliens who are ineligible to citizenship under the laws of the United States.

Scharrenberg's recommendations were not so very different from those of former Senator Phelan, who in his report "The Hawaiian Situation" had proposed to deal with the Japanese immigrants through the abrogation of the Gentlemen's Agreement, depriving the right of citizenship to second-generation Japanese Americans, and an anti-Japanese exclusion act similar to the Chinese Exclusion Act. After the publication of Scharrenberg's report, the AFL not only hardened its opposition to the renewal of the importation of Chinese labor, it switched its core argument to advocate measures against Japanese immigration.

On learning of Scharrenberg's investigation in Hawaii, Dillingham arranged an interview with President Harding. He complained that it would be unfair for the AFL, which had announced its opposition to Hawaii's bill from the start, to publicize biased results that could influence the congressional vote on the renewal of the importation of Chinese labor. He asked for the formation of a federal investigation commission appointed by the president.

In mid-November, nearly six months after Scharrenberg's visit, a five-member labor study commission arrived in Honolulu. Its members were all involved in labor issues: L. E. Sheppard, president of the Order of Railroad Conductors; H. Davies, commissioner of Conciliation for the Department of Labor; John Donlin, president of the Building Trades Department of the AFL; O. W. Hartwig, president of the Oregon Federation of Labor; and Fred Keightly, secretary of the Amalgamated Association of Iron, Steel, and Tin Workers, AFL.

After a three-week investigation, its report, submitted on January 24, 1923, concluded, "Commission did not find any serious shortage at present and in event emergency arises commission recommends that proof be furnished Congress through Secretary of Labor with a request for authority to import such alien labor as may be shown to be needed. Therefore, do not recommend adoption of pending resolution." [46] Although Dillingham had appealed directly to the president, his strategy had backfired.

Nor had Dillingham been able to win the support of the Hearst newspaper chain, which had propagated "the yellow peril" idea for years. Hearst was one of the few Americans who, at a time when most saw Germany as the greatest enemy, had already turned his gaze to the Pacific and declared that Japan was America's future enemy. In March 1917, for example, he wrote a memorandum directing the drawing of a cartoon showing a Japanese with drawn knife waiting for the chance to stab Uncle Sam in the back. But Hearst was not about to act as a tool of the Hawaiian sugar planters who wanted to import Chinese workers, also members of the same yellow race, to replace the Japanese. Although he did meet with Dillingham, who sought his cooperation, Hearst did not heed Dillingham's request for help.

Dillingham's efforts to win over the American Legion, whose support he was confident that he could obtain, also failed. Like Hearst, the

American Legion opposed any more immigration of the yellow race. Despite Dillingham's concerted efforts, the petition in the U.S. Congress did not achieve the results he had hoped for. On the contrary, the Japanese problem had become an issue of its own on the U.S. mainland. But even at this point, Dillingham had not given up. He continued to push Congress for a decision on renewing Chinese immigration, urging the solution of a new "emergency situation" created by the Japanese in Hawaii.

FUROR OVER THE FOREIGN LANGUAGE SCHOOL BILL

In the aftermath of the 1920 strike, the Foreign Language School Bill passed the emergency session of the territorial legislature in November 1920 and was implemented in July 1921. It required that Japanese-language schools in Hawaii be supervised by the Territory of Hawaii Board of Education in accordance with principles of American democracy. Japanese-language instructors were required to pass an English proficiency test, a grave matter for those who had not had to use English in the past. In November 1922 the territorial legislature also approved regulations reducing the number of grades Japanese-language schools could teach. For example, pupils would be allowed to attend language schools only after completion of fourth grade in public school. On the grounds that the Territorial Board of Education incurred additional expenses, a tax of $1 per Japanese-language school student was levied. Many in the Japanese community expressed concern over whether this was an effort to abolish the Japanese-language schools.

The *Hawaii hōchi* led the charge, stirring up debate by arguing that the matter was "a matter of life and death for the Japanese community" and "a struggle for the rights and honor of the Japanese race." Kinzaburō Makino, the newspaper's president, insisted on forcing the issue by bringing suit against the U.S. government. Since the newspaper was not directly affected by the law, it could not become a plaintiff. Instead Makino persuaded six language schools in Honolulu to file suit in late December 1922. An uproar arose over whether other Japanese-language schools should do the same, leading to lecture meetings and parents' meetings all over Hawaii, as had happened on the eve of the 1920 strike. The English-language press was also full of reports about the issue.

In the midst of this furor, the federal investigation commission appointed by President Harding visited Hawaii. The labor leaders from the mainland who were members of the commission saw with their own eyes the Japanese community demanding that Japanese be taught on

American soil and filing suit against the territory of Hawaii. It is not at all strange that they felt that the Japanese threat alleged by the territory of Hawaii was quite real.

A week before the commission arrived in Honolulu, the U.S. Supreme Court handed down its decision on the Ozawa case, ruling that a Japanese had no right to be naturalized. This decision cannot be overlooked when discussing the Japanese-language schools turmoil. The plaintiff, Takao Ozawa, had come to America when he was nineteen years old. After graduating from the University of California at Berkeley, he applied for citizenship in 1902 but was denied. Ozawa did not give up. He applied again in Honolulu, where he moved subsequently. Unbowed by denial after denial, he appealed the decision all the way to the Supreme Court. The Ozawa case had been watched with interest by the Japanese in Hawaii as a test case to determine whether Japanese would be allowed to naturalize. The Supreme Court decision, however, ruled that because Japanese immigrants were a "Mongolian race," they could not. The uproar over the suit against the Foreign Language School Bill in part sprang from the pent-up anger that the Japanese immigrants felt about this ruling.

The *Hawaii hōchi,* seemingly reawakening to its role as the defender of justice, charged that the Foreign Language School Bill was illegal. Every day the paper argued in its pages for "standing up to the attorney general of the Territory of Hawaii." When the legislature passed the Foreign Language School Bill, it also passed the Foreign Language Press Control Bill, but the *Hawaii hōchi* remained quiet only for a short while. Claiming that the U.S. Constitution guaranteed freedom of speech, the *Hōchi* reverted to its usual practice of publishing whatever it wanted. Makino was so determined that had the territorial authorities declared that the *Hōchi* was in violation of the law, he was prepared to sue, claiming that both the Foreign Language School Bill and the Foreign Language Press Control Bill were illegal.

FBI reports noted that from the summer of 1922 the *Hōchi* attempted to overcome its desperate financial circumstances by strengthening its pro-Japan and anti-American tendencies.[47] As is evident from Terasaki's diary entries, the paper's financial difficulties continued. While fanning the debate over the Japanese-language schools, Makino was making the rounds to borrow money. The *Hōchi* had not been silent about the petition for the renewal of the importation of Chinese labor. But since the action was taking place in faraway Washington, where it was difficult to grasp the details, and since its competitor, the *Nippu jiji,* had taken the same position on the issue as the *Hōchi,* its editorial arguments on the issue were more restrained than usual. Campaigning against the importation of Chinese labor was not likely to increase circulation. This was no doubt the reason that the *Hōchi* had not been more zealous in pursuing the issue of Chinese labor.

Regarding the uproar concerning the Japanese-language schools, however, *Nippu Jiji*'s position was clearly distinct from that of the *Hawaii hōchi.* On this issue, the *Hōchi* labeled the *Nippu* "moderate." *Nippu*'s president, Yasutarō Sōga, strongly opposed the suit, feeling that it would only fan the flames of anti-Japanese sentiment, but the *Hōchi*'s Makino quickly formed the Association to Support the Japanese Language Schools Suit (Nihongo gakkō shiso kiseikai), and for the next six years he fought hard on this issue. It cannot be denied that Makino's move was a business gamble for the survival of the *Hōchi,* which saw the *Nippu* as its enemy on the other front.

Judge Banks, who had nine months earlier issued the guilty verdict on the Sakamaki case, issued a temporary injunction preventing the implementation of the Foreign Language School Bill. The lawyer for the Japanese-language schools was Joseph B. Lightfoot, who had defended Makino and others during the 1909 strike. After Makino opened his "law office," Lightfoot had been Makino's adviser and worked with him on a variety of matters.

In late January 1923, less than a month after the initial submission of the suit, Emō Imamura, leader of Hawaii's Honpa Honganji sect, declared his support. Prompted by this, Buddhist-affiliated Japanese-language schools began to join the suit. Most of the schools opposing the suit were Christian-affiliated, and the *Nippu,* whose president was an ardent Christian, stood firmly on the side of the anti-suit faction.

Although the movement supporting the Foreign Language School Bill suit was a struggle against the haole territorial authorities, it tore apart Hawaii's Japanese community. Long-standing hard feelings between the Buddhists and the Christians broke through to the surface, deepening the discord. Reports of intimidation and betrayal, as both sides tried to achieve solidarity within the divided Japanese community, filled the pages of the press, and this resulted in a battle on the pages of the *Hōchi* and the *Nippu.* The dispute became so intense that it scandalized conscientious Caucasians sympathetic to the Japanese. On February 3, 1923, however, Judge Banks dismissed the suit brought by the Japanese-language schools. The association supporting the suit, led by Makino, appealed the decision.

THE FAILURE OF THE CHINESE LABOR IMMIGRATION PLAN

Three weeks later, at the opening of the twelfth session of the territory of Hawaii legislature, Governor Farrington spoke about the Japanese problem in Hawaii.

> Hawaii has a Japanese problem. To assume otherwise would be to deny the evidence of our senses. . . . [A]mong people coming to this Territory and enjoying our American freedom of thought and action, an element has arisen that interprets liberty as license and claims exceptional privilege as a right to be demanded. These malcontents and agitators have been more successful among the Japanese than with other resident aliens.
>
> A striking evidence of the operations of these agitators was the attempt to organize in 1920 a general strike among the Japanese for the purpose of dominating the laborers in the sugar industry. The spirit prompting the movement was voiced in vicious and insulting propaganda carried on by units of the Japanese language press. A natural result was a conspiracy to destroy life and property. The people of the Territory are to be congratulated on the self-control shown in effectively dealing with this situation. More exacting laws became necessary to better protect fundamental American institutions.[48]

Such outspoken references to Japanese on the public record in the Hawaiian legislature had not been heard even during the 1920 strike. A few weeks before, Farrington had sent the territorial secretary, Raymond C. Brown, to Washington with a letter describing the emergency situation in Hawaii. Accompanied by Dillingham, Brown made the rounds to various high-level government officials complaining about the furor over the the foreign-language school situation and the crisis it posed for Hawaii.

In a report to Farrington, Brown said that Albert B. Fall, secretary of the interior, reacted to the situation like "the proverbial bull to a red flag." Fall, like former Attorney General Palmer, constantly spoke of the threat of communism. Brown reported that not only Fall but other highly placed government officials who heard about the Japanese-language school suit were extremely sympathetic to the territory. In other words, as the petition for the importation of Chinese labor was reaching a critical stage in the U.S. Congress, Dillingham and the Hawaii Emergency Labor Commission pulled out a trump card—the Japanese-language schools dispute.

Even Secretary of the Interior Fall, excited though he was by the issue, fudged by pointing out that the Department of the Interior could not act by itself on an issue involving foreign policy. Despite Hawaii's petition to give "bitter medicine for Japanese," Congress did not place the resolution for the renewal of the importation of Chinese labor on its agenda. Both houses of Congress decided not to bring the issue to a vote, as Congress was in the midst of dealing with graver matters.

Dillingham, who was not about to admit defeat after working three years for the bill, hoped for direct intervention by President Harding, who was considered to be a friend of Hawaii. But on August 2 the president died suddenly. During his term countless cases of political corruption surfaced. Fall was embroiled in charges of corruption involving the oil industry. The Teapot Dome scandal, which entangled the attorney general as well, involved siphoning navy oil reserves to private oil companies in exchange for large bribes. President Harding was also mentioned in this scandal, and in the midst of disclosures he died in San Francisco on his return trip from a speaking tour of Alaska. The cause of death is still not known.

After the end of World War I the United States is said to have entered an era of moral decadence and material greed, spurred by the Prohibition Act, which led to widespread corruption throughout the country. The Republican administration under Harding, with the exception of a few officials such as Secretary of State Hughes, reflected this tendency. The Hawaiian sugar planters, with their connections to the Republican administration, thought it an opportune moment to press their case in Washington. However, the hopes of the HSPA to import lower-wage Chinese laborers were dashed by resistance from the mainland labor unions led by the AFL and by objections from the mainland sugar growers, their main competitors.

On August 10, 1923, some of Honolulu's political and economic leaders, among them Walter Dillingham, attended an "Aloha tribute" to President Harding, a man thought to have supported Hawaii's cause.

In an FBI report dated August 6, Reverend Takie Okumura, who opposed the suit brought by the Japanese-language schools, was said to have called for "complete abolition of the Japanese schools." The report cited Okumura as a "consistent worker among the Japanese for Americanization and Christianization."[49] Takie Okumura had established the first Japanese-language school in Hawaii after persuading the Japanese immigrants with little free time or money to show interest in their children's education. Twenty-six years later Reverend Okumura advocated the abolition of these schools for the nisei. In various localities of Hawaii, the furor over the Japanese-language schools continued.

Makino's *Hawaii hōchi* called Sōga of the *Nippu jiji*, which supported Reverend Okumura's position, an "enemy of the Japanese."

Beretania Street, in places a four-lane boulevard running through Honolulu today, parallels Highway 1, which cuts across Oahu east to west. West of Aala Park, from the intersection with King Street, Beretania Street changes its name to Dillingham Boulevard, which turns into Highway 1 just before Honolulu International Airport on the blue waters of Keehi Lagoon. The Oahu prison stands at the western end of Dillingham Boulevard. The prison, sitting today behind walls topped by barbed wire, consists of several buildings built over the years. In the watchtowers one can see sentries holding rifles. The old building facing Dillingham Boulevard is entirely different from the newer additions. The windows in this two-story stone structure are barred, but the side facing Dillingham Boulevard is not surrounded by a wall. It was in this stone building that Noboru Tsutsumi and the other federation leaders were incarcerated.

The prison, the only one on Oahu, had been built four years before Tsutsumi and the others entered it. Prisoners awaiting trial and those convicted were put there regardless of the severity of their crimes. The average daily number of prisoners in 1923 was 355: 119 Filipinos, 91 Hawaiians, 90 Chinese, 17 Caucasians, and 38 Japanese. In proportion to their number in the Hawaiian population, there were very few Japanese prisoners.

The crimes that the prisoners had committed, apart from violations of the Prohibition Act, were mainly robbery, sexual offenses, and drug abuse. Nearly all the drug crimes were opium-related, and those convicted for these crimes were almost all Chinese. In 1923 a large counterfeiting operation was uncovered, involving more than twenty Japanese, and an unprecedented number of arrests were made in Hawaii on charges of bribery and embezzlement. Tsutsumi and the other federation leaders found guilty of conspiracy were put in the category "other crimes."[50]

Tokutarō Hirota, who still lives in Honolulu, remembers visiting Tsutsumi at the Oahu prison. When I interviewed him in 1988, he was eighty-seven years old. A staunch member of the Nuuanu Union Church, he had been involved in many church philanthropic activities after he succeeded in business. On visits to meet Tsutsumi, Hirota accompanied Reverend Teikichi Hori, who had graduated from Dōshisha Universitry some years after Takie Okumura and later returned to Japan to become a professor at his alma mater. A popular pastor, he was greatly admired by young men like Hirota.

It was a trip of some twenty minutes in the church car to the prison. When Hirota and Reverend Hori asked to see Tsutsumi, they were immediately shown to the visiting room, where several other groups were visiting prisoners. According to Hirota, Tsutsumi always entered the room smiling in his faded denim prison garb. No guards monitored their conversation, and they were able to speak freely in Japanese. During the thirty-minute visits, conversation with Tsutsumi was hardly ever about the Bible, despite Reverend Hori's presence. Neither did Hirota recall Tsutsumi saying anything about the Japanese-language schools dispute, a topic that was nearly always raised whenever Japanese gathered at that time. "Mr. Tsutsumi talked on and on," Hirota recalled, "about his hopes and dreams of what he wanted to do after he returned to Japan."

Tsutsumi had already left Hawaii in spirit. During these visits he talked about how he wanted to lead the youth of Japan when he returned to his country. He had expanded his dreams to educating the youth of Japan, based on what he had learned from his experiences in Hawaii. In an essay he wrote a few months before he was charged in the Sakamaki house dynamiting case, he concluded,

> Amidst evergreen nature, in the morning sunlight and the dew of the stars, raised on the beneficence of Buddha and Shintō gods without distinction, working together, living together, talking together, laughing together—this is the way of a true life and a true human being. I yearn for a world without the shadow of the abominable demons like misunderstanding, defamation, calumny, discord, prejudice, and strife, for the revelations of gods and the guidance of Buddha, and for the springtime of peace and the whisperings of love.

On April 26, 1923, ten months after Tsutsumi and Hoshino entered prison, the appeals court of the territory of Hawaii dismissed the appeal of Gotō and the twelve other defendants, who were sent to prison four days later. At the time, public attention in the mainland and in Europe was focused on the appeal in the Sacco and Vanzetti case, but only a few people visited the former Federation of Japanese Labor leaders in the Oahu prison. Gotō and the others filed an appeal to the U.S. Supreme Court, but theirs was a lonely struggle with no supporters. The Japanese cane field workers showed no interest in the leaders they had looked up to three years before during the strike. The Japanese-language newspapers treated them as criminals, and both the *Hawaii hōchi* and the *Nippu jiji* published only a mere three lines about their legal appeal.

In those days leprosy was the most feared disease in Hawaii. Its unfortunate victims were forcibly sent by boat to be placed in isolation on the undeveloped island of Molokai. This was a boat trip that meant they would never be able to see their families again, as they were being sent off to die. The Japanese community in Hawaii cast off the imprisoned former federation leaders as if they were lepers.

Life in the Oahu prison for Tsutsumi and the other inmates consisted of cleaning the prison and tending the vegetable plots to grow their own food. At times they were sent out to work on road construction or trash disposal. But they had plenty of time to themselves in the afternoons. Many guards were Hawaiian and not very strict. Gotō told his wife later that during their imprisonment he studied philosophy and other subjects under Tsutsumi's instruction. Gotō had gone to Hawaii before he finished middle school, and because he had little opportunity to attend school to learn English, he was eager to study. There were no restrictions on what the prisoners were allowed to read. For Gotō, life in prison was an unexpected chance to focus on learning, which he liked, with no need to worry about being able to eat and with no concerns about the discord within the Japanese community.

The Great Kantō Earthquake struck Tokyo on September 1, 1923, some five months after Gotō and the others started serving their sentences. The tragic disaster, which caused the deaths of more than ninety thousand, brought a temporary unity to the Japanese community in Hawaii, which was still divided on the Japanese schools issue but collected tens of thousands of dollars in aid for their homeland. The Japanese-language press reported on the massacre of Korean residents in Tokyo in the wake of the earthquake, and also on the killing of labor movement activists by the military police. But one wonders to what extent the incarcerated federation leaders felt any connection with these events.

On March 14, 1924, seven months after the Great Kantō Earthquake, the Japanese-language newspapers carried front page news that Richard Halsey, head of the Bureau of Immigration in Honolulu, had committed suicide the previous night. The sixty-seven-year-old Halsey had been missing since the day before. He was reported to have killed himself by stabbing his throat with a sharp knife near the Ala Moana coast.[51] Halsey, who had been head of the Bureau of Immigration for more than twenty years, had lived in Japan as a missionary and had many acquaintances among the Japanese in Hawaii. According to the

Hawaii hōchi, he had been upset deeply by an investigation into the illegal landing of Chinese in Hawaii.

Makino's *Hōchi* had discovered that young Chinese men were entering Hawaii illegally and had demanded an investigation into the facts. In what the *Hōchi* called "perhaps a major breakthrough in the scandal," Halsey was relieved of his post as head of the Bureau of Immigration.[52] He had committed suicide just before the investigator from the Bureau of Immigration in Washington arrived. The case was left up in the air. It is impossible to know now how deeply Halsey himself was involved in this case. Corruption in the Bureau of Immigration had been rumored for a long time, however. When Halsey was relieved of his duties, three Chinese interpreters in the Bureau of Immigration were also fired. The top person among the Japanese staff, Katsunuma, as well as several under him were transferred to other assignments.

The illegal Chinese immigrants had arrived by ship from Hong Kong. It was rumored that Chinese merchants in Hawaii, convinced that Congress would pass legislation allowing the importation of Chinese labor, had made arrangements in advance. Halsey's suicide closed this case with no way of finding out whether the HSPA had been involved or not.

Among the materials presented in support of the Hawaiian effort to renew importation of Chinese labor was a letter from a Hong Kong industrialist connected to the Chinese government addressed to Walter Dillingham, indicating full support for the measure. In 1924 Dillingham was still using the title Chairman of the Hawaii Emergency Labor Commission, but after the case of the illegal Chinese immigrants ended in Halsey's suicide, he no longer used it.

SEVEN

THE JAPANESE EXCLUSION ACT

Washington, D.C.: Spring 1924

REPRESENTATIVE JOHNSON PROPOSES AN IMMIGRATION LAW

The flowering cherry trees lining the banks of the Potomac River in Washington were a gift from the Japanese government in 1911 to symbolize the friendship between Japan and America. In the spring of 1924, four years after the Oahu strike, when those same Japanese trees rooted in foreign soil were scattering their petals, both houses of the U.S. Congress were debating new immigration legislation. On December 5, 1923, Rep. Albert Johnson, chairman of the House Committee on Immigration and Naturalization, had submitted to the House a new immigration quota bill. A member of the committee for nine years and an expert on immigration issues, he might not have proposed the bill had it not been for the committee's hearings on Chinese immigrant labor. Having heard about the "Japanese conspiracy" over and over from Walter Dillingham and other Hawaiian representatives, Johnson finally decided to propose a new law prohibiting the immigration of all Asians.

Johnson had listened intently to the testimony at the hearings not because he was concerned about a temporary renewal of Chinese immigration. As a congressman from a state that was worried about "the Japanese problem," he had been interested in finding out about the Japanese in Hawaii. Despite the conveniently optimistic observations of Walter Dillingham, it was clear from the first day of the hearings that Johnson did not pay much heed to Hawaii's request for renewal of the importation of Chinese labor. As head of a U.S. eugenics research center, he was undoubtedly interested in the restriction of immigration from that perspective.

In June 1923, two months after debate on the Chinese labor question had been shelved, Albert Johnson went on an inspection tour of Hawaii, On his return to the mainland, he announced, "The Japanese problem in Hawaii remains. An attempt at solutions cannot be long deferred." [1] Having witnessed conditions more serious than he had imagined, Johnson felt that his apprehension about the Japanese could no longer be ignored.

In 1920, when the second Oahu strike took place, more immigrants than ever before had arrived at Ellis Island from impoverished European nations in the wake of World War I. The majority, who could not speak English, came from Italy and other southern European countries and from Eastern European countries in the throes of revolution. Many of these new immigrants were also Catholic or Jewish, and many were poor. Their arrival presented many social and economic problems, and in Congress demands for a new look at immigration law grew stronger. In 1920 Johnson, as chairman of the House Committee on Immigration and Naturalization, guided the passage of a temporary immigration quota law limited to a period of two years. Johnson's bill was an amendment to a bill proposed the year before by Senate Committee on Immigration and Naturalization chairman William Dillingham, who had chaired the hearings on the Hawaiian petition. Dillingham's bill set yearly immigration quotas at 5 percent of the immigrant population from each nation as recorded in the 1910 census. Johnson's bill in the House had decreased the quota to 3 percent, but it was vetoed by President Wilson, and it did not become law until the following year, when Warren Harding became president.

The main targets of Johnson's immigration quota were the southern and Eastern Europeans whose numbers had increased dramatically after World War I. For the first time the United States, an immigrant nation that had always opened its doors to people who had crossed the Atlantic to Ellis Island, was limiting the number it would let in. Representative Johnson became the central figure in the formulation of a new immigration law, to be enacted in 1924, when the time limit on the quota system would run out. The enthusiasm he had shown at the hearings on the renewal of the importation of Chinese labor stemmed from his interest in a new immigration law.

In early December 1923, six months after his trip to Hawaii, Johnson submitted a new immigration bill to the House Committee on Immigration and Naturalization. It proposed to lower quotas to 2 percent and to base them on the 1890 census figures. This was clearly meant to give an advantage to the Anglo-Saxon Protestants who were then the majority in the population. The Johnson bill also stipulated "the absolute exclusion of the aliens ineligible to citizenship." This provision meant total exclusion of all Asians, including the Japanese.

On the day after the Johnson bill was submitted to the House Committee, the Senate Committee on Immigration and Naturalization proposed an amendment to the Federal Constitution that would deprive the right of citizenship to children born in the United States to aliens ineligible for citizenship. This amendment would mean a denial of citizenship to second-generation Asians, including Japanese American nisei. The amendment, proposed by a senator from Washington, was immediately voted down. Sen. William Dillingham had passed away a few months earlier.

Concerned about these actions in Congress, the Japanese ambassador, Masanao Hanihara, who had arrived a few days earlier, met with Secretary of State Hughes. With the Christmas recess approaching, movement on the immigration law slowed down in both houses, but on January 12, 1924, after the Congress reconvened, Foreign Minister Keishirō Matsui cabled Hanihara directing him to tell Hughes that even pro-American elements in Japan were denouncing the "Japanese Exclusion Act." Three days later Hanihara handed Hughes a memorandum noting the anxiety felt by the Japanese government in its expectation of an outcry of public opinion in Japan should Congress pass Johnson's new immigration bill. Hughes, also apprehensive about what was going on in Congress, replied that the American government would pay close attention to the matter.

After some revisions, Johnson's immigration quota bill cleared the Committee on Immigration and Naturalization on January 31, and on February 1 it was sent to the House floor as the new immigration bill. Hughes sent a message to chairman Johnson and others urging reconsideration. He expressed concern that the Japanese people, who tended to react in a volatile manner to pressure from other nations, would undoubtedly express anger at what they would perceive as a national humiliation, and that would nullify the outcome of the Washington Conference.

The new immigration bill was front page news in the Japanese-language newspapers in Hawaii, but the Japanese community still perceived the bill as a "fire on a far shore," of no great concern to them. They were embroiled in the Japanese-language schools issue, and they were excited about the celebration of the marriage of the crown prince of Japan. At the grand ceremony held in the garden of the Japanese consulate in Honolulu, decorated with large crossed rising sun flags, crowds of Japanese residents spilled through a gate draped with red and white bunting inching their way to the room displaying a photograph of the imperial couple. In the next room Consul General Keiichi Yamazaki, decked out in his gold-braided dress uniform, received their congratulations.

AMBASSADOR HANIHARA'S "VEILED THREAT"

The Senate as well as the House was considering several new immigration bills. On February 16, Sen. David A. Reed, a Democrat from Pennsylvania, proposed a bill not very different from the House's Johnson bill for consideration by the Senate Committee on Immigration and Naturalization. Secretary of State Hughes sent a message urging its chairman, LeBaron B. Colt, to heed his concerns. The committee hearings on the Senate bill reached a climax during the four days from March 11 to March 15, when witnesses from various circles testified.

Sen. Samuel M. Shortridge of California, who took over where the late Senator Dillingham had left off, was active in pushing through this immigration legislation. Virgil S. McClatchy, the first witness to appear, was introduced by Shortridge as "a gentleman who has devoted many years of earnest and intelligent study to this problem."[2] McClatchy began by saying that the new immigration bill had the wholehearted support of the American Legion, the American Federation of Labor, the Grange, and the Native Sons of the Golden West. "The yellow and brown races do not intermarry with the white race," he said, "and their heredity, standards of living, ideas, psychology, all combine to make them unassimilable with the white race."

When Colt pointed out that members of the black race were admitted to citizenship, McClatchy replied, "[This is] on account of conditions which I shall not consider at this time." He then spoke at length on his views of the Japanese.

> I have a very high regard for the character and ability of the Japanese nation and the Japanese people. And I realize that it is in effect their strong racial characteristics which make them so dangerous a factor if admitted to this country as permanent residents. [I.e., even U.S.-born second-generation Japanese were not assimilable because they had been raised by Japanese parents.]
>
> With great pride of race, they have no idea of assimilating in the sense of

amalgamation. They never cease to be Japanese. They do not come to this country with any desire or any intent to lose their racial or national identity. They come here specifically and professedly for the purpose of colonizing and establishing here permanently the proud Yamato race.

Chairman Colt responded with some irritation: "Here is this great question of racial discrimination. Now, I thought Japan said to the United States, 'Don't pass a law which would denote our inferiority. Leave it to our honor' and that that was the essence of the Gentlemen's Agreement—that is, the absence of a statute of exclusion, leaving it to the honor of Japan." Colt indicated that it was necessary to pay careful attention to relations with Japan. But McClatchy, citing population statistics, did not budge from advocating total exclusion of Japanese immigrants. "Hawaii will be hopelessly Japanese," he said. "What has happened in Hawaii has already happened in some districts of California."

James Phelan, former senator from California and current chairman of the San Francisco Chamber of Commerce, appeared a few days later. He also commented on the conditions he had observed in Hawaii when he went there to investigate at Dillingham's invitation. "The people of California object to the Japanese," he concluded, "and I say it involves the whole question—because of racial and economic reasons."

For several days testimony was heard from those strenuously opposing the new immigration bill, including businessmen who opposed it on the grounds that it made no sense to restrict the source of a cheap labor force. Others opposed the bill because it violated the principle that the United States was a country that did not discriminate on the basis of race and gave equal opportunity to people of all countries. Well-respected academics and Christian leaders, such as Quakers, testified against the bill. Among them were missionaries from Hawaii who had lived many years in Japan. When Senator Shortridge said one of them had allegedly been "employed by the Japanese government," the hearings erupted in a heated clash between supporters and opponents of the bill.

The letter from Secretary of State Hughes was read. It stated, "My desire was to avoid an unfortunate violation of our international obligations by provision in the bill which I believed to be inconsistent therewith." The Italian and Romanian governments had expressed objections, but it was Japan that Hughes meant when he wrote of "an unfortunate violation of our international obligations."

In early April, after revision, the Johnson Reed Immigration Quota Law was sent to the floor of both houses. The bill did not have the full support of the administration. As it undermined the idea that the United States is an immigrant nation, neither could it expect overwhelming support in Congress. What turned Congress in favor of the bill was a letter of protest sent by Ambassador Hanihara to Secretary of State Hughes on April 10, 1924.

Masanao Hanihara, forty-eight, was an experienced diplomat who was fluent in English. He had served in Washington for eleven years and had assisted Foreign Minister Jūtarō Komura in the negotiation of the Portsmouth Treaty that ended the Russo-Japanese War in 1905. Hanihara had also dealt with immigration issues as consul general in San Francisco. Promoted to vice foreign minister, he had been a member of the Japanese delegation to the Washington Conference two years earlier, and he had been on board the *Taiyō-maru* with Honolulu Consul General Chōnosuke Yada on his return to Japan.

Hanihara's letter to Hughes at the direction of Foreign Minister Matsui began by referring to the Gentlemen's Agreement. Under the agreement, he said, Japan "voluntarily undertook to adopt and enforce certain administrative measures designed to check the emigration to the United States of Japanese laborers." It was reached because discriminatory immigration legislation proposed on the part of the United States would naturally "wound the national susceptibilities of the Japanese people." The letter went on:

> The important question is whether Japan as a nation is or is not entitled to the proper respect and consideration of other nations. In other words, the Japanese Government asks of the United States Government simply that proper consideration ordinarily given by one nation to the self respect of another, which after all forms the basis of amicable international intercourse throughout the civilized world. . . . In other words, the manifest object of the [section denying citizenship to ineligible aliens] is to single out Japanese as a nation, stigmatizing them as unworthy and undesirable in the eyes of the American people. . . . It is indeed difficult to believe that it can be the intention of the people of your great country, who always stand for high principles of justice and fair play in the intercourse of nations.

In his conclusion Hanihara reminded Hughes that he had pointed out "the *grave consequences* [emphasis added] which the enactment of the measure retaining that particular provision would inevitably bring upon the otherwise happy and mutually advantageous relations between our two countries."

It was this line of the letter that hardliners seized on to push the new immigration bill through both houses of Congress. Senator Shortridge, who had introduced McClatchy, president of the Oriental Exclusion League of California, as a "true patriot" at the Senate hearings, was the first to question the phrase "grave consequences." Others in both the House and the Senate suggested that "grave consequences" amounted to a veiled threat by the Japanese government, and the furor became front page news in papers around the country.

Taken aback, on April 18, Foreign Minister Matsui directed Ambassador Hanihara to clarify his meaning to Secretary of State Hughes and to announce publicly:

> We did not intend it to mean war or a threat. The Japanese Exclusion Act tramples on the prestige of our nation, and gives to Japanese citizens' minds the impression of deep resentment that can never be eradicated. As a result the Japanese government's effort . . . to maintain good relations between Japan and the U.S. will be nullified. . . . This is of grave consequences for the Imperial government which has been upholding the ideal of harmony among the peoples of the world and placing great weight on Japan-U.S. relations toward that end. This is the context which the term "grave consequences" was used.

The Japanese government was certain that President Calvin Coolidge, who had taken office after Harding's death, would invoke his veto power to block the new immigration bill if it passed. It was also proposed that Eiichi Shibusawa, who was highly respected in American political and economic circles, be sent as a special envoy to Washington, but in an era when it was not yet possible to travel rapidly by airplane, he would not have been able to arrive in time to have any effect.

In the end, the "veiled threat" resulted in the passage of the Johnson Reed Immigration Quota Act in both houses of Congress with overwhelming majorities: in the House 308 to 58 and in the Senate 69 to 9. In the Senate Committee on Immigration and Naturalization, Colt, its chairman, was one of the nine senators who voted against the bill. Some politicians in Congress, who accurately saw through the motives behind the hearings on the renewal of the importation of Chinese labor, were not swayed by the virulent anti-Japanese criticisms by the Hawaiian sugar planters that were fueled by self-interest. But President Coolidge did not use his veto power, dashing the hopes of the Japanese government. Nineteen twenty-four was a presidential election year, and competition within the Republican party was particularly intense. Having been thrust unexpectedly into the presidency, Coolidge had an advantage, but his power base was not yet solid. Yielding to strong pressures from West Coast congressmen, President Coolidge, despite Hughes's urging, was unable to come up with a compromise plan. The prospect of a national election, which jolted American politics once every four years, was the backdrop for the passage of the new immigration law that took effect on July 1, 1924.

PROTEST IN JAPAN

Despite his advancing years, Reverend Takie Okumura of the Makiki Church continued to promote his Americanization movement. After the passage of the new immigration act, Okumura distributed a pamphlet entitled "What Do We Do Now?" The pamphlet read, in part:

> It is important to resolve to cultivate one's own destiny by oneself. . . . There are two paths we can take. (1) Pack up and make a neat parting from Hawaii to return home, and start anew in places like South America or Manchuria. (2) Patiently endure until the U.S. awakens to justice while patiently showing the results of assimilation to make efforts until Americans recognize that we are essential elements to a prosperous society.
>
> I am taking the second path. On this occasion we should reflect deeply on our own conduct and become fully awakened to our circumstances in order to "do in Rome as the Romans do." We should be as the smile of the dandelion that blooms even when stepped upon.

The Japanese immigrant community in Hawaii reacted calmly to the new immigration law. This pleased even Okumura, who had often criticized the immigrants. "The Japanese language newspapers on the islands treated this issue calmly and seriously, and their discourse did not go beyond the bounds of common sense," he noted. In contrast, reports from Japanese consulates on the West Coast noted that passage of the law was discouraging news to local Japanese residents. The San Francisco consul general reported, "As to psychological impact, for most of the general residents it is very difficult for them to avoid being dejected." As most immigrants already had brought over their families, however, "the actual impact was felt most strongly by some 2,000 unmarried males who still had the possibility of becoming married." [3]

The Japanese community in Hawaii felt this "actual impact" less than the Japanese on the West Coast. For some time Japanese had constituted close to half of the Hawaiian population, and immigrants no longer needed to seek marriage partners from Japan. The total exclusion of Japanese immigrants posed no immediate threat to the influence of the Japanese in Hawaii. As usual, the *Hawaii hōchi* printed inflammatory editorials but showed no intention of launching a movement to protest the law; and the *Hōchi*'s president, Kinzaburō Makino, was still busily involved with the Japanese-language school dispute.

When the new immigration act passed, 88 of the 146 Japanese-language schools in Hawaii had joined the suit led by Makino. In the spring of 1924 these schools formed the Honolulu Education Association (Honolulu Kyōikukai) and decided to commission scholars in Japan to write new textbooks suitable for Hawaiian nisei. Indeed, the schools were in the midst of arguing over who should be sent to Japan for this purpose. To the Japanese in Hawaii, the immediate issue was the Japanese-language school question rather than developments in the capital. It was much easier for them to understand how this issue affected their rights than to understand the ramifications of the new immigration law.

It was not the Japanese immigrants who opposed the passage of the new immigration act in Hawaii. The first voices of protest rose from the haole community, not only from expected sources such as Reverend Palmer and the University of Hawaii's president Dean but also from those who had not been known to be protective toward the Japanese, including members of the territorial legislature and many sugar planters. In fact, one of the first organizations to send a telegram of protest to President Coolidge was the mission board whose predecessors had sent the ancestors of the sugar planters to Hawaii.

Takie Okumura, who had begun his Americanization movement in 1921, wrote in 1922, "[The] bad feelings left by the 1920 strike have not disappeared" and "[The planters] held no little feeling of displeasure toward me." By 1924, when the immigration law was passed, this attitude was greatly improved, and he felt a "spirit of cooperation" throughout Hawaii. Although the Hawaiian governing elite, with the sugar planters at its apex, attempted to "teach the upstart Japanese a lesson" after the 1920 strike by renewing the immigration of Chinese laborers, the complete exclusion of all Japanese immigrants went far beyond what they had intended.

In the summer of 1923, when anti-Japanese activists from California, former Senator Phelan and McClatchy, then Congressmen Raker and Johnson, visited Hawaii to investigate the "crisis" in Hawaii, the English-language press was fed up with their anti-Japanese agitation. Even the *Honolulu Advertiser,* the original proponent of the Japanese conspiracy theory, declared sarcastically, " 'We are going to be saved.' Congressman Raker and Johnson are going to do it! From what? 'Save' us rather from the snap judgement of these little men of narrow vision and imperfect understanding!"[4]

For the Hawaiian governing class, despite the labor strife, Hawaii remained the paradise of the Pacific that had prospered by following the Christian principles taught by their forebears and the traditional aloha spirit. The kamaaina were offended to have their "paradise" tarred by the same brush as California with its Oriental Exclusion League and other racist groups. Were they upset that while they had thought they were using the Californians for Hawaii's end, it was they who had been used by the anti-Japanese movement on the West Coast?

Whatever the case, the Japanese community in Hawaii, its attention absorbed by the Japanese-language school furor, left it to the haoles to protest the new immigration law. Only Walter Dillingham and the other members of the Hawaii Emergency Labor Commission maintained silence on Congress's decision.

Reverend Okumura was appalled by the reaction to the immigration act in Japan: "The Japanese exclusion immigration act has excited public opinion to such an extent that calls for war against the U.S. are heard in Japan. Such anti-American feelings and movements are minutely reported." He saw early on the danger that could befall Japanese immigrants such as himself: "There are those who are showing patriotic indignation and resentment in vain, engaging in radical arguments and ridiculous movements, even those who behave shamefully in an attempt to commit suicide to die in indignation. . . . Some call for the dispatch of warships to repatriate the Japanese residents."

The Japanese in Hawaii began to see the new immigration act as a "national humiliation" only after feelings of victimization reached them from their homeland. Terasaki's diary did not mention the reactions of the Japanese in Hawaii, but it did note on nearly a daily basis the reactions in Japan. On May 27, the day after the president signed the immigration law, he wrote, "In Japan, public opinion has erupted on the Japanese Exclusion Act, and military troops are clamoring." Five days later he wrote, "Upset by the Immigration Act, six people have committed suicide."

On May 31, more than four hundred Shinto priests from all over Japan gathered at Meiji Shrine in Tokyo to pledge their "opposition to the U.S. Japanese Exclusion Act." On the same day, a man in his forties, leaving a note signed by "an anonymous citizen of the Empire of Japan" that called on the American people to "repent" (*hansei*), slit his throat with a razor in the shrubbery across the street from the American Embassy in Tokyo. The Metropolitan Police Agency refused the request of the Kokuryūkai (Amur River Society), a "patriotic" society, to claim the corpse of this "indignant martyr," but his funeral on June 8 was attended by some eight hundred prominent politicians, military personnel, and businessmen, including the liberal politician Ryūtarō Nagai and several army generals. Funerary wreaths were sent by Mitsuru Tōyama, a venerable right-wing nationalist, as well as by the leaders of the two major political parties, Takaaki Katō, president of the Kenseikai, and Korekiyo Takahashi, president of the Seiyūkai. An anti-American rally organized by political parties to "display the resolute national unity of the Japanese people against the measure taken by the U.S." had already been held at the sumo wrestling stadium in Tokyo.

On the eve of the funeral, a group of "patriots" invaded the newly completed Imperial Hotel, the first international-class hotel in Japan, designed by the American architect Frank Lloyd Wright and considered one of his masterpieces. One of the registered guests was Yasutarō Sōga, president of the *Nippu jiji* in Honolulu, who had been staying at the hotel for some two months on a visit to his homeland. On the evening of June 7 a dance party attended by more than one hundred Japanese and foreigners in the hotel's main banquet room was disrupted when a group of about a dozen men calling themselves adherents of the ultranationalist Taigyōsha barged in wearing crested Japanese-style full kimono dress. Unsheathing swords, they engaged in some menacing swordplay, danced a sword dance, and demanded that the band play the Japanese national anthem. Some foreign women guests fainted dead away in their formal gowns. This "Imperial Hotel Incident," reported by the Associated Press, appeared in newspapers across America. Ambassador Hanihara cabled from Washington, "This story, published in newspapers with eye-catching headlines calling it an insult to Americans in Japan, has stirred great attention." [5]

Since he had been out late to dinner elsewhere, Sōga had not witnessed the incident, but he did note that "those on the hotel staff seemed to be keeping it as quiet as they could" and saw it as "an expression of the pent-up anti-American feelings among the general Japanese populace." [6]

The Tokyo newspapers (*Niroku shinpō, Tokyo nichinichi shinbun, Tokyo maiyū shinbun, Tokyo yūkan shinpō, Chūō shinbun, Yomiuri shinbun, Kokumin shinbun, Jiji shinpō, Hōchi shinbun, Tokyo asahi,*

Chūgai shōgyō shinbun, Manchōhō, Yamato shinbun, Miyako shinbun)
had issued a joint statement condemning the "injustice and unfairness
of the Japanese exclusion act" on April 21, a month before the president
signed it. A rally organized by a league of university students in Tokyo
issued a statement promising "to uphold the dignity of Imperial Japan
to our utmost," and meetings protesting the law were held by university
students in other cities.

Sohō Tokutomi, founder of the *Kokumin shinbun,* and considered
the dean of the press, called July 1, the day that the new immigration law
went into effect, a "day of national indignation" and urged a patriotic
anti-American patriotic Asianism. Kanzō Uchimura, a major Christian
intellectual and founder of the nondenominational "no-church" movement, declared himself "angered at the trampling of universal justice"
and urged an anti-American boycott: "At all costs, do not go to America, do not use American goods, do not accept American aid, do not
read Americans writings, do not enter American churches."

The April 21 Tokyo newspapers' statement urged the exclusion of
American materials and contractors from the reconstruction work on
Tokyo and Yokohama. The Great Kantō Earthquake had destroyed
220,000 homes in Tokyo the previous summer but reconstruction was
not moving very fast due to delays in official action. Moreover, prices
were soaring, and children were being abandoned because of unemployment and lack of jobs. The passage of the new American immigration
law provided an outlet for popular dissatisfaction about the domestic
situation in Japan.

The magazine *Tokyo*'s September issue ran a special entitled "Japan and America: Should They Fight?" Opinions from artists and
entertainers were presented to reflect the voices of the general public.
Ritsuko Mori, an actress, said, "Really, if our country were richer and
we had more confidence, we wouldn't have to bear such indignity.
Though I'm a woman, it makes me angry." And Hakusan Kanda, a professional storyteller, said, "Discriminatory treatment of races is something strange, isn't it. Of course, cats and dogs dislike each other. When
the Taikō [Hideyoshi] was ruling Japan, there was no United States of
America. It seems that the newcomer country has not yet really become
cultivated."

An anti-American mood spread rapidly through the country, almost
as though it had been orchestrated. Starting with local provincial political and commercial groups, it spread to student groups, labor groups,
and religious groups. Citizens' rallies passed resolutions to "stop the im-

porting of American goods, and effect a thorough boycott of American goods," to "abolish the importing of American cotton," or to "absolutely prohibit the viewing of American movies." The following anti-American rallies were just some of those held during the two weeks following the passage of the new immigration act: Asahikawa citizens rally; Otaru citizens rally; Muroran citizens rally; anti-American citizens rally sponsored by the Hakodate city chapter of the veterans association; lecture meeting sponsored by the Muroran Mainichi Shinbun newspaper company; lecture meeting sponsored by Hirosaki Higher School students; Kōfu reformists' standing committee; Tsuchiura City, Ibaraki prefecture, citizens rally; Akashi citizens rally; lecture meeting sponsored by the Yokohama Christian youth group; lecture meeting to impeach the U.S. Congress sponsored by the Osaka Kinnō Resshi party; lecture meeting to criticize Japan-U.S. issues sponsored by Kanazawa city Christian pastors; lecture meeting sponsored by Toyohashi town Christian pastors; emergency meeting of the Kanazawa City young lawyers group; Sakai City lecture meeting; Ōmiya town lecture meeting; lecture meeting sponsored by the Kawagoe chamber of commerce and commerce and industry association; lecture meeting on Japan-U.S. problems held jointly by the cities of Ueda and Nagano; lecture meeting sponsored by the Osaka port construction youth group with the support of Kyokutō Renmei Kyōkai (Far Eastern Federated Association); Maebashi City lecture meeting; lecture meeting the Kobe Asians Federation; Kōriyama town, Fukushima prefecture, lecture meeting; Nagasaki citizens rally; Sasebo newspaper reporters lecture meeting.

Those who resented American criticism of Japan's Siberian intervention and its demands for special interests in China used the passage of the new immigration law as an opportunity to attack pro-American elements in Japan. The anti-American movement in Japan spread, buoyed by inflammatory rhetoric: "national disgrace," "righteous indignation," "inhumanity," and "outrage against the Yamato spirit." At the time of the Washington Conference, many patriotic groups held rallies in Ueno and Shiba parks in Tokyo to protest the arms reduction agreement. It was almost like a rehearsal for this new wave of intense anti-American protest.

What had most alarmed the HSPA during the 1920 strike was the nationalistic solidarity of the Japanese laborers. The response in Japan to a new immigration act that besmirched the honor of the Japanese people seemed to underscore this concern. An extreme nationalism that saw America as its enemy spread like mass hysteria throughout Japan. There was a general public backlash against a cultural and social infatuation with America, from its sought after consumer goods such as Ford motor cars through Hollywood movies and baseball to the lifestyles of the *moga mobo,* the "modern girls" and "modern boys" who embraced Western fads.

As Gorō Sogobeya, an actor, said,

> There is too much of an American wind blowing in Japan these days: it is America first and America second. When it seems that the sun doesn't rise or set without America, we need to reconsider our situation. We can't help but have misgivings about the future of our Japanese state. The America we yearned for, longed for, and adored, has rebuffed us strongly, showing us that they dislike us and are anti-Japanese. Those of us who have even a smidgen of manly feelings must wake up to reality. I think the anti-Japanese issue in America is a good lesson for those Japanese who have come down with a fever of excessive adoration for America.[7]

Meanwhile in the United States, politicians in both houses of Congress focused on the coming election. Apart from the Imperial Hotel incident, the extreme Japanese reactions to the new immigration law hardly attracted their interest. But on July 1, 1924, the day the immigration act took effect, the American stars and stripes flown on the U.S. Embassy grounds in Tokyo was pulled down and stolen. (The perpetrator was arrested in Osaka, and the flag was returned a week later.) Former ambassador to the United States, Kijūrō Shidehara, who had become the new foreign minister, immediately sent to the U.S. government an expression of regret at this "unfortunate incident."

This apology was not enough to satisfy many on the West Coast, especially the Hearst newspapers, which used the incident as new evidence to justify their anti-Japanese position. It was Japanese immigrants on the West Coast, especially those in California, who bore the brunt of the American reaction. Shortly after the American flag incident, two Japanese were beaten to death in San Pedro, outside Los Angeles. In the same area, a large mob attacked the house of a Japanese automobile dealer and beat up the man and his wife. In a town north of San Francisco, a mob of some thirty people with rifles and pistols in hand forced themselves into the building of a Japanese cannery contractor, firing about a hundred shots into a shed where twenty-five Japanese laborers were sleeping. It was said that the local Ku Klux Klan was involved in this incident. The San Francisco consulate reported that it was "miraculous" that there were no injuries.[8] The Japanese consulate in Honolulu, in contrast, reported no incidents of violence directed at Japanese immigrants because of the new law, nor were there any other anti-Japanese incidents on the islands.

It is interesting to note that Japanese residents in Japan's colonial territories were no less fervid in their patriotic reaction to the immigration law than their compatriots in the home islands. Patriotic rallies were sponsored by Japanese nationalist groups in Korea and other overseas territories. But the Japanese colonial authorities were more concerned about the reaction of their colonial subjects than about the actions of Japanese residents. Any sign of anti-Japanese sentiment in a powerful country like the United States was bound not only to weaken Japan's image but also to encourage anticolonial nationalists in the colonies.

Despite official efforts at suppression, independence movements were stirring in Korea, supported by the overseas Korean community. The majority of Koreans overseas were laborers and political refugees who had emigrated to Hawaii and the United States, and their enmity toward Japan was also aimed at Japanese immigrants. During the 1920 strike Korean laborers, many of them said to have been political refugees, were quick to go to work as scabs for the plantations.

Sangorō Yanagiya, a comic storyteller, expressed his reactions to the passage of the immigration law: "This is a time when we should endure all things and wait for peace. . . . However, in the unfortunate instance that diplomatic relations are broken, it won't be settled by war against just Germany, it will be a major war of the entire world."[9]

What "national indignity" had the Japanese as a nation risen up to cry out against? What "justice" did Japan demand, even though it had brought Korea and Taiwan under its rule, trampling human rights with military boots?

The 1924 immigration act restricted immigrants from all countries on a quota basis. Only immigrants from Asia were "aliens ineligible to citizenship" excluded entirely. The law was clearly racially discriminatory, pushed through by hard-line anti-Japanese congressmen from California and other West Coast states. Yet Japan itself had implemented racially discriminatory policies toward its own neighbors in Asia.

The Japanese government did not protest the new immigration act on behalf of all Asians, nor did it base its appeal on the humanitarianism embodied in America's founding spirit of equality and fairness. Rather than confidently advance an argument based on ethical principles, the Japanese simply asserted they should be given the same "special treatment" as Caucasians. While affirming that the immigration act was racially discriminatory, the Japanese government insisted that an exception be made for Japan. Since American immigration policy had always given special treatment to Japanese in contrast to other Asians, the Japanese government simply pushed for recognition of its special rights by emphasizing its loyalty and friendship to the United States.

But American politics no longer permitted such an appeal. The burgeoning anti-Japanese movement on the West Coast, fueled by charges of Hawaii's Japanese problem made by the Hawaiian sugar planters who wanted to import Chinese laborers in the wake of the 1920 strike, had made it difficult for Congress to give Japan the same special treatment it had in the past. The failure of diplomatic exchanges between Japan and the United States on the new immigration act revealed not merely a gap in perception but also Japan's misperception of the situation.

The passage of the 1924 immigration law set loose an unhealthy nationalism in Japan. Although the law used the term "aliens ineligible to citizenship," and it avoided referring to the "Japanese," Foreign Ministry documents immediately called it the "Japanese exclusion act." The Japanese press followed suit, reporting on the law as though it prohibited only Japanese immigrants. The predictable reaction of the general Japanese public was that the American Congress wanted to shut out Japanese immigrants. New right-wing groups, focusing only on Japan and attacking the law as a "national humiliation," formed to take advantage of the public's emotional reaction, and older right-wing organizations like the Kokuryūkai tried to expand their bases.[10]

Shortly after President Coolidge signed the 1924 immigration law, the director of the Europe/America Bureau in the Foreign Ministry received a document entitled "An Opinion on Establishing Our Basic Foreign Policy Principles on the Occasion of the Japanese Exclusion Act." "While the Japanese Exclusion Act was a great error on the part of the U.S., I believe it provides *Japan with a heaven-sent opportunity*," it began.

> Should we let this opportunity go by, it would inevitably mean the perishing of Japan and the Japanese people. . . . I rejoice greatly because I believe this occasion points the way to Japan's future path. . . . Now is the time for the Japanese people to stop riding on the coattails of the Anglo-Saxons and feed-

ing at the same trough. Instead, Japan should bravely define itself as a savior of the Asian people, and expend our utmost sincere efforts from a humanitarian position. . . . It is clearly folly to confront the U.S. as an enemy when we do not clash on vital interests. However, we should strongly protest the Japanese Exclusion Act. This protest should not simply be based on technicalities, such as a treaty violation, but rather emphasize the racial discrimination inherent in the act.

The real purpose of the protest, the document concluded, was not the United States: "The target is *countries other than the U.S., specifically in Asia,* for whom we should use this as a 'trick' to unite the peoples of Asia."

The author of this memorandum, Tadakazu Ōhashi, was a thirty-one-year-old diplomat who had graduated from Tokyo University and was serving as Japanese consul in Seattle. Following service in Seattle, Ōhashi was posted to the Chinese mainland, eventually serving as consul general in Harbin. When Manchukuo was established in 1934 he became diplomatic affairs section chief of the state ministry, then director of the foreign affairs bureau and councillor of the foreign affairs bureau. One year before war broke out between Japan and the United States, he became vice minister in the Foreign Ministry in Japan.

The suggestions of one young diplomat could hardly have swayed Japanese policy, but one thing is certain: the ultranationalistic reaction, heightened at a stroke by the passage of the 1924 immigration act, made more plausible the utopian vision of an Asia united under the Japanese emperor. Distrust of America that took root in 1924 began to spread, and the saber-rattling of the military grew louder. The public reaction to the "Japanese Exclusion Act" was an important psychological step leading toward the epithet "American and British devils" (*kichiku Bei Ei*) that took hold in Japan after the outbreak of the Pacific War seventeen years later in 1941.

Yasutarō Sōga of the *Nippu jiji,* who learned about passage of the law while in Tokyo, was angered at the time by the stamp of "humiliation that the Japanese people felt at being slapped in the face." Yet, after he had completed a tour of China and Korea, Sōga's reaction changed. "As soon as I entered Korea," he later recalled, "I felt great apprehension about Japan's political policies. As I went to Manchuria and China, I was forced to think whether Japan's foreign policy toward its neighbors would be able to keep peace in its current form."[11] After Sōga returned to Honolulu a month after the law passed, he thought, "I was struck by how beautiful Honolulu was." It was then that Sōga reaffirmed his determination to live out his life in Hawaii.

THE SUPREME COURT DENIES THE DEFENDANTS' APPEAL

To the residents of Hilo, on the island of Hawaii, the eruption of Kilauea was of more concern than the congressional debate over the new immigration act. The eruption was so dangerous that residents on a part of Olaa Plantation located south of Kilauea were ordered to evacuate. In mid-May another major eruption sent a river of lava flowing down from its fissures. Observers near the mouth of the volcano were killed by the spewing rocks and molten ash. By June the volcano had quieted down, and there were fewer days when the sky was gray with ash over Waiakea Plantation.

After Tsurunosuke Koyama, one of the 1920 strike leaders, went to prison for his part in the Sakamaki house dynamiting, his thirty-six-year-old wife, Teru, ran their store at Waiakea. Outwardly, Teru was a typical Japanese woman—soft-spoken, with a fair-skinned, round face—but she had a keen eye for business and was a good employer, so she was able to keep the Koyama store profitable while Tsurunosuke was away. Following her husband, who was baptized while in prison, Teru also became a Christian. Her younger brother, a well-known baker in Honolulu, had become a Christian years before and had been donating surplus bread from his bakery to the Oahu prison each day.

Magotarō Hiruya, the second son of Teru's youngest brother, had come from Teru's hometown, Nakatsu in Kyūshū, to go to school in Honolulu while staying with his uncle, whose bakery he later inherited. He recalled how his Aunt Teru visited Honolulu nearly every week while Tsurunosuke was in the Oahu prison. The Koyamas were known at Waiakea Plantation as a loving couple. Teru's sole luxury was the kimonos that a dealer brought to the store, and Tsurunosuke gladly bought what she wanted. Even a half century later, her nephew could clearly remember Teru, dressed in one of these kimonos, dashing off to the prison. On each visit, Teru carried as many box lunches or sweets as she could for her husband to share with his friends. Those like Noboru Tsutsumi, who had no families to visit them, must have looked forward to Teru's visit as eagerly as her husband did.

Ala Moana, a major shopping center crowded with Japanese tourists, was one of Walter Dillingham's business projects, but in the 1920s it was the site of a refuse dump where inmates from the Oahu prison were often sent to work. When visiting her husband, Teru Koyama preferred the garbage dump to the prison visiting room. The Hawaiian guards were willing to look the other way for a bit of money.

Since Tsurunosuke had been drawn into the 1920 labor struggle as a community leader on Waiakea Plantation, Teru never felt ashamed being the wife of a prisoner. Even so, after chatting with her husband about the store as they sat on the beach near the garbage dump, Teru would feel renewed energy when she returned by boat to Hilo.

Perhaps Teru heard from her husband about the final decision made in Washington on the Sakamaki house dynamiting case. On June 2, 1924, one week after President Coolidge signed the new immigration act, the U.S. Supreme Court case no. 463. The case of I. Goto, et al., Appellants, was summarily denied. The Japanese community in Hawaii showed no interest in this final decision.

What is most noteworthy about the Supreme Court decision on the Sakamaki dynamiting case is not the decision itself, which was expected. More significant is that the plaintiff's brief was not submitted by a territorial official. Rather, it was submitted under the signature of HSPA attorney Frank Thompson, making it amply clear that the territory had brought charges against the leaders of the Federation of Japanese Labor involved in the 1920 Oahu strike under pressure from the sugar planters.

The expenses later charged to the territory of Hawaii by the Supreme Court for the appeal on the Sakamaki case totaled $118.40: $53.40 for administrative expenses, $45 for printing costs, $20 for summary preparation by the attorney. Since the trial had been for the HSPA's benefit, these expenses should have been billed to the HSPA, but they were submitted to the accounting department of the territory of Hawaii. What the thirteen defendants, including Gotō, owed remains unknown.

In early March 1925, nine months after the Supreme Court decision, Pablo Manlapit, the president of the Filipino Labor Union, joined Tsutsumi and the other former Japanese federation leaders at the Oahu prison. Just before the passage of the new immigration law, another major labor struggle had broken out in the cane fields. No doubt the new strike was what caused many Hawaiian sugar planters to send telegrams to Washington protesting the exclusion of Japanese immigrants by the new law. During the new strike the planters had to rely on the Japanese laborers, whom they looked at with new eyes. In contrast to the 1920 strike, the new strike, at the very least, was not a "bloody struggle."

In early April 1924 Pablo Manlapit, supported by George Wright's Hawaii Central Labor Council, led the Filipino laborers on Oahu plantations in a strike for wage increases. The number of Filipino laborers had increased since the 1920 strike, and more than 19,000 Filipinos worked in the cane fields. Outnumbering the Japanese laborers by 6,000, the Filipinos had become the largest ethnic group in the sugar plantation workforce. At its annual meeting in late 1920, the HSPA had decided not to rely on one nationality for its labor force in order to avoid a repetition of the 1920 strike. By the time they realized it, however, the Filipino workers had the majority.

The HSPA did not take the threat of a Filipino strike seriously. Because very few Filipinos in Hawaii were financially successful, the source of support funds for the strikers was limited. With all the federation leaders in jail, the organization had been destroyed, and the planters expected that Japanese workers would not sympathize with a strike led by Filipinos. Even as the strike spread to all the islands, the Japanese continued to work in the fields. The Filipino laborers had to carry on the fight by themselves, but in contrast to the disciplined solidarity of the Japanese in 1920, the Filipinos were fragmented, and violent incidents broke out frequently as they fought among themselves along ethnic lines.

What dealt the final blow to the 1924 strike was a confrontation with plantation security guards in mid-September. The Filipinos were armed with rifles as well as large hoes and knives used at work. It was the most violent labor clash in Hawaiian history. Four security guards and sixteen Filipino laborers were killed, and many others were wounded. One hundred sixty-two striking laborers were arrested, 72 of whom were convicted. Since the Philippines were American territory, the HSPA could not claim that the 1924 strike involved a foreign conspiracy. It was Pablo Manlapit who became their sole target. The HSPA aimed at arresting Manlapit and knocking the props out from his supporter, George Wright's Hawaii Central Labor Council.

Manlapit was arrested in a case involving the death of a Filipino laborer's child on Waipahu Plantation. The father of the dead child, who testified as a prosecution witness, said that Manlapit had forced him to tell others that the child had died because the company told him if he did not go back to work on the plantation, his gravely ill child would not be treated at the plantation hospital. It was revealed later that the father gave false testimony in return for a payment of $110, but Manlapit had already been found guilty of suborning perjury. After his release

from prison two years later, the territory of Hawaii ordered his depor-
tation. Since his children were born in the United States, he chose to go
to California rather than return to the Philippines. Five years later, after
the strike furor had died down, he returned to Hawaii and attempted to
rebuild the Filipino Labor Union that had fallen apart after he had entered prison. This time he was arrested for "suspicion of fraud" and was
forcibly deported to the Philippines.

NOBORU TSUTSUMI RETURNS HOME

For the first time in three years an Imperial Navy training fleet visited
Hawaii in late February 1925. The fleet, which was secretly gathering
intelligence on the United States as a potential enemy, had sailed to
the Marianas and other South Seas islands, the Panama Canal, Central
America, and along the west coast of the United States to Vancouver,
Canada, and was on its way home. The Japanese community in Hawaii
turned out to greet the fleet, enthusiastically waving rising sun flags at
the ports of Honolulu and Hilo, almost as though eager to put behind
them the rancor built up since the passage of the immigration act the
year before. To the nisei, and to younger Japanese such as Seiei Wakikawa, a student at the University of Hawaii, this hearty welcome appeared to reflect an insensitivity to the current situation. (Wakikawa,
who later studied at Tokyo University, returned to become editor-in-
chief at *Nippu jiji*.)

Less than two months after the visit of the Imperial Navy training
fleet, American army and navy forces engaged in a massive exercise in
Hawaii at the end of April. A total of 137 warships were lined up in the
seas from Pearl Harbor to Waikiki, including 11 battleships, 10 light
cruisers, 60 destroyers, and 11 submarines, with 45,000 men participating, including two admirals. The exercise was unprecedented in scale.
Army troops stationed in Hawaii played the role of defenders while
American army and navy forces from San Francisco and the West Coast
as well as Australia and New Zealand played the role of potential enemy
forces attacking Pearl Harbor. The exercise, which began on April 27,
lasted nearly a month. According to Yasutarō Sōga of the *Nippu,* the
Japanese in Hawaii saw the exercise as a demonstration of strength vis-
à-vis Japan.

After the exercise ended, aloha welcome festivities lasted for several
days. American servicemen participated in sports and other activities
with the local residents. Walter Dillingham, whose firm had constructed

the naval base at Pearl Harbor, was a central figure in the welcoming festivities. In 1926 Dillingham's Hawaiian Dredging Company signed a
new contract with the U.S. Departments of the Army and Navy. The
Washington Conference had put a brake on the construction of warships, but to provide for the day when the disarmament treaty might be
abrogated, expansion of docking facilities for large warships at Pearl
Harbor was to begin in 1927. Dillingham had won the contracts for expansion of a submarine base, the building of a diesel oil refinery, and
other construction.

To observe the exercises, not only a congressional delegation but
also a huge contingent of journalists visited Hawaii. The May 25 *San
Francisco Chronicle* carried a story by one of its reporters who, seeing
Japanese fishing boats and motorboats moving freely about the port at
Pearl Harbor, reported with alarm: "Foreign Spies Swarm Navy Base in
Hawaii! Parties aboard the sampans are able to secure first-hand knowl-
edge of every new activity within Pearl Harbor, the chief defense link of
the island of Oahu." He was voicing doubts later linked to the attack on
Pearl Harbor.

In June 1925, while Honolulu was full of uniformed American navy
men, Noboru Tsutsumi and Chūhei Hoshino, two of the former leaders
of the Federation of Japanese Labor, were released from the Oahu prison
early for good conduct, after serving three years of their four-year sentences.[12] As soon as they were free, the two men boarded a ship for their
homeland. When Tsutsumi's eldest daughter, eleven-year-old Michiko,
went to meet her Daddy at the pier in Yokohama, she was in the fourth
year of elementary school. Michiko's younger brother, Toshio, whom
Tsutsumi saw for the first time, was seven years old. It had been eight
years since Tsutsumi had left Japan.

While he was gone, his wife, Chiyo, had lived with her parents at the
Tsutsumi clinic in Nagahama, as she had when Tsutsumi was studying
at Kyoto University. She spent her days talking to her mother, wonder-
ing when Noboru-san would return. Masao Tsutsumi, the eldest son
of Chiyo's eldest brother, who now heads the Tsutsumi Hospital, lived
there at the time. His aunt had been able to wait eight years for her husband's return, he recalled, because of her easygoing personality. When
she received word that her husband was finally coming home, she happily headed for Yokohama with her two children.

When Michiko first saw her father, whom she had longed for for so
long, she was disappointed. He seemed so different from the "handsome

Daddy who looked like a foreigner in his photographs." Her father was terribly thin and even to a child's eyes looked tired in his rumpled suit. Her mother had promised that he would bring lots of unusual things from Hawaii, but the only present he pulled out of his single bag was a necklace made of walnuts. As he patted Michiko's bobbed head, he said, "You've gotten so big."

Michiko recalled, "Father got off the ship with some women who accompanied him from Hawaii." The reunited Tsutsumi family stayed for a while with Chiyo's sister, who had married a doctor in private practice near Waseda University in Tokyo. The women accompanying her father were visiting Japan from Hawaii, and they stayed with them a few nights. Her father spoke to them as though they were close friends, but young Michiko had no idea what kind of acquaintances they were. When the women departed, the family was together again for the first time in many years.

"Father never spoke about his life in Hawaii," Michiko recalled. "I had heard from Mother that he was put in prison in Hawaii, but since it was for something he did for other people, not for stealing or anything like that, he did not have a criminal record in Japan."

Seeing his homeland for the first time in eight years, Tsutsumi must have been amazed at how much daily life had changed. Many more women were wearing Western clothes on the street, and politics had taken a new turn. A universal manhood suffrage law had been passed by the Imperial Diet in 1925 after five years of effort, but the coalition cabinet that proposed the law was splitting apart. Amid this turmoil, Tsutsumi's attention must have been drawn to the labor strife in China. Since earlier in the year, labor struggles against Japanese businesses had erupted in the Chinese treaty ports. In late May, during a strike at Nihon Naigai Cotton Company in Shanghai, police fired on the striking workers, killing and injuring many. Laborers and students were joined by Shanghai merchants in a general strike to protest this treatment, and anti-Japanese protests spread to other cities, including Hong Kong. To suppress this movement, ground troops from Japan, Britain, the United States, and France landed in Shanghai.

For a year or so after his return, Tsutsumi quietly helped out with clerical work at Chiyo's sister's husband's clinic, but in December 1926, just about the time that the Shōwa emperor began his reign, Tsutsumi paid a visit to Toyohiko Kagawa. Many religious leaders had visited Hawaii, but, according to Yasutarō Sōga, Kagawa had "left the deepest impression." [13] Kagawa, a Christian socialist, was known to be more interested in solving social problems than in simply saving souls. He had organized the Kansai branch of the Yūaikai with Bunji Suzuki and others, and he was arrested and imprisoned as a result of his leadership in the 1921 Mitsubishi Kobe and Kawasaki dockyard strikes. Kagawa was involved in a wide range of causes, including the universal manhood suffrage movement and the organizing of tenant farmers. When Tsutsumi had heard Kagawa speak in Hawaii, it had opened his eyes. Here was a man he wished to be like. Indeed, Tsutsumi's baptism in prison may have been a result of Kagawa's influence.

Shortly after his visit with Kagawa, whom he venerated, Tsutsumi left his brother-in-law's clinic to rent a house in Honsho Fukagawa, a district of Tokyo filled with tenements where low-income laborers lived. During the day he helped out at a consumers' cooperative for laborers, and in the evening he taught English at a night school for working youth associated with Kagawa. Chiyo, who had been raised in comfort, experienced poverty for the first time in her life. Tsutsumi was kind to his wife, perhaps to make up for the long time he had been away. Happy at his caring nature, Chiyo did needlework, with her baby on her back. A year after Tsutsumi's return, a second son, Norio, was born.

Tsutsumi never raised his voice in harshness to his children. He called Michiko "Michibō," and he never tired of listening to her chatter. Michiko went to greet him every night when he returned by streetcar from teaching his night classes. But their life as a close-knit family did not last long. On many nights Tsutsumi brought home young workers who attended his night school classes, and it was not unusual for some of them to stay for several nights. Chiyo showed little interest in their discussions, peppered with words like "capitalist," "struggle," "demonstration," and "strike." She was concerned about how to feed these extra people on their meager household budget. In September 1927, two years after Tsutsumi's return to Japan, a major strike broke out at Noda Shōyu Company. Tsutsumi joined in the strike, which lasted eight months, and his absences from home grew more frequent than before.

It was in 1927 that Sacco and Vanzetti were executed by electric chair in Boston. In prison they had fought for retrial, and their appeals had gained wide public support. The state of Massachusetts, however, ignored the president's pleas for clemency and forced an end to the case seven years after it started. The execution of the two men caused a worldwide outcry. Intellectual and cultural leaders, including Nobel laureates, denounced it. In major American cities as well as in European capitals, there were demonstrations for clemency and meetings to protest the execution. In Tokyo anarchists held a lecture meeting as part of their movement for "release of Sacco and Vanzetti and opposition to troop intervention in China," resulting in some arrests by the authorities. It must be pointed out, however, that the majority of the American public believed in the authorities and accepted the execution of the "Reds" as just. Many volumes have been written about the Sacco and Vanzetti case, some of which claim their guilt. But in 1977, fifty years after their execution, Massachusetts Governor Michael Dukakis publicly acknowledged that the trial had been a mistake.

THE FATE OF THE FEDERATION LEADERS

News of the execution of Sacco and Vanzetti was reported briefly in the Japanese-language newspapers in Hawaii. It is doubtful, however, that many in the Japanese community were interested in the fate of these two Italian immigrants. They were still savoring the success of the campaign against the foreign-language school law. A news story in the *Hawaii hōchi* crowed, "Glorious victory in unprecedented suit against the foreign language school control act targeting the eradication of Japanese language schools. Banzai, Banzai, Banzai. Faith is heard in heaven, justice is ultimately victorious."

The decision against the territory of Hawaii was handed down five months before the execution of Sacco and Vanzetti. The Supreme Court ruled that because "freedom of education" was guaranteed by the U.S. Constitution, the territory had no right to meddle in the management of the Japanese-language schools as they were privately operated institutions. The outcome of the five-and-a-half-year suit ended in defeat for the territory of Hawaii. When the news arrived from Washington, Makino and others in the *Hōchi* editorial room hugged each other and cried tears of joy. The *Hōchi* hired an airplane to drop copies of its "Victory Extra" edition from the sky that day.

The "Victory Extra" chided the competition: "What will the *Nippu jiji* faction, who belittled the cause by refusing to contribute even five cents, say against the decision?" Makino finally had a chance to attack his rival paper, which always took a "reasonable" editorial stance. For Makino, victory on the Japanese-language school suit meant the defeat of his old enemy Yasutarō Sōga, of the *Nippu jiji,* a central figure in the faction accepting control over the language schools.

The victory was also a victory for the Honganji sect in Hawaii, and a defeat for the Christians who did not support the suit. For five years

Hawaii's Japanese community had been deeply divided over the issue. Families were ostracized, and children taunted each other. Discord surrounding the Japanese-language schools furor continued for years, leaving a deep wound that the Japanese community found difficult to heal. The Japanese-language school suit support association placed a full-page announcement in the *Hawaii hōchi,* "We express our heartfelt feelings of respect and gratitude to the sincere efforts for the struggle shown over many years by the *Hawaii hōchi* company." Kinzazaburō Makino, the troublemaker in Hawaii's Japanese community, had finally achieved the hero's status that he had not during the 1920 strike. Some, like Reverend Takie Okumura, who feared the decision would reverse the efforts of his Americanization movement, cautioned against excessive rejoicing in the Japanese community. The Japanese consul general warned, "I would hope that on this occasion care would be taken as to behavior so that the relations between the peoples of Japan and America that have deteriorated due to this issue will not further deteriorate." Makino completely ignored them.

For the next few months Makino toured the islands lecturing on the victory of the lawsuit. Everywhere he was applauded. Parents of children who attended the Japanese-language schools welcomed him as a champion who had fought for their rights. They adorned Makino with colorful flowered leis and shouted choruses of "Banzai" at his lectures at the Japanese-language schools. It stirred their patriotism all the more. For Makino, the lecture tour was also an opportunity to increase circulation of the *Hawaii hōchi:* he sold company bonds to the Japanese-language school parents. When the *Hōchi* victory commemorative issue was published a few years later, it alleged that the bonds took the form of donations to the *Hōchi* for a "renewed show of gratitude to President Makino." According to Kiyoshi Ōkubo, Hilo bureau chief for the *Hawaii hōchi* at the time, a more accurate description of the situation was that Makino ordered the staffs of local *Hōchi* bureaus to make the rounds coercing purchasers into treating the bonds as donations to the company.

After the news of the victory came from Washington, Ichiji Gotō, former secretary of the Federation of Japanese Labor and a defendant in the Sakamaki house dynamiting case, answered congratulatory telephone calls in the editorial department of the *Hōchi.* In May 1926, one year after Tsutsumi and Hoshino returned to Japan, Gotō and eleven other defendants were released early on good behavior. Tsunehiko Murakami, named by two prosection witnesses as the man who had set and lit the fuse of the dynamite, was released one month after the others because of a violation while in prison.

Gotō had been a reporter for the *Nippu jiji* before he became involved in the strike. After his release from prison, Yasutarō Sōga refused to rehire him because of his prison record, but Makino told him, "If you feel like working, come on by." Although Makino was overbearing, he had a warm heart. Makino also hired George Wright, who had earned the even greater ire of the HSPA by helping the Filipinos' strike in 1924, when no one else would. He added an English-language page to the *Hōchi* and put Wright in charge of it.

Like Gotō none of the former federation leaders participated in the labor movement after release from prison. Neither did they speak much about the strike or about the trial to their families. Indeed, more than two-thirds of them were divorced while in prison. Unable to make a living while their husbands were in prison, some wives returned to Japan with their children. But since it was not difficult for women, fewer in number than men in the Japanese immigrant community, to find a new mate, others simply abandoned their husbands and divorced them. The powerful HSPA had sought to disarm the leaders of the Federation of Japanese Labor, who had stood up to them, by charging them with the Sakamaki house dynamiting, but it ruined their family lives as well.

Hiroshi Miyazawa, who along with Noboru Tsutsumi and Ichiji Gotō was a secretary of the federation, was one of those divorced by his wife. As a man with a prison record, he could not return to his work as a pastor. Using his facility in English, he eked out a living as an interpreter and an agent.

The only two defendants able to resume their former occupations were Tsurunosuke Koyama and Chikao Ishida, both members of the Hawaii Island union. With the help of his wife, Teru, who had faithfully waited for him, Koyama made his business at Waiakea Plantation more successful than before. After World War II, Koyama returned to live in Miyazaki in the hometown of his second wife, whom he married after Teru's death. He died there at age seventy-four.

Ishida returned to his position as principal of a Japanese-language school at his former plantation on Hawaii, but his wife had returned to Japan with their son while he was in prison, then divorced him. His school backed the lawsuit, and he was active locally on its behalf. When Gotō accompanied Makino on his victory tour of the island, Ishida, who led the welcome party, met Gotō again for the first time since they were in prison. The other defendant from Hawaii, Sazō Satō, died in a traffic accident shortly after his release.

Honji Fujitani had organized the first union on Oahu at Waialua Plantation, but his wife was evicted from plantation housing. She was able to survive somehow with four children, the oldest of whom was five. Fujitani could not return to the plantation after his release, so he worked at various jobs in Honolulu. Tokuji Baba, also from Waialua Plantation, went to work as a head clerk at a small inn in Honolulu.

The leaders from the Waipahu Plantation union, where trouble with scabs often occurred during the strike, could not return to their plantation. Kan'ichi Takizawa made his living by assisting a group that sponsored Japanese performing artists, such as storytellers, singers, and sumo wrestlers, and after World War II he returned to Japan. Unable to settle in his hometown, Nagano, he moved to Hokkaido, where he died. Fumio Kawamata, also from the Waipahu union, whom the prosecution accused of being a gigolo during the trial, was welcomed back by the woman innkeeper he had lived with before.

Shōshichirō Furushō, another defendant from Waipahu Plantation, left Hawaii in 1932, a year after the Manchurian incident, to return to his hometown in Kumamoto prefecture with his wife and children. Leaving work on the family fields to others, he opened an American-style supermarket in front of the railroad station, a venture that had great success. Furushō liked being involved in local politics. According to his granddaughter, he was always busy running around at election time, and he died at age sixty-five after World War II.

The fish farm run by Seigo Kondō, who had become involved with the security pickets while aiding evicted laborers in Pearl City, fell on hard times while in prison. He was married and had a daughter, but after a divorce he returned to his hometown in Niigata, where he ran a factory making ropes to tie barrels for the Kikkōman Shōyu (Kikkoman Soy Sauce) company. During election campaigns, he was so busy supporting local candidates that he spent hardly any time at home. Only Kondō and Furushō occasionally spoke of their involvement in "a strike that stunned the capitalists in Hawaii" during their later years. Kondō, like Furushō, known as a curmudgeon, died at age eighty-one.

Of the remaining defendants in the Sakamaki dynamiting case, Shunji Tomota of Waimanalo Plantation was listed in the *Hawaii Nihonjin meibo* (Hawaii Japanese Directory) three years after his release from prison as "Honolulu resident; odd jobs." In the same directory, Tsunehiko Murakami, released a month after the others, was listed as "Hono-

lulu resident; store owner." Their names do not appear in later direc-
tories, or in any other materials, and their subsequent lives remain unknown. Chūhei Hoshino's whereabouts after he returned to Japan with
Tsutsumi remain unknown as well.

On May 23, 1930, eight months after the start of the worldwide depression triggered by the October crash of the New York stock market,
a farewell party was held in Tokyo for U.S. Ambassador William R.
Castle. Masanao Hanihara, the former Japanese ambassador to the
United States, warned the departing Castle that the only way to restore
amicable relations between Japan and the United States was to amend
the Immigration Act of 1924. He continued to feel answerable for his
statement that passage of the law would have "grave consequences."
    Shortly after Hanihara's remarks were reported in Washington, Rep.
Albert Johnson, the author of the act and still chairman of the House
Committee on Immigration and Naturalization, held a press conference.
He announced that he wished to wipe away the hard feelings aroused
between the United States and Japan by passage of the Immigration Act
of 1924 and that he hoped in the near future to present an amendment
that would permit a proportionate quota for immigrants from Japan. In
effect, Johnson announced that he had reevaluated the law that he had
pushed through Congress six years earlier, causing a major rift between
the United States and Japan. The statement stunned congressmen.
    Johnson was a representative from the state of Washington, where
lumber was the main industry. As the depression spread, causing major
social problems, the export of lumber to Japan took on increasing importance to the state. The Japan-America Society in Seattle, which had
not been pleased by Johnson's role in the passage of the 1924 Immigration Act, encouraged lumber industry leaders interested in trade with Japan to put pressure on Representative Johnson to amend the law.
    An old school conservative on the right wing of the Republican party,
Johnson had fought a tough campaign to win his previous election. He
foresaw that his next one would be even more difficult, and he needed
to promise local leaders that he would propose an amendment to the
1924 Immigration Act at the right time. Given his previous position on
the issue, however, he had to find an appropriate way to bring it to Congress again. Hanihara's plea to Castle had given him the chance to state
his intention to do so. When Ambassador Castle bid farewell to Foreign
Minister Shidehara on May 25, 1930, he said that since understanding

of the issue was gradually spreading throughout America, a satisfactory solution to the immigration issue was possible.

Two weeks later, on June 10, the Honolulu Chamber of Commerce, which had strongly supported the importation of Chinese labor when Walter Dillingham had been its president, backed Johnson's proposal to amend the Immigration Act. It sent a telegram to President Herbert Hoover urging that Japanese immigrants be given a quota. Following the lead of the Honolulu Chamber of Commerce, other chambers quickly issued similar statements in Seattle, Tacoma, and other cities in Washington, as well as in Portland, Oregon. Even in California, the chambers of commerce in San Francisco and Los Angeles announced resolutions supporting the amendment.

The strength of American politics is the willingness to admit past mistakes and to learn from them. Many recognized the role that racial discrimination had played in passage of the Immigration Act six years earlier. The American Legion and the AFL both continued to view Japanese immigrants as a potential threat and firmly opposed any amendment, but by the summer of 1931, a year after Johnson's announcement, pressure to revise the law had reached the point that the Japanese embassy in Washington reported to Tokyo, "Most of the informed people in the U.S. are favorably disposed to the movement to amend the Immigration Act to give Japanese a 'quota.'"[14]

Unfortunately, on September 18, two months later, the Kwantung Army launched its plans to occupy Manchuria, the three northeastern provinces of China, by blowing up a section of track on the South Manchurian Railway at Liutiaogou, just outside Mukden. Claiming that the explosion was the work of Chinese saboteurs, Japanese military forces made an all-out assault on the Mukden barracks and arsenal, the main fortification of the Chinese troops. In less than a day the Kwantung Army occupied Mukden, and within the next five months it gained control over most of Manchuria. The invasion, proclaiming a new phase of Japanese imperial aggression, killed any chance for the passage of an amendment to the Immigration Act of 1924. Those who had backed the amendment in the hope of improving U.S.-Japan relations would not support the actions of the Japanese militarists. The Manchurian incident was a turning point when a "sense of crisis toward Japan" spread from the West Coast to the rest of the country.

It could be said that the Manchurian incident also ended Representative Johnson's political career. In 1932, the year Japan recognized the new "independent" state of Manchukuo and Japanese emigration to Manchuria was encouraged, Johnson lost his bid for reelection to a young, liberal Democratic candidate, ending a twenty-year career in Congress. Returning to work at his newspaper, Johnson energetically wrote pieces from his nationalistic perspective until he died thirty-six years later at the age of eighty-eight.

WAR BETWEEN JAPAN AND THE UNITED STATES

The only reference in the literature of the Japanese left to Noboru Tsutsumi's history of the 1920 Japanese plantation workers' movement in Hawaii (*1920nen Hawaii satō kōchi rōdō undōshi, jō*) is a brief mention in *Suzuki Mosaburō zenshū* (The Complete Works of Mosaburō Suzuki). After working with Sen Katayama's left-wing group in New York, Suzuki visited postrevolution Moscow, and on his return to Japan, he worked as a newspaper reporter while joining a movement to launch a proletarian party. The proletarian party movement went through several splits and mergers among its rightist, leftist, and centrist factions before the formation of the National Masses party (Zenkoku Taishūtō) in 1930. Among the party's advisers were Toyohiko Kagawa and Toshihiko Sakai. Mosaburō Suzuki, along with Kanjū Katō, Chōzaburō Mizutani, Jōtarō Kawakami, and others, became a member of the central executive committee. It is most likely that that is when Suzuki and Noboru Tsutsumi became acquainted.

Tsutsumi was closer to Ryūsuke Miyazaki, a left-wing politician better known for having eloped with the poet Byakuren Yanagihara rather than for his radical socialist activities at Tokyo Imperial University. Tsutsumi damaged his throat so badly while campaigning for Miyazaki that he took to bed. His daughter, Michiko, who later became a doctor, thought his throat problem must have been a symptom of tuberculosis, an illness that he may have brought back with him from Hawaii. When he returned to Japan, Tsutsumi was already quite thin and often perspired in his sleep. Tuberculosis was a major cause of death in Hawaii, as it was in Japan.

Since his involvement in the Noda Shōyu company strike, Tsutsumi's movements had come under police surveillance. After his health deteriorated, the family had trouble feeding itself, so they moved to Chiyo's family's clinic in Nagahama. Tsutsumi's older brother, Ekan Kurokawa, who had returned from his studies in Germany, had opened up his medical practice near Kyoto University. When Tsutsumi recovered somewhat in 1932 he did administrative chores at his brother's clinic. In May 1932 Chiyo died of acute meningitis. Tsutsumi wept aloud, not minding that his children saw him, as if to apologize for having acted selfishly for so long. In 1933 Shigenao Konishi, Tsutsumi's mentor during his student days, became president of Kyoto University, and through his influence Tsutsumi became director of administration at his alma mater, but he had to sign a statement promising not to involve himself in labor movement activities.

In November 1933 Sen Katayama died in Moscow, just before the Stalinist purges began. Although called stubborn and narrow-minded, Katayama had lived his life according to his ideology.

One year later, in December 1934, Japan announced that it would abandon the Washington Naval Limitation Treaty. In this same year Tsutsumi married his second wife, Tsuruyo, who had just graduated from a women's normal school. She was just three years older than his daughter. According to Tsuruyo, her husband's health was so delicate that she wondered if she had married him simply to become his nurse. Yet it was Tsuruyo who had sought out Tsutsumi, drawn by his calm gentleness and the erudition with which he answered her every question. By this time, in addition to his duties at Kyoto University, Tsutsumi had also become business manager of Kitano Hospital in Osaka, which was affiliated with Kyoto University.

Spirited and cheerful, Tsuruyo did not want to be Tsutsumi's nursemaid. Unlike Chiyo, she had the intelligence and interest to respond to his talk of politics and the world. It was the first time that he had found a partner willing to enter his world. In 1938, the year that the National General Mobilization Law was decreed, Tsuruyo gave birth to a son, Tamotsu, the third son for Tsutsumi.

In the summer of 1933, the year Japan withdrew from the League of Nations, Franklin D. Roosevelt became the first American president to visit Hawaii. He was making an observation tour to check the country's front line of defense in the Pacific, but publicly it was reported that he was on a fishing vacation with his sons. The Japanese community in Hawaii, seeing this as a good opportunity to improve strained relations between Japan and the United States, participated with enthusiasm in the events welcoming the president. When the cruiser *Houston*, with the president aboard, and several accompanying vessels first put in to the port of Hilo, they were greeted offshore by a fleet of more than fifty Japanese fishing boats colorfully decked out. This seemed to have the opposite effect of what was intended, for it gave the impression that the Japanese immigrants in Hawaii were boasting of their influence.

Yet the Japanese immigrant community was making an all-out effort, and the stars and stripes were flown from all the Japanese shops along the road through Olaa Plantation as the president's convertible passed on its way to Mount Kilauea. Nisei schoolchildren and Japanese laborers at Olaa took the day off to wave small American flags by the roadside. Despite the midday heat, elderly immigrants of the Olaa Buddhist association stood at the roadside clad in black formal dress kimonos.

Jūzaburō Sakamaki, the company interpreter on Olaa Plantation, was not among those paying their respects to the president. Sakamaki had arranged for his eldest son, who as a high school student had stood guard with a pistol until dawn on the night of the dynamite blast, to take over his work as interpreter and postmaster. Shortly after his retirement Sakamaki suffered a stroke that left him partially paralyzed and bedridden. Six years after the president's visit to Hawaii, Sakamaki died at the age of seventy-one.

President Roosevelt received an even more elaborate welcome in Honolulu. On the last night of his visit a group of Japanese girls in cotton yukata danced a "Banzai dance" during a lantern parade. The president, whose legs were paralyzed by polio, pulled himself higher in the open car to watch them with great interest. The *Nippu jiji* noted that he was smiling throughout "like a doting father." When President Roosevelt toured the facilities at Pearl Harbor, the sole civilian among the high-ranking officers of the army and navy who escorted the president was Walter Dillingham, the former chairman of the Hawaii Emergency Labor Commission.

Eight years later the surprise attack by Japanese air forces on Pearl Harbor, the base of the U.S. Pacific fleet, sank five battleships, including the *Arizona,* and damaged three more. Casualties numbered 2,403 deaths and 3,478 wounded. A declaration of war from Japan arrived in Washington thirty-five minutes after the attack formally opened hostilities with the United States. In 1924 Sohō Tokutomi had called the day that the Immigration Act of 1924 took force a "day of national humiliation." President Roosevelt now called December 7, the day of the Pearl Harbor attack, a "day of infamy."

Roosevelt appointed a commission to determine why the U.S. Navy was unable to foresee the Japanese attack and requested a thorough review of U.S.-Japan relations leading to "this cowardly attack." The first item the commission checked out of the Library of Congress as a reference was the transcript of hearings of the House Committee on Immigration and Naturalization. It is not difficult to imagine that the Hawaii Labor Committee's opening statement on "Labor Problems in Hawaii" must have attracted the most attention in the record. The commission's allegation that the 1920 strike was a Japanese conspiracy once again came to the attention of the federal government. This transcript was sent to FBI Director Hoover who was charged with overseeing domestic security issues.

In February 1942, two and a half months after the Pearl Harbor attack, President Roosevelt signed an executive order requiring evacuation to relocation camps of some 110,000 Japanese and Japanese Americans, including many American citizens, from states on the West Coast. The Hawaiian Islands had already been placed under martial law, and a military administration was established. A document proposing relocation of Japanese in Hawaii was sent to the military governor, Lieutenant General Delos C. Emmons, but Hawaiian leaders, who appealed to the aloha spirit and a sense of fair play, took quick action to assure that the Japanese community in Hawaii was not relocated. Pastors, academics, and the major kamaaina industrialists without exception opposed the internment of Japanese. Even Walter Dillingham was among them.

On the day after the Pearl Harbor attack, however, local FBI agents acting under orders from headquarters in Washington arrested Japanese community leaders thought to be loyal to their homeland, Japan, the new enemy. Buddhist and Shinto priests, Japanese-language school instructors, members of the chamber of commerce, and members of prefectural organizations were sent to Sand Island, where the Bureau of Immigration was located, and some seven hundred of them were then dispatched in ten different groups to internment camps on the mainland.

The Japanese and Japanese American population of Hawaii at the time was 160,000, of whom only 35,000 were first-generation Japanese. It was they who occupied leadership positions in the Japanese community. After the FBI roundup leadership inevitably shifted to the nisei. The first measure taken by the younger generation was voluntarily to close the Japanese-language schools, whose numbers had increased after the victory in the suit against the territorial control law. The Japanese-language schools in Hawaii were destroyed by this act, and even after the war ended they did not reopen.

One of those arrested by the FBI was *Nippu jiji* president Yasutarō Sōga. Since he was an earnest Christian, known for years to be pro-

American, news of his arrest shocked the Japanese community. Sōga had many friends in haole society, but he faithfully attended events such as welcoming parties for the Imperial Navy fleet and he was also close to influential Japanese in Hawaii, such as the consul general, the branch heads of the Sumitomo Bank, the Specie Bank, and so on. Such "suspicious" behavior may have prompted the FBI to arrest him. During the war Sōga was forced to live behind barbed wire in a desert camp on the mainland. When he regained his freedom at war's end, he returned to Hawaii. The *Nippu jiji* had been shut down at the start of the war, but he started publishing it again under a new name, the *Hawaii Times*. Turning his work over to his only son, he obtained U.S. citizenship and died at age eighty-three.

The most well known Japanese in Hawaii, Reverend Takie Okumura, was not arrested by the FBI. Until the start of the war he had single-mindedly pushed for Americanization, and he was too frail to arrest due to his advanced age. He died five years after the war ended, at age eighty-six, without witnessing the right of naturalization granted to Japanese. Since Okumura had constantly regarded the Buddhists as the enemy of his Americanization movement, the Japanese community in Hawaii remains reluctant to show much appreciation for his efforts.

Among those sent on the first ship to the U.S. mainland relocation camps from Sand Island was former Waialua union president Tokuji Baba, who had made a meager living as an innkeeper after his release from prison. He was one of eighty Hawaiian internees who chose to return to Japan during the war. Although he had given up his inheritance to his nephew, who succeeded to the family business, as an eldest son Baba retained his rights to become the head of the family. After spending twelve years idling away his days at his family home, he returned to Hawaii where he died at the age of ninety-two.

Chikao Ishida, who had returned to his post as Japanese-language school principal after release from prison, was relocated to the mainland along with his second wife and two preschool children. As the Japanese-language schools remained closed after the war, he had to put his children through school by working in a Honolulu macaroni factory. Ishida died at age seventy-nine, after obtaining American citizenship.

Many in the Japanese community in Hawaii wondered how Kinza-burō Makino, president of the *Hawaii hōchi*, evaded arrest by the FBI. He led the campaign on behalf of the Japanese-language schools suit, and he constantly badgered the haole governing class by asserting the rights of Japanese residents. In contrast to Sōga of *Nippu jiji*, however,

Makino was not involved with the Japanese Consulate, nor did he have any dealings with the elite Japanese businessmen who looked down on immigrants. According to Yoshimi Mizuno, who served as a maid in the Makino household for many years (and was treated like a daughter), Makino packed his necessities in a suitcase in the trunk of his car so that he would be prepared in case he was arrested.

According to Mizuno, after the war began a "Mr. Shivers" often visited the Makino house. Robert Shivers, head of the FBI's Hawaii office, had been posted to Hawaii as relations between the United States and Japan declined. "Mr. Shivers would drop by on weekend evenings on his way back from a drive with his wife," she recalled. "He would talk for a bit with Uncle [Makino] and then go home. He never did stay for dinner." Mizuno took these lightly, as casual visits by a friend, but no one at Makino's newspaper knew of his association with Shivers, not even Kumaichi Kumazaki, who for decades worked closely with Makino and was in charge of accounting and other matters. Makino's residence, an isolated house facing the ocean at a distance from central Honolulu, was far from the gaze of others, ideal for clandestine meetings. Kinzaburō Makino had personally invested the profits from his Makino law office in real estate, not in the *Hawaii hōchi* newspaper company. When he died at age seventy-six, eight years after the war, Makino left a large inheritance for his wife, far greater than others had imagined he had. If, at the end of his life, he thought that he had lost to Sōga, his main regret must have been that, despite being very fond of children, he did not leave any successors.

Ichiji Gotō, who assisted the aging Makino until the end, shouldered the editorial work of the *Hawaii hōchi*. Gotō never forgot his debt of gratitude to Makino for hiring him after his release from prison. He too evaded arrest after the war began. Shortly after Makino's death, Gotō left with his second wife to retire to Kannawa hot springs in Beppu City, Kyūshū. A deeply religious man, he spent each day reading a verse from the Bible until his death at age eighty-eight.

Hiroshima was the home prefecture of the greatest number of Japanese immigrants in Hawaii, so many returned there before the war broke out. Many experienced the atomic bombing of Hiroshima, among them Hiroshi Miyazawa, secretary of the Federation of Japanese Labor during the 1920 strike, and Jirō Hayakawa, who was secretary general of the association after the strike. Unable to work as a pastor after his release from prison, Miyazawa had left Hawaii for Hiroshima, his wife's hometown. During the war he found himself under harsh police surveillance because he had lived abroad, but the atomic bomb liberated him. Fortunately Miyazawa survived the blast to live nearly twenty years more; he died at age seventy-seven.

After Japan's defeat, the Allied Occupation forces arrived in Japan to bring democracy to Japan's burned out cities and devastated population. The first general election under democracy was held in April 1946. In the first electoral district of Shiga prefecture thirty-five candidates ran for six seats, numbers that reflected public enthusiasm for the new political era. Seven of these candidates belonged to the newly organized Japan Socialist party. Two of the Socialist candidates won. One was Kizaburō Yao, president of Shiga Nichinichi Tsūshin press, who had been in the prefectural assembly for many years; the other was Noboru Tsutsumi, an unknown candidate.

Tsutsumi ran as a Socialist but was not officially recognized as a candidate by the party. When Tsutsumi saw his comrades from the prewar proletariat movement declare their candidacy (Mosaburō Suzuki in Tokyo, Suehiro Nishio in Osaka, and Chōzaburō Mizutani in Kyoto), he could not remain a bystander. Although he had neither campaign funds nor physical strength, he wished to be part of the new era. He declared his candidacy from his childhood home, the temple at Kōzuhata. Carrying rice balls in a lunchbox tied to his waist, he campaigned on a bicycle with a megaphone in hand. His eloquence of twenty-six years earlier came to life again, as he spoke of his experience leading the Hawaiian sugarcane workers in their demands for a wage increase. At first his only ally was his wife, Tsuruyo, but later his second son, then a university student, and the cousins he had grown up with plunged in to help with the campaign. In the end, beating all predictions, Tsutsumi won election with 39,225 votes, the third largest number.

Since food was still scarce, Tsutsumi, the newly elected Diet member, left his wife and family in Kyoto. He boarded the packed train to Tokyo alone, carrying rice and soy sauce on his back and finding a seat only in the rest room. His throat, which he injured in the campaign, never recovered. At the end of the year, he collapsed in the National Diet building. Tsuruyo, who had just given birth to a daughter, Mihoko, in January 1947, rushed to Tokyo with the new baby on her back. With difficulty she purchased penicillin on the black market, but Tsutsumi's tuberculosis had progressed too far. On February 20, 1947, Noboru Tsutsumi died at age fifty-seven. The inscription on his gravestone at the temple at Kōzuhata, his family home, reads "Remains of Noboru

Kaishinin Shakuhō, third son of fifteenth-generation head priest Rei-zui." Tsutsumi had never told Tsuruyo that he had been baptized as a Christian.

Widowed at the age of thirty-four, Tsuruyo decided to fulfill her husband's dreams as a politician, despite opposition from those around her who thought it ill-advised. Undiscouraged by defeat in her first attempt, she was elected to the Diet two years later, her little daughter Mihoko at her side. She carried on her husband's political legacy for three terms. From a woman's perspective she pursued such issues as the repatriation of Japanese emigrants from abroad, aid for war widows and surviving families, and the curbing of prostitution. She also served as director of the Socialist party's Shiga prefecture union women's department.

In 1951 Tsuruyo Tsutsumi was a member of the Japanese delegation to the signing of the San Francisco Peace Treaty and the U.S.-Japan Security Treaty that marked the end of the six-year Occupation of Japan. On her trip back to Japan Tsuruyo was able to realize her husband's dream of visiting Hawaii once again.

More than thirty years had passed since the second Oahu strike. Although the six-month strike had shaken the haole governing class in Hawaii, Tsuruyo could not find anyone who remembered Noboru Tsutsumi's name. The Hawaii that Tsuruyo saw on her visit was no longer the Hawaii that Noboru had known. During the war Hawaii's military-dependent economy had grown, with accompanying rapid changes, such as new roadways on a par with the mainland. Thousands of American servicemen had passed through the islands during the war, and on the mainland the public now saw Hawaii as a "tropical Paradise." Air travel accelerated Hawaii's growth as a tourist mecca, and from 1945 income from tourism grew 20 percent per year on average. At the time of Tsuruyo's visit tourism was about to overtake the sugar industry as the major source of revenue for Hawaii.

In the cane fields mechanization progressed, resulting in annual decreases in the labor force. The number of Japanese laborers declined drastically. The issei who had gone to Hawaii to work the cane fields were now elderly, and the nisei had acquired education that freed them from backbreaking physical labor. The vast majority of nisei employed on the sugar plantations now worked in the company's business office or as skilled workers in the mills.

The majority of the field laborers were Filipino, many of whom had left the plantations during the war to work on military construction sites.

Construction jobs were plentiful and pay scales were the same as on the mainland. In 1946 organizers sent by the International Longshoremen Workers' Union (ILWU) to unionize the sugar plantation workers in Hawaii staged a major strike. It centered on Olaa Plantation, the site of the Sakamaki house dynamiting, where second-generation Japanese Americans organized a local labor struggle. The strike victory telegram sent to ILWU headquarters on the mainland declared that Hawaii was no longer a "feudal" territory and that paternalism had been overthrown.

As the labor union movement spread, the wages in Hawaii's sugar plantations became the highest in the world for sugar industry labor. Indeed, rising wages were a major factor in the decline of the Hawaiian sugar industry, which had to compete with cheap labor elsewhere. As tourism supplanted the sugar industry in economic importance, plantations were reduced in size or closed down. All over the Hawaiian Islands, cane fields were turned into housing developments, airports, golf courses, and resort facilities. By the 1980s many of these projects were financed by Japanese capital.

Olaa Plantation (now called Puna Sugar Company), one of the few plantations left on the island of Hawaii, closed down in 1984. It was not only the Japanese community that changed as leadership passed from one generation to another after Pearl Harbor. With Hawaii placed under military control after the war began, the kamaaina, the plutocracy that dominated prewar Hawaii, lost their clout overnight.

Walter Dillingham was an exception. After the war he expanded his businesses even further. Not only did he sell his land and plantation to the military at an opportune time, he developed the Hawaiian Dredging Company into a construction company to build tourist facilities. Many high-rise hotels and major shopping centers that Japanese tourists have visited over the years were built by Dillingham's company. A nine-page article in the February 10, 1961, issue of *Life* magazine introduced Walter Dillingham's family as "Hawaii's first family." A photograph of the entire clan showed that even at eighty-five Dillingham remained the powerful head of the family. According to the article, Dillingham still went to his office several times a week to look after his various enterprises.

In 1962, the year after the *Life* article appeared, Dillingham's third son ran for the Senate as a Republican party candidate. The campaign became the most costly ever waged in Hawaii. Despite predictions to the contrary, he was defeated by the Democratic candidate, Daniel Inouye, a second-generation Japanese American.

When the war began the nisei, despite their American citizenship, were given a draft classification as "enemy aliens," which kept them out of military service. Swallowing this humiliation, many nisei from Hawaii and mainland detention centers volunteered for military service to prove their loyalty to the United States. The 442d Regimental Combat Team, made up of nisei troops, became the most highly decorated unit in the wartime history of the United States and ensured future standing for the nisei as loyal Americans. Dan Inouye, the son of an immigrant field worker from Fukuoka prefecture, was a member of the nisei battalion and lost an arm on the Italian front.

The Walter-McCarran Immigration and Naturalization Act of 1952 finally gave to Japanese and other Asians the right to naturalize. What swayed Congress in favor of this bill was the war record of the nisei battalion. Nisei soldiers who returned safely from the front used the GI bill to go to college, opening the way to positions that their parents never imagined possible.

In Hawaii, many nisei veterans used their war records to go into politics. Voted in by the Japanese American population majority in Hawaii, these nisei politicians were so influential that they practically took over the Hawaiian political world. Dan Inouye, the most successful, entered politics as a member of the House of Representatives in the first Congress after Hawaii gained statehood, and two years later, he successfully ran for Senate.

Walter Dillingham, the last surviving member of the powerful kamaaina governing elite, died at age eighty-eight the year after Inouye defeated his son in the Senate race. His entry in the Hawaii *Who's Who* runs several pages, longer than any other, and it mentions what may be his only failure, the petition for renewal of the importation of Chinese labor. The entry notes that he did his utmost on the issue but does not mention what the result was.

In his autobiography Yasutarō Sōga described the 1920 strike as follows:

> The strike was settled after some difficulties. But the aftereffects of the Olaa dynamiting incident were not allowed to remain untouched. After the earnest effort of investigation by the district attorney's office, fifteen members of the Federation of Japanese Labor including Tsutsumi were arrested for conspiracy. . . . They were all declared guilty . . . and sent to prison. . . . Not all of the defendants had conspired to commit the crime. Among those Federation

leaders who were imprisoned, apparently some know nothing of the incident. . . . It is unknown how much was gathered during the second great
strike for the strike fund from the islands. It was said that the amount was at
least $200,000–$300,000.[15]

The discrepancy between the figures publicly reported by the federation at the time of the strike and the amount noted by Sōga indicates that
he had not necessarily checked the facts. Sōga was more than seventy
years old when he wrote his recollections, based on his memory of the
trial twenty-one years earlier, but his comments appear to justify the testimony of Matsumoto and Saitō, the two key prosecution witnesses.[16]
As a record of the recollections of a respected newspaper editor who was
knowledgeable about the events of his day, Sōga's comments on the
1920 strike and the trial of the Federation of Japanese Labor leaders
who led it have been treated as fact by others.

In 1964 members of Hawaii's Japanese-language press published
Hawaii Nihonjin iminshi (History of Japanese Immigration in Hawaii)
to commemorate the centennial of Japanese immigration to Hawaii. An
important volume that traced the footprints of the Japanese immigrants
for the first time, it was regarded as historically factual, but it treats the
Sakamaki case very much as Sōga did: "The Sakamaki house dynamiting case was detrimental as the strike had gone on in a just and fair manner without any incidents of violence. After this incident, the situation
changed entirely."[17] The entry was even shorter than Sōga's, and concluded that the federation had certainly been involved in the Sakamaki
house dynamiting case. It also noted that reasons for the failure of the
strike were "the lack of character and aptitude among some of the leaders [and] misappropriation of funds. . . . The local labor unions organized by them disappeared after the end of the strike." This last sentence
is the only one that is close to being accurate.

NOTES

PROLOGUE

1. Territory of Hawaii v. I. Sato et al., Circuit Court of the First Circuit Court, Territory of Hawaii (February 2, 1922).

2. *Tobei*, November 12, 1907.

3. E. Alexander Powell, "Are We Giving Japan a Square Deal?" *Atlantic Monthly*, no. 1281 (December 1921): 536–544.

1. THE JAPANESE VILLAGE IN THE PACIFIC

1. Edward D. Beechert, *Working in Hawaii: A Labor History* (Honolulu: University of Hawaii Press, 1985), 159–169.

2. *Nippu jiji*, May 31, 1909.

3. *Labor World* changed its name to *Shakaishugi* (Socialism), and would later be reissued as *Tobeikyōkai kikanshi* (Going to America Society Magazine).

4. Foreign Ministry Archives, *Tokubetsu yōshisatsunin jōsei ippan*, August 31, 1909.

5. The *Tokubetsu yōshisatsunin jōsei ippan* described the IWW as "established in 1905 in the Northern United States [*sic*] with the aim of improving the status of workers, its headquarters are in Chicago with branches in the U.S. as well as in newly settled areas such as Australia and it engages in extremely radical activities."

6. *Hikari*, March 28, 1906.

7. Ibid.

8. *Berkeley Daily Gazette,* December 16, 1906.
9. *Nichibei,* June 28, 1909.

2. A PERSON TO BE WATCHED

1. Here is the information regarding persons with the name "Tsutsumi" to be found in roll numbers 919, 921, 945, and 949 of the Investigative Case Files of the Federal Bureau of Investigation (1908–1922), National Archives:

> H. Tsutsumi; subject Yoshie Takahashi is connected with above.—subject is engaged in business in New York. (October 1, 1921)
> Hideo Tsutsumi; subject age 32 arrival in San Francisco. Is Professor of Electricity and Engineering at Waseda University, Tokio. Will remain in U.S. 3 months. Information on back of photo. (February 25, 1921) [Prof. Hideo Tsutsumi was renowned in the field of electrical physics and nuclear engineering.]
> M. Tsutsumi; subject registered at William Penn Hotel (N.Y.) on 5–26–21.
> H. Tsutsumi; Suzuki Tadashi is connected with the above Japanese . . . (illegible) organization. (October 1, 1921)

All of these men entered the United States on the mainland.

2. National Archives, Investigative Case Files of the Federal Bureau of Investigation, January 28, 1921, report on Japanese Affairs (Honolulu and Hawaii Islands); referring to *Los Angeles Weekly Intelligence Report* for January 13, 1921, pp. 26, 27, 28.

3. Yasujirō Tsutsumi, the founder of the Seibu group of companies, hailed from a nearby village. Though unrelated, he was of the same generation as Noboru Tsutsumi and his brothers.

4. The character Noboru can also be pronounced "Ryū," a homophone for the word "dragon."

5. Interview, Kimiko Kurokawa.

6. *Honolulu Star Bulletin,* June 22, 1918.

7. Hawaii kyōikukai hensanbu, ed., *Hawaii Nihongo kyōikushi* (Honolulu, 1937), 6.

3. THE OAKU STRIKE BEGINS

1. "Nyū Yoriku yori," *Shin shakai,* February 18.
2. Beechert, *Working in Hawaii,* 196–197.
3. *Hawaii hōchi,* November 10, 1919.
4. Ibid., November 4, 1919.
5. By the beginning of the strike one additional plantation was included.
6. *Honolulu Advertiser,* December 13, 1919.
7. *Nippu jiji,* December 15, 1919.
8. National Archives, Investigative Files of the Federal Bureau of Investigation, Japanese Affairs (Honolulu and Hawaiian Islands), Report dated February 5, 1921.
9. *Hawaii hōchi,* January 5, 1920.

10. *Hawaiian Annual,* 1910.
11. *Hawaii hōchi,* January 30, 1920.

4. THE JAPANESE CONSPIRACY

1. *Jiji shinpō,* January 31, 1920.
2. The *Jiji shinpō* reported on February 11, 1920, "Korean and Chinese were called in as replacements for Japanese on strike." Rather than stress the fact that Japanese laborers had caused disturbances in American territory, the Japanese press focused on the actions of the Koreans to the disadvantage of Japanese.
3. National Archives, Investigative Files of the Federal Bureau of Investigation, Japanese Affairs (Honolulu and Hawaiian Islands), Washington, D.C., Report dated January 18, 1921.
4. *Nippu jiji,* October 28, 1919.
5. Sam Nishimura, Oral History Project, University of Hawaii.
6. National Archives, Investigative Files of the Federal Bureau of Investigation, Japanese Affairs (Honolulu and Hawaiian Islands), Report dated January 22, 1921.
7. Interview, Tsuneichi Yamamoto.
8. Interview, Ryōkin Toyohira, former *Nippu jiji* reporter.
9. Interview, Takeshi Haga.
10. Foreign Ministry Archives, Kurusu to Uchida, March 22, 1920.
11. Oral History Project, University of Hawaii.
12. Oral History Project, University of Hawaii.
13. Interview, Violet Fujinaka.
14. Serphine Robello, fifteen at the time, later an electrician. Oral History Project, University of Hawaii.
15. Sam Nishimura, Oral History Project, University of Hawaii.
16. Antone Camacho, Oral History Project, University of Hawaii.
17. Seiichi Miyasaki, seventeen years old at the time, later a physician. Oral History Project, University of Hawaii.
18. *Hawaii hōchi,* February 4, 1920.
19. *Nippu jiji,* February 23, 1920.
20. Ibid., February 25, 1920.
21. Ibid., November 8, 1919.
22. John E. Reinicke, *Feigned Necessity* (San Francisco: Chinese Materials Center, 1974), 40.
23. Foreign Ministry Archives, Furuya to Uchida, February 26, 1920.
24. *Pacific Commercial Advertiser,* February 28, 1920.
25. *Honolulu Star Bulletin,* February 24, 1920.
26. S. Robello, Portuguese at Waialua Plantation, Oral History Project, University of Hawaii.
27. *Pacific Commercial Advertiser,* February 14, 1920; March 3, 1920.
28. Interview, Ryōkin Toyohira.
29. *Hawaii hōchi,* March 23, 1920.
30. Ibid.

31. Foreign Ministry Archives, Ueno to Foreign Minister, July 14, 1909.
32. Ibid.
33. Ibid., June 17, 1909.
34. Foreign Ministry Archives, Arita to Katō, July 23, 1915.
35. *Honolulu Advertiser,* April 2, 1920.
36. *Hawaii hōchi,* April 4, 1920.
37. Foreign Ministry Archives, Furuya to Uchida, April 6, 1920.
38. *Hawaii hōchi* April 3, 1920.
39. *Hawaii shinpō,* April 4, 1920.
40. *Honolulu Star Bulletin,* April 4, 1920.
41. Foreign Ministry Archives, Furuya to Uchida, April 6, 1920.
42. *Jiji shinpō,* May 2, 1920.
43. Ibid.
44. *Hawaii Star Bulletin,* May 20, 1920.
45. Federation of Japanese Labor, *Tsutsumi benmeibun* (Honolulu, 1920).
46. Sōtōshū Hawaii kaikyō sōhonbu, ed., *Sōtōshū Hawaii kaikyō nanajū-gonenshi* (Honolulu: Hawaii Sōtōshū kyōkai, n.d.).
47. Foreign Ministry Archives, Furuya to Uchida, July 3, 1920. Emphasis added.
48. Ibid.
49. An English translation may be in *Pacific Commercial Advertiser,* July 2, 1920.
50. *Nippu jiji,* August 16, 1920.
51. *Honolulu Star Bulletin,* July 10, 1920.
52. *San Francisco Chronicle,* August 20, 1920.
53. *Honolulu Star Bulletin,* July 10, 1920.
54. Hawaiian Sugar Planters' Association, *Proceedings of the Fortieth Meeting* (Honolulu: Honolulu Star Bulletin, 1921). Waterhouse spoke on November 29, 1920.
55. *Hawaii hōchi,* August 14, 1920.
56. Ibid., September 2, 1920.
57. Ibid., August 27, 1920.
58. The Sōtō sect's history gives an example of his expansive personality: Isobe, during his later posting in Los Angeles, invited a parishioner to a restaurant. The parishioner had only $20 and caused a commotion when he found that Isobe had splurged and the bill came to $60. *Sōtōshū Hawaii kaikyō nanajū-gonenshi,* 6.
59. Foreign Ministry Archives, Yada to Uchida, August 20, 1920.
60. Hawaii Sugar Planters' Association, *Proceedings,* 1920.
61. *Hawaii hōchi,* October 16, 1920.
62. Ibid., October 20, 1920.
63. Ibid., October 23, 1920.
64. *Honolulu Advertiser,* January 1, 1921.
65. *Hawaiian Annual,* 1921.
66. Interview, Tazuko Iwasaki.
67. Foreign Ministry Archives, Yada to Uchida, October 20, 1921.

68. Norio Koga, Oral History Project, University of Hawaii.
69. Oral History Project, University of Hawaii.
70. Foreign Ministry Archives, Yada to Uchida, March 9, 1921.

5. THE CONSPIRACY TRIAL

1. *Honolulu Advertiser,* August 1, 1921.
2. *Honolulu Star Bulletin,* August 2, 1921.
3. *Hawaii hōchi,* August 2, 1921.
4. The first names of these Japanese defendants were not used in the trial records. All of the defendants are identified only by first initial from the time of the indictment. Of the 21 men charged, 15, including N. (at times referred to as "T.") Tsutsumi, appeared for the arraignment. Three of the absent men (Y. Satō, K. Miyamura, E. Yokoo) had already returned to Japan, and Jinbo's whereabouts were unknown.
5. The testimony quoted is from the transcript of the Sakamaki house dynamiting case trial. Contemporary newspaper articles were referred to for the portions indicating the atmosphere of the courtroom. *Territory v. I. Sato et al.*
6. Prosecution exhibits (A–D)—the plan of the Sakamaki house, which was the site of the crime, the photograph of the side of the house that had been destroyed (the same one printed in the *Advertiser* at the time of the indictment), an enlargement of a portion of it, and a map of Olaa Plantation—had already been submitted by H. T. Lake, a detective detailed to the legal department of the city and county of Honolulu.

Detective Lake, who went to the Sakamaki house on the morning after the incident to investigate the premises, had later been transferred to the Honolulu police department but had been sent to Olaa just before the indictment to gather details about the case from Sakamaki. The map of Olaa and the plan of the Sakamaki house had been prepared by Lake with Sakamaki's help at the time of this reinvestigation one year after the crime. Lake testified, "I first met him (Sakamaki) when I was senior captain of police of the Island of Hawaii . . . about twenty-two years" ago. This meant that the prosecution had gathered the facts of the case by sending to the scene of the crime a detective who was acquainted with the victim.
7. Eldest son, Paul (Fukuo), 18 (ages were given in the traditional Japanese method of counting the first year as age 1); second son, George (Jōji), 16; third son, Shunzo (Shunzō), 13; eldest daughter, Masa, 8; fifth son, Uuroku (Urio in the transcript; actually Yūroku), 4. Of his last child, Noboru, he said only that he was a one-year-old boy.

Including his seventh son, Ben, who was born after the incident, Sakamaki eventually was able to send all of them to the University of Hawaii. For a time three of his sons were boarding in Honolulu at once. For the Japanese immigrants the education of children was a paramount concern, but most were barely able to send their children through local public high school. This put Sakamaki in the position of being envied and resented by other Japanese.

8. Interview, Masao Koga; from Olaa, graduated from the University of Hawaii.

9. Although the name had already been changed to the Hawaii Laborers' Association, the court used "Federation" throughout, so Federation will be used here.

10. Ryūgai Aoki, *Hawaii jinbutsu hyōron* (Hilo: Seikisha, 1914).

11. Matsumoto was mistaken about these figures also. The amounts announced by the federation were $1,328 for newspapers and magazines and $9,045 for printing and advertisements.

12. *Honolulu Star Bulletin*, August 2, 1921.

13. National Archives, Office of the Assistant Chief of Staff, Military Intelligence, Headquarters, Hawaii Department, Report dated October 2, 1922.

14. Ibid.

15. University of Hawaii, Sinclair Library, Teisuke Terasaki, "Terasaki Teisuke nisshi," 1917-1956, entry dated December 13, 1920. Hereafter cited as Terasaki diary.

16. *Hawaii nenkan*, 1929, lists in the Wainaku district of Hilo "Okinawa, car business, Ineushi Aragaki"—who is most likely the same person.

17. Then Furushō said to him, "'I may have to ask you some other things.'" Saitō said, "He told me that, 'That Hōsen Isobe went in as a go-between to have the strike settled, but he is not speeding the thing up, that we are going to ask him to withdraw from this matter, and I want you to go along with us to his place.'" (There is no testimony as to what happened.)

18. The August 2, 1921, *Honolulu Advertiser* speculated, "One Jinbo, whose full and true name is to the grand jurors unknown, might have been Y. Kosaki who had already went back to Japan." August 2, 1921.

19. *Honolulu Advertiser*, February 16, 1922.

20. Ibid.

21. *Honolulu Star Bulletin*, August 25, 1920.

22. *Hawaii hōchi*, March 5, 1920.

23. From the material at the archives of the Hawaiian Sugar Planters' Association, it is clear that at the time of the strike the HSPA had an exceedingly high fire insurance coverage—$20 million.

24. National Archives, Investigative Files of the Federal Bureau of Investigation, Japanese Affairs (Honolulu and Hawaiian Islands), Report dated February 5, 1921.

25. Ibid.

26. An article in the *Nippu jiji* of that date noted, "Baba's frail figure looked miserable as he weakly waved his hat in encouragement."

27. The *Honolulu Advertiser* published as front page headlines: "Labor Official Is Witness, In the Olaa Dynamite Trial: His Testimony Not Shaken" and "Secretary of Japanese Federation, Enters Complete Denial of State's Witnesses' Stories on Stand."

28. After confirming that it was Tsutsumi who had written the Federation of Japanese Labor report on the strike (prosecution exhibit J), Lymar asked Tsutsumi to read a portion of it. Interpreter Maruyama was unable to interpret this,

so Tsutsumi left the witness stand while S. Shirai, an interpreter assisting the defense, took the stand to interpret the text.

29. *Hawaii hōchi,* April 24, 1920.

30. Ibid., December 23, 1920.

31. Ibid.

32. *Honolulu Advertiser,* March 4, 1922.

33. National Archives, Investigative Files of the Federal Bureau of Investigation, Japanese Affairs (Honolulu and Hawaiian Islands), Report dated February 5, 1921.

34. Instruction No. 25.

35. National Archives, Investigative Files of the Federal Bureau of Investigation, Japanese Affairs (Honolulu and Hawaiian Islands), Report dated February 25, 1922.

36. *Hyōron-no Hyōron,* October 2, 1922.

37. National Archives, February 18, 1922.

6. REOPENING CHINESE IMMIGRATION

1. U.S. House of Representatives, *Labor Problems in Hawaii, Hearings . . . on H. J. Res. 158 and H. J. 171, pt. 1,* 67th Cong., 1st sess. (1921).

2. Foreign Ministry Archives, Moroi to Motono, December 4, 1917.

3. *Honolulu Advertiser,* January 24, 1920.

4. U.S. Senate, *Japanese in Hawaii, Hearings on S. 3206 . . . ,* 66th Cong., 2d sess. (1920).

5. In chapter 3, on the Japanese conspiracy, I mentioned that Senator Phelan gave a speech that seemed to predict war between the United States and Japan. This speech was delivered ten days after he met with Governor McCarthy.

6. *Los Angeles Examiner,* March 20, 1921.

7. Ibid., March 25, 1921.

8. Foreign Ministry Archives, Transcript, Shidehara 'Morris' Conference.

9. Kijūrō Shidehara, *Gaikō gojūnen* (Fifty Years of Diplomacy) (Tokyo: Yomiuri shinbunsha, 1951).

10. National Archives, Investigative Files of the Federal Bureau of Investigation, Japanese Affairs (Honolulu and Hawaiian Islands), Report dated January 22, 1921.

11. *Hawaii hōchi,* April 30, 1921.

12. Foreign Ministry Archives, Kawahara to Foreign Minister, July 3, 1920.

13. Reinicke, *Feigned Necessity,* 80.

14. *Honolulu Advertiser,* May 23, 1921.

15. *Hawaii hōchi,* October 18, 1920.

16. *Honolulu Advertiser,* June 22, 1921.

17. *Kokumin shinbun,* November 5, 1920.

18. Foreign Ministry Archives, Yada to Uchida, iNovember 13, 1920.

19. *Honolulu Advertiser,* June 30, 1921.

20. Reinicke, *Feigned Necessity,* 202-204.

21. U.S. House of Representatives, *Labor Problems in Hawaii*. Other material quoted in this section is taken from this source.

22. *Honolulu Advertiser*, April 1, 1920; *Honolulu Star Bulletin*, July 10, 1920.

23. U.S. House of Representatives, *Labor Problems in Hawaii*.

24. Foreign Ministry Archives, Yamakazi to Uchida, June 15, 1922.

25. Reinicke, *Feigned Necessity*, 224.

26. Yuji Ichioka, *The Issei: The World of the First-Generation Japanese Immigrants, 1885-1924* (New York: Free Press, 1988), 102.

27. U.S. House of Representatives, *Labor Problems in Hawaii*.

28. Ibid.

29. Reinicke, *Feigned Necessity*, 237-244.

30. *Honolulu Advertiser*, August 2, 1921.

31. *San Francisco Chronicle*, August 3, 1921.

32. U.S. Senate, *Immigration into Hawaii. Hearings on S. J. Res. 82 ...*, Pt. 2, 67th Cong., 2d sess. (1922). Other material quoted in this section comes from the same source.

33. Reinicke, *Feigned Necessity*, 305.

34. *Honolulu Star Bulletin*, November 16, 1921.

35. National Archives, Assistant Chief of Staff, Military Intelligence, Hawaii Department, Report dated February 18, 1922.

36. Foreign Ministry Archives, Uchida to Shidehara, March 25, 1922.

37. National Archives, Investigative Files of the Federal Bureau of Investigation, Japanese Affairs (Honolulu and Hawaiian Islands), Report dated January 16, 1922.

38. It has already been mentioned that in the immigration card file preserved at the Consulate the cards for Kan'ichi Takizawa and Chūhei Hoshino were marked in red ink: "Warning: dangerous person who attempted to bring charges against Consul General Yada." Although the specific details cannot be known, it appears that the "attitude of the Consul General" seen as problematic by the federation representatives at this meeting with Shibusawa was not unrelated to the incident with Takizawa and Hoshino.

39. National Archives, Investigative Files of the Federal Bureau of Investigation, Japanese Affairs (Honolulu and Hawaiian Islands), Report dated January 16, 1922.

40. *Tokyo asahi*, January 30, 1922.

41. Thereafter, the Sakamaki house dynamiting case was handled as *Territory of Hawaii v. I. Goto et al.*

42. James Phelan, "The Hawaiian Situation," *Congressional Record*, April 13, 1922.

43. Foreign Ministry Archives, Saburi to Uchida, April 24, 1922.

44. U.S. Senate, *Immigration into Hawaii*, Pt. 2. Other material quoted in this section comes from the same source.

45. *Nippu jiji*, June 28, 1922.

46. Reinicke, *Feigned Necessity*, 462. Judging that Japanese were incapable of becoming assimilated, the commission report also warned: "Commission fully appreciates dangers of menace of alien domination by one race and strongly rec-

ommends question of national defense should receive prompt remedial legislation." As the report dealt with foreign policy matters, it was classified top secret.

47. National Archives, Investigative Files of the Federal Bureau of Investigation, Japanese Affairs (Honolulu and Hawaiian Islands), Report dated August 7, 1922.

48. Message of the Honorable W. R. Farrington, Governor of Hawaii, to the Legislature, Territory of Hawaii, February 21, 1923, 13.

49. National Archives, Investigative Files of the Federal Bureau of Investigation, Japanese Affairs (Honolulu and Hawaiian Islands), Report dated August 6, 1923.

50. Yasutarō Sōga of the *Nippu*, who had been sent to the same prison some ten years earlier due to his actions in the first Oahu strike, noted in his reminiscences: "Although I had resigned myself, it was still with a sense of unutterable loneliness that I first entered prison." *Gojūnenkan no Hawaii kaiko*.

51. *Hawaii hōchi*, March 14, 1924.

52. Ibid.

7. THE JAPANESE EXCLUSION ACT

1. Reinicke, *Feigned Necessity*, 481.

2. U.S. Senate, *Japanese Immigration Legislation. Hearings . . . on S. 2576*. 68th Cong., 1st sess. (1924).

3. Foreign Ministry Archives, Ōyama to Shidehara, August 3, 1924.

4. *Honululu Advertiser*, June 26, 1923.

5. Foreign Ministry Archives, Hanihara to Shidehara, June 10, 1924.

6. Yasutarō Sōga, *Gojūnenkan no Hawaii kaiko* (Recollections of Fifty Years in Hawaii) (Honolulu, 1953).

7. *Tōkyō*, September 1924.

8. Ichioka, *The Issei*, 250–251.

9. *Tōkyō*, September 1924.

10. Leading the protest were Kokuryūkai (Black Dragon Society; Amur River Society), Zuihokai, Ōkoku seinendan (Imperial Youth Group), Shishintō, Kinnōresshitō, Asia kyōkai, Yūkoku seishinkai, Taibei dōshikai, Tōyō renmei kyōkai, and Dainihon rokuji gun.

11. Sōga, *Gojūnenkan no Hawaii kaiko*.

12. Tsutsumi and Hoshino had begun serving their sentences a year before Gotō and the others who had appealed, so their release was earlier as well. This meant that Tsutsumi and Manlapit, president of the Filipino Labor Union, the two leaders who had struggled together against the HSPA, had overlapped at the Oahu prison for three months.

13. Sōga, *Gojūnenkan no Hawaii kaiko*.

14. Foreign Ministry Archives, Satō to Shidehara, July 12, 1931.

15. *Gojūnenkan no Hawaii kaiko* is meaningful to read to observe Sōga's experiences and impression of events but is problematical as a record of fact.

16. Sōga, *Gojūnenkan no Hawaii kaiko*.

17. Hawaii Nihonjin iminshi kankō iinkai, ed., *Hawaii Nihonjin iminshi* (Honolulu: Hawaii Nihonjin rengō kyōkai, 1964).

BIBLIOGRAPHY

ARCHIVES

Foreign Ministry Archives, Consulate General of Japan, Honolulu, Reports on immigration, 1908–1924, Tokyo, Japan.

Foreign Ministry Archives, Materials on immigration to the United States, 1910–1924, Tokyo, Japan.

Foreign Ministry Archives, Materials on passage of 1924 Immigration Act, Tokyo, Japan.

National Archives, Investigative Files of the Federal Bureau of Investigation, Japanese Affairs (Honolulu and Hawaiian Islands), 1917–1925, Washington, D.C.

National Archives, Office of the Secretary, U.S. Department of the Interior, Materials on Japanese immigration and activities in the territory of Hawaii, 1919–1924, Washington, D.C.

National Archives, U.S. Department of State, Materials on relations with Japan 1920–1924, Washington, D.C.

Territory of Hawaii v. I. Sato, M. Miyazawa, C. Ishida, T. Murakami, T. Koyama, S. Kondo, T. Baba, H. Fujitani, K. Furusho, F. Kawamata, K. Takizawa, S. Tomoda, C. Hoshino, T. Tsutsumi, et al., Circuit Court of the First Judicial Circuit, Territory of Hawaii, January Term, 1922. Transcript. (Copy in possession of author.)

University of Hawaii, Oral History Project, Social Science Research Institute, Honolulu. (Interviews of Antone Camacho, Barbara Gibson, Noriyu Koga, Seiichi Miyazaki, Nobuyuki Nakatsu, Sam Nishimura, William Rego, Seraphine Robello)

GOVERNMENT PUBLICATIONS

Foreign Ministry of Japan. *Nihon gaikō monjo* (1919–1924). Tokyo: Gaimusho.

——. *Nihon gaikō monjo: Tai-Bei imin mondai keika gaiyō*. 2. vols. Tokyo, 1980.

——. *Nihon gaikō monjo: Washington kaigi gumbi seigen mondai*. Tokyo, 1974.

State of California. Reclamation Board. *Report, 1912*. Sacramento: California State Printing Office, 1913.

——. *Report, 1916*. Sacramento: California State Printing Office, 1916.

U.S. House of Representatives. *Japanese Immigration. Hearings Before the House Committee on Immigration and Naturalization. Part 1*. 66th Cong., 2d sess. (1920).

——. *Japanese Immigration. Hearings Before the House Committee on Immigration and Naturalization. Part 2*. 66th Cong., 2d sess. (1920).

——. *Japanese Immigration. Hearings Before the House Committee on Immigration and Naturalization. Part 3*. 66th Cong., 2d sess. (1920).

——. *Labor Problems in Hawaii. Hearings Before the House Committee on Immigration and Naturalization on H. J. Res. 158 and on H. J. Res. 171. Part 1*. 67th Cong., 1st sess. (1921).

——. *Labor Problems in Hawaii. Hearings Before the Committee on Immigration and Naturalization, House of Representatives on H. J. Res. 158 and on H. J. Res. 171. Part 2*. 67th Cong., 1st sess. (1921).

——. *Labor Problems in Hawaii. Hearings Before the Committee on Immigration and Naturalization, House of Representatives on H. J. Res. 158 and on H. J. Res. 171. Part 3*. 67th Cong., 1st sess. (1921).

——. *Labor Problems in Hawaii. Report to accompany H. J. Res. 171*. 67th Cong., 4th sess. House Report Nr. 1717 (1923).

U.S. Senate. *Immigration into Hawaii. Hearings on S. J. Res. 82 Before the Senate Committee on Immigration*. 67th Cong., 1st sess. (1921).

——. *Immigration into Hawaii. Hearings on S. J. Res. 82 Before the Senate Committee on Immigration. Part 2*. 67th Cong., 2d sess. (1922).

——. *Immigration to Relieve an Emergency Caused by a Shortage of Labor in Hawaii*. 67th Cong. 4th sess. Senate Report Nr. 1252 (1923).

——. *Japanese in Hawaii. Hearings on S. 3206 Before the Senate Committee on Immigration*. 66th Cong., 2d sess. (1920).

——. *Japanese Immigration Legislation. Hearings Before the Senate Committee on Immigration on. S. 2576*. 68th Cong., 1st sess. (1924).

NEWSPAPERS AND PERIODICALS

Hawaiian Annual. Honolulu.
The Hawaiian Planters' Record. Honolulu.
Hawaii hōchi. Honolulu.
Hawaii shinpō. Honolulu.
Honolulu Advertiser.
Honolulu Star Bulletin.

Jiji shinpō. Tokyo.
Nippu jiji. Honolulu.
Tobei. Tokyo.

ENGLISH-LANGUAGE PUBLICATIONS

Adler, Jacob. *Claus Spreckels: The Sugar King of Hawaii.* Honolulu: University of Hawaii Press, 1966.

Beechert, Edward D. *Working in Hawaii: A Labor History.* Honolulu: University of Hawaii Press, 1985.

Bottomley, W. T. *A Statement Concerning the Sugar Industry in Hawaii: Labor Conditions on Hawaiian Sugar Plantations; Filipino Laborers Thereon, and the Alleged Filipino "Strike" of 1924.* Honolulu: Hawaiian Sugar Planters' Association, 1924.

California Farmers Co-operative Association. *Japanese Immigration and the Japanese in California: California Farmers Co-operative Association.* N.p., n.d.

Conroy, Francis Hilary. "The Japanese Penetration into Hawaii, 1868–1898." Ph.D. dissertation, University of California, 1949.

Damon, Ethel. *Koamalu: A Story of Pioneers in Kauai and What They Built in That Garden Island.* Privately published, 1931.

Dean, Arthur L. *Alexander Baldwin, Ltd., and the Predecessor Partnerships.* Honolulu: Alexander & Baldwin, 1956.

Dubofsky, Melvyn. *Big Bill Haywood.* New York: St. Martin's. 1987.

Dubofsky, Melvyn, and W. Van Tine. *Labor Leaders in America.* Urbana: University of Illinois Press, 1987.

DuPuy, William A. *Hawaii and Its Race Problem.* Washington, D.C.: Government Printing Office, 1932.

Ehrmann, Herbert B. *The Case That Will Not Die: Commonwealth vs. Sacco and Vanzetti.* New York: Little, Brown, 1969.

Emmet, Boris. *The California and Hawaiian Sugar Refining Corporation.* Stanford: Stanford University Press, 1928.

Foner, Philip S. *History of the Labor Movement in the United States.* Vols. 6–8. New York: International Publisher, 1982.

Frankfurter, M. D., and G. Jackson, eds. *The Letters of Sacco and Vanzetti.* New York: Viking, 1928.

Hawaiian Sugar Planters' Association. *Proceedings of the Fortieth Meeting.* Honolulu: Honolulu Star Bulletin, 1921.

————. *The Sugar Industry of Hawaii and the Labor Shortage: What It Means to the United States and Hawaii.* Honolulu: Hawaiian Sugar Planters' Association, n.d.

Hawaii Laborers' Association. *Facts About the Strike on Sugar Plantations in Hawaii.* Honolulu: Hawaii Laborers' Association, 1920.

Ichioka, Yuji. *The Issei: The World of the First-Generation Japanese Immigrants, 1885–1924.* New York: Free Press, 1988.

Johannessen, Edward. *The Hawaiian Labor Movement: A Brief History.* Boston: Bruce Humphries, 1956.

Kanzaki, Kiichi. *California and the Japanese.* N.p., n.d.

Kent, Harold W. *Charles Reed Bishop.* Palo Alto, Calif.: Pacific Books, 1965.

Kinney, W. A. *Hawaii's Capacity for Self-Government All But Destroyed.* Salt Lake City: F. Jensen, 1927.

Krauss, Bob, and W. P. Alexander. *Grove Farm Plantation.* Honolulu: Pacific Books, 1976.

Kuykendall, Ralph S. *The Hawaiian Kingdom.* Vol. 3. *1874–1893: The Kalakaua Dynasty.* Honolulu: University of Hawaii Press, 1967.

MacDonald, Alexander. *Revolt in Paradise: The Social Revolution in Hawaii after Pearl Harbor.* New York: Steven Day, 1944.

McGovern, George S., and Leonard F. Guttridge. *The Great Coalfield War.* Houghton Mifflin, 1972.

Montgomery, David. *The Fall of the House of Labor.* Cambridge: Cambridge University Press, 1987.

———. *Worker's Control in America.* Cambridge: Cambridge University Press, 1979.

Porteus, Stanley D. *A Century of Social Thinking in Hawaii.* Palo Alto, Calif.: Pacific Books, 1962.

Powell, E. Alexander. "Are We Giving Japan A Square Deal?" *Atlantic Monthly,* no. 1281 (1921).

Reinicke, John E. *Feigned Necessity.* San Francisco: Chinese Materials Center, 1974.

Russell, Francis. *Tragedy in Dedham: The Story of the Sacco and Vanzetti Case.* New York: McGraw-Hill, 1971.

Sacramento Bee. *Our New Racial Problem: Japanese Immigration and Its Menace.* Sacramento: Sacramento Bee, 1920.

Sakamaki, Shunzo. *Japan and the United States, 1790–1853.* Tokyo: Asiatic Society of Japan, 1940.

Samuels, Frederick. *The Japanese and the Haoles of Honolulu.* New Haven, Conn.: College and University Press, 1970.

Smith, Gibbs M. *Joe Hill.* Salt Lake City: University of Utah Press, 1969.

Thurston, Lorrin A. *Memoirs of the Hawaiian Revolution.* Honolulu: Honolulu Advertiser Publishing, 1936.

Vandercook, John W. *King Cane: The Story of Sugar in Hawaii.* New York: Harper and Brothers, 1939.

Worden, William L. *Cargoes: Matson's First Century in the Pacific.* Honolulu: University of Hawaii Press, 1981.

Yardley, Paul T. *Millstones and Milestones: The Career of B. F. Dillingham.* Honolulu: B. F. Dillingham Co., 1981.

Zalburg, Sanford. *A Spark Is Struck.* Honolulu: University of Hawaii Press, 1979.

JAPANESE-LANGUAGE PUBLICATIONS

Aikawa, Masao. *Hawaii Nihonjin meikan.* Honolulu, 1927.

Akaishi, Seiichi. *Beikoku imin hō kōwa.* Tokyo: Hakubundo, 1929.

Aoki, Ryūgai. *Hawaii jinbutsu hyōron.* Hilo: Seikisha, 1914.

Hawaii hōchi, comp. *Nihongo gakkō shōso jisshūnen kinen shi*. Honolulu: Hawaii hōchi sha, 1937.

Hawaii kyōikukai hensanbu, ed. *Hawaii Nihongo kyōikushi*. Honolulu, 1937.

Hawaii Nihonjin iminshi kankō iinkai, ed. *Hawaii Nihonjin iminshi*. Honolulu: Hawaii Nihonjin rengō kyōkai, 1964.

Hawaii shinpōsha. *Hawaii Nihonjin nenkan*. Honolulu: 1921–1924.

Hayashi, Saburō. *Hawaii jitsugyō annai*. Kona: Kona hanyōsha, 1909.

Hayashi, Yoshimitsu, ed. *Hawaii jijō*. Honolulu, 1921.

Honda, Ryokusen. *Densha nisshi o kataru*. N.p.: Ryokusen Honda, 1956.

Imamura, Emō. *Hawaii kaikyōshiyō*. Honolulu: Honpa Honganji Mission, 1918.

Isobe, Hōsen. *Bukkyō kaigai dendō shi*. N.p.: Hokubei sanzenshūji, 1932.

Katayama, Sen. *Jiden*. Tokyo: Iwanami shoten, 1954.

———. *Tobei annai*. Tokyo: Rōdō shinbunsha, 1901.

Kawazoe Kenpū kankō kyōkai, ed. *Imin hyakunen no nenrin*. N.p.: Kawazoe Kenpū kankō kyōkai, 1968.

Kihara, Ryūichi, ed. *Hawaii Nihonjinshi*. Tokyo: Bunseisha, 1935.

Kishimoto, Eitarō, Watanabe Haruo, and Koyama Hirotake. *Katayama Sen*. 2 vols. Tokyo: Miraisha, 1959.

Kokumin shinbunsha, ed. *Kokumin nenkan*. Tokyo: Minyūsha, 1917.

Makino Kinzaburō den hensan iinkai, ed. *Makino Kanzaburō den*. Honolulu, 1965.

Murasaki, Namitarō, ed. *Saikin Hawaii annai*. Honolulu: Hawaii annaisha, 1920.

Nerai, Genshi. *Hawaii hōki ruishū*. N.p.: Motoshige shosekibu, 1909.

Nippu jiji, ed. *Hawaii nenkan*. Honolulu: Nippu jiji, 1919–1929.

Okumura, Takie. *Onchō shichijūnen*. Honolulu, 1935.

Ōsumi, Asanori. *Saishin no Hawaii jijō*. Tokyo: Kaigai kenkyūsha, 1932.

Ōuchi, Hyōe, and Kōsaka Etsurō, eds. *Suzuki Mōsaburō senshū*. Tokyo: Rōdō daigaku, 1970.

Shidehara, Kijūrō. *Gaikō gojūnen*. Tokyo: Yomiuri shinbunsha, 1951.

Sōga, Yasutarō. *Gojūnenkan no Hawaii kaiko*. Honolulu, 1953.

Sōtōshū Hawaii kaikyō sōhonbu, ed. *Sōtōshū Hawaii kaikyō nanajūgonenshi*. Honolulu: Hawaii Sōtōshu kyōkai, n.d.

Terasaki, Teisuke. "Terasaki Teisuke nisshi." 1917–1956. Manuscript. University of Hawaii, Sinclair Library, Honolulu.

Tsutsumi, Noboru. *1920nen Hawaii satō kōchi rōdō undōshi, jō*. Vol. 1. Honolulu: Hawaii rōdō renmeikai honbu, 1920.

INDEX

Aala Park (Honolulu), rallies at, 108–9, 110, 122, 126
Abe, Isoo, 21
Advertiser Publishing Company, 248
AFL. *See* American Federation of Labor (AFL)
African Americans: AFL exclusion of, 258, 271; citizenship of, 303–4; as laborers, 261
Aiea Plantation: evictions from, 85–86; location of, xii–xiii (maps); money sent to Japan from, 69; strikebreakers at, 95–96; workers' return to, 122, 126
Akamine, A., 170–71, 218–19
Ala Moana (shopping center), 317–18
Albany Knickerbocker Press (newspaper), 268
Alcara (laborer), 187, 206, 213
Alexander, Arthur C., 287
Alien Land Law: call to amend, 112; debates over, 252; passage of, 136, 237; revision of, 238; support for, 251, 259, 285; U.S.-Japan relations and, 123–24, 236
American Cane Growers Association, 261
American Emigration Association (Japan), 21
American Factors, Ltd., 248
American Federationist (magazine), 288–89

American Federation of Labor (AFL): allegations against, 268; Asian immigration opposed by, 257–60, 266, 287–90; conventions of, 43, 237, 257, 258–59; goals of, 258; Hawaiian problems linked to, 269–70; immigration quota bill supported by, 303, 329; membership in, 23; Oahu strike ignored by, 265; racial discrimination by, 258, 271, 288–89; support for, 256; WWI support from, 42
Americanization. *See* assimilation
American Legion: Asian immigration opposed by, 290–91; immigration quota bill supported by, 303, 329; on Japanese-language press and schools, 88, 245, 287; on Japanese strikers, 68; members of, 214, 249; national meeting of, 274
American Sugar Beet Company, 260
anarchists, 59, 138–39, 269
Andrews, Lorrin, 41
Ang Filipinos (newspaper), 48
Anglo-Japanese Alliance, lapse of, 275
Aragaki, I., 166–68, 346n16
Aragaki, Yasuki, 143
Arahata, Kanson, 67–68
Arita, Hachirō, 106
Arizona (ship), 332
arson, allegations of, 186–87

Asahi Theater (Honolulu), events at, 49–50, 95, 99
Asama (ship), 289
Asano, Hitoshi, 243
Asia: attitudes toward, 251; immigration law as opportunity to unify, 316; missionaries in, 72
Asian immigration: under Hawaiian monarchy, 263–64; opposition to, 257–60, 287, 290. *See also* Chinese immigrants; Japanese immigrants; Johnson Reed Immigration Quota Law; Korean immigrants
assassination, 24–25, 140
assimilation: encouragement of, 25, 36, 41, 50–51, 90, 239–43, 307; impossibility of, 284–86; obstacles to, 245, 251, 254, 295, 303–4
Association to Support the Japanese Language Schools Suit, 293
Atherton, Frank C., 242–43
automobiles, 97, 178

Baba, Hiroshi, 4, 9–10
Baba, Tokuji, fig. 4; alibi of, 191, 213, 225; appearance of, 142, 148, 190, 346n26; background of, 190; on explosion, 155; indictment of, 221; leadership of, 147; Matsumoto on role of, 158–60, 162–63; Miyazawa on role of, 183; postprison life of, 327; testimony of, 190–92, 221; WWII relocation of, 334
Baku, N., 213
Baldwin, Harry A., 178, 283, 284, 285, 287
Bank of Hawaii, 248
Banks, James J.: background of, 141–42; court rules set by, 141, 173; impatience of, 150, 168, 180, 211, 213; injunction issued by, 293; instructions to jury, 216–17, 225; on language, 181, 183; rulings of, 155–56, 185, 187, 190, 196, 198, 224
beet sugar industry, laborers for, 260–61
B. F. Dillingham Company, 248
Big Five. *See* Hawaiian Sugar Planters' Association (HSPA); sugar planters
Bishop Trust Company, 247–48
Board of Immigration (Hawaiian Kingdom), 13, 14–15
Board of Public Health, 76
bombs, as impetus for Palmer raids, 59. *See also* explosion
Boston Globe (newspaper), 268
Brooks, Francis M.: Baba questioned by, 191; background of, 179; closing arguments of, 216; Hasegawa questioned by, 179–80; Miyazawa questioned by, 181, 182–83, 190; objections of, 196; role of, 142
Brown, Arthur M., 142, 207
Brown, Raymond C., 294
Buddhism: affiliation with, 144, 190; Christian feuds with, 37, 293; as control mechanism, 254; federation support from, 75; rejection of, 242, 334; schools associated with, 39. *See also* Honganji sect
Buddhist Youth Association, 190
Bureau of Investigation (later FBI). *See* Federal Bureau of Investigation (FBI)
Butler, Jack, 262, 267, 287–88

California: anti-Japanese feelings in, 10, 112, 237–39, 241, 244, 254, 304; Chinese laborers in, 14; immigration law and, 307, 329; Japanese safety in, 278, 313–14; political refugees in, 22–23. *See also* Alien Land Law
California and Hawaiian Sugar Company (C&H Sugar), 114, 260
California Japanese Exclusion League, 17, 237
Camacho, Antone, 85
cartoons, fig. 5, 67, 71, 97
Castle, William R., 110–11, 328–29
Castle and Cook (sugar planters), 111
Cathcart, John W.: background of, 180; cross-examination by, 180–81; death of, 195–96, 227; illness of, 183; language and, 181; role of, 142, 165
Central Union Church (Honolulu), 144
Chillingworth, Charles F., 230, 245, 249, 261–62, 274
Chilton, Wilmot, 261, 265–68, 270
China: anti-Japanese agitation in, 322; Japanese occupation of, 72, 239, 275, 316; territorial integrity of, 275–76; U.S. and Japanese interests in, 38–39, 71. *See also* Manchuria
Chinese Exclusion Act (1882): AFL and, 257–60; move to liberalize, 232–33; passage of, 14, 258; reconsideration of, 233–35, 244, 256, 260, 283, 291; upheld, 294–96
Chinese immigrants: characterization of, 271; encouragement of, 232–33, 244, 245, 249, 253–54, 256, 260, 284; illegal entrance of, 299; number of, 232–33; opposition to, 14, 232, 244–45, 259, 260–62, 267; as strikebreakers, 94; voting by, 235. *See also* Chinese Exclusion Act (1882)

Chōbei Ban-zuiin (novel), 104
Christianity: Buddhist feuds with, 37, 293; conversion to, 144, 181–82, 183, 207, 281–82, 317; emphasis on, 144, 145, 242; schools associated with, 39
citizenship: of African Americans, 303–4; dual, 234, 240, 273; legal assistance in obtaining, 104; naturalization for, 292, 339
Colt, LeBaron B., 272, 303–4, 306
communism: fear of, 32, 43; influence of, 44–45
Communist party: crackdown on, 138–39; outlawed, 112; raids on offices of, 58–62
Congressional Committee on Immigration, visit by, 123–24. *See also* House Committee on Immigration and Naturalization; Senate Committee on Immigration and Naturalization
conspiracy trial: alibis in, 179–81, 191, 192–93, 194–97, 213, 225; appeal after, 282, 297, 318, 348n41; Aragaki's testimony in, 166–68; atmosphere of, 142–43; Baba's testimony in, 190–92; bail in, 140; closing arguments in, 214–16; defendants in, 220–24, 325–30; defense concerns in, 142, 222–23; exhibits in, 166, 170–71, 181, 198, 218–19, 345n6, 346–47n28; Gotō's testimony in, 206–7; Hamai's testimony in, 166; Hamamoto's testimony in, 195; Hoshino's testimony in, 196–97; indictments in, 140, 141, 150–51, 168, 220, 268–69, 281; indifference to, 226–27; Inoguchi's testimony in, 192–93; Kawamata's testimony in, 204–6; Koyama's testimony in, 207–8; language difficulties in, 149–50, 158, 180, 181, 199–200, 217–18, 346–47n28; legal concerns of, 169; Matsumoto's testimony in, 146–61; Miyazawa's testimony in, 181, 182–87, 189–90; Mizutari's testimony in, 193–95; motives for, 268–69, 318; pistol's role in, 166–67, 170, 175, 198–99, 222; prosecution concerns in, 142, 218–19; Saitō's testimony in, 168–73; Sakamaki's testimony in, 143–46, 161; Satō's testimony in, 209–10; sentencing in, 226, 280–81; Suzuki's testimony in, 174–78, 213–14; Takizawa's testimony in, 203–4; Tsuda's testimony in, 211–12; Tsutsumi's testimony in, 197–99; verdict in, fig. 6, 224–25, 280. *See also* Banks, James J.;

explosion; Japanese conspiracy; jury; *specific defendants*
Consulate General of Japan in Honolulu: agents for, 7–8, 143, 235; allegations against, 111; on Japanese immigrants, 34; Japanese-language schools and, 37; records kept by, 26, 33, 196, 203–5, 342n1, 348n38; red flag incident and, 68–69; on rice riots, 45; statement on strike from, 82–83; "Tsutsumi statement" and, 79–82; war bonds sales by, 235
consumer goods, price increase in, 114–15, 132
Cook, James, 13
Cooke, Clarence H., 287
Coolidge, Calvin, 306, 315
Council of National Defense, 42, 257
counterfeiting operation, 296
Cuba, sugar from, 114

Davies, H., 290
Davis, Charles, 207–8
Dean, Arthur L., 90, 92, 286–87
Debs, Eugene, 137
Democratic National Convention (1921), 239
DeWitt, Gen. John, 285
Dillingham, Benjamin Franklin (Frank), 246–47, 249–50
Dillingham, Louise, 249
Dillingham, Walter Francis: activities of, 252, 274, 283–84; AFL and, 257, 259–60; background of, 245–49, 317; criticism of, 289; death of, 339; family of, 272, 287, 338–39; House hearings and, 252–53, 256, 271–72; mainland relations of, 250; military contacts of, 320–21; persistence of, 282–83, 290–91, 294–95; post-WWII business of, 338; on racial balance, 263; relocation opposed by, 333; role of, 230, 268, 299, 332; Senate hearings and, 272–74, 285; Shidehara's communication with, 276–77; strike mediation and, 248; Wright's testimony and, 262, 267
Dillingham, William P., 272, 301–2
disease: bubonic plague, 246–47; leprosy, 298; tuberculosis, 330, 336. *See also* influenza epidemic
Dole, Sanford (company president), 118
Donlin, John, 290
drug crimes, 296
Dukakis, Michael, 324
dynamite, uses of, 11, 169–70, 222, 269–70

earthquakes, 23, 298, 311
Eckart, Charles F., 2, 9–10
Edward VIII (King of England), 108
Eight Eight Fleet (Japan), 276
Eight Mile Camp, 4
Emmons, Lt. Gen. Delos C., 333
Endman, John P., 287
English-language newspapers: anti-Japanese articles in, 238, 254, 268, 290; on congressional visits, 308–9; on conspiracy trial, 173; on explosion, 269; fear of Japanization in, 67–72; on Foreign Language School Bill, 291–92; on Hawaii Emergency Labor Commission, 286–87; on Hawaii's statehood, 74; on Imperial Hotel Incident, 310; Japanese-language schools opposed by, 38; labor organizing and, 52–53; on mediation plan, 91; on Palmer raids, 58–60; on 77-cent flag parade, 111; on "Tsutsumi statement," 79–82; UWH attacked in, 288. See also specific newspapers
English Law School (Japan), 102
Espionage Act (1917), 43
eugenics research, immigration and, 300
European immigrants, quota for, 301–2. See also Italian immigrants; Johnson Reed Immigration Quota Law
Ewa Plantation: evictions from, 85; explosion at, 187, 281; fire at, 186; laborers at, 147, 159, 162, 173, 192–93, 211, 223; location of, xii–xiii (maps); parade participants from, 109; rally at, 95; stockholders of, 248; strike at, 19, 63, 64; strikebreakers at, 95–96; strike leaders fired from, 126; union at, 53, 148, 222; workers' return to, 122
Exclusion Act (1924), 12
explosion: context of, 11–12; description of, 1–3, 139–40, 143–44, 155; federation implicated in, 147–51, 154–57, 159–61, 165–66, 171–73; mainland newspapers on, 269; meeting following, 9–10; motive for, 220; planning of, 151–54, 157–58, 162–63, 172, 174–76, 178; preparation of dynamite for, 169–70, 222; suspects arrested for, 8–9, 10; timing of, 167–68. See also conspiracy trial

Fall, Albert B., 294–95
Farrington, Wallace R.: background of, 139; on Japanese problem, 294; news-paper of, 267; reports to, 273, 283; testimony for House hearings, 253–54, 256; UWH rejected by, 288
Federal Bureau of Investigation (FBI): on federation, 190, 192, 220–21, 228–29; on Hawaii hōchi, 292; Japanese arrested by, 333–35; on Japanese immigrants, 241; on Matsumura, 164; radical activities tracked by, 26–28, 62; raids by, 43, 58–62, 112, 269; records of, 342n1; on Tsutsumi, 83–84; on Yamazaki's arrival, 227–28. See also Palmer, A. Mitchell
Federation of Japanese Labor: aftermath of strike and, 126–28; conditions for ending strike and, 125–26; criticism of, 97–101, 107, 115, 122–24, 126–27, 133–34, 243–44; defense of, 162; dissolution of locals of, 281; divisions in, 210; emergency shelters of, 85–87, 128; finances of, 60–61, 97–100, 127–29, 157, 163, 171, 192, 215, 228, 340, 346n11; formation of, 49, 52; goals of, 81; Honolulu Central Labor Union's link to, 267–68; implicated in cane fires, 187; implicated in explosion, 147–51, 154–57, 159–61, 165–66, 171–73; Japanese government influence denied by, 69, 80–83; leaders of, fig. 4, 88, 97–98, 140, 324–25; on Matsumura, 164–65; mediation plans and, 90–93; meeting minutes of, 202; name of, 113, 132–33, 346n9; offices of, 56–57; reports on, 27–28, 228–29; 77-cent flag parade of, 108–11; stop strike order by, 118–22; on strikebreakers, 95–96; strike called by, 61–62, 64–66; structure of, 52–53, 57, 129–31; unity ensured by, 69–70, 83, 224, 235–36, 255; wage increase demands of, 53–55, 58. See also Hawaii Laborers' Association
Fern, Joseph James (Keo Kimo Pana), 89
Filipino immigrants: encouragement of, 250, 261; evictions of, 86–87; Japanese distrusted by, 133; number of, 232, 282, 288, 319; occupations of, 337–38; as parade participants, 109; as strikebreakers, 94; strike by, 63–65; support for, 182; war bonds purchased by, 235
Filipino Labor Union of Hawaii: cooperation of, 53; divisions in, 48; rally for, 49; strike ended by, 76–77; strikes called by, 56, 62, 78, 318–19; support

for, 68, 113, 182; wage demands of, 48, 56, 133
First Circuit Court (Honolulu), 141. *See also* conspiracy trial
Fletcher, Henry P., 273–74
Ford Motor Company, 51
Foreign Language Press Control Bill, 137, 287, 292
Foreign Language School Bill: context of, 236; furor over, 291–93, 294; injunction against, 293; passage of, 138; proposal for, 40–41; suit against, 292–95, 324–25. *See also* Japanese-language schools
Frear, Walter F., 51, 287
Free, Arthur Monroe (representative), 264–67
Fujii, N., 175, 178
Fujimoto, Hajime, 180
Fujimura, allegations against, 190
Fujinaka, Violet, 86
Fujioka, G., 8–9, 10
Fujita, allegations against, 187
Fujitani, Honji, fig. 4; appearance of, 142; associates of, 190; Baba on role of, 191; dispute with Makino, 204; on explosion, 155; indictment of, 140, 221, 281; lack of testimony by, 222; Matsumoto on role of, 147, 149, 150, 156, 162; named on passenger list, 170, 219; postprison life of, 327; Saitō on role of, 169; speeches of, 185
Fukunaga, T., 206
Furukawa, Hajime, 28–29, 30–31
Furushō, Shōshichirō, fig. 4; allegations against, 187–88; appearance of, 142, 148; arrest of, 188; background of, 188–89, 222; on explosion, 155; indictment of, 221; Matsumoto on role of, 157–58; postprison life of, 327; role of, 168–69; Saitō on role of, 169, 171–72, 188; Suzuki on role of, 174, 175, 213; Tsuda on role of, 211–12
Furuya, Eiichi: on conditions for ending strike, 125; Japanese government connection denied by, 69, 96; on mediation plans, 91, 118–19, 121; role of, 122–23, 228; on 77-cent flag parade, 109, 111; Tsutsumi questioned by, 79–83

Gaiety Theater (Hilo), 49
gannen mono, definition of, 13
Gentlemen's Agreement (1908): components of, 17–18, 27, 278, 304; as con-

text, 19; criticism of, 289; effects of, 37; revision of, 239–40
Gompers, Samuel: Asian immigration opposed by, 257–58, 259, 262, 287; labor conference and, 51; strike intervention by, 49; testimony for House hearings, 261, 270–71; war position for, 42; as worker, 282
Gotō, Ichiji, fig. 4; appearance of, 142, 148; background of, 56–57, 207, 281; evictions and, 86; on explosion, 155; incarceration of, 297–98, 349n12; income of, 206–7; indictment of, 140, 220; instructions from, 148–49; mediation plans and, 92, 124–25; postprison life of, 325–26, 335; role of, 61, 62, 65, 66, 99, 190; testimony of, 206–7, 221
Gotō, Shinpei, 50–51
Grange, immigration quota bill supported by, 303
grape pickers, strike by, 25
Great Britain, arms race and, 274–76
Great Depression, 328
Great Earthquake (San Francisco), 23
Great Kantō Earthquake (Japan), 298, 311
Griffiths, Arthur F., 90

Haga, Takeshi: criticism of, 53; federation leaders and, 97–98; mediation plan and, 116–18; newspaper role of, 103–4, 107–8; speech by, 50; on Tsutsumi, 84
Haleiwa Hotel Company, 247
Halsey, Richard, 298–99
Hamai, Goichi, 166
Hamamoto, Take, 195
Hamano (Satō's friend), 209–10
Hanihara, Masanao: alleged threat by, 305–7; background of, 305; immigration quota bill and, 302; on Imperial Hotel Incident, 310; on U.S.-Japan relations, 328; Washington Conference and, 275, 279
Hara, Takashi, 275
Harada, T., 190, 213, 280
Harding, Warren G.: appeals to, 226; appointments by, 245; assistance from, 252, 290; background of, 250–51, 253; death of, 295; election of, 137–38, 238, 285; Hawaiian interests of, 250–51; immigration quota and, 301
Hartwig, O. W., 290
Hasegawa, Genshō, 179–80, 191–93, 213–14

Hattori, Takeshi, 68–69, 91
Hawaii: as American, 231; annexation of, 15–16, 17, 232, 234; birthrate in, 37–38; business interests in, 247–48, 285; climate of, 34, 85–86; court expenses paid by, 318; as exception, 274; gender relations in, 205; guns in, 175; illegal immigrants in, 299; Japanese ships welcomed to, 82, 96, 236, 264, 276, 289, 320; labor study commission in, 290, 291–92; legislature in, 41, 294–95; politics in, 72, 73, 224, 283; social structure in, 14; statehood for, 74, 233; as stepping-stone, 14, 33; U.S. military exercises in, 320–21; WWII changes in, 337–38. See also Hilo; Honolulu; sugar industry
Hawaiian Dredging Company, Ltd., 247, 248–49, 321, 338
Hawaiian Hume Concrete Pipe Company, 247
Hawaiian Pineapple Company, 118
Hawaiian Sugar Planters' Association (HSPA): Chinese immigrants desired by, 232–33; defendants' appeal and, 318; on 1920 economy, 134–36; evictions by, 76, 85–87; experiment station of, 10; on federation, 70–71; on Filipino laborers, 63; Hattori's association with, 68–69; immigration law and, 312–13; insurance coverage of, 346n23; on Japanese conspiracy, 71–72; legal suit against, 105–6; Makino's paper and, 227; Manlapit targeted by, 319–20; members of, 55; negotiations with, 54, 61–62, 65–66, 73, 90–93, 119–25, 233, 244; opposition to, 74, 104; political power of, 73; posters distributed by, fig. 5; support for, 51, 60, 165–66, 249; tactics of, 83–85, 93–95, 97, 99, 108–9, 114–15, 129, 319; UWH attacked by, 288; wage increase demands and, 54–56, 58, 65; wages raised by, 131–33, 156; wages reduced by, 228–29; Wright's credibility attacked by, 267–68. See also Hawaii Emergency Labor Commission; sugar planters
Hawaii Central Labor Council, strike support from, 319. See also Honolulu Central Labor Union
Hawaii chōhō (newspaper), 165
Hawaii Emergency Labor Commission: AFL opposition to plan of, 257–60; criticism of, 285–89; establishment of, 244–45; House hearings and, 252–56, 264, 333; Japanese-language schools issue and, 294–95; members of, 230, 245, 249, 283, 299; Senate hearings and, 234–37, 272–74; tactics of, 260, 261, 266–68, 283–84. See also Dillingham, Walter Francis
Hawaii hōchi (newspaper): on back to work order, 76–78; on Baldwin's statement, 287; competition for, 103; on conspiracy trial, 187, 201–2, 226–27, 297; on explosion and arrests, 8, 140; on federation, 61, 70, 101, 107–8, 126–30, 228; finances of, 227, 292, 325; on Foreign Language School Bill, 291–93, 296, 324–25; founding of, 102; on Halsey's suicide, 299; on immigration, 245, 292–93, 307–8; on Isobe, 129; on Kawamata, 204–5; on newspapers' role, 52; popularity of, 106–7; president of, 73; reporters for, 97–98, 325–26, 335; on 77-cent flag parade, 109–10; staff labor union and, 62; on strike, 65–66, 70, 125–26; on strikebreakers, 94; on strike mediation, 89, 91, 116; on traitors to strike, 83; on wage increase, 132, 133
Hawaii Island Education Research Group, 35–36
Hawaii jinbutsu hyōron (newspaper), 152
Hawaii Laborers' Association: government report on, 27–28; leaders of, 140–41; name of, 113, 132–33, 346n9; newspaper of, 138; post-trial weakness of, 228–29; Shibusawa's meeting with, 279–80; stop strike order by, 122; on wage increase, 133. See also Federation of Japanese Labor
Hawaii Macadamia Nut Company, 248
Hawaii mainichi shinbun (newspaper), 41, 53
Hawaii shinpō (newspaper): on Baba, 191; on Kawamata, 204–5; on mediation plan, 91; owner of, 138; red flag incident and, 68–69; on 77-cent flag parade, 110; on wage increase, 132
Hawaii Times (newspaper), 334
Hayakawa, Jirō, 140–41, 279–80, 288, 335
Hay Market incident, 269
Haywood, "Big Bill," 42–43, 138, 282
Hearst newspapers, as anti-Japanese, 238, 290, 313–14
Heen, William H.: Aragaki questioned by, 167; Baba questioned by, 191–92; background of, 142; Gotō questioned by, 206–7; Hamamoto questioned by, 195; Hoshino questioned by, 196–97;

inability to identify defendants, 167; Inoguchi questioned by, 193; Kawamata questioned by, 205–6; Koyama questioned by, 209; Matsumoto questioned by, 146–49, 155, 156, 157, 160; Miyazawa questioned by, 183–90; Mizutari questioned by, 194; opening statement by, 142; praise for, 225; Saitō questioned by, 171–72; Sakamaki questioned by, 143–44, 145, 146; Satō questioned by, 210; Suzuki questioned by, 174–76, 213–14; tactics of, 150–51; Takizawa questioned by, 203–4; Tsuda questioned by, 211–13; Tsutsumi questioned by, 199–202

Heimin (Common Man, magazine), 44

Heiminsha (organization), 23

Higginbotham, Joseph, 101

High Treason incident, 31, 68

High Wage Association, 102

hiimin, definition of, 27

Hilo: hotels in, 150–56, 166, 218–19; Japanese establishments in, 34–35; labor rally in, 49

Hiroshima, immigrants' link to, 335–36

Hirota, Tokutarō, 296–97

Hiroyama, T., 190

Hiruya, Magotarō, 317

Holmes, Oliver Wendell, 59

Honganji mission, 86, 89

Honganji sect: hostility toward, 242; mission priests in, 6; popularity of, 120; school suit and, 324–25; temples and schools established by, 37, 39, 213, 293

Honolulu: buildings burned in, 246–47; businesses in, 34, 102, 245–46, 247, 317–18; celebrations in, 57–58, 88, 108, 111, 303; churches in, 144, 241, 242, 281, 296, 307; clubs in, 52, 98, 103, 123, 284; court in, 141; evicted families in, 86–87; hotels in, 141, 156; immigration office in, 33, 298–99; influences on, 49; media in, 35; prison in, 296–98, 317–18; rallies in, 108–9, 110, 122, 126; schools in, 36–37; as stopping point in travel, 50–51; theater in, 49–50, 95, 99. *See also* Consulate General of Japan in Honolulu; Kyōrakukan hotel/restaurant

Honolulu Advertiser (newspaper): on anti-Japanese in California, 254; on Chinese immigration, 233, 250; on conspiracy trial, 152, 155, 162, 173–75, 184, 193, 195, 196, 202, 208, 212, 214, 216, 225, 346n18; on 1920 economy, 134; on explosion, 139–40; on federation leaders, 108; on governors, 74, 230; on House hearings, 268; on Koyama, 208; on mediation plan, 92; on Palmer raids, 58, 60; on Pearl Harbor, 249; publisher of, 246; reporters for, 139; on strike, 64, 67, 69, 70–71, 125; on "Tsutsumi statement," 79, 264

Honolulu Board of Health, 87

Honolulu Bond and Mortgage Company, 247

Honolulu Central Labor Union: Chinese immigration opposed by, 259; contributions to, 265–68; criticism of, 270; membership of, 261–62; Oahu strike ignored by, 265. *See also* Hawaii Central Labor Council

Honolulu Chamber of Commerce, 119, 249, 266, 283, 329

Honolulu Club, 52

Honolulu Japanese Physicians' Association, 87

Honolulu Plantation Labor Supporters' Association: evicted families and, 86; formation of, 49; influence of, 75; labor organizing and, 52–53; mediation and, 248; meeting of, 49–51

Honolulu Rapid Transit Company, 248

Honolulu Star Bulletin (newspaper): on anti-Japanese in California, 254; on conspiracy trial, 158, 268; on explosion and arrests, 8, 140; on immigration, 124; on Palmer raids, 60; publisher of, 253; reporters for, 89, 139; on strike, 67, 77, 125; on Wright's credibility, 267

Hoover, Herbert, 260, 329

Hoover, J. Edgar, 26, 27, 59–60, 110

Hopwood, John, 287

Hori, Teikichi, 281, 296–97

Horner, Albert: background of, 245; on Dillingham, 250; return to Hawaii, 274; role of, 230, 253; Wright's meeting with, 261–62

Hoshino, Chūhei, fig. 4; alibi of, 179–81, 192–93, 196–97, 225; appearance of, 142, 148; background of, 196; as dangerous, 196, 348n38; on explosion, 155; federation finances and, 128; incarceration of, 297, 349n12; indictment of, 140, 221; instructions from, 148–49; Matsumoto on role of, 156–57; Miyazawa on role of, 183; postprison life of, 321, 328; Suzuki on role of, 174–75; testimony of, 196–97, 221

Hosoi Funeral Home, 89

House Committee on Immigration and Naturalization: AFL and, 257–60; conspiracy trial indictments and, 268–69; Dillingham's visits to members of, 252; hearings on Hawaii's labor problems, 252–56, 259–66, 270–72, 333; immigration quotas and, 300–303; Kuhio's outburst to, 262–64; statement distributed to, 230–32

Houston (cruiser), 331–32

HSPA. *See* Hawaiian Sugar Planters' Association (HSPA)

Huber, S. C., 114–15, 119

Hughes, Charles Evans: Dillingham's meeting with, 273–74; Hanihara's letter to, 305–6; immigration quota bill and, 302, 304; role of, 239, 295; Washington Conference and, 275–76, 277–78, 285

Hyōron no Hyōron (Review of Review), 228

Iaukea, Curtis: influenza concerns of, 76, 85, 87; on mediation plan, 91–92, 186–87; strike and, 73–74, 108

ILWU (International Longshoremen Workers' Union), 338

Imamura, Emō, 6, 164, 293

immigrants: differences among, 15, 19; encouragement of, 5, 7. *See also* Chinese immigrants; European immigrants; Filipino immigrants; Italian immigrants; Japanese immigrants; Johnson Reed Immigration Quota Law; Korean immigrants; Mexican immigrants; Portuguese immigrants

Imperial Hotel (Tokyo), 310–11

Industrial Workers of the World (IWW): demise of, 138; description of, 34n15; influence of, 48; outlawed, 112; raids against, 43, 59–60, 269; role of, 23–25, 44, 47; Tsutsumi on, 81; WWI opposed by, 42–43

influenza epidemic: Board of Health concerns with, 76; cost of, 96; deaths from, 87–89; evictions during, 85–87; federation concerns with, 62

Inman, J. M., 237, 239

Inoguchi, Sajo (Sayo?), 192–93, 201

Inomata, Tsunao, 44

Inoue, Etsuta, 88–89, 174, 177, 193

Inouye, Daniel, 339

Inter-Island Navigation Company, 34

International Labor Conference (League of Nations), 51, 60

International Longshoremen Workers' Union (ILWU), 338

International Socialist and Trade Union Congress, 24

Iron Molders' Union (Honolulu), 259, 260

Irwin, Harry, 75, 76

Ishida, Chikao: appearance of, 142, 148; Aragaki on role of, 166–67; Hoshino on role of, 197; indictment of, 221; Koyama on role of, 209; lack of testimony by, 221–22; Matsumoto on role of, 150–51, 154–56; postprison life of, 326–27; WWII relocation of, 334

Ishigaki, Eitarō, 44

Isobe, Hōsen: background of, 120; criticism of, 129; mediation by, 118–20, 121, 130; questions about, 126–27; role of, 141, 346n17; Waterhouse confronted by, 124–25

Italian immigrants, hostility to, 139

Iwasa, Sakutarō, 24, 25

Iwasa, Sueji, 8–9, 10

Iwasaki, Jirokichi (Jirō), fig. 1; competition for, 9; concerns of, 255; status of, 5–6; work duties of, 16–17

Iwasaki, Tazuko, 9, 135, 255

Iwate (ship), 289

IWW. *See* Industrial Workers of the World (IWW)

Izumo (ship), 289

Izumo Taisha shrine, 86

James, Frank, 224–25

Japan: arms race and, 274–76; business interests in, 243; declaration of war by, 332; discipline in, 224, 236, 255; earthquake in, 298, 311; education in, 29–30; gifts from, 300; Harding's election and, 251; homogeneity of, 218, 232, 254; immigrants' return to, 96, 321–23; immigration quota law and, 305–7, 309–17; imperialism of, 16, 17, 71–72, 111–13, 329–30; influenza epidemic in, 87; labor movement in, 51, 78–79, 257–58, 323, 330–31; leftist incidents in, 30–31; nationalism of, 20, 50, 264–65, 276, 289, 312–13, 315–16; politics in, 22–23, 330, 336–37; red flag incident in, 67–68; rice riots in, 44–47; U.S. occupation of, 336, 337; wages returned to, 15, 69; in WWI, 38. *See also* U.S.-Japan relations

Japan-America Society (Seattle), 328

Japanese Americans. *See* nisei

Japanese Association (Honolulu), 49

Japanese Chamber of Commerce (Honolulu), 63, 103, 123, 266

Japanese conspiracy: allegations of, 79,
84–85, 123–24, 134, 234–36, 255,
268, 273, 284; countermeasures to,
113, 123; denial of, 73–75, 259; evidence for, 123, 277, 285, 294; fears
of, 67–72, 90, 238, 241, 253–56;
motives for, 220, 243; Pearl Harbor
attack and, 332–33; planning and,
151–54; response to, 230–32. See
also conspiracy trial
Japanese Contractors' Association, 47
Japanese Educational Association of
Hawaii, 39–40, 41
Japanese Exclusion Act. See Johnson
Reed Immigration Quota Law
Japanese Federation Strike Investigation
Committee, 25
Japanese Fresno Federation of Labor, 25
Japanese Hospital (later Kuwakini Hospital): influenza epidemic and, 88, 179,
180–81; Tsutsumi's baptism at, 281;
workers at, 148
Japanese immigrants: annexation's impact on, 17; arrival of, 33–36; attacks
on, 313–14; birthrate and, 234, 237–
38; characterization of, 81, 241, 270,
273; conditions for, 15, 17–18, 264;
context of, 13–18; earthquake and,
298; exodus from Hawaii, 231–32;
families of, 240, 256, 326; Franklin D.
Roosevelt welcomed by, 331–32; goals
of, 36, 136; guides for, 5, 21–22, 33–
34; history on, 340; immigration law
and, 307–9; Japan's interests in, 123–
24; legal assistance for, 104–5; nationalism of, 75, 78; naturalization of,
292, 339; number of, 34, 233–34; opposition to, 17–18, 20–21, 24–25,
71, 90, 233, 258–59, 264–65, 289–
90; as political refugees, 22–23; recruitment of, 13, 14–15; rice riots
and, 44–47; savings of, 135; as strikebreakers, 95; terminology of, 35; U.S.
support from, 38–39; war bonds
purchased by, 235; on Washington
Conference agreement, 276; WWII
relocation of, 285, 333–34. See also
laborers; nisei
Japanese-language newspapers: on conspiracy trial, 173; on Hawaii Emergency Labor Commission, 285–86;
immigrant history by, 340; on immigration quota bill, 302–3, 307–8, 312,
315; on Imperial Hotel Incident, 310–
11; labor organizing and, 52–53, 254–
55; opposition to, 88, 214; red flag
incident and, 67–68; role of, 41, 75;

Sacco and Vanzetti case in, 324; on
strikes, 47, 83, 125. See also Foreign
Language Press Control Bill; specific
newspapers
Japanese-language schools: closure of,
333; curriculum and texts in, 37, 39;
as emergency shelters, 86–88; establishment of, 36–37; number of, 39;
opposition to, 25, 38, 88, 234–35,
244, 245; rationale for, 39–40; types
of, 35. See also Foreign Language
School Bill; teachers
Japanese Nationality Act, 240
Japanization. See Japanese conspiracy
Jernegan, Prescott F., 286–87
Jiji shinpō (newspaper), 310–11, 343n2
Jinbo, arrest of, 172, 346n18
Jōdo sect, 39, 276
Johnson, Albert: background of, 252,
300; committee actions of, 264–66,
270–71; death of, 330; Hawaii visit
of, 308–9; immigration quota bill and,
300–302, 328–30; telegrams for,
259
Johnson, Hiram W., 237, 238, 284–85
Johnson Reed Immigration Quota Law:
amendment of, 328–29; background
of, 300–307; enactment of, 306–7;
Japanese attack linked to, 332–33;
Japanese immigrants' response to,
307–9; Japan's protest of, 309–17;
overturned by new law, 339
Judd, Albert F., 40–41
jury: judge's instructions to, 216–17,
225; language barriers for, 217–18;
questions by, 146, 151, 217, 225;
election of, 141, 217

Kagawa, Toyohiko, 322–23, 330
Kagoshima Commercial School, 123
Kahuku Plantation: evictions from, 85–
86; labor organizers at, 44, 223; location of, xii–xiii (maps); rally at, 95;
strike at, 63, 95; strikebreakers at,
96; workers return to, 122
Kakumei (Revolution, journal), 24–25
Kalihi, hospitals for workers in, 128
kamaaina, definition of, 14. See also
sugar planters
Kamada, Eikichi, 60
Kamehameha I (King of Hawaii), 14, 47
kanaka, definition of, 14
Kanda, Hakusan, 311
Katayama, Sen: associates of, 21, 24;
background of, 7; death of, 331; defection of, 138; on emigration, 5, 21–22;
on Japanese occupation, 112–13; on

Katayama, Sen (continued)
  labor movement, 43–44; role of, 31,
  181, 206, 258, 330
Katō, Kanjū, 330
Katō, Takaaki, 106, 201, 310
Katō, Tomosaburō, 275, 279
Katsunuma (immigration official), 299
Katsura Tarō, 68
Kauai Federation of Labor, 79
Kawahara, Masao, 90, 92, 115–16,
  118–19, 248
Kawakami, Hajime, 30
Kawakami, Jōtarō, 330
Kawamata, Fumio: appearance of, 142,
  148; background of, 204–5; indict-
  ment of, 140, 221, 281; Matsumoto
  on role of, 148–49, 155, 164; post-
  prison life of, 327; Saitō on role of,
  169, 171, 172; Suzuki on role of,
  174, 175, 213; testimony of, 204–6,
  221
Kazan (Volcano, newspaper), 145–46,
  220, 243
Keightly, Fred, 290
Kido, Kōichi, 30
Kilauea, Mount, xii (map), 3, 317
Kimura, Torakichi, 99
Kingsley Hall (settlement house), 21
Kitano Hospital (Osaka), 331
Kobayashi, allegations against, 187
Kobayashi Hotel, 159, 172
Koike, Ryōsaku, 205
Kokumin shinbun (newspaper), 310–11
Kokuryūkai (Amur River Society), 310,
  315
Komura, Jūtarō, 106, 305
Kona, sugar refinery at, 255
Kondō, Seigo: appearance of, 142, 148;
  background of, 158–59, 222; indict-
  ment of, 221; Matsumoto on role of,
  155, 158, 159–60, 163–64; post-
  prison life of, 327; Saitō on role of,
  172
Konishi, Shigenao, 30, 33, 331
Konno, Tomekichi, 255
Konoe, Fumimaro, 30
Korea: Japanese control of, 71–72, 239,
  316; Japanese nationalism in, 314
Korean immigrants, as strikebreakers,
  94, 314
Kosaki, Y., 346n18
Kōtoku, Denjirō (Shūsui), 21, 23–25,
  141
Koyama, Teru, 208, 317–18, 326
Koyama, Tsurunosuke: appearance of,
  142, 148; background of, 208; incarceration of, 317–18; indictment of,

221; Matsumoto on role of, 150–51,
  154, 156; postprison life of, 326; role
  of, 121–22; testimony of, 207–9,
  221–22
Kuhio Kalanianaole: background of, 263;
  death of, 283; House hearings and,
  262–64, 272; HSPA communications
  and, 266–67; on Japanese conspiracy,
  268
Ku Klux Klan, 43, 313–14
Kumazaki, Kumaiichi, 106, 335
Kumazawa (consulate secretary), 79,
  80, 82
Kurokawa, Ekan, 29, 31, 32–33, 330–31
Kurokawa, Eseki, 29, 31
Kurokawa, Kimiko, 32
Kurokawa, M., 227–28
Kurokawa, Masano, 28–29, 32
Kurokawa, Noboru. See Tsutsumi,
  Noboru
Kurokawa, Reizui, 28–29, 32
Kurusu, Kazuo, 180–81
Kurusu, Saburō, 85
Kyōrakukan hotel/restaurant: assault
  incident at, 157, 163, 177, 182–83,
  188, 198–99, 202, 219, 223; descrip-
  tion of, 61–62; doctor's visit to, 179;
  meetings at, 52, 171–72, 174; workers
  at, 192
Kyoto Imperial University, 28, 30–32,
  331

labor contractors: background of, 188–
  89; duties of, 16; profits of, 135; tax
  on, 17
laborers: bango numbers for, 2; children
  of, 36–37; clothing for, 109; conditions for, 4, 25, 51, 54, 133, 264; criticism of, 114–15, 133–34, 250; House
  hearings on problems with, 252–56;
  interpreters for, 7–8, 182, 184; living
  expenses of, 54; for navy base, 236–
  37; origins of, 231–32, 335–36; post-
  trial indifference of, 226–27; protests of, 18; reports on, 230–32, 241,
  290, 291–92; representation of, 43;
  as strike leaders, 126; support for,
  49–51; work hours for, 4. See also
  plantations; strikes; wages
labor movement: as block to Chinese
  immigration, 257–60, 266, 289–90;
  conference on, 51, 60; as context, 11–
  12; "dynamite" linked to, 11, 269–
  70; radical elements of, 23–24; rice
  riots' impact on, 44–47; WWI's impact on, 42–44. See also American
  Federation of Labor (AFL); Federation

of Japanese Labor; Filipino Labor
Union of Hawaii; Honolulu Central
Labor Union; Industrial Workers of
the World (IWW)
Labor World (Rōdō sekai, newspaper),
21–22
Lahaina Plantation, strike at, 19
Lake, H. T., 8, 345n6
land: haole ownership of, 14; Hawaiian
ownership of, 233, 263; nisei owner-
ship of, 112, 237. *See also* Alien Land
Law
Lane, Franklin N., 36
Lansing, Robert, 236
Lansing-Ishii Agreement, 38
Laupahoehoe Plantation, laborers at, 209
League of Nations: Japan and, 277, 331;
labor conferences of, 51, 60
legal cases: against Foreign Language
School Bill, 292–95, 324–25; *Makino
v. HPSA*, 105–6. *See also* conspiracy
trial
Lenin, V. I., 43
Lightfoot, Joseph B., 104–5, 107, 117,
130, 293
Liliuokalani (Queen of Hawaii), 73
Lincoln, Abraham, 109, 110–11
longshoremen, strike of, 48
Los Angeles Examiner (newspaper), 238,
254, 268
lunas (overseers), abusiveness of, 18
Lymar, William B.: Aragaki questioned
by, 167–68; background of, 142; closing arguments of, 216; concerns of,
222–23; Gotō questioned by, 206; instructions from, 205; Matsumoto questioned by, 161–66; on Matsumoto's
testimony, 149, 155–56; objections
of, 189, 211, 214; Saitō questioned
by, 172–73; Sakamaki questioned by,
145–46, 161; Suzuki questioned by,
176–78; Tsutsumi questioned
by, 197–99

Mabuchi, Jūtarō, 113
MacArthur, Gen. Arthur, 247
MacCaughley, Vaughan, 287
Makiki Japanese Church (Honolulu),
241, 242, 307
Makino, Eijirō, 101
Makino, Jō, 101
Makino, Kin, 101
Makino, Kinzaburō (Fred), fig. 2; back-
ground of, 101–3; federation and,
97–98, 100–101, 107–8, 227; in first
Oahu strike, 73, 102; on Foreign
Language School Bill, 291–93, 296,

324–25; Fujitani's dispute with, 204;
HPSA sued by, 105–6; immigration
and, 299, 308; Isobe criticized by, 129;
leadership of, 107; legal assistance
from, 104–6; on Manlapit and HSPA,
76–77; Matsumura's relation with,
165; mediation plan of, 116–18, 130;
newspaper of, 91, 103–5, 326; 77-cent
flag parade and, 108; Tsutsumi and,
282; Wright's encounter with, 265,
267; in WWII, 334–35
Makino, Michie, 102, 105
Makino Drug Store (Honolulu), 102
Maloney, Robert S., 252
Manchuria, Japanese occupation of,
329–30
Manlapit, Pablo: arrest of, 319; back
to work order by, 76–77, 84–85; de-
portation of, 320; on HSPA wage increase, 132–33; incarceration of, 318,
349n12; labor organizing by, 48–49,
53; new strike call by, 78; Scharrenberg's meeting with, 288; strike vote
and, 62, 63; Thompson's relations
with, 76–78, 219; unity appeal from,
66
marriage: as adoption into family, 31–
33; obstacles to, 307; "picture bride,"
18, 37, 104, 182, 237, 240
Martin, Henry, 2, 8
Maruyama, Kin'ichirō: background of,
149–50; as interpreter for trial, 157–
58, 168, 180, 197, 200, 217–18,
346–47n28
Massachusetts, explosion in, 1. *See also*
Sacco, Nicola; Vanzetti, Bartolomeo
Masuda, Seishi, 57, 61, 107
Matano Hotel (Hilo), 151, 153–56, 166,
219
Matsonia (ship), 77–78, 230
Matsui, Keishirō, 302, 305, 306
Matsumoto, J. (picket), 211
Matsumoto, Junji (witness): allegations
against, 190; appearance of, 174; Aragaki on role of, 167–68; Baba on role
of, 191; background of, 161–62; confession of, 268; defense and, 161–66,
176, 216; employer of, 180; Gotō on
role of, 206; Hoshino on role of, 196–
97; Koyama on role of, 209; Miyazawa on role of, 183; name on passenger list, 170–71; prosecution and,
215–16, 218–20; Saitō on role of,
169–72; suicide attempt of, 162;
Suzuki on role of, 177–78; Takizawa
on role of, 203; testimony of, 146–61,
182, 185, 194, 203, 210, 222, 223,

Matsumoto, Junji (continued)
225, 275, 340; Tsutsumi on role of,
198–99
Matsumoto, Y., 187, 211
Matsumoto, Z., 187
Matsumura, Tamotsu: appearance of,
196; background of, 164; employer
of, 183; Matsumoto on role of, 164–
66; Miyazawa on role of, 183; Suzuki
on role of, 177–78
Matsuura, Gyokuei, 129
Maui, longshoremen's strike on, 48
Maui shinbun (newspaper), 57
Maunakea (steamship), 154, 169,
170–71, 188, 198, 219
Mauna Loa (volcano), 49
May Day rally (Japan), 113
McCarthy, Charles: appointments by,
230, 245; background of, 234; on
Japanese characteristics, 75, 235; on
Japanese immigration, 233–37, 241;
Japanese-language schools and, 41;
land laws and, 233; mediation plan
and, 116–17, 130; statehood and, 74,
233; testimony for Senate committee,
234–37; Washington trip of, 58,
73–74, 107–8, 283
McClatchy, Virgil S., 284, 286, 303–4,
306, 308–9
McDuffie (detective), 160, 172
Mead, Royal D.: background of, 72; evictions enforced by, 76; federation contributions and, 99, 100; negotiations
by, 54, 65, 73, 244; successor of, 119,
262; testimony for House hearings,
252–53, 254–55; on workers, 282
Mexican immigrants, in beet sugar
industry, 261
Min (Queen of Korea), 120
miners, strike of, 49
missionaries: in Asia, 72; in Hawaii,
13, 72, 231; Japanese Christians as,
181–82. See also Honganji mission
Mission Centennial Celebration, 108,
111, 142
Miyake (laborer), 160, 187
Miyamura, Kaichi: Koyama on role of,
209; Matsumoto on role of, 150–54,
156–57, 160, 223–24; prosecution on
role of, 215–16; return to Japan, 148,
223–24; Saitō on role of, 169, 172,
223–24
Miyasaki, Seiichi, 85, 343n17
Miyazaki, Ryūsuke, 330
Miyazawa, Hiroshi, fig. 4; allegations
against, 99; appearance of, 142, 148;
appointment for, 57; background of,

181–82, 183–84, 281; evictions and,
86–87; on explosion, 155; income of,
201; indictment of, 140, 220, 221; instructions from, 148–49; mediation
plan and, 92; postprison life of, 326,
335–36; prosecution on role of, 215;
Saitō on role of, 171; strike vote and,
62, 64–66; testimony of, 181, 182–
87, 189–90, 221; Tsutsumi on role
of, 198–99
Mizuno, Yoshimi, 105, 335
Mizutani, Chōzaburō, 330, 336
Mizutari, Yasuyuki, fig. 4; background
of, 193; Hamamoto on role of, 195;
testimony of, 193–95, 198, 225
Moana Hotel (Honolulu), 141
Mochizuki Club (Honolulu), 98, 123
Mokuleia Ranch and Land Company,
247
Molokai island, leprosy cases sent to,
298
Moore, Fred, 138–39
Moori, Iga, 90, 92, 115, 119, 248, 280
Morgan, J. P., 59
Mori, Ritsuko, 311
Morikawa, M., 178
Morita, Sakae, 113
Moroi, Rokurō, 35, 40, 68, 79, 233
Morris, Roland, 239–41, 251, 257, 278
Murakami, Tsunehiko: appearance of,
142; lack of testimony by, 222–23;
Matsumoto on role of, 150–54, 159–
60, 168; postprison life of, 325–26;
prosecution on role of, 215–16, 218–
19; Saitō on role of, 169–70, 172;
Suzuki on role of, 176, 213
Mutō, Sanji, 60
Mutsuhito (Emperor of Japan), 22
Myōjō (periodical), 276

Naalehu Plantation, merchant at, 101
Nagai, Ryūtarō, 310
Nakabayashi, Kiyofumi, 79, 80, 281
Nakahashi, Tokugorō, 113
Nakano, Seigō, 50
Nakazawa, Hayaji, 187–88, 203,
211–12
Naniwa (ship), 82
National General Mobilization Law
(Japan), 331
National Masses party (Japan), 330
Native Sons of the Golden West, 303
Negoro, Motoyuki, 102, 108
newspapers. See English-language news-
papers; Japanese-language newspapers;
specific newspapers
Nichibei (newspaper), 25

Nine-Party Treaty. *See* Washington Conference, treaty from

Nippu jiji (newspaper): on Baba, 346n26; on Baldwin's statement, 286, 287; on Chinese labor, 292–93; closed in WWII, 334; competition for, 103; on conspiracy defendants, 297; editor of, 73, 102–3, 320; on explosion, 197; on Franklin D. Roosevelt's visit, 332; Foreign Language School Bill and, 293, 296, 324; on military exercises, 320; popularity of, 106–7; reporters for, 57, 326; on 77-cent flag parade, 110; on strike, 65, 89, 91, 116, 125–26; subscriptions for, 147, 162, 222; on wage increase, 132; on Washington Conference, 275

nisei: allegations against, 252–53; Americanization and, 242–43; appeal to, 286–87; definition of, 35; dual citizenship for, 234, 240, 273; on federation support, 135; hostility to, 284, 285; land ownership by, 112, 237; military service of, 339; occupations of, 337; political concerns of, 320, 339; voting and, 72, 235; WWII relocation of, 285, 333–34

Nishida, Kitarō, 30

Nishimura, Sam, 78

Nishio, Suehiro, 336

Noguchi (clerk), 173

Nuuanu Union Church (Honolulu), 281, 296

Oahu, restaurant in, 95, 99, 175

Oahu Ice and Cold Storage Company, 285

Oahu Island strike (first) (1909): context of, 19–22, 25; failure of, 25, 44; leaders of, 73, 102–3; legacy of, 52

Oahu Island strike (second) (1920): acting governor's statement on, 73–75; aftermath of, 122–31, 240–41, 339–40; beginning of, 65–66; Chinese immigration and, 233; conditions for ending, 124–25; congressional hearings and, 252–53, 264, 270, 272–73; context of, 11–12, 51–52, 67–69, 93–94, 112–14; criticism of, 70–72, 114–15; divisions in, 76–78; Filipinos' role in, 47–49, 56; Japan's interest in, 72, 113, 343n2; mediation of, 89–93, 115–18, 130, 186–87, 233, 248, 279–80; organizing for, 47–54, 56, 95; pickets in, 147, 148, 163, 169, 174, 177, 185–86, 199, 204, 211; planters' description of, 254–55;

planters' profits in, 134–36; posters about, fig. 5; 77-cent flag parade in, 108–11; songs in, 94–95, 99, 116; stop strike order in, 118–22; strikebreakers in, 94–97, 174–75; Thompson's machinations during, 76–78; traitors denounced in, 83; "Tsutsumi statement" and, 78–85. *See also* conspiracy trial; Federation of Japanese Labor; influenza epidemic

Oahu Railway and Land Company, 193, 247, 248

Oahu Shōkai (cooperative), 189

Oahu Sugar Company, 248

Ogata, Manpachi, 83, 187–89, 203, 222

Ōhashi, Tadakazu, 316

Oka, Shigeki, 23

Okazaki (pineapple grower), 214

Okino Hotel (Hilo), 150, 152, 166, 218

Ōkubo, Gen'ichi, 194, 198

Ōkubo, Kiyoshi, 325

Okumura, Takie: Americanization movement of, 241–43, 334; associates of, 90, 242–43; background of, 36; immigration act and, 307, 309; on Japanese-language schools, 295–96, 325; as mediator, 115, 280; status of, 103; strike opposed by, 243–44

Olaa Japanese Christian Church, 144, 153

Olaa Japanese Temperance Union, 144–45

Olaa Nine Mile, site of, 144

Olaa Plantation: closure of, 338; development of, 16–17; evacuation of, 317; improvements at, 134–35; laborers at, 161; location of, xii (map); owner of, 246–47; schools at, 36, 39; strike at, 18–19, 209, 338; temple at, 36. *See also* conspiracy trial; explosion

Olaa Sugar Company: church building funded by, 144; current facilities of, 3–5; employees of, 2, 7, 143; proposed purchase of, 255; vice president of, 248

Onodera, Tokuji, 172, 266

Open Door Policy, 275

Oriental Exclusion League of California, 284, 306, 309

Ōsugi, Sakae, 24, 67–68

Oxnard, Henry T., 260–61

Ozaki, Yukio, 50

Ozawa, Takao, 292

Pacific Bank, 56, 61

Pacific Savings Support Corporation, 128

Paia Plantation, laborers at, 177–78

Palmer, A. Mitchell: Bureau of Investigation established by, 26; investigations by, 134; prediction of, 113; presidential bid of, 119, 137; raids by, 58–62, 112, 269; reports to, 114–15; strikes and, 49, 75

Palmer, Albert W.: background of, 89–90; on Chinese immigration, 244; church of, 241; letter to nisei, 286–87; mediation plan of, 90–93, 186–87, 233

Pan-American Association, 112

Pan-Pacific Commercial Conference, 251

Papala sugar mill, 196

Paris Peace Conference, 50, 236, 277

Pearl City, rally at, 95

Pearl Harbor: attack on, 285, 332–33; dry dock at, 236–37, 248–49, 250; expansion of base at, 276, 321; Franklin D. Roosevelt's tour of, 332; Navy facility at, 47, 194

Phelan, James P.: background of, 237; campaign of, 237–38; on Hawaiian situation, 284, 286, 308; Japanese immigration and, 234–37, 289; role of, 239, 258, 260; Senate testimony of, 304; on U.S.-Japan relations, 112, 347n5

Philadelphia Record (newspaper), 268

Philippine Labor Bureau, 84

Philippines: as exception, 274; unification of, 48. See also Filipino immigrants

Pineapple Association, 245

pineapple production, 115, 245

Pioneer Plantation, laborers at, 193

plantations: doctors on, 18; housing on, 4–5, 19, 55, 76, 85–87; location of, xii–xiii (maps); managers of, 15, 247; mechanization on, 337; overseers on, 18; schools on, 36–37; stores on, 45–46, 317, 326. See also labor contractors; laborers; sugar industry; *specific plantations*

Portsmouth Treaty, 305

Portuguese immigrants: settlement of, 20; strike and, 63

Prince Fushimi Memorial Scholarship Association, 103

prison: activities in, 298; description of, 296, 317–18; people in, 296–97, 318

Prohibition, 129, 144–45, 295–96

proletarian party movement (Japan), 330

prostitution, allegations of, 238

Puerto Ricans: recruitment of, 244; strike and, 63

Puerto Rico, as exception, 274

Puna Sugar Company, 338. See also Olaa Plantation

racial conflict, emphasis on, 71–72, 73

racial discrimination: of AFL, 258, 271, 288–89; justification for, 273; ubiquitousness of, 19–20; in wage increases, 75. See also Johnson Reed Immigration Quota Law

Railroad Brotherhoods, 75, 114–15

railroad workers: in Hawaii vs. mainland, 75, 193; strikes of, 110, 112

Raker, John F.: Hawaii visit of, 308–9; House hearings and, 254, 256, 262, 263, 266, 271–72

Realty Syndicate, 247

red flag incident (1908), 67–68

Reed, David A., 303–4

Rego, William, 135–36

religion. See Buddhism; Christianity; missionaries; *specific churches*

Renown (cruiser), 108

Republican party, sugar planters' support for, 137–38

rice riots (1918), 44–47

Robello, Serphine, 343n14

Rōdō (Labor, magazine), 25

Rōdō sekai (magazine), 206

Rogers, John M., 261

Rolph, George M., 260

Roosevelt, Franklin D., 331–33

Roosevelt, Theodore, 17

Rotary Club (Honolulu), 103, 284

Russo-Japanese War, 17, 20, 37, 38, 71, 305

Saburi, Sadao, 284

Sacco, Nicola: arrest of, 1, 26; draft evasion by, 42; execution of, 323–24; trial of, 138–39, 226, 297

Saikaiya Hotel (Honolulu), 156

Saikin Hawaii annai (guidebook), 33–34

Saionji, Kimmochi, 22, 68

Saito, Y., 206

Saitō, I.: appearance of, 174; Baba on role of, 191; background of, 168–69, 173; confession of, 268; defense and, 216; employer of, 180; Gotō on role of, 206; Hoshino on role of, 196–97; Koyama on role of, 209; Matsumoto on role of, 150–57, 159–60, 168; Miyazawa on role of, 182–83; prosecution and, 215–16, 218–20; Suzuki on role of, 177–78; Takizawa on role of, 203; testimony of, 169–73,

185, 188, 189, 194, 210, 225, 340;
Tsutsumi on role of, 198
Saitō, Seikan, 214
Sakai, Toshihiko, 43, 67–68, 141, 330
Sakamaki, Ben, 5, 6, 345n7
Sakamaki, George (Jōji), 5, 8, 345n7
Sakamaki, Haru, 5
Sakamaki, Hisao, 6
Sakamaki, Jūzaburō (Frank), fig. 1; activities of, 144, 151–53, 183, 220,
243; background of, 5–7, 143, 144–
45; death of, 332; description of home,
4–5; explosion in home of, 2–3, 118,
139–40; laborers' request for dismissal of, 19; Matsumoto's relations with,
160–61; status of, 5–6, 9, 217; testimony of, 143–46, 161; Tsutsumi on,
197; work duties of, 7–8, 16–17. See
also conspiracy trial; explosion
Sakamaki, Masa, 5, 345n7
Sakamaki, Noboru, 5, 345n7
Sakamaki, Paul (Tokuo), 5, 8, 345n7
Sakamaki, Shunzō (Shunzo), 5, 345n7
Sakamaki, Yūroku (Charles), 5, 345n7
San Francisco: earthquake in, 23; immigration law and, 307; mayor of, 237;
school segregation in, 17
San Francisco Chronicle (newspaper):
on House hearings, 268; on "Japanese colonization," 124; on military
exercises, 321; on Oahu strike, 269
San Francisco Peace Treaty, 337
San Francisco School Board, 17
Sarminento, Juan, 48, 76–77
Satō, Sazō: appearance of, 142; death of,
327; on explosion, 155; Hoshino on
role of, 197; indictment of, 221; Matsumoto on role of, 156, 223; Suzuki
on role of, 174–76, 223; testimony
of, 209–10, 221
Satō, Yōkichi, 148, 155, 213, 221, 223
Sawayanagi, Seitarō, 30
Scharrenberg, Paul, 237, 259, 260,
287–90
schools, segregation in, 17. See also
Japanese-language schools
Seaside Club (Hilo), 151
Seibu group (companies), 342n3
Senate, Phelan's speech for, 284
Senate Committee on Immigration and
Naturalization: Hawaii's labor problems hearings, 233–35, 272–74,
284–85; immigration quota hearings,
301–5, 306
Senate Committee on the Philippines,
250

Shakaishugi (Socialism, newspaper),
341n3
Shaw, Guy L., 253, 264
Sheldon, William, 78
Sheppard, L. E., 290
Shibayama, Tokuzō, 117–18, 130
Shibusawa, Eiichi: federation leaders'
meeting with, 279–80; immigration
quota bill and, 306; on Japanese immigrant laborers, 258; Okumura's
meeting with, 243; role of, 43, 61;
at Washington Conference, 277
Shidehara, Kijūrō: on American flag incident, 313; Chinese immigration and,
276–77; meetings of, 239–41, 251,
257, 278; at Washington Conference,
275
Shingle, Robert, 235
Shirai, S., 346–47n28
Shivers, Robert, 335
Shortridge, Samuel M., 303, 304, 305–6
Shunyō-maru (steamship), 33, 192
Siberia, Japanese occupation of, 111,
112–13, 239, 275
Siberia-maru (ship), 96, 267
silk industry, description of, 29
Sino-Japanese War, 37. See also China
Smith, John Mott, 118, 130
socialism: advocates of, 21–24; Palmer
raids and, 59; red flag incident and,
67–68; in WWI, 43–44
Socialist Party (Japan), 336–37
socialist revolutionary party, 24–25
Society for Formation of Labor Unions
(Rōdō Kumiai Kiseikai, Japan), 258
Society for the Study of Socialism
(Japan), 21, 24
Sōga, Yasutarō: background of, 102–3;
in first Oahu strike, 73; Foreign Language School Bill and, 293, 296, 324;
immigration act and, 310, 316–17; on
military exercises, 320; newspaper of,
91, 326; on prison, 349n50; on religious leaders in Japan, 322; on strike,
339–40; on Washington Conference,
275; WWII relocation of, 333–34
Sogobeya, Gorō, 313
Sōma Inn, 163
Sōtō sect, 39, 120, 129, 141, 344n58
Soviet Union (USSR): establishment of,
32, 43; nonintervention in, 111; U.S.
reports on, 27
Stafford, Harold: background of, 214;
closing arguments by, 214–16; foreign-
language schools control act and,
245; judicial requests by, 210–11;

Stafford, Harold (continued)
letter to nisei, 287; praise for, 225;
role of, 142
Stephens, William D. (Calif. governor),
124
Stevenson, Robert Louis, 246
strikes: in China, 322; extent of, 47–49;
government reports on, 27; in Japan,
79, 323, 330; money-raising for, 61;
origins of, 18–19, 25, 47; of railroad
workers, 110, 112; "silent send-off"
tactic in, 96, 182. See also Oahu
Island strike (first) (1909); Oahu
Island strike (second) (1920)
sugar: beet vs. cane production of,
260–61; price of, 93, 114, 126, 132,
134–35, 228; tariffs on, 250
sugar industry: control of stock in, 80–
81; dynamite used in, 11; expansion
of, 14; fear of Japanization in, 67–72;
innovation in, 10; investment in, 246–
47; postwar changes in, 337–38;
profiteers arrested in, 114; rainfall
needed for, 93–94; terminology in, 16.
See also laborers; plantations; sugar
planters
sugar planters: annexation sought by,
15–16; Filipinos' relations with, 48;
Japanese as threat to, 20–21; other
business interests of, 247–48; paternalism of, 56, 254; political connections of, 137–38, 262; power of,
16, 44, 55, 73–74, 262; profits for,
131–36, 260–61; racial discrimination of, 19–20; railroads operated
by, 75; strike described by, 254–
55; worker negotiations with, 126.
See also Hawaiian Sugar Planters'
Association (HSPA)
Suigorō restaurant (Waiau), 121, 124–
25, 127, 194–95, 198, 225
Sumitomo Bank, 56–58, 84, 99
Sumizawa, Suzuki on, 213–14
Suzuki, Bunji: convention attended by,
43, 237, 258–59; Kagawa's link to,
323; rice costs and, 45; role of, 31;
support for, 279
Suzuki, D., 171
Suzuki, J., 171
Suzuki, Mosaburō, 44, 330, 336
Suzuki, Seiichi: background of, 176–77;
defense on role of, 216; employer of,
180; Satō on role of, 210; testimony
of, 174–76, 177–78, 212–14, 223;
Tsutsumi on role of, 198–200
syndicalism, advocates of, 24

Tabata, H., 170
Taiwan, Japanese control of, 71
Taiyō-maru (ship), 279, 305
Takahashi, Korekiyo, 310
Takano, Fusatarō, 258
Takeda (doctor), 153
Takematsu (picket leader), 169, 187, 189
Takeuchi, Tetsugorō, 25
Takizawa, Kan'ichi: appearance of, 142,
148; background of, 203; as danger-
ous, 203, 348n38; indictment of, 140,
221, 281; Matsumoto on role of,
148–49, 155, 163; postprison life of,
327; Saitō on role of, 169, 171–72;
testimony of, 203–4, 221
Tanaka, Kikuzō, 33
Taniguchi, M., 150, 170
teachers: examinations for, 40–41, 138;
on language education, 39–40; legal
assistance for, 104; organizations for,
35–36, 39, 41; role of, 26, 33, 164,
187, 201, 291
Teapot Dome scandal, 295
temples, as emergency shelters, 86
Tenyō-maru (ship), 122
Terasaki, Teisuke: on conspiracy trial,
227, 280–81; diary of, 60, 89; on
Dillingham, 285; on immigration
act, 309; on labor union, 62; on
Matsumura, 165; on mediation, 91,
118, 130; on newspaper, 292; role
of, 103–4; on strike, 63, 67, 73, 97,
108
Terauchi Masatake, 45
Territory of Hawaii Board of Education,
291, 324
Territory of Hawaii v. I. Goto et al.
See conspiracy trial, appeal after
Thompson, Frank: associates of, 180; de-
fendants' appeal and, 318; employees
of, 172–73, 180; House hearings and,
260, 266–67; machinations of, 76–
78, 165–66, 178, 219–20, 268, 270;
newspapers watched by, 73
Thompson Cathcart law firm, 180, 183
Thurston, Lorrin A., 246
Tobei (magazine), 5
Tobei annai (Guide to Going to America,
Katayama), 21–22, 181, 206
Tobeikyōkai kikanshi (Going to America
Society Magazine), 341n3
Togashi, Tomiji, 6, 213
Tōgō, Capt. Heihachirō, 82
Tōhoku Hotel, 158–59, 171–72
Tokimatsu, role of, 213
Tokiwaen restaurant (Oahu), 95, 99, 175

Tokonami, Takejirō, 113
Tokugawa, Ietatsu, 275
Tokutomi, Sohō, 311, 332
Tokyo, U.S. Embassy in, 313
Tokyo (magazine), 311
Tomota, Shunji: appearance of, 142; on explosion, 155; indictment of, 221, 281; lack of testimony by, 221; Matsumoto on role of, 156; postprison life of, 327
tourist industry, 111, 337, 338
Tōyama, Mitsuru, 310
Toyohira, Ryōkin, 97
Tōyō Steamship (company), 33
Treasure Island (Stevenson), 246
Trotter, Frederick, 76
Tsuchiya, Seiichi, 106
Tsuda, Bunkichi, 211–12
Tsutsumi, Chiyo (Noboru's wife): background of, 31–33; children of, 32, 282; death of, 331; living situation of, 321–23, 330
Tsutsumi, Hideo, 342n1
Tsutsumi, Koto, 31
Tsutsumi, Masao, 321
Tsutsumi, Michiko, 32, 33, 321–22, 323, 330
Tsutsumi, Mihoko, 336–37
Tsutsumi, Noboru, figs. 3 and 4; alibi of, 194–95; alleged warship statement by, 79–85, 264; appearance of, 142, 148; appointment for, 57–58; arrival of, 33–36; Baba's relation with, 191; background of, 28–33, 200–201; baptism of, 281–82; criticism of, 100–101, 243–44; death of, 336–37; on explosion, 155; federation and, 57, 127–30, 157; goals of, 297; government reports on, 241; Hamamoto on role of, 195; history written by, 330; incarceration of, 296–98, 317, 349n12; income for, 201–2; indictment of, 140, 220–21; instructions from, 148–49; labor organizing and, 45–47, 49, 83–85, 95, 108–9, 185; Matsumoto's altercation with, 157–58, 163, 166; mediation plan and, 92, 117–18; Miyazawa's relation with, 182; Mizutari on role of, 193–94; name of, 342n4; as newspaperman, 41, 53; postprison life of, 321–23, 330–31, 336–37; request to judge, 226; Saitō on role of, 169, 171–72; stop strike order and, 118–19, 121; strike vote and, 56–57, 61–62, 65–66; as suspicious person, 26–27;

Suzuki on role of, 174–78, 213; testimony of, 197–202, 221, 225, 346–47n28; Tsuda on role of, 211–12; on U.S.-Japanese cooperation, 39–40; on wages and conditions, 54–55, 60–61
Tsutsumi, Norio, 323
Tsutsumi, Taizō, 31, 32, 33
Tsutsumi, Takashi, 27–28
Tsutsumi, Tamotsu, 331
Tsutsumi, Toshio, 33, 321
Tsutsumi, Tsuruyo, 331, 336–37
Tsutsumi, Yasujirō, 342n3
Twenty-one Demands, 38, 71

Uchida, Kōsai (foreign minister): Americanization and, 243; instructions from, 122; reports to, 82, 85, 91, 109, 111, 118; on Washington Conference, 277–78
Uchida, Yasuya, 106, 113
Uchimura, Kanzō, 311
Ueda, Sachiko, 189
Umemoto (federation director), 194
United States: anti-Japanese feelings in, 10, 12, 71–72, 111–12, 123; arms race and, 274–76; exports of, 328; Far Eastern policy of, 275–76; geography knowledge in, 251–52; ideals of, 304–5; imperialism of, 16; indentures in, 15, 17, 256. *See also* assimilation; California; citizenship; Federal Bureau of Investigation (FBI); Hawaii; immigrants
U.S. Army, 236, 320–21
U.S. Congress, Oahu strike's impact on, 12. *See also* House Committee on Immigration and Naturalization; Senate Committee on Immigration and Naturalization
U.S. Constitution, proposed amendment to, 302
U.S.-Japan relations: Americanization movement and, 243; Chinese immigration and, 233; crisis in, 329–32; discussions on, 239–41, 251, 257, 278; immigration quota bill and, 305–7; issues in, 124, 239, 277, 280; Japan's misperceptions of, 315; Phelan's speech on, 112, 347n5. *See also* Johnson Reed Immigration Quota Law; Washington Conference
U.S.-Japan Security Treaty, 337
U.S. Navy: exercises of, 320–21; expansion of, 111–12, 236; workers supported by sailor from, 110. *See also* Pearl Harbor

U.S. Supreme Court: appeal denied by, 318; on Foreign Language School Bill, 324–25; on Ozawa case, 292
United Workers of Hawaii (UWH), 288

Van Reed, Eugene, 13, 18
Vanzetti, Bartolomeo: arrest of, 1, 26; draft evasion by, 42; execution of, 323–24; trial of, 138–39, 226, 297

wages: bonus system in, 55, 56, 126, 131–32, 184, 231; calls for increased, 41, 44–45, 47–49, 51–58, 65, 133; for contract workers, 15; discrimination in, 19, 25, 75; for first-year arrivals, 13; gender differences in, 54, 109, 131, 133; increased by HSPA, 131–33, 156; for mainland laborers, 54; planters' evidence of sufficient, 69–70; poststrike, 126; postwar increase in, 338; reduced by HSPA, 228–29
Wahiawa Plantation, pickets at, 147, 187
Waiakea Plantation: labor contractors at, 223–24; laborers at, 208; store at, 317, 326
Waialua Plantation: evictions from, 86, 191, 327; fire at, 186; influenza epidemic and, 87–88; labor contractors at, 188–89; laborers at, 147, 162, 188, 190, 192; location of, xii–xiii (maps); organizing at, 44, 52, 95; strike at, 19, 94, 164–65, 199; strikebreakers at, 95–96
Waianae Plantation: location of, xii–xiii (maps); rally at, 95
Waiau: hotel in, 121, 192; restaurant in, 121, 124–25, 127, 194–95, 198, 225
Waikiki, development of, 234
Waikiki Water Company, 248
Waimanalo Plantation: fire at, 186; labor organizer at, 48, 221; location of, xii–xiii (maps); strikebreakers at, 96
Wainaku Plantation, contractor at, 152
Waipahu Plantation: evictions from, 86; explosion at, 187; fire at, 186; laborers at, 168–69; location of, xii–xiii (maps); parade participants from, 109; photography studio at, 113; pickets at, 169, 204; rally at, 95; stockholders of, 248; strike at, 19, 63, 64, 66, 200, 203–4; strikebreakers at, 95–96, 327; traitors at, 83; union dissolved at, 281
Wakabayashi (pineapple dealer), 119, 121
Wakikawa, Seiei, 102–3, 320

Walter-McCarran Immigration and Naturalization Act (1952), 339
Washington (state), depression's effects on, 328
Washington, D.C., cherry trees in, 300
Washington Conference: immigration concerns and, 277–79, 312; proposals in, 274–75; Senate hearings postponed for, 274; treaty from, 275–76, 282, 331
Waterhouse, John: background of, 119; on 1920 economy, 134; family of, 176; on Filipino immigration, 94; Isobe's confrontation with, 124–25; motives of, 123–24; negotiations and, 55, 118–19, 121, 130, 148, 192; poststrike posters distributed by, 126; questions about, 127; on strike, 71, 125; on sugar profits, 131, 250; workers criticized by, 133–34
Wilson, J., 287
Wilson, Woodrow: Alien Land Law and, 285; idealism of, 137, 251; immigration quota bill and, 301; on labor conference, 51; League of Nations and, 59; on racial equality, 236; reelection of, 42
Wobblies. See Industrial Workers of the World (IWW)
women, suffrage for, 137
women workers: as percentage, 109; wages of, 54, 109, 131, 133
Woodlawn Stock and Dairy Company, 247
workers. See laborers
World War I: as context, 32–33, 35–36; German-language schools closed during, 38; U.S. labor movement during, 42–44
Wright, Frank Lloyd, 310
Wright, George W.: background of, 261; credibility of, 267–68, 270–71; Filipino strike and, 319; job for, 326; leadership of, 259, 261–62; Scharrenberg's meeting with, 288; testimony for House hearings, 262, 264–67

Yada, Chōnosuke: appointment for, 79, 122–23; associates of, 164, 305; conflicts with, 196, 203, 348n38; departure of, 227–28, 253, 279; on federation after strike, 131; on Harding's election, 251; influence on, 280; Isobe's mediation and, 127; on Japanese-language press bill, 138; on 1920 economy, 135; strike condemned by, 123; on wage increase, 132

Yakumo (cruiser), 82, 96, 236, 264
Yamagata, Aritomo, 22
Yamaguchi, Kumano, 105–6
Yamakawa, Manjirō, 70
Yamamoto, Tsuneichi, 41, 84, 97–98
Yamamura, Kōhachi, 145–46, 172
Yamato shinbun (later *Nippu jiji,* newspaper), 102, 311
Yamazaki, Keiichi, 227–28, 253, 255–56, 303
Yanagihira, Byakuren, 330
Yanagiya, Sangorō, 314
Yao, Kizaburō, 336

Yap (island), Japanese mandate over, 239
Yokohama Specie Bank, 61, 255
Yokoo, Eijūrō: on explosion, 155; fired from job, 126; indictment of, 152, 221; mediation and, 148; return to Japan, 223; strike declaration read by, 122; Suzuki on role of, 176; Tsuda on role of, 211
Yokoo, Toyo, 148, 152, 223
Yoshimura (laborer), 151–52, 169, 215
Young Hotel (Waiau), 121, 192
Yūaikai (Friendly Society, Japan), 31, 43, 45, 237, 258–59, 279, 323

Text: 10/13 Sabon
Display: Gill Sans
Compositor: G & S Typesetters, Inc.
Printer and Binder: Haddon Craftsmen, Inc.